RECENT DEVELOPMENTS IN THE THEORY OF INDUSTRIAL ORGANIZATION

Recent Developments in the Theory of Industrial Organization

Edited by
Alfredo Del Monte
Professor of Industrial Economics
University of Naples

MACMILLAN

First published 1992 by
THE MACMILLAN PRESS LTD
Houndmills, Basingstoke, Hampshire RG21 2XS
and London
Companies and representatives
throughout the world

ISBN 0–333–53158–2

A catalogue record for this book is available
from the British Library

Printed in Hong Kong

Contents

Acknowledgement

Particular thanks are due to Ash Amin and David Storey for their suggestions on the structure and content of the book.

ALFREDO DEL MONTE

Notes on the Contributors

Nicola Acocella is Professor of Economic Policy at the University of Rome 'La Sapienza'. He has been Senior Visitor, or Visiting Professor, at the Universities of Cambridge (1970–1, 1984 and 1985), Oxford (Fellow of the British Academy, 1977), Toronto (Fellow of the Canadian Social Sciences and Humanities Research Council, 1980), Harvard (Fellow of the American Council of Learned Societies, 1980), Stanford (1986). He has published several articles in academic journals on industrial economics issues, as well as *Le Multinazionali italiane* (1985) and *Teorie dell'Internazionalizzazione e Realtà Italiana* (1989).

Alfredo Del Monte is Professor of Industrial Economics at the University of Naples. His publications include various articles in academic journals on development, regional and industrial issues and *Il Mezzogiorno nell'Economia Italiana* (1978), *Politica Regionale e Sviluppo Economico* (1977) and *Finanza d'Impresa* (1989).

Keith Cowling is Professor of Economics, University of Warwick. He is the editor of the *International Review of Applied Economics*, was managing editor of the *International Journal of Industrial Organization*, 1982–7, was president of the *European Association for Research in Industrial Economics*, 1987–9, and is the author of *Mergers and Economic Performance* (with others), *Monopoly Capitalism* (1982), *Transnational Monopoly Capitalism* (with Roger Sugden, 1987), and *A New Economic Policy for Britain* (edited with Roger Sugden, 1990).

Giovanni Dosi is Professor of Economics, University of Rome, and Visiting Fellow, SPRU, University of Sussex. He is the author of several works in the fields of the economics of innovation, industrial economics and international trade, including: *Technical Change and Industrial Transformation* (1984) and *The Economics of Technical Change and International Trade* (with K. Pavid and L. Soete, 1990).

Fabio M. Esposito is a PhD student in economics at the University of Naples at the Centro di Specializzazione in Ricerche Economiche Agrarie.

John D. Hey is Professor of Economics and Statistics at the University of York. He is editor of the *Economic Journal* and on the editorial boards of the *Journal of Risk and Uncertainty*, *Journal of Behavioral Decision-Making*, *Empirica*, the *Journal of Behavioral Economics* and *Managerial and Decision Economics*. He has published many books – a forthcoming one is *Experimental Economics* – and some fifty journal papers. His main interests are in the economics of uncertainty and experimental economics.

Neil Kay is Professor of Economics at Strathclyde University, Glasgow, Scotland. He is the author of three books and numerous articles in the area of industrial economics and corporate strategy. He has held two visiting associate professorships at the University of California, Irvine (1980–2), and was visiting professor at the European University in Florence (1987–8).

Roberto Marchionatti teaches economics at the University of Urbino. He is author of *Rilevanza e Limiti del Neoricardismo* (1981) and co-author of *Montedison 1966–1989: L'Evoluzione di una Grande Impresa al Confine tra Pubblico e Privato* (1990).

Riccardo Martina is Lecturer in Economics at the Department of Public Economics at the University of Naples. His main research interests are in the fields of industrial organization and public economics. His published work include co-authored papers on oligopoly theory and the economics of tax evasion which have appeared in the *Scottish Journal of Economics* and in the *Journal of Public Economics*.

Niall O' Higgins is a PhD candidate at the European University Institute in Florence, and Lecturer in Mathematics and Econometrics on the MSc in public sector economics in Naples. His main research interest is the microeconometrics of the labour market, although he has also published work on the progressivity of government taxation and expenditure and industrial economics.

Malcolm C. Sawyer is Professor of Economics at the University of Leeds. He has published extensively in the areas of industrial economics (including industrial policy) and macroeconomics (especially post-Keynesian economics), including *The Economics of Industries and Firms* (1985) and *The Economics of Michal Kalecki* (1985). He is managing editor of the *International Review of Applied Economics*.

Patrizia Sbriglia is Lecturer in the Department of Economics at the University of Naples, from where she received her doctorate in 1988. She has published articles on theoretical and applied aspects of oligopoly theory, x Notes on the Contributors

market structure and innovation, and general industrial economics.

Damiano Silipo is Lecturer in Economics at Università della Calabria. His main interests are in the economics of uncertainty and technical progress decisions.

Francesco Silva is Professor of Industrial Economics at the University of Torino. He is author of *Il mercato Italiano dell'Auto nel Contesto Europeo* (1981) and *Impresa, Concorrenza e Organizzazione* (1980).

Paul Stoneman is Research Professor in the School of Industrial and Business Studies at the University of Warwick. His publications include various articles in academic journals on technology-related issues and *The Economic Analysis of Technological Change* (1983) and *The Economic Analysis of Technology Policy* (1987).

John Sutton is Professor of Economics at the London School of Economics, where he directs the Economics of Industry Research Group. He has published extensively in the recent game-theoretic I.O. literature, and has been particularly concerned with the empirical implementation of these ideas, as described in his recent book *Sunk Costs and Market Structure* (1991). During 1991 Professor Sutton was a Marvin Bower Fellow at the Harvard Business School.

Introduction: Recent Developments in Industrial Organization

Alfredo Del Monte

INTRODUCTION

Industrial organization theory has made substantial progress in the past decade. New tools and new approaches have been developed, and the purpose of this volume is to review and present some of these developments. The material is organized into four sections: recent approaches to industrial organization; the behaviour of individual firms and the characteristics of industrial systems as a whole; new theories of the firm and market structure; and technical progress and market structure – some special issues.

RECENT APPROACHES TO INDUSTRIAL ORGANIZATION

The theory of industrial organization has focused on the concept of the market, defined as a collection of buyers and sellers who produce and buy goods which are close substitutes for one another. Markets or industries are seen as the appropriate unit of study.

The traditional approach to the study of the markets in industrial organization has been based on the 'structure–conduct–performance' paradigm. Here market structure, defined as the number of firms in the market, the degree of product differentiation, etc., determines the conduct of firms, which in turn determines market performance (rate of profits, innovation rate, efficiency, etc.).

In order to test the predictions of this theory, empirical econometric work has analysed the existing links between indicators of performance (such as profit rates, innovation rates, etc.) and indicators of market structure, in particular the degree of concentration. However, this approach has been subjected to several criticisms. First, links must be interpreted as 'descriptive statistics', rather than as a reflection of causal relationships, since there are strong interactions between market structure, conduct and performance.

1

Hence the variables that enter into the correlation are determined simultaneously, given basic conditions in technology and demand (exogenous variables).

In order to overcome this criticism several new approaches have been developed. Within them the most important aim has been to explain firstly the working of markets, focusing on the relationship between firms and on the role of potential entrants, and secondly the determinants of the number of firms within the market. Exogenous variables such as the characteristics of technology (irreversibilities and convexities), demand and the strategies of firms to deter entry, are regarded as the most relevant determinants of market strategies, particularly when markets are dominated by few firms.

The literature has grown rapidly in recent years, and game theory, which is the standard tool for the analysis of strategic conflict, has become so central that most of the traditional problems are reinterpreted in terms of this theory 'thus bringing a unified methodology to the field' (Tirole, 1988, p. 3). Since game theory is considered such a powerful tool that it can be used to illuminate many social and economic situations and can be applied both to conflict and/or co-operation situations, many authors believe that its use opens new frontiers to industrial organization. It is useful for the analysis of any situation where the choice of the single unit is made by taking account of the reactions of the other units (firms, groups of interests, etc.). Game theory in industrial organization has been applied not only to oligopoly situations but also to develop a theory of the internal organization of the firm.[1]

The general use of game theory in industrial organization has been defended by Tirole and Fudenberg (1987, p. 176) 'The reason it has been embraced by a majority of researchers in the field is that it imposes some discipline on theoretical thinking. It forces economists to clearly specify the strategic variables, their timing, and the information structure faced by firms.' This is the obvious merit of any mathematical model in economics: it is an expedient way of detecting errors in some mental operations. However, such an approach has been criticized (Georgescu-Roegen, 1971) on the basis that it can work negatively: if the model does not reveal an error, it does not mean that the argument or the arithmetical calculations are wholly correct.

The same criticism can be applied to what Sutton calls the *strong* defence of the use of theory of games in industrial organization: industrial economics involves a departure from perfect competition to a situation where there are very few firms. If there are few firms, this is only interesting analytically if they are concerned with others' reactions. But if the reactions of firms are to be modelled, then game theory is the only way in which we can model them, because game theory, by definition, is the study of agents, each of whose maximization problems depends upon the actions or strategies chosen by others.

The chapter in this volume by Sutton offers a second defence. Sutton points out that the use of the game theory is justified if it allows us to understand better the working of markets and the industrial system. The usefulness of the game theory must be evaluated on the basis of its predictive content.[2] Sutton suggests that, at micro-level, game theory has been very successful: empirical results are consistent with predictions of theoretical game models. However, some problems remain: the first concerns multiple equilibria. Almost every non-trivial game has many (sometimes infinitely many) different equilibrium points. If we do not have a theory selecting a single equilibrium point[3] as the solution to the game, then the problem of multiplicity makes the testing of theories very difficult.

A further problem is that for most applications of game theory to industrial organization there are many alternatives to the design of the appropriate game form to be used. Many of the results are highly dependent upon the rules of the game to be played. Sutton, in his chapter answers the above criticisms and argues that the predictions of the game theory hold not only in the context of 'single industry studies' but that game-theoretic concepts could be used to explain statistical regularities in the context of inter-industry cross-sections.

In spite of these arguments many authors believe that it is very difficult to assess whether game theory is a correct representation of the behaviour of firms in non-competitive markets.

A completely different approach, critical of the hypotheses of neoclassical economics, has developed. Many authors have recognized that evolutionary elements predominate in every concrete economic phenomenon of significance.[4] This new emphasis is also the result of revolutions in natural science. Evolution is recognized to be a phenomenon that interests researchers in both physics and biology. Only 30 years ago the theory of the universe by H. Bond and T. Gold was one of a stationary universe. Now it is possible to see evolutionary phenomena at the level of physical universe. On the other hand the recognition that organisms have evolved and that the behaviour of living systems is one of increasing complexity and self-organization is a unifying principle of modern biology.[5] This approach rejects the hypothesis that in economic life man acts mechanically and that it is possible to derive economic laws from a single logical foundation. It is the evolutionary nature of the economic process that precludes the understanding of all its relevant aspects by deductive models. Georgescu-Roegen claims that economic process could not be seen as a mechanical analogue: 'In this representation the economic process neither induces any qualitative change nor is affected by the qualitative change in the environment into which it is anchored. It is an isolated self-contained and ahistorical process – a circular flow between production and consumption with no outlets, as elementary textbooks depict it' (1971, p. 2). Therefore the study of the processes of change, rather than the processes towards equilibrium, are the relevant considerations of economics.

One of the most important consequences of this approach is the criticism of the optimization principle on which neoclassical theory is founded. This principle is claimed not to be adequate to explain the behaviour of individuals and the observation of what happens in the sphere of economic organization or between organizations and individuals. The observation of the reality suffices to reveal phenomena that do not consist of *tatonnements* with given means towards given ends according to given rules.

In industrial organization this criticism concerns primarily the theory of the firm. Neoclassical theory of the firm is based on the concept of *substantive rationality*, a term coined by Simon (1976) who argues: 'Behaviour is substantially rational when it is appropriate to the achievement of a given goal within the limit imposed by given conditions and constraints' (p. 68). However, this concept can be easily criticized. In a world characterized by imperfect information, problems of 'bounded rationality' arise so that the assumption of 'substantive rationality' has to be abandoned in order to understand the true behaviour of the firm.

On the other hand, it must be recognized that the assumption of substantive rationality does have a number of advantages for the theory of industrial organization, and continues to be used in much current work. It allows the study of how markets function without requiring a 'realistic' theory of the firm. In the traditional approach the firm is viewed as an abstract entity characterized simply by a production function and an objective function to be maximized. The organization of the firm is treated as given in analysing the functioning of the markets. However when we assume a different concept of rationality, such as the 'procedural rationality'[6]), it is much more difficult to separate a realistic theory of the firm from a theory of market.[7] The internal organization of the firm and market structure have to be regarded as the result of a dynamic process in which both interact. Despite its appeal, it is difficult to analyse this dynamism, which is why theories that have followed this approach have obtained imprecise results and have been difficult to verify.

On the other hand there is a long tradition which contends that optimization on the part of business firms is an unnecessary and even unhelpful concept for the purpose of scientific explanation and prediction.[8] The evolutionary approach should not be confused with the natural selection argument, which has been used by neoclassical economists to show that, in the long run, the only firms that survive are those whose decisions are compatible with neoclassical theory.[9] Enke (1951) suggested that, given sufficient intensity of competition, all policies except for the optimum would in time fail the survival test. In the *long run, viability* dictates optimality. Consequently, for long run predictive purposes (under conditions of intense competition) the analyst is entitled to assume that firms behave 'as if' they were optimizing. However, as Hirschleifer (1977) observes, if the situation is not *objectively* deterministic, so that some or all of the strategies available generate probability distributions rather than definite deterministic numbers for the outcome, there may not exist any unequivocal optimum.

A different position is taken by Alchian, Simon, Nelson and Winter who suggest that the environment plays a selective role in rewarding the choice of *viable* (positive realized profit) strategies. Viability, and not optimality, hence becomes the relevant success criterion.[10] This is the criterion on which the evolutionary theory of the firm is founded. Nelson and Winter (1982) see the firm as characterized largely in terms of the routines that it has. Nelson and Winter attempt to provide a unified theory of the behaviour of the firm and of the working of the markets. The paper by Dosi, in the present volume, illustrates the main difference between the different schools (the neoclassical and the evolutionary) and also presents some of the results obtained by the evolutionary approach. Although much relevant progress has been made by the research in this field, the chapter suggests that we are still a long way from a comprehensive theory of the firm and its markets.

The difficulty of gathering data to facilitate accurate tests of industrial organization theories is a very familiar problem. The chapter by Hey indicates the contributions we could expect from experimental economics in order to test the theory. Experimentally generated data could be used to test different theories and, in particular, assumptions about the behaviour of the agents. One of the positive aspects of this approach is that the 'environment' can be controlled in such a way to allow us to understand better some limits of the neoclassical theory of the firm. In real life, agents in the industries are not single individuals but firms managed by a board and by managers with experience. The key problem is to replicate in a laboratory the same conditions and pressures involved in the decision-making processes of the firm; in any event, the subjects of the experiments must be teams of managers, rather than individuals. For the time being it therefore appears that, whilst laboratory experiments may have a useful role when examining relatively simple decisions, they do not yet offer clear insights into more complex matters.

THE BEHAVIOUR OF INDIVIDUAL FIRMS AND THE CHARACTERISTICS OF INDUSTRIAL SYSTEMS

A second very important difference between the evolutionary and the standard approach to economy is that the first does not hypothesize that the properties of a macro-system are deducible from the elemental properties of its components. As Hahn and Hollis (1979) claim 'throughout pure theory macro-movements are thus explained as the collective work of rational individuals and the pedagogic reasons why the pure economist starts with micro-analysis also reflect his deepest ontological commitments' (p. 3).

The evolutionary approach, on the other hand, recognizes that in economics, as in biology or physics, the whole is never equal simply to the sum of its various parts (Max Plank in Georgescu-Roegen, 1971 p. 328.)

The basic hypothesis in traditional industrial organization theory is that the natural forces of competition inherent to the market lead to an efficient allocation of resources and to socially acceptable revenue distributions. Therefore the optimal performance of the economic system is ensured by a public policy apparatus that guarantees the structural prerequisites of perfect competition.

The relationship between market structure and the characteristics of the industrial system as a whole are discussed by less orthodox approaches. The analysis makes very little use of the concept of general equilibrium and does not assume that there is any tendency for the firm to achieve long-run equilibrium. The Schumpeterian analysis of the relationship between monopoly and technical change, or the Kaleckian analysis of the effect of the degree of monopoly on the level of aggregate demand are the starting-points of several recent works on this subject.

In his chapter, Sawyer argues that, contrary to much recent literature, the price–output decisions of firms operating in imperfectly competitive markets do not generate unemployment of labour, although excess capacity may occur. The author suggests that in order to develop a thorough analysis of imperfectly competitive markets the role of aggregate demand must be explicitly considered. He shows that the impact of industrial structure comes through the firms' investment, research and development decisions and their consequences for the distribution of income rather than through their price–output decisions.

There is a long tradition which postulates a positive relationship between, on the one hand, the growth of giant firms and oligopolistic market structures and, on the other, the tendencies within the capitalistic system toward stagnation. In his chapter, Cowling extends the analysis developed in his book *Monopoly Capitalism* (1982) to take into account recent developments in industrial organization. Cowling claims that recent work on the stability of collusive arrangements reinforces the hypothesis of rivalry and collusion in the oligopoly case, and that the collusive outcome within oligopoly groups would not be undermined by potential entrants. Therefore high monopoly prices could be maintained for a long periods. On the other hand, given the structure of the labour market, the tendency for price-cost margins to increase as concentration increases cannot be easily reversed in the process of wage bargaining, thus leading to an increase in the propensity to save. Therefore Cowling concludes that the large development of monopolistic and oligopolistic markets has had a negative impact on the functional income distribution, and reinforces the tendencies to stagnation of the capitalist system.

Recently, a new approach to industrial organization which links the economic system as a whole to the behaviour of the firm at micro-level has been developed. This approach has seen the convergence of thought between scholars from economics (e.g. Freeman, Boyer, Nelson, Piore, etc.), geography (e.g. Storper, Scott), and sociology (e.g. Sabel). Each has contributed to the study of technical and institutional change within a framework of economic analysis and policy-making, rather than regarding technological and organizational change as a residual or 'exogenous' factor. This approach tries to relate aspects of the economic system as a whole to microeconomic behaviour. Technological change in this paradigm is explained at the micro-level by reference to the evolutionary theory of the firm pioneered by Nelson and Winter (1982). At macro-level, the notion of 'technology paradigm' or 'trajectory' implies a mechanism of dynamic adjustment of the economic system that is radically different from that considered by neoclassical theory.

This approach to technological change and industrial organization is clearly illustrated in the chapter by Dosi. Dynamic mechanisms other than those of equilibrium are considered by economists who try to explain the change in the forms of productive activity in the actual phase of capitalism. This approach tries to explain evolutionary changes in the advanced economies not through the movement from one point of equilibrium to another, but through the complex interrelationship of social, economic and institutional forces. The transition from the Fordist regime of accumulation to a new regime of flexible accumulation is said to be occurring and is theorized as a reflection of dynamics that revolve for the most part around the social division of labour, the formation of external economies, and the dissolution of market rigidities. More recently, some aspects of the social divisions of labour have been partially explained at micro-level through the use of the 'transaction costs approach'.

The chapter by Del Monte and Esposito examines the concept of flexibility at both the macro- and micro- level and develops a model of a competitive industry under uncertain demand, based on the Stiglerian notion of flexibility. It is generally held, in the economic literature, that the growing importance of flexible specialization reflects increased uncertainty in markets. The paper concludes, however, that a well-defined relationship between the uncertainty of the external environment and the choice of a firm's organizational structure does not exist. The relationship will depend upon the kind of uncertainty which prevails, and will also differ from one socioeconomic environment to another. The complexity and multiplicity of forces favouring alternative types of plants and/or organizational modes makes it very difficult to build a macroeconomic theory of flexibility based on the observation of the microeconomic behaviour of the single firm.

Finally, the chapter by Marchionatti and Silva, using the Italian case as an example, illustrates the impact of public intervention policies for industrial development. It argues that, during the 1950s and 1960s, these forms of intervention reflected a fundamental distrust of the effectiveness of the market mechanism in Italy. By the 1970s, however, Italian industrial economists were arguing that the appropriate unit of study ought to be the 'industrial district' rather than the industrial sector or firm (Becattini, 1979; 1987). Hence local industrial policy is increasingly becoming the key issue for economic development.

NEW THEORIES OF THE FIRM

Industrial organization developed as a theory of market structure but, until very recently, it lacked a theory of the firm. The firm was regarded as a black box that transforms the factors of production into outputs. However, in recent years a theory of the internal organization of the firm has been developed within the neoclassical framework. Here the firm is viewed as an organizational structure in which a centralized planned authority replaces the impersonal forces of the market. The new theory tries to answer questions that are central to any theory of the firm. For instance:

1.   What determines the boundaries of the firm, and is there an appropriate degree of vertical, lateral or horizontal integration? New theories of the firm try to provide a rigorous analysis of such questions, following the transactions cost approach (Tirole, 1986; Hart and Holstrom, 1987). Moreover, new emphasis is given to the effects of uncertainty on the size of the firms and on the market structure.

2. Which subjects determine, through their actions, the behaviour of the firm? The new approach sees the firm as a coalitional structure comprising different constituents, including stockholders, managers and employees (Aoki, 1984).

Following this approach, a very large literature has analysed the principal–agent problem in the context of the firm. Its aim is to articulate a reward structure within which workers and managers pursue the objectives of the firm.

Another problem which has been studied through the transaction cost approach (Williamson, 1975; 1985) is the existence of a large number of organizational structures. These range from short and long term contracts, joint ventures, quasi-integration and other forms of collaborative agreements.

The transactional cost approach assumes that amongst the many possible forms of internal organization, those tending to predominate over time are the ones that minimize production and transaction costs. Some authors assume the prevailing organizational structures are the most efficient. But it is possible that the search to maximize long-run profit leads to an organizational form which, though not cost-minimal, nevertheless achieves maximum profits through market power.

Observation shows that *viable* alternative organization modes exist in the same industry and in the same country. This phenomenon is similar to what is termed 'polymorphism' by biologists.[11] The Del Monte and Esposito chapter referred to above, also analyses the possibility that there is not an evolution towards a unique type of firm structure. The case of the Italian textile industry in which vertically integrated firms and network firms coexist is an illustration of polymorphism in industrial organization.

The papers by Kay and by Acocella examine these matters with reference to two rather different cases. The Kay paper focuses on a particular form of collaborative activity, the joint ventures (JV) which is an organizational form that cannot be explained solely in terms of the transaction costs approach. Kay suggests that JVs are generally more costly than alternative forms of economic organization, at least for the geographical area in which the venture is located. This is because JVs rarely manage to combine the advantages of the market and hierarchy elements of their structure. Therefore there must be other reasons that induce economic agents to choose this organizational form. As Kay suggests, 'even though JVs may be the most expensive form of economic organization considered at local level of the venture itself, once system wide effects are recognised it may be a relatively cheap way of pursuing the venture looked at from the level of the firm itself'.

The Acocella chapter summarizes and examines critically the main theories of multinational enterprises based on the efficiency paradigm. It stresses the need for a more general theory of multinational enterprises which takes into account both efficiency and strategic issues.

The study of the effects of uncertainty on the behaviour of the firm has been for a long time on the research agenda of industrial economists and of micro-theorists. Papers in this area have significantly contributed to our understanding of the firm's behaviour and of the working of markets. Within the large body of contributions, an interesting set of papers share the assumption of risk-averse attitudes of firms. Since the seminal work by Sandmo (1971) on the effects of price uncertainty on the output decision of a competitive firm, research on this topic has been extended to other market configurations. However, it has been only very recently that attention has been paid to the relationships between risk preferences of firms and market equilibrium in the context of a duopoly setting. This research has highlighted a crucial feature of this model: risk-averse firms behave both as risk-averse agents and as strategic players; as a consequence, the equilibrium outcome will be interestingly affected by the simultaneous working of these two forces.

In his chapter, Martina reviews the development of this recent literature and examines the effects on the output decisions of firms of an increase in the degree of risk aversion. He shows that risk preferences do influence firms' behaviour and, therefore, market equilibrium, thus suggesting an explanation of the structure of industries different from those based on a 'technological' view.

TECHNICAL PROGRESS AND MARKET STRUCTURES

One of the main emphases in the innovation literature has been to explain the characteristics of technological change in terms of a relationship between market structure and innovative activity. Empirical observations have suggested that there is a positive association between the degree of concentration in an industry and the extent of innovation, provided concentration is not unduly high (Dasgupta, 1986). Recently a new literature has examined why the relationship between research and development expenditure and market structure is less clear than might be expected, i.e. the effect of spillover on the intensity of R & D expenditure (Hartwick, 1984; Katz, 1986; D'Aspremont and Jacquemin, 1988).

The role of small industrial firms in influencing the rates of technological change, however, remains controversial. Research has shown that the

Schumpeterian hypothesis, according to which large firms would have an advantage because of increasing returns to scale in R & D, does not seem to be empirically supported. A significant number of basic innovations have originated in small firms, which often play an important role – especially in the United States – in industries characterized by high rate of growth and technological change (Acs and Audretsch, 1988). Empirical evidence also suggests that larger firms do not engage in more R & D activity, relative to their size, than smaller firms (Kamien and Schwartz, 1982). The chapter by Sbriglia and O'Higgins confirms these findings with reference to Italy, a country which is characterized by an industrial structure that is much more dominated by small firms than, for example, the United States.

Theorization of innovative activity generally presumes that the number of firms in an industry is given. Only recently have Dasgupta and Stiglitz (1980; 1981) and Levin (1978) developed theoretical models in which industrial structure is assumed to be endogenous.

Most of the literature on technological progress has focused on invention, and less emphasis has been placed on the adoption of new technologies. The traditional approach to adoption was outlined by Griliches (1957) and Mansfield (1961) who assumed that the diffusion path of innovations was S-shaped and driven by an epidemic process. This suggested that a few firms adopted the innovations early, that the diffusion accelerated as other firms learnt about the invention, and that the process decelerated when most firms had adopted. Mansfield (1968) and others have shown that the S curve, although not necessarily the epidemic theory, does indeed have considerable empirical validity. This approach has analysed the diffusion of innovation within a static context in which technology itself, and the size distribution of firms, are static over time. Most of the subsequent works have analysed the strategic aspect of adoption (Dasgupta and Stiglitz, 1980; Fudenberg and Tirole, 1985).

The chapter by Stoneman allows the size distribution of firms to be endogenous but takes the existence of the technology as predetermined. *Inter alia*, the paper uses a framework developed by Reinganum (1981), in which the gain from adoption is related to the extent of adoption. The Stoneman paper analyses how market structure is both influenced by and affects the diffusion process. Although the paper does not reach a consistent set of findings from the various models developed, it does confirm the need to analyse the diffusion of innovations as part of a theory of technological competition.

Uncertainty is inherent to the process of R & D: the success or the failure of a project is, in fact, crucially determined by luck, as well as by the rational behaviour of the agents. In this context, attitudes towards risk of the entrepreneur play an important role in determining the rate and the direction of inventive activity. In his paper, Silipo examines how the search for a successful discovery is affected by risk aversion; moreover, the author shows that this effect operates whatever the nature of the project undertaken is.

CONCLUSION

The central lesson to be learnt from the papers presented at the conference is that industrial organization can no longer be seen as a discipline which examines only the functioning of the market. Standard approaches to industrial organization have been quite effective in understanding equilibrium situations and in describing processes that are not far from the equilibrium situation. In a modern economy, the complexity of the industrial system requires that other topics are studied. Many of these concern the processes by which new economic means, new organizational modes and new economic relations are created (e.g. growth and birth of firms), the evolution of economic organizations and industrial structures, and the coexistence in the same industry of very different organizational modes over long periods of time. Some of these topics have been covered in this volume, while others have not been considered. Currently, there is no unified methodology for studying these topics. The basic hypotheses of the standard approach (optimality principles, the representative agent, the slow change of the environment in relation to the endogenous variables of economic models, etc.) do not seem appropriate to the study of evolutionary aspects of industrial organization. This explains why different approaches have been developed. Each is appropriate for the particular topic which it addresses, and should not be viewed as a weakness in the theory of industrial organization.

The absence of any integrating framework for these new developments remains very clear. It has not been our purpose to provide that framework. Rather our intention has been to bring together the wide variety of the different approaches adopted by scholars of industrial organizations. It is hoped that this may be the first step towards greater cross-fertilization of ideas and approaches within these sub-disciplines in economics.

Notes

1. Chapter 1 of the Tirole book, 'The Theory of Industrial Organization', is a very interesting review of this literature.
2. There is a well-known debate on the general principles of economics: many economists (Friedman, 1953) argue that the only test of a theory (a theory is a set of logically linked, high-order generalizations) is the success of its prediction. Others hold the view that there are two dimensions to the development of scientific knowledge: the forecasting and the explanation. They do not believe that these two aspects necessarily coincide. A model could provide good forecasts and yet only a weak explanation. Conversely, a theory that explains phenomena adequately may not facilitate forecasting.
3. In the last years some authors have tried to offer rational criteria for selecting one equilibrium point as the solution of the game: e.g., J. Harsanyi and R. Selten, (1988).
4. Marshall was one of the first authors to recognize that biology and not mechanics was the true Mecca of the economist (Georgescu-Roegen, 1970).
5. The entropy law has been seen as the law that could be used as the unitary element of interpretations of basic evolutionary processes in different fields; in his 1971 book *The Entropy Law and the Economic Process*, Georgescu-Roegen analyses the intimate relationship between the entropy law and the economic process. In biology, a recent book by D.R. Brooks and E.O. Wiley, *Evolution as Entropy: Towards a Unified Theory of Biology* (1988), claims that a causal relationship between information flow and energy flow in organisms is clarified by the second law of thermodynamics.
6. 'Behaviour is procedurally rational when it is the outcome of appropriate deliberation. Its procedural rationality depends upon the process that generated it' (Simon, 1976, p. 68).
7. At least for the time being, theory of the market and theory of the organization of the firm as studied by game theory appear to be two separate fields of research.
8. Many economists share the Machlup view that optimality arguments are used not to predict the behaviour of the individual firm but to explain the observable consequences of the observed change of conditions. 'The type of action assumed to be taken by the theoretical actor in the model under specified conditions need not be expected and cannot be predicted actually to be taken by any particular real actor. The empiricist's inclination is to verify the theoretically deduced action by testing individual behaviour, although the theory serves only to explain and predict effects of mass behaviour'. (Machlup, 1967).
9. Modern biology has already shown that natural selection is only one of the mechanisms that explain the process of evolution from a population with given characteristics to another population with different characteristics. The other two processes of evolution are *genetic drives* and *molecular drives*.
10. This position is shared by many biologists and ecologists: Lewontin (1977) argues that 'the dynamics of natural selection does not include foresight, and there is no *theoretical principle* that assures *optimization as consequence of selection*'.
11. Stable polymorphisms are established when the reproductive linkage patterns between phenotypes are equally probable (no selection against heterozygotes),

when heterozygotes are selected for, or when gene-frequency-dependent selection is operating. The existence of different blood groups is an example of polymorphism.

Bibliography

ACS, J.Z. and AUDRETSCH, D.B. (1988), 'Innovation in Large and Small Firms: An Empirical Analysis', *American Economic Review* 78, pp. 678–98.

AOKI, M. (1984) *The Co-operative Game Theory of the Firm*, Oxford: Clarendon Press.

BECATTINI, G. (1979) 'Dal Settore Industriale al Distretto Industriale', *Rivista di Economia e Politica Industriale,* 1, pp. 7–22.

BECATTINI, G. (ed) (1987) *Mercato e Forze Locali: Il Distretto Industriale,* Bologna.

BROOKS D.R. and E.O. WILEY, (1988) *Evolution as Entropy: Towards a Unified Theory of Biology,* University of Chicago Press.

COWLING K. (1982) *Monopoly Capitalism,* London: MacMillan.

DASGUPTA, P. (1986) 'The Theory of Technological Competition', in Mathewson, G.F. and Stiglitz, J. (eds) *New Developments in the Analysis of Market Structure,* London: MacMillan.

DASGUPTA, P. and STIGLITZ, J. (1980) 'Uncertainty, Industrial Structure, and the Speed of R & D', *Bell Journal of Economics* 11, pp. 1–28.

DASGUPTA, P. STIGLITZ, J. (1981) 'Entry, Innovation and Exit: Towards a Dynamic Theory of Oligopolistic Industrial Structure', *European Economic Review* 15, pp. 137–58.

D'ASPREMONT, C. and JACQUEMIN, A. (1988) 'Cooperative and Noncooperative R & D in Duopoly with Spillovers', *American Economic Review* 78, pp. 1133–7.

ENKE, S. (1951) 'On Maximizing Profits: A Distinction between Chamberlin and Robinson', *American Economic Review* 41, pp. 566–78.

FRIEDMAN, M. (1953) *Essays in Positive Economics,* University of Chicago Press.

FUDENBERG, D. and TIROLE, J. (1985) 'Preemption and Rent Equalization in the Adoption of a New Technology', *Review of Economic Studies* 52, pp. 383–401.

GEORGESCU-ROEGEN, N. (1971) *The Entropy Law and the Economic Process,* Cambridge, Mass: Harvard University Press.

GRILICHES, Z. (1957) 'Hybrid Corn: An Exploration in the Economics of Technological Change', *Econometrics* 25, pp. 509–22.

HAHN, F. and HOLLIS, M. (eds) (1979) *Philosophy and Economic Theory,* Oxford University Press.

HARSANYI J. and SELTEN R. (1988) *A General Theory of Equilibrium Selection Games,* Boston: MIT Press.

HART, O. and HOLSTROM, B. (1987) 'The Theory of Contracts', in T. Bewley (ed.) *Advances in Economic Theory – Fifth World Congress,* Cambridge University Press.

HARTWICK, J.M. (1984) 'Optimal R & D Levels When Firm j Benefits From Firm i's Inventive Activity', *Economics Letters* 16, pp. 165–70.

HIRSCHLEIFER, J. (1977) 'Economics from a Biological Point of View', *Journal of Law and Economics* 20(1), pp. 1–52.

KAMIEN, M. and SCHWARTZ, N. (1982) *Market Structure and Innovation,* Cambridge University Press.

KATZ M.L. (1986) 'An Analysis of Cooperative Research and Development', *Rand Journal of Economics* 17(4), pp. 527–43.

LEVIN, R.C. (1978) 'Technical Change, Barriers to Entry and Market Structure', *Economica* 45, pp. 347–61.

LEWONTIN, R.C. (1977) 'Fitness, Survival and Optimality', in D. Hain, R.D. Mitchell and G.R. Stairs (eds) *Analysis of Ecological Systems,* Columbus: Ohio State University Press.

MACHLUP F. (1967) 'Theories of the Firm: Marginalist, Behavioural, Managerial', *American Economic Review* 57, pp. 1–33.

MANSFIELD, E. (1968) *The Economics of Technological Change,* New York: Norton.

MANSFIELD, E. (1961) 'Technical Change and the Rate of Imitation', *Econometrica* 29, pp. 741–66.

NELSON, R. and WINTER, S. (1982) *An Evolutionary Theory of Economic Change,* Cambridge, Mass.: The Belknap Press.

REINGANUM, J. (1981) 'Market Structure and the Diffusion of New Technology', *Bell Journal of Economics* 12, pp. 618–24.

SANDMO, A. (1971) 'On the Theory of the Competitive Firm under Price Uncertainty', *American Economic Review* 61, pp. 65–73.

SIMON, H. (1976) 'From Substantive to Procedural Rationality', in S. Latsis, (ed.), *Method and Appraisal in Economics,* Cambridge University Press, reprinted in Hahn and Hollis (eds) (1979).

TIROLE, J. (1986) Hierarchies and Bureaucracies, *Journal of Law, Economics and Organization* 2, pp. 181–214.

TIROLE, J. and FUDENBERG, D. (1987) Understanding Rent Dissipation: On the Use of Game Theory in Industrial Organization, *American Economic Review,* Papers and Proceedings, 77, pp. 176–184.

TIROLE, J. (1988) *The Theory of Industrial Organization,* Boston: MIT Press.

WILLIAMSON, O.E. (1975) *Market and Hierarchies: Analysis and Antitrust Implications,* New York: Free Press.

WILLIAMSON, O.E. (1985) *The Economic Institutions of Capitalism,* New York: Free Press.

Part I

Recent Approaches to Industrial Organization

1 Implementing Game-Theoretic Models in Industrial Economics: Levels of Attack

John Sutton

Up to ten years ago, industrial economics in the Anglo-Saxon tradition was a heavily 'empirical' subject. Following the tradition laid down by Bain and his successors, industrial economists focused particular attention on the investigation of a small number of statistical regularities, which were usually investigated by means of cross-sectional regressions carried out across a group of independent industries.

A glance over the journals of the past decade indicates a sea-change of a quite dramatic kind in the balance of research work in this field, however. Throughout the 1980s, the large bulk of research effort has been devoted to the development of a new body of theory which rests upon use of game-theoretic oligopoly models.

Until quite recently, there seemed to be little contact between the older tradition and this new body of work. The reasons for this were quite fundamental. It was not merely that the new theoretical approaches sometimes led to perspectives which were at variance with the traditional structure–conduct–performance paradigm. Rather, the new theories led many observers to respond by challenging the usefulness of any research programme based on a search for cross-industry regularities. The reasons for this response go to the root of the new theoretical approach; and in order to explain what is at issue, we first need to look at some basic features of game-theoretic models.

'EXPLAINING EVERYTHING . . .'

Game-theoretic models, as such, are no novelty within industrial economics. The classic Bertrand and Cournot models have been standard undergraduate fare for decades.[1] Why, then, was there such a sudden upsurge of

19

interest in the development and use of formal game-theoretic oligopoly models from the late 1970s onwards?

The impetus for this development lay in the appearance, in the late 1970s, of a series of independent applications of game-theoretic models to various standard problems in the field. A particularly influential contribution was the series of investigations of predatory pricing by Kreps (1982) and Wilson and Milgrom and Roberts (1982). The study of patent races and technological competition using game-theoretic models was also important (see Dasgupta and Stiglitz, 1980, for example). At around the same time, new interest developed in the area of product differentiation; in this regard, both the theoretical contribution of d'Aspremont, Gabszewicz and Thisse (1979) in correcting Hotelling's (1929) error, and the motivation provided by Schmalensee's (1978) analysis of the US antitrust case involving RTE (ready-to-eat) breakfast cereals played an important part.

Lying behind many of these developments was an important development within applied game theory generally. One of the major factors which appears to have limited the scope and usefulness of game-theoretic models up to the late 1970s, was the fact that simple 'one shot' games failed to offer a sufficiently rich and flexible vehicle within which to capture many intuitively appealing distinctions which appeared to be of central relevance to industrial economists. These intuitions could however be captured by working with a richer class of extensive form games than had hitherto been investigated. For example, the use of 'two-stage games', particularly in the product differentiation literature, permitted a neat distinction between 'long-run' and 'short-run' decision variables, and offered a simple way of capturing the notion of 'sunk costs'. Multi-stage games were essential in permitting an analysis of predatory behaviour in a multi-market setting. Within games of this kind, however, the employment of the basic 'Nash equilibrium' concept typically led to the appearance of multiple equilibria. The introduction of 'refinements' of the Nash equilibrium concept, first in the form of Selten's Perfect Equilibrium[2] and later Kreps and Wilson's sequential equilibrium[3] played a key role in reducing the set of acceptable or 'sensible' equilibria.

Throughout the 1970s the literature was dominated by the application of extensive form games to an extremely wide range of problems. A major success which may be claimed for this literature relates to its role in providing a satisfactory rationale for a wide range of observed phenomena. For example, the use of predatory pricing, which had come to be regarded as highly 'unlikely' on the basis of *a priori* theoretical arguments (McGee, 1958; Telser, 1965), was shown to have a clear and coherent theoretical basis, whether by way of 'reputation effects' (Kreps and Wilson, 1982), or by way of 'long purse arguments' (Benoit, 1984). Another example relates to the use of vertical restraints by manufacturers in their relations with retailers: here, the use of game-theoretic models could provide a detailed rationale for various forms of behaviour observed (Matthewson and Winter, 1984).

Now in many cases, including the two just mentioned, it could be argued that the game-theoretic models merely formalized long-standing intuitive arguments which could be found in the traditional literature. On the other hand, the development of these models has in some cases induced a substantial change in the conventional wisdom surrounding the issue (as in predatory pricing), while in other cases it has substantially enriched our understanding of the phenomenon (as in the case of vertical restraints, where the rationale underlying different combinations of standard restraints has been more fully explained).

'. . . EXPLAINING NOTHING?'

One of the main attractions of this class of models, then, is that many forms of widely observed behaviour can be rationalized by reference to a suitably designed game. But this flexibility, which has lent itself to the provision of 'explanations' for such a wide class of phenomena, lies at the very root of the most serious criticism which can be advanced against these models: to what extent does this approach generate specific testable predictions? Quite apart from the fact that any specific game-theoretic model may admit multiple equilibria, it is almost always the case that a wide range of choice exists as to the design of the appropriate game form to be used. Moreover, the results of the analysis often depend very delicately on the precise specification chosen. For example, the qualitative features of the results often depend on the way in which price competition is modelled (Bertrand, Cournot, etc.). They are also likely to depend on the presence or absence of strategic asymmetrics (first mover advantages, etc.).

Now in *some* contexts, a judgement may be made on *a priori* grounds as to which game form is appropriate to that particular setting. One reaction which has become extremely widespread over the past few years, runs as follows: since results are delicately dependent on the details of these models, the 'right' way to implement them empirically is to focus attention on one specific market, and to 'tailor make' the oligopoly model to fit that situation.

In practice, there are situations in which the institutional setting constraints the game so tightly as to leave us with a rich set of specific predictions, and the result is a pleasingly clear-cut exercise in 'testing the theory'. This happens for example in the analysis of certain auction markets (Hendriks and Porter, 1988). On the other hand, there are areas in which the class of admissable models is extremely wide, and we are left with an exercise in 'model selection' (see for example Gasmi, Laffont and Vuong, 1990).

It is this line of argument which underlies the new empirical literature in industrial economics which has begun to develop over the past three or four years (see the Journal of Industrial Economics Symposium of June 1987).

Allied to this view is a widespread feeling that the new game-theoretic literature leads to a viewpoint inimical to the traditional use of cross-industry studies. Implicit here is the belief that few results of interest are likely to hold over a class of candidate models sufficiently broad to justify their empirical implementation over a run of industries whose detailed characteristics may vary widely.

The central argument of the present paper is that this view represents an over-reaction. What is argued here is that an obvious but fundamental trade-off exists between the *precision* of predictions available and the *robustness* of such results to variations in the detailed structure of the underlying model. In the light of that trade-off, it is reasonable to try to proceed along two complementary paths:

1. By looking to those weak but robust results which hold across a broad class of models we may hope to find a basis for explaining such limited statistical regularities as hold good over a cross-section of different industries; while
2. Within the broad class of models thus defined it may then be possible to define special cases within that general framework which correspond to specific markets – and at this level we may hope to test more precise predictions in the context of 'single industry studies'.

The point of view set out above is not one which can be usefully defended in the abstract. What is at issue is not whether such as 'trade-off' exists: that point is one which would command widespread assent. What is at issue is whether *any* results of substantial interest can be shown to hold over a sufficiently broad class of models to warrant their application as a basis for cross-industry studies; and whether, within that class of models, a sufficiently rich menu of special cases can be identified which generates precise predictions for specific industries.

This kind of argument is best defended by appeal to a specific illustration, and in the remainder of this chapter I would like to turn to one specific research programme which follows this path.

INDUSTRIAL STRUCTURE I: ROBUST RESULTS AND CROSS-INDUSTRY REGULARITIES

The issues addressed in this section and the next relate to a general question which has been the focus of continued attention in the industrial economics literature: to what extent do industry characteristics such as the level of set-up costs (or the degree of scale economies), consumer tastes (and in particular the effectiveness of advertising), or the scope for technical improvements (and so the importance of R & D activity) influence or constrain the equilibrium structure of the industry?

The present section outlines one recent framework of analysis within which these questions may be addressed. This framework derives from the work of Shaked and Sutton (1987); see also Sutton (1990).

The class of models on which this analysis rests share one central feature. Equilibrium is modelled within the framework of a two-stage game: firms incur fixed outlays at stage 1 associated with acquiring a plant (set-up costs) and developing and establishing a product line (possibly incurring advertising and R & D outlays). These fixed outlays incurred in stage 1 of the game are treated as 'sunk cost' once we turn to analysing the second stage. At that stage of the game, the number of firms and their respective product offerings are taken as given, and firms compete in price.

Now the sunk costs incurred at stage 1 are of two kinds. The set-up costs incurred in acquiring a plant can be taken as exogenously given by the underlying technology of the industry. On the other hand, the levels of advertising and R & D incurred by firms is endogenously determined, as part of the outcome of the game played by firms in 'stage 1'.

Suppose, to begin with, that the only sunk costs involved are the exogenously given 'set-up costs' associated with establishing a plant. Within this case it is useful to distinguish two sub-cases. The first sub-case is that in which the various firms produce a homogenous product. For simplicity, assume that all firms incur the same sunk cost σ on entering the industry. The size of this sunk cost may in practice be proxied by the cost of acquiring a single plant of minimal efficient scale, net of any resale or scrap value which could be realized following closure. Suppose that, once this plant is established, all firms operate subject to the same constant level of marginal cost.

Now consider how the equilibrium number of firms in the industry varies as the size of the market (as measured by the population of consumers, and denoted S) increases.[4] It is easy to see that as market size increases in this model the equilibrium number of firms n increases, and so concentration – which we can measure simply as $1/n$ – declines indefinitely. For, at equilibrium, entry occurs up to the point where the profits of the last entrant cover the sunk cost σ. But these profits are given by $(\bar{p}-MC)$. $Sf(\bar{p})/n$, where $(\bar{p}-MC)$ is the unit mark-up, and $Sf(.)$ represents the market demand schedule, which expands proportionately with S. Thus n increases to infinity with S, so long as we assume that $(\bar{p}-MC)$ is non-increasing and remains strictly positive for all n.[5]

This case, then, corresponds to some familiar 'limit theorems' of the standard theoretical literature; and it offers one way of characterizing a traditional idea within industrial economics: that scale economies become unimportant as a constraint on equilibrium structure in 'large' economies.

The above remarks relate to the sub-case in which firms offer a homogeneous product. The second sub-case to be considered is that in which firms offer products which are differentiated, but in which sunk costs are still exogenously determined. This case has been widely explored in the 'horizontal product differentiation' literature: the archetypal example of this case arises in simple 'locational' models of the Hotelling kind. In these models, consumers are spread over some geographic region, and they incur (psychic or transport) costs in purchasing from distant suppliers. Each firm may establish any number of plants, and it incurs a fixed set-up cost of σ per plant. Consumers thereafter make their purchases from the 'lowest cost' supplier, where the cost of the consumer consists of the price paid to the firm, plus a 'transport cost' which depends on his distance from the supplier in question.

Now in models of this kind, multiple equilibria are endemic. In general, for any given market size, we may find 'fragmented' equilibria in which a large number of firms each sell at one location, and 'concentrated' equilibria in which a small number of firms each sell at many locations.

In the next section, we will look at the factors underlying the appearance of these two types of equilibria; and we shall see that these factors are likely to vary widely from one industry to another. Thus, if we are interested in finding properties 'robust' enough to be of interest in cross-industry studies, then we cannot constrain possible equilibrium configurations here, beyond saying that the bound corresponding to the 'most fragmented' configuration ('single product firms') form a *lower bound* to equilibrium concentration. This bound declines with market size in the manner of the schedule described above for the homogenous product case.

To sum up, then: in the case in which sunk costs are exogenous, an increase in the size of the market may lead to the appearance of indefinitely low levels of concentration (Fig. 1.1(i)).

We now turn to the second case, i.e. where *endogenous* sunk costs are present, whether in the form of advertising or R & D.

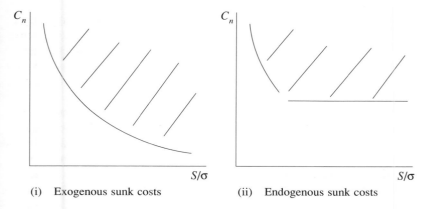

(i)   Exogenous sunk costs   (ii)   Endogenous sunk costs

Figure 1.1   A schematic representation of a general result concerning equilibrium concentration as a function of market size

Suppose that, by incurring greater fixed costs at stage 1 of the game, a firm can enhance the demand for its product at stage 2 (i.e. for any prices set by other firms, the demand schedule of the firm in question shifts outwards). Then it is fairly obvious that the game played at stage 1 might involve a competitive escalation of outlays by firms, leading to higher sunk costs being incurred at equilibrium. It is also fairly obvious that, the larger the size of the market – and so the profits achievable at stage 2 – the greater might be the sunk costs incurred in stage 1 at equilibrium.

What is not obvious is that this is not merely a *possible* outcome: rather, in turns out on examining a range of different oligopoly models that an unusually robust result arises in this case, which runs contrary to that found in the 'exogenous sunk cost' case. What this result says is that under very general conditions a lower bound exists to the equilibrium level of concentration in the industry, no matter how large the market becomes.

The level of this lower bound depends upon the degree of responsiveness of the demand faced by an individual firm to increases in its fixed (advertising or R & D) outlays at stage 1 of the game. The higher that degree of responsiveness, the higher will be the lower bound to equilibrium concentration levels in the industry.

Under these circumstances, increases in market size cannot lead to a fragmented market structure as the size of the market increases (Fig. 1.1(ii)). Rather, a competitive escalation in outlays at stage 1 of the game raises the equilibrium level of sunk costs incurred by incumbent firms in step with increases in the size of the market – thus offsetting the tendency towards fragmentation.

Now the importance of this simple but basic result, in the present context, lies in the fact that it holds over an extremely wide class of oligopoly models. For example, the result holds good independently of whether each firm offers a single product, or a range of products. It holds independently of the form which price competition takes at stage 2 of the game (Bertrand, Cournot, etc.). It is not affected by altering the 'sequence of moves' in the entry stage of the game (simultaneous entry, sequential entry, etc.). The degree of robustness of this result to changes in model specification makes it a suitable candidate for investigation in a cross-industry setting.

What this property implies, then, is that if we confine attention to some set of 'homogeneous good' industries, in which advertising and R & D outlays are insignificant, and examine how concentration varies with the size of the market across different countries, then we should expect concentration to fall as the size of the market rises relative to the set-up costs incurred in entering the industry. It is a key prediction of the theory, moreover, that this relationship should break down among 'advertising-intensive' industries.

This property has been investigated in some recent work by the present author (reported in Sutton, 1991) within the context of 20 food and drink markets in each of six countries. It is shown that the relationship between market size and concentration differs as between the group of 'homogeneous goods' industries (salt, sugar, flour, etc.) as against 'advertising intensive' industries (frozen food, coffee, confectionery, etc.) in the manner predicted.

Now in the earlier literature on cross-sectional differences in structure, there are few statistical regularities which appear consistently across different studies. One attraction of the present approach is that these few regularities which have appeared can be shown to follow from the simple 'robust' proposition derived above (for details, the reader is referred to Sutton, 1991b).

By investigating each of the industries in the sample in some detail, moreover, it is possible to confirm that the mechanisms influencing the evolution of structure in these two groups of industries appear to be closely in line with those implicit in the simple game-theoretic models. It is also possible to see that, beyond the broad and simple characterization embodied in this 'robust' result, there is little scope for generalization. Strong differences in experience from one industry to another exist, which reflect such factors as (institutionally determined) differences in the intensity of price competition, the presence or absence of 'first mover advantages', and so on.

Nonetheless, by looking at these industries or groups of industries which appear on *a priori* grounds to conform to some particular special case within the model, it is possible to show how industry-specific factors (such as first-mover advantages, say) lead to differences in the structure of a given industry between one country and another. In this way some progress can be made in going beyond the weak and general characterization which can be achieved independently of such considerations.

This appear, however, to be as far as one can go in seeking principles applicable across a fairly broad cross-section of industries. Further progress in understanding the evolution of structure is best achieved by way of a complementary approach directed towards 'single-industry studies'.

INDUSTRIAL STRUCTURE II: SPECIFIC RESULTS AND SINGLE MARKET STUDIES

We now turn to the second line of attack, in which the aim is to focus on some specific market for which we can 'fine tune' the appropriate oligopoly model.

The context in which we do this is one which our preceding discussion has shown to be particularly 'problematic', in the sense that the kind of 'general' or 'robust' arguments described in the preceding section exclude very few forms of structure as possible equilibria. Specifically, we look at a case in which a homogeneous good is sold at various locations. The appropriate model here is one of 'horizontal product differentiation'. The reason that little can be said *in general* regarding equilibrium structure, is that a wide range of possible configurations exist, ranging from 'fragmented' structures in which a large number of producers each sell at one location, to 'concentrated' structures in which a small number of producers each sell at many locations.

The range of such configurations which actually form equilibria will depend on two types of consideration, both of which will differ widely from one market to another.

The first type of consideration relates to the *cost* side of the model. In so far as economies of scope exist, this will work in favour of the appearance of more concentrated outcomes. In what follows, we will confine ourselves to the special case in which such scope economies are not significant.

The second type of consideration relates to the *demand* side of the model. Here, the range of configurations which constitute equilibrium outcomes can be determined by reference to a quite simple and intuitively appealing criterion, developed in Shaked and Sutton (1990), which runs as follows:

Suppose, to fix ideas, that the product is initially supplied at only one outlet (location). Imagine a situation in which market demand expands, by way of an increase in the population of consumers. Consider the difference in the incentives to introduce a second outlet faced by the incumbent 'monopolist', and by some 'potential entrant', respectively. To the incumbent the set-up cost of establishing a new outlet must be outweighed by the net addition to its profits, which will accrue because new customers, who hitherto did not purchase from its old outlet, will now be drawn into the market. This 'market expansion effect', which can be measured by the proportionate increase in the monopolist's profit, is the first of the two effects which determine equilibrium structure.

The second effect which we need to examine arises when we turn to look at the incentives facing a potential entrant. When the entrant sets up a new outlet, part of his sales arise at the expense of the incumbent's existing outlet. What matters to the new entrant, however, is the level of demand for the new variety: he escapes the negative externality which must be taken into account by the monopolist, and this strengthens his incentive to introduce the new outlet. Working against this, however, is a second factor: if the second outlet is introduced by a new entrant, then prices will tend to be lower in the resulting competitive environment than would be the case were the two outlets operated by a monopolist. This 'competition effect' may be measured by the ratio of duopoly profit to the profit of a monopolist operating two outlets. The stronger is the 'competition effect', the weaker is the entrant's incentive to open a second outlet, relative to the incumbent's.

In general, then, the set of configurations which are supportable as equilibria in this setting will depend upon the relative strength of the 'market expansion effect' and the 'competition effect' respectively.

What I wish to argue, in what follows, is that within some specific market context it may be possible to pin down the relative importance of these two effects, and so derive some quite specific testable predictions regarding equilibrium structure.

The kind of predictions which we describe below concern the relationship between market size (as measured by the population of consumers) and the set of equilibrium configurations.

As market size (the population of consumers) increases, we move through a succession of critical values at which different configurations become supportable as equilibria. For a sufficiently small size, no outlet will be viable. At some critical level S_1 a single outlet becomes viable. Thereafter, two cases arise:

(i)   either we next reach a critical level $S_{1,1}$ beyond which the unique equilibrium configuration involves two different sellers each operating one outlet; or

(ii)   we reach a critical level $S_{2,0}$ beyond which the unique equilibrium involves one seller operating two outlets. (In labelling equilibria, the notation (x, y) reads: seller 1 operates x outlets and seller 2 operates y outlets.)

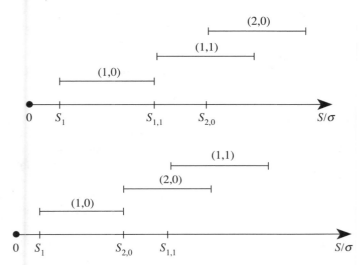

Figure 1.2   *How equilibrium configurations are related to market size. The notation (x, y) reads: seller 1 operates x outlets and seller 2 operates y outlets*

As size increases further, we move into a region involving *both* these 'two outlet' configurations as equilibria. Thereafter, further increases in market size lead to the appearance of configurations involving three outlets, four outlets, and so on (Fig. 1.2).

What determines whether we are in case (i) or case (ii), i.e. whether (1, 1) or (2, 0) enters first? This depends on the relative strength of the 'expansion effect' and 'competition effect'. If the expansion effect is strong, and the competition effect is weak, then the 'monopoly' solution (2, 0) enters first. If the relative strength of these two effects is reversed, then (1, 1) enters first.

The reason for this follows directly from our earlier remarks on the way in which these two effects determine the incentives for the incumbent, as against the potential entrant, to open a second outlet. The point is a general one; and it may be extended to equilibria involving any number of products. If the expansion effect is weak relative to the competition effect, then the more 'fragmented' equilibria involving n products will appear at lower market sizes (population levels) than will the more 'concentrated' n-outlet equilibria.

In other words, if we can decide within some particular context, either that the expansion effect is very weak relative to the competition effect, or else that it is very strong relative to the competition effect, then we obtain a clear testable prediction as to the ordering of the critical market size values $s_{1,1}$, $s_{2,0}$, etc.[6] To implement this model, then, we need to find a context within which (*a*) the maintained assumptions of the model are valid, and (*b*) the setting is such that the expansion effect is either very strong, or very weak, relative to the competition effect, so that a clear-cut prediction can be made.

One further feature of these models, not illustrated in Figure 1.2, is as follows. As the expansion effect becomes weaker, the range of market sizes over which the 'monopoly' configurations appear tends to shrink – and for a sufficiently small 'expansion effect', these configurations may not appear at all.

Now recent empirical work by Bresnahan and Reiss (1990) has drawn attention to the idea of looking at the relationship between town populations (together with some ancillary measures of demand) and the number of retail outlets of a given type which the town supports. What the above discussion suggests is that there may be some scope in this context for testing a relatively precise set of predictions relating not only to the number, but also to the ownership configuration, of outlets.

In looking at a set of 'isolated towns', of course, we would expect that the 'expansion effect' may be very small, at least for certain types of product. Under these circumstances, we might simply expect few observations of the 'monopoly' type to occur. Beyond this, is there scope for probing any further implications of the theory?

Even in this setting, considerable scope may exist for testing one key idea: as the 'competition effect' becomes stronger, the interval of market size over which a given number of outlets can be supported is shifted upwards.

In some settings, it may be possible to test this implication directly. Consider, for example, the case of retail petrol. Here, even if the ownership configuration in all towns is 'fragmented', in the sense that all stations are independently owned, an interesting distinction arises between those cases in which all the town's outlets obtain their supplies from the same petrol company as against the situation in which they obtain their supplies from rival producers. Given the producers' control over the wholesale price at which outlets obtain supplies, we would expect less intense price competition in the former setting. The theory predicts that the range of town sizes which supports a given number of outlets will then be shifted downwards.[7]

The central theme of the present section may be summed up succinctly: once we confine attention to some single industry, it may be possible to take advantage of the special features of that industry, to specify the underlying oligopoly model tightly on *a priori* grounds, and so obtain a set of relatively precise testable predictions.

CONCLUDING COMMENTS

The two illustrations set out above correspond to two different but complementary approaches to a fundamental difficulty raised by the new generation of game-theoretic models in industrial economics. The level of attack involved in the first approach is similar to that which characterized most empirical work in industrial economics in the 1960s and 1970s. The latter approach, on the other hand, is typical of the 'single industry studies' which have become popular over the past few years.

Viewed from a theoretical perspective, the two approaches can be seen as deeply complementary, however. Once it is accepted that a basic trade-off exists between the precision of some set of predictions and their breadth of applicability (in terms of 'robustness' to detailed changes in the specification of the underlying model), then it seems natural to attempt this kind of two-pronged attack.

The potential fruitfulness of such a strategy cannot be gauged in advance. This clearly depends on the problem in hand, and specifically on the extent to which some results can be obtained which are both reasonably robust, and substantively interesting. What has been argued here is that the study of the determinants of cross-sectional differences in industrial structure offers one example in which this strategy appears attractive.

Notes

The support of the Leverhulme Foundation, the ESRC and STICERD (LSE) is gratefully acknowledged.

1.   A 'game' consists of three objects: a set of players; a set of strategies for each player; and a pay-off function specifying the pay-off to each player as a function of the set of strategies chosen by all players.
   The basic equilibrium notion is that of a Nash equilibrium: viz. a set of strategies form a Nash equilibrium if each player's strategy is an optimal (payoff-maximizing) reply to the strategies chosen by rival players.
   The familiar 'Bertrand equilibrium' is a 'Nash equilibrium in prices' (i.e. the

        strategy of each player is simply to choose a price). The 'Cournot equilibrium' is a 'Nash equilibrium in quantities'.

2.   A (subgame-) perfect equilibrium is a Nash equilibrium which has the additional property that the strategies used by players in each subgame form a Nash equilibrium in that subgame. Thus, for example, if a game takes place in two stages, the 'perfectness' requirement means that *whatever* actions players take at stage 1, the strategies employed in stage 2 of the game form a Nash equilibrium in that subgame. Intuitively, this can be seen as excluding the use of any 'empty' threats or promises at stage 1 (i.e. ones which would not be carried out should the eventuality in question actually arise at stage 2). More delicate considerations arise once imperfect information is introduced (Selten, 1975).

3.   The 'sequential equilibrium' notion offers one way of extending the 'subgame perfectness' notion to a setting of incomplete information. For an application, see Kreps and Wilson (1982).

4.   i.e. by 'replication', so that the distribution of consumer tastes remains unchanged, and so for any set of prices charged by firms the level of market demand faced by each firm is multiplied by s_1/s_0, where population rises from s_0 to s_1.

5.   Though it may of course approach zero asymptotically as $n \to \infty$. This excludes the limiting 'Bertrand' case (see Sutton, 1991).

6.   These two effects have been defined above in terms of relative profit levels for the two-outlet case.

7.   The above discussion relates to a setting characterized by strategic symmetry ('simultaneous entry'). This should be distinguished from the case in which one firm enjoys a first-mover advantage. In the latter setting, 'monopoly' configurations may appear even when the 'expansion effect' is zero: the first mover may pre-empt subsequent entry by opening multiple outlets.

References

BENOIT, J-P. (1984) 'Financially Constrained Entry in a Game with Incomplete Information', *Rand Journal of Economics* 15, pp. 490–9.

BRESNAHAN, T.F. and REISS, C. (1990) 'Entry in Monopoly Markets', *Review of Economic Studies*.

DASGUPTA, P. and STIGLITZ, J. (1980) 'Industrial Structure and the Nature of Innovative Activity', *Economic Journal* 90, pp. 266–93.

D'ASPREMONT, C., GABSZEWICZ, J. J. and THISSE, J-F. (1979) 'On Hotelling's "Stability in Competition"', *Econometrica* 47, pp. 1145–50.

GASMI, F., LAFFONT, J.J. and VUONG, Q. (1990) 'An Econometric Analysis of a Dynamic Duopoly Model', *European Economic Review*, forthcoming.

HENDRIKS, K. and PORTER R.H. (1988) 'An Empirical Study of an Auction with Asymmetric Information', *American Economic Review* 78 (14), pp. 301–14.

HOTELLING, H. (1929) 'Stability in Competition', *Economic Journal* 39, pp. 41–57.

KREPS, D. and WILSON R. (1982) 'Reputation and Imperfect Information', *Journal of Economic Theory* 27, pp. 253–79.

MCGEE, J.S. (1958) 'Predatory Price Cutting: The Standard Oil (N.J.) Case', *Journal of Law and Economics* 137, pp. 138–43.

MATTHEWSON, G.F. and WINTER, R.A. (1984) 'An Economic Theory of Vertical Restraints', *Rand Journal of Economics* 15, pp. 27–38.

MILGROM, P. and ROBERTS, J. (1982) 'Predation, Reputation and Entry', *Journal of Economic Theory* 27, pp. 280–312.

SCHMALENSEE, R. (1978) 'Entry Deterrence in the Ready-to-Eat Breakfast Cereal Industry', *Bell Journal of Economics* 9, pp. 305–27.

SELTEN, R. (1975) 'A Re-Examination of the Perfectness Concept for Equilibrium Points in Extensive Games', *International Journal of Game Theory* 4, pp. 25–55.

SHAKED, A. and SUTTON, J. (1987) 'Product Differentiation and Industrial Structure', *Journal of Industrial Economics* 36, pp. 131–46.

SHAKED, A. and SUTTON, J. (1990) 'Multiproduct Firms and Market Structure', *Rand Journal of Economics*, forthcoming.

SLADE, Margaret (1990) 'Strategic Pricing Models and Interpretation of Price-War Data', *European Economic Review*, forthcoming.

SUTTON, J. (1990) 'Endogenous Sunk Costs and Market Structure', in G. Bonanno and D. Brandolini (eds), *Industrial Structure in the New Industrial Economics*, Oxford University Press.

SUTTON, J. (1991) *Sunk Costs and Market Structure*, Cambridge, Mass.: MIT Press.

TELSER, L. (1965) 'Abusive Trade Practices: An Economic Analysis', *Law and Contemporary Problems* 488, pp. 494–6.

TIROLE, J. (1988) *The Theory of Industrial Organization*, Cambridge Mass.: MIT Press.

2 Performances, Interactions and Evolution in the Theory of Industrial Organization[1]

Giovanni Dosi

INTRODUCTION

I can think of two ways of introducing the reflections that follow on the achievements, limitations and promises of current theories of industrial organization. One is with reference to some major empirical phenomena that economic theories of industrial organization have addressed (or, in some cases, ought to address). Another one refers to the actual developments of industrial economics, in particular in the post-war period. This contribution is not intended by any means as a survey: rather, I am simply going to present some reflections on the current 'state of the art', in a perspective which, surely, many practitioners of the field will consider as somewhat biased toward 'evolutionary' and 'institutionalist' themes. (For more general surveys and modelling attempts, with a variety of interpretative approaches, see Schmalensee (1988), Stiglitz and Mathewson (1986), Jacquemin (1987), Scherer (1980), Kreps and Spence (1986), Tirole (1988), Schmalensee and Willig (1989), and Kreps (1990).[2]

As Herbert Simon once ironically said, beginning with sheer 'facts' demands some apologies. Sharing that outdated inclination, I too will start with some empirical phenomena which industrial economics ought plausibly to address:

1. Why do industries in contemporary economies strikingly depart from the characteristics which competitive economic models assume?
   What accounts for the rather general existence of industrial oligopolistic markets?
2. Under conditions of oligopolistic interactions, and thus also of strategic behaviours by individual firms, how do agents behave?
   Which variables determine their strategies?
3. What explains industrial performances across industries and over time?

In particular, how does one explain (*a*) the observed profit levels; (*b*) the relative insensitivity of industry-level mark-ups over the business cycle; (*c*) the significant intra-industry variance in production costs and profits; (*d*) the persistency of old time of these differences; and (*e*)the inter-industrial differences in average profitabilities?

4. Obviously, industries change over time in the efficiencies with which they utilize their inputs and also in their output mixes. What are the sources, processes and effects of these changes in production methods and product characteristics? That is, how does one account for various forms of process-, product- and organizational innovations?

5. In contemporary mixed economies most firms are diversified across a range of different products and, quite often, also vertically integrated in the production of some of their own inputs: why is that? Moreover, despite integration and product diversification, why do most firms appear to have rather recognizable limits to their expansion across product lines (i.e. why, for example, General Motors makes trucks but not biscuits)?

6. What accounts for the observed size-distribution of business firms which appears to have persistently resembled a Pareto-distribution despite major changes in technologies, relative sectoral shares and relative firm shares in manufacturing output?

7. What explains the observed evolution over time of the patterns of internal organization of business firms and also the coexistence of different patterns of any one time (e.g. U-forms, M-forms, conglomerates, 'network firms', etc.)?

8. How do technological and organizational changes interact with the growth and decline of firms and, generally, with the changes in market structures?

Putting it more succinctly, the empirical phenomena on which industrial economics focuses have to do with (*a*) the explanation of the (moving) *boundaries between markets and organizations*; (*b*) the nature of *behaviours and of co-ordination*, generally among strategic agents; and (*c*) the determinants of changing individual and aggregate *performances*.

At a more theoretical level, an assessment of the contemporary achievements of industrial economics reasonably ought to trace the progress of different approaches in interpreting at least some of the above empirical phenomena. (In fact some of them are not uncontroversial in the discipline: still, I personally consider the available evidence to be strong enough). I will mainly focus here on the relative interpretative merits and limitations of, *lato sensu*, 'standard', 'structuralist', and 'evolutionary' theories of industrial organization (a more precise meaning of these categories is given below).

First, I shall suggest a sort of reconstruction of the main themes, methodologies and empirical conclusions of these theoretical approaches to industrial economics. Secondly, I will present my assessment of these different analytical perspectives. Finally, I will outline some directions of research which, in my view, are highly challenging and promising.

STRUCTURES, CONDUCTS, PERFORMANCES AND THE DYNAMICS OF INDUSTRIES

There is probably a common recognition behind the early explorations of the features of industry in this century, namely: first, the prevalent forms of industrial organization involve at least some producers that show a size big enough to enjoy some indivisibilities and/or increasing returns; and, second, market interactions plausibly imply strategic behaviours and various sorts of oligopolistic interaction or monopolistic competition. These phenomena, as known, are underlying early critiques of Marshall's canonic interpretations of industrial equilibria, such as those of Sraffa (1925 and 1926), as well as A. Young's emphasis on increasing returns (Young, 1928), and Chamberlin (1933) and J. Robinson (1933) on strategic behaviours implicitly based on spatial and product differentiation. In a somewhat different stream of analysis, it is well known that models such as those of Cournot, Bertrand and von Stackelberg pioneered the investigation of the 'rational' interactive strategies and their possible outcomes.

By the mid-twentieth century the discipline of economics had widely recognized the generalized existence of non-purely-competitive forms of market organization.

Moreover, empirical evidence (such as Hall and Hitch, 1939) added puzzling pieces of evidence on corporate behaviours (e.g. on pricing) which would not confirm with theory-based predictions on competitive interactions and not even with the simplest predictions of oligopolistic models. Relatively fixed mark-up pricing is probably the best-known case, but also rather widespread 'rules of thumb' for scrapping, and 'fixed-percentage-of-sales' rules for R & D investment, belong to this category of evidence.

Facing these phenomena and theoretical puzzles, with hindsight, one can recognize in the history of economic analysis a sort of 'bifurcation', around the 1950s and 60s.

One rather broad and heterogeneous set of analyses focuses on *the structural conditions* which determine what I would call persistent *asymmetries* between incumbents and potential entrants in any one industrial sector and among incumbents themselves. Size-related economies of scale and other absolute-cost advantages were identified among the main sources of differential competitive advantages. Then one proceeded to establish some direct links between structural conditions, the degrees to which firms can exercise oligopolistic power and, as a consequence, also with the average price and profit performances of various industries (cf. Bain, 1956; Mason, 1939; Sylos-Labini, 1967). I call a *structuralist approach* that set of interpretative models which assume that the features of industrial technologies and organization can be a proximate predictor of industrial performances, irrespective of any explicit representation of 'rationally deducted' strategic decision procedures. In a language possibly nearer to current industrial organization theories, these approaches assumed throughout some sort of von Stackelberg interactions involving asymmetric pay-offs of a nature such that they would have approximately determined the diverse 'equilibrium' behaviours of the various actors, identifiable even without any explicit representations of optimizing micro-strategies.

Conversely, a seemingly diverging stream of analysis investigated primarily the problems of *rational calculation* under strategic interactions and focused on the properties of notional equilibria which such interactions would have yielded. 'Structuralist' analyses, in this perspective, have been criticized for the lack of explicit micro-foundations and for what is sometimes called 'implicit theorizing' (for example, how does one justify rather fixed mark-ups? Is it optimizing for the incumbent to charge entry-deterring prices? etc.). In fact, the 'structure–conduct–performance' paradigm – grown, especially in the USA, since the 1960s – identifies the 'conduct' dimension in literally profit-maximizing behaviours. By applying such a conduct on specific context conditions, in principle derived from empirical observation (the 'structure'), the paradigm promises a micro-founded account of 'performances'. (For a general synthesis in this perspective see Scherer, 1980).

For the purposes of the present work, note two things. First, the emphasis on 'micro-foundations', which I *do* consider very important and very challenging, focuses the attention on questions such as: What are the behaviours underlying certain observed industry-wide performances? More generally, why do agents do what they do? Second, note also the beginning of an irresistible tendency towards identifying the micro-foundations with literally maximizing behaviours.

To be fair, the 'structure–conduct–performance' paradigm attempts to strike some balance between the attention to 'structural' conditions (e.g. the characteristics of the various agents, their cost functions, etc.) and the analysis of 'rational conducts'. With hindsight, however, one observes in the discipline a trend towards an almost exclusive focus on 'conducts' and an increasingly casual account of the constraints to rational behaviours. From structure–conduct–performance analyses to more recent 'new industrial organization' models of the 1970s and 80s, one observes a significant theoretical simplification of the contexts in which decisions take place (treated sometimes as an embarrassing link with history-specific phenomena), and, conversely, an increasing complexity of the postulated rational conducts.

Within this broad tendency the focus on 'rational' micro-foundations has led, as we know, to two broad classes of models, based on decision-theoretic and game-theoretic frameworks. For a very simple illustration, consider the profit-maximizing problem for any one i-firm involving a quantity control variable (q_i), so that the first order condition is

$$\frac{dc_i}{dq_i} = p + \frac{dp}{dQ} \frac{dQ}{dq_i} q_i$$

where $c_i = c(q_i)$ are the production costs, p is the price and $Q = \sum_i q_i$. Surely, even if one accepts any 'rational' representation of conducts, the shape of the cost function and demand elasticities for the industry affect performances. However, since they are 'exogenous' to the strategic problem facing each i-firm, the theory has increasingly focused on the second right-hand term. Of course, one modelling strategy is to remain rather agnostic on (dQ/dq_i) and allow, at least in principle, a theoretically undetermined set of conjectures. On the other hand, one may 'close' the system by rewriting the profit-maximizing conditions for each firm in game-theoretic terms. In general, one defines a set of strategies that the agents can follow, the associated pay-offs, and explores the existence and properties of equilibria. Then, in so far as the model is used for interpretative rather than normative purposes,[3] one generally adds the deceptively innocent assumption that *the agents also know* or come to know about this same set of strategies and pay-offs (this is often part of the so-called 'common knowledge' assumption in game theory). All that certainly *is* a behavioural micro-foundation, but in my view it is achieved at a rather high price.

First, one generally achieves a neat 'rational' interpretation only by representing *structurally identical agents*. Second, the latter are assumed to have the computing capabilities to allow them to work out their optimal strategies. Third, note that the nearer one gets to a 'realistic' degree of environmental complexity, the higher the demands on the computational and cognitive abilities of the agents (in fact, the dimensionality of the strategic problem increases more than linearly in the number of interacting agents and in the number of control variables, i.e. output, quantities, investments, R & D, advertising, etc.).

Simplifying greatly: 'rational' equilibrium models of industrial organization have tended to steadily amplify the demands on the assumed 'rationality' of corporate decision-makers, while seemingly constraining the degrees of (history-dependent) specifications on the nature and characteristics of the agents. Conversely, the older 'structuralist' tradition, although empirically more plausible in the asymmetry assumptions, has turned out to be rather weak in its behavioural micro-foundations[4] and in the explanation of the asymmetries themselves. (More precisely, the 'American' tradition, à la Bain, has quite often taken the latter as given, without explicit theoretical justifications, while one finds quite rich interpretations based on scale-biased technical progress, especially in Downie, 1958; Sylos-Labini, 1967; and Steindl, 1976).

More recently an 'evolutionary' approach has developed, still in its infancy, but with some illustrious ancestors in spirit: Schumpeter, von Hayek, the more micro-analytical parts of Marx, and also, in several places, A. Smith. In my view the key elements that an evolutionary approach to industrial economics emphasizes are the following:

1. The permanent diversity amongst the agents, not only in terms of size and scale economies, but more importantly, in their capabilities of innovating and imitating. (Of course, this requires a theory of production which is different from the standard one based on freely available information, but a good deal has been done in that direction.)[5]
2. The generalized inadequacy of agents to correctly compute the equilibrium strategies (which might or might not exist), but also their ability to discover and implement new technologies, products, organizational set-ups.
3. The frequent occurrence of some forms of dynamic increasing returns.
4. An explicit market interaction also involving the *ex post selection* amongst heterogeneous behaviours, technologies, firms.

Compared with the other two approaches mentioned earlier, it certainly embodies – and also tries to explain – the evidence on persistent asymmetries in efficiency and performances. It is inherently dynamic, and hence seemingly fit for the analysis of the evolution of industrial structures. It assumes less computational ability, more behavioural inertiality, but also more creative potential of the agents than the standard 'rational' models (I shall discuss some implications of that later). Admittedly it yields less elegant models which generally cannot be analytically solved but only simulated, since it generally implies highly non-linear processes of corporate learning and market selection (with all the known problems in interpreting simulations . . .).

So far I have sketched three archetypes, so simplified as to be inevitable caricatures. However, what I want to convey is an extreme picture of different basic methodologies, with their different emphases on what is important and what is not and, crucially, their implicit assumptions on what, in the last resort, 'explains' the phenomena under investigation. Again, to be heroically brief, 'structuralist' approaches have based their explanations of observed performances on the features of the underlying industrial structures, seen as rather invariant and powerful enough to shape individual behaviours. 'Rational'/micro-founded/equilibrium models are inclined to account for whatever is analysed in terms of the consistency among rational decision processes of strategic agents. Evolutionary models attempt a joint account of performances and industrial dynamics by focusing on disequilibrium processes of learning and market selection.

Of course, as the modern philosophy of science has taught us, each research programme tries to fulfill its promises of 'explaining' by progressively refining its instruments and by being applied to ever-new problems. Indeed, industrial economics in the post-war period has rapidly developed in its modelling activities (and also in its empirical analyses, although at significantly lower rates). Let me move a few steps beyond the foregoing archetypes and discuss what kind of 'progress' has been made and whether the different streams of analyses have converged or further departed in their objects of enquiry and in their 'explanations' of industrial phenomena.

STRATEGIC RATIONALITY, MARKETS AND INDUSTRIAL EVOLUTION

Let me first discuss some developments in what I earlier called, in a shorthand, 'rational' equilibrium theories, and then compare them with 'evolutionary' theories.

At the risk of being roughly oversimplistic, I believe that its decision-theoretic version does not seem analytically very promising, or rather it can be promising only at the cost of embodying a lot of those empirically based auxiliary assumptions which were part of the earlier critiques of 'structuralist' approaches. In fact, without any further assumptions, what determines agents' beliefs about other agents' beliefs? How are these beliefs made to be *ex ante* consistent? How does one avoid infinite regresses? Overcoming these difficulties implies, indeed, detailed empirical analyses of context-specific behaviour formation: history and institutions, somewhat surreptitiously, regain a central role in the determination of performances. In this respect, Hahn's works on 'conjectural equilibria' are illuminating on the general dependence of such equilibria (whenever they exist) on the nature of beliefs which cannot themselves be 'rationally' derived, but rather must be given from a domain outside the theory (see Hahn, 1977; 1978; 1988).

Game-theoretical models of (generally, non-cooperative) coordination appear *prima facie* more promising to industrial analysis. After all, many of the decisions that modern oligopolistic firms take can be represented as parts of strategic interactions with other players. Also it is reasonable to assume that each player makes the best use of information that he can. And, needless to say, he will prefer, other things being equal, higher returns to lower returns strategies. Apparently it is a perfectly adequate set-up for game-theoretical representations. In fact a rapidly growing stream of economic literature has applied game-theoretic models to oligopolistic behaviours, dealing with issues such as competition versus collusion, product differentiation, price discrimination, entry deterrence, patenting. I shall not attempt any review of this wide set of works here (for this purpose see Tirole, 1988; Kreps, 1990; Schmalensee, 1988; Binmore and Dasgupta, 1986, and the chapters by Hey and Sutton in this volume). I do share with a few practitioners of these endeavours the view that these exercises may help in *rationally reconstructing* the possible existence of *consistency conditions* amongst decentralized strategic behaviours. However, the exploration of the conditions for the *existence* of consistency (that is, the existence of equilibria) under highly stylized theoretical assumptions is still very far from any claim that such a 'rational reconstruction' is by itself an 'explanation' (whatever that means in social sciences) of what one observes. (In fact, stability of equilibria – at least a local one – jointly with some criteria of selection among multiple equilibria, would be required, but nothing like that is likely to be delivered.) I am personally rather distant from the Hegelian belief that 'whatever is real is rational and whatever is rational is real'. Hence I am equally sceptical on empirical interpretations based on the *ex ante* rationality of the 'Spirit of the World' of classical German philosophy, as well as, by the same token, on the magic of decentralized self-seeking shopkeepers on Main Street.

Let me consider some of the necessary conditions for more direct *interpretative* utilizations of game-theoretic models. To start with, even when the external analyst knows all the possible strategies, the exhaustive list of events of nature and also that (possibly locally) stable equilibria exist, one should ask whether one should suppose that the agents know it too. (A similar point is made in Hey's contribution to this volume). The question is crucial because only an affirmative answer provides grounds to the conjecture that what we empirically observe is the outcome of an *ex ante* coordination among rational agents. As hinted earlier, I am rather sceptical about a yes answer: it requires identity in the rational power of all agents, no 'competence gap' in information processing,[6] no computational limitations – irrespective of the complexity of the problem-solving tasks – and stationarity (no unexpected events, such as innovations).

Of course, a negative answer does not necessarily mean that game-theoretic models lose their interpretative importance; but if the answer to the earlier question is no – e.g. because agents are largely uninformed, have computational limitations, have 'competence gaps' – then one must account for the learning process through which agents 'eventually get there' (i.e. to the equilibria whose existence is deductively demonstrated by economic theory). Sequential and 'evolutionary' games have tackled precisely this problem. In fact J. Sutton's contribution is a very stimulating challenge to compare them with evolutionary approaches, as defined earlier. The general structure of an 'evolutionary game' does not demand the *ex ante* consistency of micro-plans at all, but searches for the possible existence of evolutionary stable strategies (ESS) which, in turn, can be shown to bear close analogies with Nash equilibria. Agents may well learn over time about their best strategies, but if ESS exist they can reasonably be assumed to converge there, possibly via some mixture of learning and selection processes – i.e. essentially the same process postulated by 'disequilibrium' evolutionary models. Further, these results substantiate the claim that *particular behavioural institutions* (rules of decision, collective norms, etc.) *are nothing but the solution concepts of particular games*. I have no difficulty in recognizing that in several empirical circumstances explicit ('disequilibrium') analyses of the evolutionary processes, on the one hand, and game-theoretic models – more focused on the existence and properties of equilibria and of the related ESSs – on the other, are essentially equivalent. Indeed, the latter are more parsimonious in their hypotheses and more elegant in the derivation of the results. Moreover, there have recently been promising theoretical results based on 'genetic algorithm' simulation methods, showing the emergence of highly efficient strategies, simply as a result of *recombination, mutation, selection* processes, and starting from very little strategic rationality of individual agents (see for example, on a repeated 'Prisoner Dilemma', Miller, 1989). So, yes, I do agree that in several cases 'evolutionary games' and 'evolutionary disequilibrium models' overlap in their conclusions. Here, however, I also want to highlight the class of cases when the two approaches *do not* coincide.

Perhaps significantly, as Sutton mentions, a lot of examples of successful applications of evolutionary games come from biology. In my view, this is not only due to a simpler identification of the selection criteria (although obviously important), but also crucially to (*a*) a much greater stationarity of the selection environment as compared to the across- and within-population rates of mutation in social environments, and (*b*) the very slow and non-teleological processes of innovation (mutation) within and across species. Even in the biological world these conditions do not always apply. Dinosaurs might have had an ESS for a long while, but if two of Gould's conjectures are right on the role of 'sex and drugs' in their disappearance, the evolution of climate might have made reproduction difficult and eating habits might have poisoned them (Gould, 1985). I, too, like to cite biological examples as illustrations and metaphors, but I am a little worried when they are perhaps taken too closely as analogies to extremely complex social processes of convergence to equilibria whose very identification requires a lot of restrictions and theoretical imagination, even for the specialists. Indeed, I am deeply puzzled when, in a different context, R. Lucas (1986) cites the case of Pavlovian conditioning of pigeons as evidence for the robustness of an adaptive process of convergence to sophisticated rational expectation models! More seriously, I suggest that the search for ESSs and the explicit exploration of evolutionary processes closely converge only when the environment, for analytical purposes, is nearly stationary: that is, the rate of change in the environment is much slower than the rates of adjustment/selection of the population of agents. Otherwise asymptotic ('equilibrium') properties lose importance in the interpretation of what one actually observes. As Binmore and Dasgupta put it,

> . . . whether the equilibrating process is carried out in the minds of the player, as in the theory of rational agents, or in real time, as in evolutionary game theory, it still does not follow that game theory is an appropriate tool if the underlying environment is changing too rapidly for things to settle down (Binmore and Dasgupta, 1986, pp. 6–7).

Indeed, I suggest that this is often the case in contemporary industry. This is my first point.

Second, it seems to me that most of game-theoretical or, for that matter, evolutionary-game-theoretical models – irrespective of the amount of *computational* rationality that they attribute to the agents – underplay innovative capabilities of the latter. Pushing the illustration to the extreme, most game-theoretic models depict agents who, no matter how much information they are assumed to possess, would not pass a Turing test: they are logically indistinguishable from computers. Conversely, the 'evolutionary agents', seemingly 'more stupid' than computers, generally with much less computing power, are nonetheless sometimes capable of 'creation' and 'discovery'. What would happen, for example, in Sutton's example on the spiders, if the weakest of them were unexpectedly able to invent a knife or a machine gun? What would become the ESS for the other ones?

Again it seems to me that equivalence between the two evolutionary 'philosophies' does not apply when *unexploited opportunities are present in the system and innovations may endogenously emerge.*

Third, consider the case, also emphasized in biology by Allen (1988), whereby selection criteria endogenously depend on the frequency distributions of a different behaviours. Some initially rare characters may be 'symmetry-breaking' in the sense that their growth may be self-reinforcing and, relatedly, the whole landscape of the selection environment may be permanently changing via endogenous processes of 'mutation'/innovation (more on this issue in Silverberg, 1988).

Seemingly, one can go some way in interpreting equilibria *cum* frequency-dependent selection processes in terms of *mixed* strategies. However, I find it very hard to believe that one may seriously describe empirical behaviours in such circumstances as a conscious randomization process on pure strategies based on structured beliefs on probability distributions of the rivals' characteristics. Everyone vaguely acquainted with the 'deterministic' certainty with which business actors decide their actions under conditions of gross ignorance (as compared to the requirement of the theory) will find my doubts no surprise. In my view, a much more credible interpretation of mixed strategies is in terms of frequency distributions over populations of agents which *ex ante* choose, rightly or wrongly, *pure* strategies. But then we are back to the problems discussed above: under what selective circumstances do the frequency distributions converge to the equilibrium ones? Indeed, the requirements for convergence are plausibly stricter than those implied by equilibria in pure strategies, since one can primarily advocate environmental *selection factors but not learning factors* (it seems to me rather awkward to postulate that, within the same environment, within a group of homogeneous rational decentralized agents, ex ante, an equilibrium number of them would learn to converge to strategy A and others to strategy B). Again, it appears more plausible to use mixed strategy equilibria as metaphorical representations of biological environments rather than social ones.[7] In the latter, the foregoing limits of interpretations based on mixed strategy equilibria are further highlighted by all those cases whereby selection criteria change with the emergence and the endogenous frequency variations of a *previously unknown* 'event' or 'strategy'. How can one define an ESS for a firm in the computer industry which holds *before and after* the entry of Apple Computers? Or, in the microelectronics industry, before and after the invention of integrated circuits and 4-bit and 8-bit and 6-bit . . . microprocessors?

From a game-theoretic point of view, consider a generic stochastic set-up whereby the maximand for each *i*-player is a function $v_i = v_i (a_1 \ldots a_n;$ $e_1 \ldots e_m)$ with $a \epsilon A$ (the space of feasible strategies) and $e \epsilon E$ (the space of events). The foregoing discussion of evolution *cum* innovation implies that individual agents may unpredictably add to their menu of strategies new superior ones and, *relatedly*, generate new events (this is precisely what electricity, diesel engines, new chemical compounds, microprocessors, etc., were, when originally introduced).

Of course, in the game-theoretical language, all this involves *incomplete information* games (there is no common knowledge on the nature of the other players). Certainly, in repeated interactions, there are processes of learning and selection at work. However, note first that, if players can continuously generate new strategies, learning processes cannot be such as to reduce the incomplete information game to a complete information one. Second, on the selection side, one has recently analysed selection processes which plausibly do not yield, in general, stable ESSs. Let me briefly recall, for example, the selection process amongst different technologies with endogenous increasing returns, formalized by Arthur (1983; 1988a; 1988b), and Arthur, Ermoliev and Kaniovski (1987), whereby the returns to, say, two technologies (*A* and *B*), for two heterogeneous groups of adopters (*R* and *S*) are also a function of the number of past adoptions of each technology (n_A and n_B). Suppose also that at time zero the return of Technology *A* to *R*-agents is greater than *B* ($a_R > b_R$) and, *vice versa* of *B* for *S*-agents ($b_S > a_S$), and that the 'entry' of *R*- and *S*- varieties of agents follows a random process. In the case of linear increasing returns to adoptions, 'switching' from *A* to *B* by *R*-agents will occur whenever ($b_r + rn_b$) > ($a_r + rn_a$). The converse holds for the 'switching' of *S*-agents to the *A*-technology.

For the purposes of this essay, Arthur–Ermoliev–Kaniovski's theorem on the conditions of convergence with probability one to either technologies *A* or *B* implies, in these circumstances, the non-existence of an ESS, either in pure or mixed strategies: the asymptotic ('equilibrium') state emerges as a *system property* and small initial random fluctuations are amplified via the increasing return process.

Silverberg (1987) and Silverberg, Dosi and Orsenigo (1988), analyse another selection process, whereby firms grow or shrink in their market shares (f_i) according to their competitiveness (E_i) relative to the industry-average competitiveness $(E = \sum_i f_i E_i)$, that is: $f_i = A(E_i - \bar{E})f_i$. Innovation, imitation, organizational changes, various kinds of scale economies, etc., imply in principle a complex dynamics in the E_i's and, as a consequence, also in the *market selector* $(\bar{E})$. Again, I suggest that only particularly demanding restrictions on the dynamics of the E_i's allow the existence of ESSs. In fact, in Silverberg, Dosi and Orsenigo (1988) we present a rather simple case with two competing technologies and endogenous learning: there, one finds simulation examples where no equilibrium in pure strategies exists. I am prepared to argue that, with a sufficiently rapid innovative dynamics, there is no economically meaningful sense in which even equilibria in mixed strategies have an interpretative power in the evolutionary dynamics.

To summarize, I suggest that there is a whole class of empirically very relevant processes of industrial change wherein the equivalence between equilibrium/'rational' accounts of evolution, on the one hand, and 'disequilibrium' analyses of evolutionary *processes*, on the other, does not hold. Having said that, I do not want to underestimate the analytical importance of a good deal of recent game-theoretic endeavours. Indeed, whenever the environment is nearly stationary, they may turn out to be a rather parsimonious ways of interpreting observed phenomena as strategic equilibria. Even when the environments are non-stationary, such an analytical perspective may be very useful as a sort of 'thought experiment', highlighting important incentive-compatibility aspects, by making use of rather simple and 'artificial' assumptions on behaviours and forms of interaction.

Still, the general interpretative non-equivalence between the two approaches whenever technologies and organizations change rather rapidly also implies that the 'explanation' of observed phenomena differs. I have no intention of presenting here yet another 'book of complaints' on the limitation of standard theories of industrial organization. I am rather more optimistic and I would like to make a case for the basic analytical ingredients of evolutionary interpretations, for the promise that I believe they hold, and also for some achievements that are already there.

THE ORGANIZATION AND EVOLUTION OF INDUSTRIES

Let me briefly present what I consider some basic properties of an evolutionary approach, as I see them.

Basic Methodology

By that I mean here that set of profound (often implicit) methodological norms and beliefs, loosely speaking, on the 'real essence' of phenomena, which philosophers of science sometimes call 'influential metaphysics'. For example, in 'rational' game-theoretic models it is a rather common practice to start by some strict separation between available strategies and an unchanging context or a non-playing actor ('nature'), stylize some interaction scheme among the agents, attribute to them all the 'rational power' that the analyst himself is putting in the construction of the model, and finally study the properties of possible equilibria. Well, the 'evolutionary methodology', on the contrary, is keener on representing *empirically derived* generalizations on behavioural patterns and modes of interaction, writing them up in an explicit dynamic form and then studying the characteristics of the process so generated. In one case you say: I want to know whether a set of reciprocally consistent actions exists; then you prove the existence theorems, etc. In the other case you say: I start from what I consider plausible generalizations on behaviours and interactions, write the corresponding difference/differential equations, and then I see where the entire process leads to. Sometimes it might end up in a similar place, but sometimes it might not. From the foregoing discussion it should be clear that, in my view, only in particular circumstances a standard 'rational' equilibrium is the asymptotic state of such an evolutionary process. In many other circumstances, no such state may exist (like when the system continuously undergoes various sorts of innovation). Or, even when it exists, it might not be very relevant for the interpretation of the empirical phenomena under investigation (if they cannot be assumed to be the outcomes of equilibrium behaviours). Professor Costa, in his comments on my oral presentation of this work, was absolutely right in pointing out that the evolutionary methodology faces a crucial problem of choice among particular 'empirical generalizations' (how does one choose the stylized behavioural regularities? etc.). However, in my view it is an *unavoidable* challenge for any empirically relevant theory, and, in fact, more 'deductive' models which seemingly rely less on empirical assumptions indeed face an even more serious problem of arbitrariness in the selection of their auxiliary assumptions: e.g. What priorities do agents hold? What is the form of their utility functions? Do they play Cournot or Bertrand games?, etc.

Behavioural Patterns: Routines and Learning

A rather common theme of evolutionary approaches, linking them with Simon's contributions on 'bounded rationality' (cf. Simon, 1965) and with institutionalist analyses of organizations, concerns the *routinized* features of a good deal of corporate behaviours. Elsewhere I have discussed the origins and performance implications of behavioural rules which are, to some extent, *event-independent*, but are *robust*, in the sense that they apply problem-solving procedures to entire classes of *ex ante* unpredictable circumstances (Dosi and Egidi, 1991; general references on these issues are Simon, 1965; Cyert and March, 1963; March, 1988; Nelson and Winter, 1982; Heiner, 1983). Here let me just emphasize that the more complex and volatile the environment, the more one finds an evolutionary efficiency of relatively *invariant behaviours*. It is indeed a seemingly counter-intuitive proposition, based on (*a*) the computational limitations of empirical agents; (*b*) their 'competence gaps' in attributing informational signals to 'true' states of natures; (*c*) the 'procedural' uncertainty stemming from the general difficulty of problem-solving tasks; (*d*) the 'opaqueness', in complex environments, of the relationship between actions and consequences.

My view of evolutionary processes argues for the evolutionary robustness of seemingly mindless repetitious ('institutionalized') behaviours. Note that *their development is* in every respect *an innovative event*. Putting it somewhat provocatively, social and economic dynamics always involve the intelligent and creative generation of behavioural rules which can thereafter be mindlessly repeated; and they are efficient precisely because of the subsequent automatic stupidity that they allow. After all, the reader should simply recall how much of the social fabric of human societies is made of inertial institutions, from national parades to marriages, collective rites, rules on virginity, football games, bureaucratic procedures . . . . Or, conversely, think of how little empirical content there would be in answering the question, say, on 'What do I generally do on Saturday night?', by stating that 'I maximize my utility function'!

In this steady coexistence between 'creation' and 'stupidity' rests also the continuous presence of unexploited opportunities: that is, in the economic context, of Schumpeterian entrepreneurship, unavoidably associated with 'deviant' (innovative) behaviours.

Some consequences of this view are quite important. First, note the links between this view and all other social disciplines (generally with the exception of economics) which try to understand behaviours precisely by looking at the nature and causes of some *invariances* in, for example, cognition, value formations, actions, organizational rules, etc.

Second, all this links very easily with the experimental evidence on the *framed* nature of cognitive and decision processes, even in very simple circumstances (see Tversky and Kahnemann, 1986).

Third, this view directly implies an analysis of corporate organizations also in terms of the behavioural rules that they embody, their 'strategies' for rule modification, their particular learning procedures. In this respect, the 'evolutionary' view of industrial change outlined here is consistent and, indeed, highly complementary with those 'behaviourist' analyses of corporate organizations and strategies emphasizing the degrees of discretionality in corporate decision-making and their firm- and context-specificity (see Penrose, 1959; Marris, 1964; Porter, 1990; and the vast literature from business economics and organization theories).

Fourth, note that, empirically, relatively event-invariant rules are precisely what one observes even in strategic decision variables. Business firms typically use relatively stable mark-ups to set prices, pay-back rules to decide scrapping and replacement investment, ratios on sales to determine R & D expenditures, etc. Where these rules come from is itself an evolutionary question, but certainly firms do not often undergo any explicit optimization exercise to find them. Are these rules also ESSs? Sometimes they might well be, other times not. In any case they seem to be empirically there, and are one of the building blocks of evolutionary modelling, and demand a theoretical interpretation of their endogenous emergence.

The Importance of Empirical Taxonomies, Innovation and the Role of History

There are obviously many conceivable evolutionary processes and many structures that they can generate. It holds in biology and even more so in the social domain. In this respect, I attribute a fundamental importance to taxonomic exercises on the characteristics of (*a*) micro structures (firms), (*b*) environments and (*c*) modes of interactions.

In a biological analogy, taxonomies on observed structures are loosely equivalent to Linnean classifications of species, families, etc. The taxonomies of forms of interaction ought to 'map' the observed structures in the processes which generated them. (Note that in social evolution one easily finds a wide range of mutation-generating processes, unlike biology where the prevailing ones appear to be random genetic mutation and recombination through sexual reproduction. Moreover, the forms of interaction are obviously more complex and differentiated in the social domain.) After all, the patterns of co-ordination/competition/change among farmers are different from those among steel producers, which are different from those prevailing in the computer industry . . . etc. Certainly some differences are captured by the general categories of 'pure' versus 'oligopolistic' competition, etc. However, there are finer differences which are nonetheless essential in explaining the inter-sectoral variety in industrial organization and performance dynamics. For example, within the broad category of 'oligopoly', industries differ with respect to the strategic variables at their disposal, the ways they access the markets, their relationships with their suppliers and customers, etc. Specific historical factors are certainly behind these inter-industry differences. However, as Kreps and Spence (1986) put it, 'to understand properly the role of history, we must first study the process of industrial dynamics' (pp. 341–2). This is precisely one of the central tasks of evolutionary models.

Further, I would like to emphasize the importance of mapping taxonomies of observed industrial structures and of evolutionary processes into the specific characteristics of technological change in each sector. A lot of work has been done recently in the analysis of innovative activities, and elsewhere I have tried to define some of their basic features (an interpretative survey is in Dosi, 1988a). For example, studies have been made on intersectoral differences in the knowledge bases on which innovations draw, in the degrees of opportunities that they offer, in the cumulativeness with which advances occur, in the levels of private appropriability of innovation. Well, I suggest that these differences are crucial in explaining the differences in industrial structures and performance dynamics between, say, textiles, computers, automobiles, aerospace . . . . Evolutionary theories, it seems to me, present a particularly fruitful link with the economics of innovation and, in that, hold the promise of interpreting some of the 'stylized facts' on industrial dynamics mentioned in the introduction to this chapter.

Learning, Selection and the Notion of Equilibrium

As in 'evolutionary' versions of game-theoretic analyses, the class of evolutionary approaches that I am discussing here also rests fundamentally on *learning and selection processes*. However, I do not see evolution as a sort of convergence to equilibria which guarantees the *ex ante* consistency of beliefs and behaviours. Rather, I am keener on interpreting the aggregate order (whenever observed) as an *out-of-equilibrium system-level property*. By 'order' here I mean, rather loosely, (1) the capability of each market to coordinate without major disruptions; and, dynamically, (2) the relatively smooth pattern of change in performance variables such as prices, productivity, etc.; and finally also (3) the persistence of particular industrial structures (as revealed, for example, by the size distribution of firms or by inter-firm intra-industry variances in production efficiencies and product performances). I suggest that such order is precisely the outcome of (a) diversified learning processes by individual agents, (b) persisting 'disequilibrium' behaviours (that is, behaviours yielding unexpected outcomes and which would have been generally different if each agent knew the behaviours of the others), and (c) *ex post* selection in the product and financial markets.

As a term of reference, compare this definition of 'order' with the standard definition of equilibrium either in 'objective' terms, as a terminal state where the system eventually converges, or in 'subjective' terms as the fulfilment of expectations of all agents (see, for example, Hahn, 1984). Well, my point is that aggregate evolutionary 'order' does not imply equilibrium in either of the two versions. Indeed, I would claim that 'order' is precisely an outcome of *out-of-equilibrium behaviours*. The reader will probably find in this statement strong 'Prigoginian' tunes (see Prigogine and Stenger, 1985). Well, yes, I believe that the property identified in chemistry, physics, biology, etc., that nature becomes 'self-organized' as an out-of-equilibrium phenomenon, applies *even more so* to the domain of social interactions. Let me emphasize this point: if my hypothesis is correct, then the characteristics of a 'disequilibrium' world are *not* those of an equilibrium one plus the effects of some disturbances. On the contrary, it is precisely its being *far* from equilibrium which determines its orderly properties (if and when one observes them). So for example agents may continue to explore, make mistakes, find their plans unfulfilled, but, *precisely through these disequilibrium behaviours*, generate *collectively* a relatively coherent evolutionary path (in Silverberg, Dosi and Orsenigo, 1988, we study this property in a case of innovation diffusion).

Note also that each individual 'disequilibrium' behaviour may show varying levels of inertiality: at the extreme, agents may stick to a certain strategy (see the earlier references to routinized behaviours) irrespective of whether it is an ESS. In fact the evidence from business history provides strong hints on the inertial characteristics of corporate strategies, and the money that business consultants make should be considered good circumstantial evidence that these strategies are not ESSs . . . . The crucial point is that to have a coherent evolution of the system you do not need to have consistent micro-behaviours. Indeed, following the earlier argument, the opposite may well be true: you need a continuous generation of mistakes in order to keep the system running! For example, one can think of a dramatized version of the evolutionary dynamics discussed by the 'early' Schumpeter (more on that in Dosi, 1988b): a great number of new companies, 'carriers' of would-be innovations, continue to come to the market, some are selected in, many are selected out, and over time the older ones are eventually 'killed' by newer ones since their rate of learning rests stochastically behind the rate at which new companies innovate. In all that, you may have an evolutionary system which exhibits a rather orderly evolutionary path, for example in its average productivity growth, even if at the micro-level you observe a seemingly messy distribution of disequilibrium strategies. Or, nearer to the empirical evidence, does the reader believe that one would have still observed the hectic innovative activities of the Silicon Valley, California, if firms (old and new ones) were told *ex ante* the 'true' probability distributions of success and the related 'true' pay-offs? My conjecture is that, indeed, distributions of systematically 'wrong' Bayesian priors are fundamental ingredients of the innovative process of search that we observe in contemporary capitalist economies.

In the evolutionary environments sketched here, firms which are heterogenous in technologies, behaviours and performances permanently compete with each other. Hence, a crucial question concerns the selection process: What is selected by the environment? Firms? Strategies? Technologies? Products?

In the first instance, final markets select products and financial markets select organizations (firms). Indirectly, via the selection of products and firms, the environment selects technologies, strategies and organizational traits. Precisely because of the 'opaqueness' and complexity of the relationship between what is selected and the determinants of its differential 'fitness', one is likely to observe in every instance a lot of variety, 'slack', persistent inefficiency. However, in my view, it is precisely this 'redundant' and 'sub-optimal' coexistence of diverse strategies, organizational traits, beliefs, knowledge bases, which make for the evolutionary strength of contemporary capitalist economies. Or, putting it somewhat provocatively, if industrial evolution were simply a huge process of dynamic optimization, Mr Gorbachev would do better to stop his painstaking *perestroika* plans and simply try to buy a few Cray super-computers . . . .

Asymmetries, Performances and Evolution

It is straightforward that evolutionary processes of the kind proposed here always imply asymmetries among firms in terms of efficiency and product performances. 'Better' and 'worse' firms/products/techniques always coexist (I discuss the sources and implications of these asymmetries in Dosi, 1984; 1988a). It is a fundamental property of industrial evolution that the rates at which novelties emerge seem to be systematically higher than the rates at which selection occurs. Hence one observes *distributions*, e.g. of input productivities across firms within similar product lines, of product qualities, of production costs and profit rates.

Here, in my view, rests also a possible link between evolutionary theories and earlier 'structuralist' models. One could consider the latter as a set of conjectures on the short-term performance properties of industrial evolution. For example, one can reformulate the 'structuralist' analysis of the determinants of observed profitabilities as follows: the average level of profitability in any one industry is a function of the variance in the production efficiencies and innovative capabilities (that is, the asymmetries) among incumbents and between incumbents and potential entrants. In turn, these *asymmetries* depend on the *technological regimes* characteristics of each industry. It is a non-trivial proposition which obviously expands on the original analyses mainly based on economies of scale and entry barriers. However, it saves some of the original 'structuralist' spirit in that it tries to identify possible correspondences between environmental characteristics and observed performances. In a way, evolutionary models are the (microfounded) 'film' of the dynamic process, while some properly modified 'structuralist' analysis is a 'picture' which approximates the way the whole course of past evolution shapes and constrains current behaviours and performances. At each point in time, oligopolist firms do have some degree of strategic freedom. For example, they can trade-off unit profits for market shares. However, the degree to which they can do so depends on their relative competitiveness *vis-à-vis* other firms (their positive or negative asymmetries) which in turn are a result of the past evolutionary process. Does the distribution of asymmetries tell us something about the *boundaries* of the feasible strategies and, by implication, also the overall short-term performance of any one industry? I suggest that *it does* and, hence, one can test non-trivial propositions on the links between distributions of structural variables (including, of course, technological characteristics) and performances.

Obviously a fundamental implication of evolutionary models is that, dynamically, *structures* themselves *are endogenous*. Relatedly, such a class of models holds the promise of accounting for the observed structural variety in terms of underlying evolutionary variables, that is, in terms of the rates and modes of innovation and the patterns of interaction (i.e. competitive selection and inter-firm learning). As an example, I suggest that the observed size distribution of firms could in principle be 'explained' by particular combinations of selection and learning processes.

More generally, it seems to me that evolutionary models promise to account theoretically for all those dynamic processes where *learning opportunities and selection criteria are* themselves *endogenous*: that is, when agents are always able to innovate and the survivability criterion is *not* equivalent to the convergence, at micro-level, to optimizing behaviours and, at the collective level, to some dynamic version of Nash equilibria.

CONCLUSIONS

In the foregoing discussion I hope I have conveyed a picture of some building blocks of evolutionary approaches to industrial economics, at least the way I see them, showing some analogies and differences with the earlier 'structuralist' analyses and with contemporary models which rely much more on 'equilibrium' and 'rationality' assumptions.

Certainly, each approach to industrial analysis entails a lot of model-building which is 'appreciative' in nature. Paraphrasing Akerlof, it involves the development of 'theoretical tales' which, at best, help in the exploration of some stylized properties of the environments wherein the assumptions of the models approximately apply. This holds for evolutionary models as well as game-theoretic or decision-theoretic ones. Indeed, it is astonishing to find economists who consider any theorem-proving activity even vaguely equivalent to dirert exercises of 'validation' of the theory. However, fruitful theories do yield non-trivial empirically testable propositions. This is, in my view, the case with evolutionary approaches, which, in principle, can generate interpretative hypotheses on the stylized phenomena mentioned in the introduction to this work. In this respect, a lot of the foregoing discussion should be considered as an outline of a huge research agenda, but also a sort of map through the empirical evidence and the (admittedly preliminary) analytical results on the diverse – albeit somewhat orderly – patterns of change of industrial activities.

Notes

1.   Prepared for the Conference on 'Recent Developments in the Theory of Industrial Organization', Naples (Italy), 28–29 April 1989. Support for the research which led to this work, given by the Designated Research Centre of the ESRC at the Science Policy Research Unit (SPRU), University of Sussex, and by the Italian Ministry of Education ('Fondi 40%') is gratefully acknowledged.

2.   Outside the English language literature, see Gaffard (1990), Momigliano and Dosi (1973), Possas (1987).

3.   Relevant discussions of different interpretations of game-theoretical models are in the Introduction to Binmore and Dasgupta (1986); Binmore (1987) and (1988), Kreps (1990).

4.   See for example Scherer's argument on the 'irrationality', in certain circumstances, from a decision-theoretic point of view, of Sylos-type limit pricing (Scherer, 1980).

5.   For a survey and an interpretation, see Dosi (1988a).

6.   In the sense of Heiner (1983) and (1988) and Dosi and Egidi (1991).

7.   On the former, see Maynard Smith (1982).

Bibliography

ALLEN, P. (1988) 'Evolution, Innovation and Economics', in Dosi *et al.* (1988).

AMENDOLA, M. and GAFFARD, J.L. (1988) *The Innovative Choice*, Oxford: Basil Blackwell.

ARTHUR, B. (1983) *Competing Technologies and Lock-in by Historical Events: The Dynamics of Allocation Under Increasing Returns*, Laxenburg, Austria: IIASA Working Paper WP–83–90.

ARTHUR, B. (1988a) 'Competing Technologies', in Dosi *et al.* (1988).

ARTHUR, B. (1988b) 'Competing Technologies, Increasing Returns, and Lock-in by Historical Events', *Economic Journal*, 99 (39h) pp. 116–131.

ARTHUR, B. ERMOLIEV, Y.M. and KANIOVSKI, Y.M. (1987), 'Path-dependent Processes and the Emergence of Macro-structures', *European Journal of Operational Research* Vol 30, pp 29h–303.

BAIN, J.S. (1956), *Barriers to New Competition*, Cambridge, Mass.: Harvard University Press.

BINMORE, K. (1987) 'Modelling Rational Players. Part I', *Economics and Philosophy* October 3(2), pp 179–214.

BINMORE, K. (1988) 'Modelling Rational Players. Part II', *Economics and Philosophy* April h(1), pp. 9–55.

BINMORE, K. and DASGUPTA, P. (1986) (eds) *Economic Organizations as Games*, Oxford: Basil Blackwell.

CHAMBERLIN, E.H. (1933) *The Theory of Monopolistic Competition*, Cambridge, Mass.: Harvard University Press.

CYERT, R.M. and MARCH, J.G. (1963) *A Behavioural Theory of the Firm*, Englewood Cliffs, NJ: Prentice-Hall.

DOSI, G. (1988a) 'Sources, Procedures and Microeconomic Effects of Innovation', *Journal of Economic Literature,* pp. 1120–71.

DOSI, G. (1988b), *Finance, Innovation and Industrial Change*, Brighton: SPRU, University of Sussex, DRC Discussion Paper; prepared for the Conference on 'The Market for Innovation, Ownership and Control', Stockholm, IUI, June 1988; rev. version in *Journal of Economic Behavior and Organization,* 1990.

DOSI, G. and EGIDI, M. (1991) 'Substantive and Procedural Uncertainty. An Exploration of Economic Behaviours in Changing Environments', *Journal & Evolutionary Economics*.

DOSI, G. FREEMAN, C. NELSON, R. SILVERBERG, G. and SOETE, L. (eds) (1988) *Technical Change and Economic Theory*, London: Francis Pinter; New York: Columbia University Press.

DOWNIE, J. (1958), *The Competitive Process*, London: Macmillan.

ELIASSON, G. (1964) 'Microheterogeneity of Firms and the Stability of Industrial Growth', *Journal of Economic Behaviour and Organization*.

FEIWEL, G.R. (ed.) (1986) *Issues in Contemporary Microeconomics and Welfare*, London: Macmillan.

GEROSKI, P. and JACQUEMIN, A. (1988) 'The Persistence of Profits: A European Comparison', *Economic Journal* 98 (391), pp. 375–89.

GOULD, S.J. (1985) *The Flamingo's Smile. Reflections in Natural History*, New York: Norton.

HAHN, F. (1977) 'Exercise in Conjectural Equilibria', *Scandinavian Journal of Economics* 79(2), pp. 210–26.

HAHN, F. (1978) 'On Non-Walrasian Equilibria', *Review of Economic Studies*

45(1), pp. 1–17.

HAHN, F. (1984) *Equilibrium and Macroeconomics*, Oxford: Basil Blackwell.

HAHN, F. (1988) 'Information, Dynamics and Equilibrium', *Scottish Journal of Economics*.

HALL, C.J. and HITCH, R.H. (1939) 'Price Theory and Business Behaviour', *Oxford Economic Papers*.

HANSEN, R.G. and SAMUELSON, W.F. (1988), 'Evolution in Economic Games', *Journal of Economic Behavior and Organisation*.

HEINER, R. (1983) 'The Origin of Predictable Behavior', *American Economic Review*, 73(4) pp. 560–95.

HEINER, R. (1988) 'Imperfect Decisions and Routinized Production: Implications for Evolutionary Modeling and Inertial Technical Change', in Dosi *et al.* (1988).

JACQUEMIN, A. (1987), *The New Industrial Organization*, Cambridge, Mass.: MIT Press.

KREPS, D.M. (1990), *A Course in Microeconomic Theory*, Princeton: Princeton University Press.

KREPS, D.M. and SPENCE, A.M. (1986) 'Modelling the Role of History in Industrial Organization and Competition', in Feiwel (1986).

LUCAS, R. (1986) 'Adaptive Behaviour and Economic Theory', *Journal of Business* 59(4), Part 2, pp. 401–26.

MARCH, J.G. (1988) *Decisions and Organizations*, Oxford: Basil Blackwell.

MARRIS, R. (1964) *The Economic Theory of Managerial Capitalism*, London: Macmillan.

MASON, E.S. (1939) 'Price and Production Policies of Large Scale Enterprises', *American Economic Review* (March) pp. 61–74.

MAYNARD SMITH, J. (1982) *Evolution and the Theory of Games*, Cambridge: Cambridge University Press.

MILLER, J.H. (1989) *The Evolution of Automata in Repeated Prisoner's Dilemma*, Sante Fe: Sante Fe Institute Working Paper.

MOMIGLIANO, F. and DOSI, G. (1983) *Tecnologia e Organizzazione Industriale Internazionale*, Bologna: Il Mulino.

NELSON, R. and WINTER, S. (1982), *An Evolutionary Theory of Economic Change*, Cambridge, Mass.: The Belknap Press of Harvard University Press.

PAVITT, K. (1984) 'Sectoral Patterns of Innovation. Toward a Taxonomy and a Theory', *Research Policy*.

PENROSE, E. (1959) *The Theory of the Growth of the Firm* Oxford: Basil Blackwell.

PORTER, M. (1990), *The Competitive Advantage of Nations*, London, Macmillan.

POSSAS, M. (1987) *Estruturas de Mercato em Oligopolio*, Sao Paulo: Editora Hucitec.

PRIGOGINE, I. and STENGER, I. (1985) *Order Out of Chaos*, New York: Bentham.

ROBINSON, J. (1933) *The Economics of Imperfect Competition*, London: Macmillan.

RUMELT, R. (1988) *How Much Do Industries Matter?* Los Angeles: Graduate Business School, UCLA.

SCHERER, F.M. (1980), *Industrial Market Structure and Economic Performance* 2nd edn, Chicago: Rand McNally.

SCHMALENSEE, R. (1988) 'Industrial Economics: An Overview, *Economic Journal*.

SCHMALENSEE, R. and WILLIG, R.D. (1989) (eds) *Handbook of Industrial Organization*, Amsterdam: North-Holland.

SILVERBERG, G. (1987) 'Technical Progress, Capital Accumulation and Effective Demand: a Self-Organization Model', in D. Batten, J. Casti and B. Johansson (eds) *Economic Evolution and Structural Adjustment*, Berlin/New York: Springer Verlag.

SILVERBERG, G. (1988) 'Modelling Economic Dynamics and Technical Change: Mathematical Approaches to Self-Organization and Evolution', in Dosi *et al.* (1988).

SILVERBERG, G. DOSI, G. and ORSENIGO, L. (1988) 'Innovation, Diversity and Diffusion: A Self-Organization Model', *Economic Journal* 98 (393), pp. 1032–54.

SIMON, H. (1965) *Administrative Behaviour*, 2nd edn, New York: Free Press.

SRAFFA, P. (1925) 'Sulle Relazioni Tra Costo e Quantita, Prodotta', *Annali di Economia* n.1 pp. 328–77.

SRAFFA, P. (1926) 'The Laws of Return Under Competitive Conditions', *Economic Journal* 36, December, pp. 501–20.

STEINDL, J. (1976), *Maturity and Stagnation of American Capitalism*, 2nd edn, New York: Monthly Review Press.

STIGLITZ, J.E. and MATHEWSON, G.F. (eds) (1986) *New Development in the Analysis of Market Structure*, London: Macmillan.

SYLOS-LABINI, P. (1967) *Oligopoly and Technical Progress*, 2nd edn, Cambridge, Mass: Harvard University Press.

TIROLE, J. (1988) *The Theory of Industrial Organization*, Cambridge, Mass.: MIT Press.

TVERSKY, A. and KAHNEMAN, D. (1986) 'Rational Choice and Framing of Decision', *Journal of Business* 59(4), Part 2, pp. 251–78.

WINTER, S. (1964) *Economic 'Natural Selection' and the Theory of the Firm*, New Haven: Yale University, Yale Economic Essays.

YOUNG, A. (1928) 'Increasing Returns and Economic Progress', *Economic Journal.* 38, pp. 529–50.

3 Experiments in Industrial Organization

John D. Hey[1]

This chapter overviews the application of experimental methods in the field of industrial organization (IO). It begins by making the case for the use of such methods in this important field, arguing that experimental methods give a unique opportunity to the IO theorist to test theories under controlled conditions which exactly reproduce the theoretical environment in the laboratory. Some broader methodological points are also made. The chapter then gives an overview of past and present experimental work in industrial organization and demonstrates that such work has provided important insight into key theories and concepts in IO. A number of illustrations are given, both past and potential. The chapter concludes by discussing those areas of industrial organization which have not yet benefitted by exposure to experimental investigation but which could fruitfully be so exposed, and by arguing that such investigation could ultimately lead to a transformation in the way theorists view the field of IO.

As Charles Plott remarks at the beginning of his updated (Plott, 1989) survey (Plott, 1982) on the use of experimental methods in the field of industrial organization, 'From the very beginning laboratory experiments in economics were motivated by theories of industrial organisation'. As should be obvious from the contents of the other chapters in this volume, the reasons are not hard to find. More than in most other areas of economics, the field of IO cries out for experimental investigation: its theories lack precision, its conclusions lack unanimous support, and useful non-experimental data is conspicuous by its paucity.

For some reason, the recent past has been plagued – if that is the word – with surveys on the use of experimental methods in economics in general and in specific fields. Without stopping to think I can list Plott (1982 and 1989), Roth (1986, 1987 and 1988), Loomes (1989) and Butler and Hey (1987). For *some* specific detail, I can most efficiently simply refer the interested reader to one or other of these surveys. What I want in *this* survey is primarily to do two things:

1.   Overview the contributions that have already been made by experimen-

tal economists to the field of industrial organization; and
2. Indicate where important contributions can and should be made in the future. It is my belief that experimental work in industrial organization – although by now very well established and with a fine tradition – has only begun to nibble away at the problems posed to the economic theorist in the area of industrial organization.

First, however, I must make some preliminary remarks to bring what follows into perspective for those who are not yet familiar with the use of experimental methods in economics. To those who are familiar, I apologize for the necessity to make such remarks.

EXPERIMENTAL METHODS IN ECONOMICS

To depressingly many economists, economics is a *non-experimental* subject. Indeed, many econometric texts start with a statement to that effect: for example, 'the data available to the economist has been generated by the workings of the economic system under non-controlled circumstances'. This allows the econometrician to motivate his obsession with a non white-noise error term: by pointing out, quite correctly of course, that the *ceteris paribus* of the theory was not respected by the data.

But this is all a plot to keep the sacred art of econometrics revered by the profession. Yet at the same time it is a very dangerous plot. Just imagine the same arguments being invoked in the natural sciences! Quite rightly, such arguments would be dismissed as arrant nonsense in the physical sciences: how would chemists, physicists, biologists and the like have made the great inroads that they have over the centuries without the use of controlled experiments? The methodology of experiments is central to these disciplines: it enables the scientist carefully to test alternative theories, to control for extraneous factors and to isolate the key determinants of scientific processes. Indeed, it is probably the case that *precisely the opposite argument* to that used by economists underlies the currently accepted scientific methodology: if a theory has *not* been tested under controlled conditions, then its validity or otherwise is considered as indeterminate by the scientific community.

I see no reason why any area within the field of industrial organization can and should not be subject to experimental investigation. There are – as the rest of this conference bears witness – a plethora of different theories in the various sub-branches of the subject. The onus must surely be on the theorist to subject his theories to empirical tests – and, moreover, to empirical tests that are sufficiently discriminating to allow the relative superiority of competing theories to be evaluated. But this is all too rarely done.

There are reasons and excuses why this is the case. The usual excuse is that 'the available data are not sufficiently rich'. The real reason is usually that the theorist is solely interested in the theory – it constituting a most satisfying intellectual form of exercise – and prefers to leave the sordid matter of empirical investigation to lesser mortals. At best, such theorists present some anecdotal evidence: some broad generalizations, some stylized facts, or as Partha Dasgupta put it in his handout to the Royal Economic Society's 1989 Easter School, 'some rumours reported by applied economists'.

But this is not good enough: there are important policy issues related to these theoretical problems. Governments, whether passively or actively, necessarily employ some kind of industrial organization strategy. We, as economists, are surely concerned that such policy is motivated by the best available theory. And how can we discover that without extensive empirical testing of competing theories?

I asserted above that no part of the field of industrial organization could claim exemption from that empirical investigation being *experimental*. I now need to justify that claim. For some parts of IO – those parts which have already been subjected to such tests – the evidence speaks for itself. I will survey that later. For the other parts, I need to give some substance. This can most illuminatingly be done by giving an example.

Let me take the important field of *technological progress*. Here enormous theoretical upheavals have taken place in recent years. In particular, one can think of all the work done by 'bright young things' on R & D and patent races. Here there are lots of exciting 'applications' of the new dynamic game theory.

Now the hallmark of all this new theory is that it is very well and very tightly specified: the 'rules of the game' are tautly drawn. (This is in marked contrast to so-called evolutionary theories, where – of necessity, I will argue later – the 'rules of the game' are very vaguely drawn.) So, for example, we have patent races where the probability distribution of the time to the discovery of the to-be-patented invention is a well-specified function of the volume of resources devoted to R & D for each of the participants or potential participants in the race. The interest in the theory essentially lies in this specification rather than in the solution to the problem, since it is invariably assumed that the participants or potential participants in the race are amazingly clever at solving complicated dynamic games (in contrast to the poor theorist who has probably struggled for several months in order to derive – and explore the implications of – the optimizing conditions!).

Now let me ask the question: what is the purpose of the theory? To be fair to the theorist, one should answer: it hopefully provides an approximation to a real-life phenomenon. The obvious conclusion then is that it should be subject to empirical investigation. Suppose then that some appropriate real-life non-experimental data can be found. Except in the most bizarre circumstances, this real-life data will have been generated under conditions – a specification, to use the term employed above – different from that of the theory. In familiar terms, the *ceteris paribus* of the theory will not be satisfied in the data.

Consider then what is being tested. There are two components:

1. That the theory is correct given the appropriate specification (that is, under the given conditions);
2. That the theory survives the transition from the world of the theory to the real world.

Normally the theorist assumes that (1) is true – usually without discussion. Thus attention focuses on (2). So, effectively, the theorist is arguing that the theory isolates the essential features of the problem in so far as it relates to the real world. Admittedly the theory is an abstraction – but what is being abstracted away is inessential.

To most economists, then, whether they would tacitly admit it or not, a test of a theory is not a test of that theory *per se* but a test of whether it survives intact the transition from the world of theory to the real world. But consider the implications of this position: the outcome of the test will be either positive or negative. If it is positive, what can one conclude: that the theory is correct? Surely not, for that was taken for granted. That the theory survived the transition? Well maybe, if it was indeed correct to take it for granted that the theory was correct. But how do we know that that was so? Perhaps both the theory was wrong and its transition to the real world imperfect – and conveniently so for the two errors to cancel each other out?

And what if the outcome of the test was negative: do we conclude that the theory was wrong or that its transition to the real world was imperfect? Usually the latter. And what is the theorist's response?

Experimental methods enable the economist to separate out the first of the two components discussed above. If the theory survives that test, one can then proceed to the second component. One can therefore determine whether the theory is indeed correct under the *ceteris paribus* conditions, and, if it is, whether it survives the transition to the non *ceteris paribus* world.

So what does the experimental economist do in the context of the patent race example? Simply creates the theoretical model in the laboratory, under controlled conditions, and observes the outcome. So if the theory is a model of a two-firm race to some patentable discovery under well-specified stochastic conditions, then one simply sets up an experiment in which there are two participants, each of which has been told the relevant rules of the game. So, for example, they are told that they can spend money (either their own, or some given to them by the experimenter on commencement of the experiment, or some to be deducted from their eventual payment) which will influence the probability of them being the one to gain a prize of a specified sum of money. They are also told what pay-off they get if the other participant is the one who gains the prize (some patent race models have the loser getting nothing; others allow them to get some modest consolation prize). The precise way in which the instructions are expressed will, of course, have to depend upon the sophistication of the participants, but a form of words can usually be chosen for even the most naive of participants. So one way or another, the participants are told how the probability of their getting the prize at any specified point in time depends on the amount of money they expend, and on the actions of the other participant.

The participants are then left to get on with the game. At the end, the experimenter pays the participants (giving the winner the prize net of expenses and giving the loser the consolation prize net of expenses), and the experiment for that particular pair of participants is over. *The experimental economist has precisely replicated the theory in the laboratory.*

In this particular example, the method is clearly operational; those who are familiar with the two-firm R & D patent race literature will realize that all the necessary ingredients are there: there is a well-defined objective, usually conveniently specified in money terms, well-defined inputs – again usually conveniently specified in money terms – and well-defined relationships between objective and inputs. The only vague parts are in the behavioural responses of the firms/participants, but it is this that the solution to the theory itself specifies. If you like, the theory *is* the behavioural responses, particularly when it is a game-theoretic model (as much of the recent literature is).

While this argument appears perfectly clear to me – and a perfect rationale for the use of experiments in economics – it all too often provokes a negative response, along one or other of the following lines:

1. 'What you suggest is a pointless exercise as it is obvious what the participants will do: they will behave in accordance with the predictions of the theory; if they do not do so immediately than they will after a little practice. (I admit that it took me several months to work out the solution myself, but real-life players of the game will employ experts

– OR people, management scientists and the like.)'
2.   'What you suggest is valueless since the experiment is so unrealistic – the real world is much more complicated.'

The second response is bizarre: if the experiment was too simple then *a fortiori* the theory was too simple! The solution then surely is to make the theory specification more complex ('more realistic') and then provide an experimental test of the more complex specification. Note that this is always possible with modern neoclassical theories as they are always precisely specified. In contrast, the situation is more difficult with evolutionary theories since their specifications are *deliberately* vague: it is the very essence of the evolutionary school that their models are incompletely specified. Either the environment is incompletely specified or the agents' objective function is (or both), for if *both* of these are *completely* specified then we would be back in a neoclassical world and we would be obliged to use neoclassical methodology.

In this respect it is instructive to note that experimental investigations of evolutionary theories are conspicuous by their rarity. The problem here for the experimenter is that the experiment too – like the theory – must be set up in an incompletely specified fashion. So the participants should not be told all the rules of the games, or they should be in some doubt as to what their objective is. There are some experiments along these lines – which I shall mention briefly – but they are relatively rare. I do not think this is a good thing; it probably simply reflects the relative numbers of economists in the neoclassical and evolutionary camps, and the predominant neoclassical methodology.

PAST AND PRESENT EXPERIMENTAL WORK IN INDUSTRIAL ORGANIZATION

I hope I have now said enough to motivate the reader to read on. I will now give some flavour of the kind of experimental work that has already been done in the field of industrial organization. This will not be a comprehensive survey: that can be found elsewhere, most notably in Plott's two splendid surveys (Plott, 1982; 1989). I shall begin this section by following Plott's categorization (which is broadly the same in both the original and the updated survey); and conclude it by appending comments on and references to other pieces of experimental work to which Plott gave relatively little attention.

The meat of Plott's survey is contained in three sections: competitive market models, imperfect competition and product quality. The third is by far the shortest. The section on competitive market models reports on experiments motivated by theoretical interest in competitive markets 'without the auctioneer'. As is well known, the equilibrium price and quantity in perfectly competitive market models are theoretical entities at best: the theory says that such an equilibrium pair exists (under certain assumptions) and that it has certain desirable welfare properties. At the same time, the theory does not claim that the equilibrium pair will be *reached* or *attained* in such markets – simply that it exists. The interpretation of this is as follows: in such markets all participants are price-takers; if the prevailing price (that all participants take) is equal to the equilibrium price, then the aggregate quantity demanded by the demanders will equal the aggregate quantity supplied by the suppliers and both will equal the equilibrium quantity. There is quite clearly no notion here of the actual operation of a market – of the actual process of attainment of the equilibrium. The equilibrium concept is simply a static one: it is not intended to be a description of the outcome of a dynamic process.

While this result is of theoretical interest, it is not of much practical relevance. To make it so, we would need some assurance that the equilibrium point will be reached in actual markets. As a description of an actual market, however, the perfectly competitive story is incomplete since all participants are price-takers, and there is no one whose job it is to set the price. We need therefore to change the rules of the game so that the price-setting behaviour is well specified.

This can be done in a number of different ways. We see many examples in everyday life: there could be some kind of real-world Walrasian auctioneer; there could be some kind of auction mechanism; there could be price-setting by one side of the market with the other side responding passively; there could be a series of individual pairwise negotiations; and so on. There is, however, relatively little theory concerning such market forms, so the answer to the question 'Does the market converge to the equilibrium?' remains unanswered. Yet the answer is crucially important.

Experimental methods allow us to approach an answer. Most of the above market forms have been experimentally investigated, and there is now an impressive body of evidence. The most striking of such evidence relates to the market form known as the *oral double auction*. This is one of a class of structures known as *open outcry markets*. In this, participants on both sides of the market shout out (if they so wish) offers to buy or sell the commodity, which may or may not be accepted by the other participants, who can of course respond instead with alternative offers. This market form has been extensively investigated by experimentalists, with the 'overwhelming result that these markets converge to the competitive equilibrium [very quickly] even with very few traders' (Plott, 1989, p. 14).

Let me be more specific about the experimental set-up in such an investigation. Participants are divided into two sets, buyers and sellers. An imaginary commodity is traded in the market, with the commodity being given a value to the participants by the rules of the experiment. Specifically, buyers are individually given a *redemption schedule* showing how much the experimenter will pay to the participant for any units of the commodity that he or she buys during the experiment; sellers are individually given a *cost schedule* showing how much the participant has to pay the experimenter for any units of the commodity that he or she sells during the experiment. So buyers make money from the experiment by buying units of the commodity for less than their redemption values; sellers make money by selling units for more than they cost. These profits correspond exactly to consumer surplus and producer surplus respectively. We have precisely reproduced the demand and supply apparatus in the laboratory with appropriate incentives.

The market form can, of course, be varied by the experimenter while retaining the basic demand-and-supply apparatus. The experimenter can therefore investigate whether trading converges (if at all) to the competitive equilibrium under various market forms. As noted above, numerous experiments have shown that oral double auctions are very efficient, and usually converge very fast to the competitive equilibrium even with relatively few traders. This is an important result. (It also carries over to one-sided oral auctions, wherein just one side of the market shouts out bids or offers and the other side just passively responds.) We now await a theoretical explanation.

Other market forms have also been extensively investigated by experimentalists. In contrast with oral auctions – in which trade usually takes place at a multiplicity of prices – *one price mechanisms* are market forms which require that trade takes place at just one price. The obvious example is a real-life auctioneer process; another is a *sealed bid-offer mechanism*.

More conventional *auction* models have also been studied, with particular attention paid to the effect of the auction rules on the outcome. There are numerous different auction forms, but the most familiar are the *English auction, the Dutch auction, the first-price sealed bid auction and the second-price sealed bid auction*. In the English auction, successively higher bids are made until all except one bidder drop out; in the Dutch auction successively lower prices are called out until one bidder agrees to pay that price; in the first-price sealed bid auction the bidder with the highest sealed bid gets the item, paying his bid for it; while in the second-price sealed bid auction the bidder with the highest sealed bid gets the item, but only paying the second highest bid price for it. According to theory, the English and the second-price auction are equivalent, the Dutch and first-price auction equivalent, and the revenue from the latter pair should exceed that from the former pair. As Plott summarizes (1989, p. 23):

> Many experiments with these auctions indicate that the English and second-price auctions behave substantially the same, and prices and efficiencies of these two exceed those of the other two. The Dutch and first-price auction are not the same, with prices and efficiency of the latter greater. The models capture some of the data but paradoxes and contradictions exist.

There have also been numerous studies of bargaining solutions to the market problem, and indeed of bargaining generally. A survey is given in the useful book by Roth (1987). Bargaining theory is another splendid example of an area of economics which is used extensively throughout industrial organization and which cries out for experimental investigation. The simple cake-eating problems and the like are ideal for experimental investigation. A simple bargaining problem is outlined on page 440 of Tirole's *The Theory of Industrial Organization*:

> A buyer and a seller negotiate over one unit of a product (or a contract). The seller makes an initial offer of p_1 which the buyer either accepts or refuses. If the offer is refused, the seller makes a second offer, p_2. If the second offer is also refused, each party goes his own way, and the seller keeps his product. The value of the product is s for the seller and b for the buyer.

This almost sounds exactly like a description of a simple experiment! But Tirole's analysis is entirely theoretical.

However, numerous authors *have* carried out experimental investigations of such bargaining stories. Perhaps of particular interest is the work carried out by Binmore and his associates, especially in view of Binmore's thoughtful articles (Binmore, 1987; 1988) on the use of backward induction in both bargaining models and other dynamic games of various forms. As Tirole eloquently emphasizes (Tirole, 1988), the applications of dynamic game theory and bargaining theory in economics rely heavily on the logic of backward induction to find the appropriate solutions. Binmore shows that this logic is flawed: the backward induction 'solution' to a dynamic game relies on each player asking him or herself at each potential point in the game what he or she should optimally do at that point under the assumption that all the rival players were behaving rationally. The flaw is that the players would not find themselves at certain points if they were behaving rationally.

This problem reveals itself most acutely in game theorists' attempts to model, say, the bargaining process between management and workers over wages. According to the solution to the dynamic game theory, both sides would work out the optimal strategy *and accordingly reach agreement immediately*. There would never be a period of strike or lockout. Unfortunately, this solution not only lacks realism but it also contains the logical flaw outlined above: it (the solution) is reached by asking what would be the optimal strategy after, say, 10 weeks of strike or lockout on the assumption that the rival is rational. But the participants will never find themselves in such a position if all participants are rational: agreement would have been reached immediately! We have a logical contradiction.

The use of backward induction, and related concepts such as subgame perfect equilibria, in IO was motivated by the desire to reduce the often embarrassingly large number of theoretical equilibria in dynamic games. In some cases its use led to some awkward conclusions. A good example is the repeated 'Prisoner's Dilemma' (which is often used by IO theorists to describe the behaviour of oligopolist markets). As is well known, the only (theoretical) equilibrium of the one-off repeated game is 'confess' (that is, non-cooperation), and backward induction 'shows' that this is also the only equilibrium in *finitely* repeated Prisoner's Dilemma games. This is the case irrespective of the number of repetitions: as long as there is a finite end-point the equilibrium in that final period will be mutual non-cooperation, which means that the equilibrium in the penultimate period is also mutual non-cooperation, and so on back to the first period. In stark contrast is the *infinitely* repeated game or the game with a *random* horizon: according to the theory (which, note, is based on a subtly different kind of argument) mutual co-operation in every period is also an equilibrium.

This suggests that one should be suspicious of the finite horizon 'solution' for several reasons, though perhaps mainly because of Binmore's demolition of the backward induction argument. In any event one is left with the feeling that the theory is in a state of profound disarray, so it is fortunate that a considerable volume of experimental work has been done on the problem. (I must confess, as an aside, that I cannot see how present theoretical tools can *ever* solve game-theoretic problems: there seems to be an underlying logical impossibility in the notion that both players in a two-person game can both be behaving rationally in the strict sense used at present in game theory. I have a belief that in time there will be an Impossibility Theorem to this effect, and that then economists will turn to evolutionary-type models based on experimental and other empirical evidence. But that is in the future.)

An introduction to the experimental investigation of various game-theoretic and bargaining models can be found in Roth's various works, most notably Roth (1987) and (1988). In the latter, he discusses (p. 998) the 'hundreds of experiments' on the Prisoner's Dilemma problem in various forms. These include one-off games, repeated finite horizon games, supergames, and random horizon games. In these random horizon games, theory suggests that mutual co-operation should be the equilibrium if the probability of continuing (from one game to the next) is sufficiently large. Roth reports on an experiment in which 'sufficiently large' was 'more than 0.5' and in which subjects played three games with probabilities of continuing of 0.1, 0.5 and 0.9. He found that (Roth, 1987, p. 999) 'significantly more cooperative choices were made in the two higher probability conditions . . . than in the low probability condition. However, even in the high[est] probability condition, only 36% of first period choices were cooperative [instead of the theoretical 100%]'. Naturally he concluded that 'the results remain equivocal'.

Roth also reports on an illuminating set of experiments carried out by Selten and Stoecker (1986) in which subjects played 25 'supergames', each of which was a 10-period repeated Prisoner's Dilemma. This repeated play of the repeated game gave the subjects considerable experience of the 10-period game. Roth summarizes the results as follows (Roth, 1988, p. 1000):

> In the initial rounds players learned to cooperate (and consequently exhibited more periods of mutual cooperation starting from the very beginning and breaking down only near the end.) In the later rounds, players learned about the dangers of not defecting first, and cooperation began to unravel. There is a sense in which this observed behaviour mirrors the game-theoretic observation that the equilibrium recommendation is not a good one, but that all other patterns of play are unstable.

There has been some theoretical response to these types of results. Learning models and 'trembling hand' models try and capture some of the empirical findings. Yet I supposed that 'equilibrium-based' models will continue to be doomed to failure.

Modern industrial organization theory also draws heavily on dynamic game theory for its treatment of *imperfect competition*. The experimental work in this area is surveyed in the third section of Plott (1989). He begins his discussion with monopoly and in particular with the effect of market organization on market performance. Experimental methods enable the economist to assess the relative merits of different forms of market regulation. Amongst such forms are various new suggestions for regulation based on the theory of incentive compatibility (again based, note, on backward induction methodology). While such suggestions may appear very clever when couched in theoretical terms, their practical implementation may be fraught with difficulties; experimental investigation allows any such difficulties to be identified. Plott reports on such a study carried out by Cox and Isaac (1986) who were investigating various alternatives to rate of return regulation for the *Arizona Corporations Commission*. In particular they experimentally investigated a theoretical proposal which neither requires the regulator to know the market demand function nor the firm's cost function. Cox and Isaac (1986, p. 133) concluded that 'even though the . . . mechanism has theoretically desirable optimal properties, it is a mechanism which is permanently "unforgiving" of errors. In our laboratory markets, this feature proved to be important, with three of four sellers going bankrupt because of errors off the theoretically optimal path.'

This example shows nicely how experimental methods can be useful, not only for theory but also for policy. Another example is provided by work planned at the University of York (with co-operation between the Centre for Experimental Economics and the York Health Consortium) on the appropriate organization of the recently proposed *internal markets* in the British National Health Service.

Oligopolistic markets have also been extensively investigated using experimental methods. An interesting recent example is that of Holt (1985) who compared Cournot–Nash solutions to the duopoly problem with the consistent-conjectures solution. An important feature of his experimental design was that these two solutions were clearly separate. Plott (1989) summarizes the results of this experiment as strongly supporting the Cournot–Nash equilibrium over the consistent-conjectures equilibrium. This echoes earlier findings that the more 'sophisticated' solution concepts are less often observed in experiments than theorists would have us expect – perhaps because they are less robust (as the findings of Cox and Isaac could be interpreted). The same point is made by Roth (1988, p. 987) after summarizing the results of numerous bargaining experiments: 'Overall, although the data reveal some striking regularities, the perfect equilibrium predictions do poorly both as point predictions and in predicting qualitative differences'.

Plott's final survey section deals with experiments concerned with *product quality*, particularly those where asymmetric information is thought to play a crucial role. Obvious example include Akerlof's 'lemons' story and the Rothschild–Stiglitz account of adverse selection in the insurance market. A rather interesting experimental study in this area – and one which further indicates the potential of experimental methods for policy prescriptions – is one carried out by Plott and Wilde (1982) and commissioned by the Federal Trade Commission. This experiment concerned the behaviour of markets in which professional diagnosis plays a special role. As Plott (1989, p. 50) remarks, 'The idea was to create a market that failed in the theoretical sense [because of asymmetrical information] and use it as a baseline to study tools used by the FTC to detect failures and as a baseline for additional experiments with policies under consideration by the FTC'. Unfortunately the markets failed to fail: 'the markets worked very well even though they were not supposed to work well according to accepted theory' (Plott, 1988, p. 50)!

In experiments designed to capture Akerlof's 'lemons' market, it has been shown that the theoretical predictions may be correct in one-off games but once they are repeated, the prediction (of the blackward induction argument) that the bads will drive out the goods in all periods is not verified: sellers build up reputations and reputation effects prove to be important. Once again, experimental work highlights empirical deficiencies with theoretical constructs.

FUTURE EXPERIMENTAL WORK IN INDUSTRIAL ORGANIZATION

Although there is an impressive volume of experimental work already done on various aspects of industrial organization, much remains to be done. A comparison of Tirole's *The Theory of Industrial Organization* (which impressively defines the present-day concerns of IO theorists) with Plott's 'An Updated Review of Industrial Organization Applications of Experimental Methods', shows large gaps in the experimental (and indeed other empirical) coverage. Whether these will be filled by the IO theorists themselves is doubtful: Tirole (1988, p. 4) rather disparagingly remarks: 'another method of collecting evidence that can benefit from the theoretical developments is the running of controlled experiments in laboratories'. Not the other way round!

One obvious gap that needs too be filled with some urgency is that relating to the theory of R & D and technological invention, innovation and diffusion. The patent race stories of the new dynamic game theorists would seem to be the greatest innovation made by economists, judging from some of the excitement that they have generated. But most of these stories leave me cold, as they seem to abstract *away* the very essence of the R & D problem. At least they need to be subject to empirical testing.

The obvious method is through experimental work, since, as I have already argued, the model descriptions read just like a set of experimental instructions. I suspect that we would find (if previously related experiments' results carry over) that the theoretical predictions are poorly supported, even in the tightly constrained (unrealistic?) world of the theory. Real-life players, it would seem, do not play games the way dynamic game theorists say they ought. If the experiments led us to such a conclusion, we would have made a major step forward. The logical next step at that stage would be to look for a new theoretical paradigm, but I fear that there will be a delay before that arrives.

In the mean time, we can usefully do R & D experiments of a different kind – of an evolutionary kind. These would appear to be particularly appropriate for the encapsulation of the R & D problem, since the very essence of that problem is that the environment *cannot* be precisely specified in the way that current theorizing requires. The stochastic function relating discovery to R & D expenditures is *not* known to practising R & D departments, nor can it be subjectively estimated in the way that current theory needs. Practising R & D departments get surprised (which optimizing theory does not allow), make mistakes, get things wrong and violently change direction. Even if we cannot yet theorize about such matters (particularly using our present methodology), we could begin to do some experimental investigations. Such experiments would need to be more loosely structured than the present *genre* of experiments, and this will not be easy.

A few experiments of this type have been done, though not in this area. I myself have done search experiments where the participants were given no information about the offer distributions, Reynolds (1988) has explored the product-marketing strategies of firms in an incompletely specified market, and Keasey and Moon (1988) have looked at the tendering process in a situation where participants were not given complete information about the 'rules of the games', nor indeed about what kinds of questions they might ask the experimenter.

Such experiments are difficult to conduct because it is difficult to control for the unspecified parts of the experiment: if participants are not told everything, then they must 'fill in the gaps' themselves. This they could do in a variety of ways. It would obviously be useful to the experimenter to know how they do this, but it is difficult to control for (if indeed one wants to) and difficult to observe. In this context questionnaires might be useful, or tape-recorded thinking-aloud protocols (though one might be naturally suspicious about the reliability of such evidence), or one could simply ask the participants. There is also the difficulty that, in the absence of any theory about such situations, there are no theoretical hypotheses to test; so the experiments initially will not *test* hypotheses but rather *generate* them. This, however, is not a bad thing: experience has shown in other areas – most notably that of individual decision-making under uncertainty – that experiments can lead the theorist to new theoretical insights. The experimental evidence in that area has led to numerous new theories as alternatives to Expected Utility Theory: Prospect Theory, Regret Theory, Disappointment Theory, Implicit Weighted Utility Theory, Generalized Expected Utility Theory, Rank Dependent Utility Theory, Dual Expected Utility Theory, and so on. And now experimental methods are helping economists to test and distinguish between these theories. This is a splendid example of a genuinely scientific method being used in economics: one that could usefully be employed in other areas, particularly that of R & D.

A further area in which much recent theoretical work (usually of a game-theoretic nature) has been done is that of 'Entry, Accommodation and Exit' (to borrow one of Tirole's (1988) chapter headings). This is another area in which the theoretical specifications read like instructions for experiments and in which convention data are rather unilluminating. Many of the new models are two-period models which ideally lend themselves to testing by experimental methods. 'Consider, for example, the following two-period, two-firm model' in Tirole:

> In period 1, firm 1 (the incumbent) chooses some variable K_1 (for example, capacity). We will call K_1 an investment, although, as we will see, that word must be taken in a very large sense. Firm 2 observes K_1 and decides whether to enter. If it does not enter, it makes zero profit. The incumbent then enjoys a monopoly position in the second period. . . . If firm 2 enters, the firms make simultaneous second-period choices x_1 and x_2 (1988, p. 323)

Tirole then goes through several pages of algebra, in which he illustrates Deterrence of Entry, Accommodation of Entry and Inducement of Exit (using a rather evocative terminology involving 'Puppy dog', 'Top Dog', 'Fat Cat' and 'lean and hungry' strategies!). All good rousing stuff, and ideal for experimental investigation.

I have much the same comments to make about this branch of the recent IO literature as I had about the R & D branch: while the models may be intellectually satisfying, they would appear to me to have abstracted away the very essence of the Entry, Accommodation and Exit problem. At the very least, one would like to think of firms existing for more than two periods, preferably for a random number: how many firms in the real world plan to exist for two periods, or indeed for a fixed finite number of periods? Yet much of the theory is confined to a well-specified two-period world. Here again, the theory is specified in an unrealistic fashion which could possibly be demolished *on its own ground* by the use of experimental methods. The same methods could then be used in more loosely structured models to search for new theories about Entry Accommodation and Exit.

At this stage it might be illuminating to list the chapters of Tirole's book (which I take to define the state of modern industrial organization theory), and to estimate the proportion of the material in each chapter which already been subjected to experimental investigation. This I do in the following table, which could be taken as indicating the research agenda for experimental work in IO.

Chapter 1, on Monopoly, has been extensively studied by experimental economists, the one possible major omission being the material relating to

Table 3.1   The main chapters in Tirole's *Theory of Industrial Organization*

No. Title	Percentage covered by existing experi mental work*
Part I: *The Exercise of Monopoly Power*	
1 Monopoly	90
2 Product Selection, Quality and Advertising	50
3 Price Discrimination	60
4 Vertical Control	10
Part II: *Strategic Interaction*	
5 Short-Run Price Competition	95
6 Dynamic Price Competition and Tacit Collusion	50
7 Product Differentiation: Price Competition and Non-Price Competition	10
8 Entry, Accommodation and Exit	2
9 Information and Strategic Behaviour: Reputation, Limit Pricing and Predation	10
10 Research and Development and the Adoption of New Technologies	2
11 Noncooperative Game Theory: A User's Manual	†

* This is a *highly approximate* figure!
† See Note 2

multiproduct firms. References to the most important work can be found in the second substantive section (Section III) of Plott's surveys (1982 and 1989). Chapter 2, on Product Selection, Quality and Advertising, is a rapidly growing area in experimental economics. I have discussed this briefly above, and further references to the literature can be found in the third substantive section (Section IV) of Plott (1982 and 1989). The Price Discrimination material of Chapter 3, particularly that involving regulatory practices has also been well investigated; here there are important examples of policy questions being answered using experimental methods. However, there has been very little work done on the material of Chapter 4 on Vertical Control; despite it being ideally suited for experimental methods – certainly given the nature of the theory.

Of the second part of the book, Chapter 5, on Short-Run Price Competition in oligopolistic markets, is the most intensively investigated using experimental methods. Of course, much of this work has involved the testing of various games structures, rather than the application of the game theories in oligopoly context. So the 50 per cent I have attached to the material of Chapter 6, on Dynamic Price Competition and Collusion, should be interpreted with some care. In addition to the references cited in Plott (1982 and 1988) useful references and an extensive discussion will be found in Roth (1988).

So far, relatively little work has been done on Chapter 7's Product Differentiation, except in so far as the work reported in Plott's third substantive section (Section IV) on Product Quality is relevant.

Once again, the experimental evidence related to games – particularly repeated games – is relevant to the three remaining substantive chapters[2] (Chapters 8, 9 and 10) of Tirole's book, though I have deliberately marked down the percentages to convey the (correct) impression that little work of *direct* relevance has yet been done. But, as I have remarked above, these are areas ripe for experimental investigation. Indeed, for a student embarking on a doctoral thesis on experimental work in industrial organization, these final three chapters of Tirole (and indeed the rest of the book except in so far as it has already been subjected to investigation) read like a research agenda. Let us hope that students take up the challenge.

CONCLUSIONS

If this paper reads more like a cry for action than a survey, I suppose I should apologize. In my defence, I would say that such surveys already exist. But I hope that I have given a flavour of what has been done and what can be done: given the nature of present mainstream theorizing in economics, and particularly in the field of industrial organization, and given the almost inevitable state of the 'relevant' data, almost the only way of testing the multitude of new theories currently being offered in the major journals to the profession by the 'bright young things' of today is through experimental methods. As I have repeatedly argued above, such new theories sound exactly like a set of experimental instructions: the models are tautly specified, are well defined and have a well-defined objective function. They can easily be translated into the laboratory, and moreover have associated clearly defined testable hypotheses. Here is the chance for the economist, *qua* social scientist, to earn the world *scientist*.

At the same time, there has been a second theme running throughout the paper: and that is a cry for a different form of theorizing in economics, particularly in the field of industrial organization. To a certain extent this cry has already been headed – by the evolutionary economists, the institutional economists and the behavioural economists. But these are on the fringes: the way to convince the mainstream (if indeed one wants to) is to provide a new paradigm. Given the intellectual grasp on the profession of the prevailing optimizing paradigm, I suspect that the only way of doing this is through empirical evidence. And I further believe that only experimentally generated data – directly testing the current batch of mainstream theories – can and will convince a somewhat complacent mainstream. Experimental methods can then be used constructively, to first identify and then test the new paradigm using loosely structured experiments. Let us hope that we move on to this next stage soon.

Notes

1. I am particularly grateful to Charles C. Plott for sending me a pre-publication copy of Plott (1989), on which I draw heavily. It should really have been he who was enjoying the pleasures of Naples!
2. As the title suggests, Chapter 11 is an account of game theory, rather than its application to IO. As such, much the material has been tested experimentally.

References

BINMORE, K. (1987) 'Modelling Rational Player I', *Economics and Philosophy* 3, pp. 179–214.

BINMORE, K. (1988) 'Modelling Rational Players II', *Economics and Philosophy*, 4, pp. 9–55.

BUTLER, D.J. and HEY, J.D. (1987) 'Experimental Economics: An Introduction', *Empirica* 14, pp. 157–86.

COX, J.C. and ISAAC, R.M. (1986) 'Incentive Regulation: A Case Study in the Use of Experimental Analysis in Economics', in S. Moriarity (ed.) *Laboratory Market Research*, Norman, Oklahoma: University of Oklahoma, Center for Econometrics and Management Research.

HOLT, C.A. (1985) 'An Experimental Test of the Consistent Conjectures Hypothesis', *American Economic Review* 75, pp. 314–25.

KEASEY, K. and MOON, P. (1988) 'Information Search and Competitive Tendering: An Exploratory Study', University of Warwick Discussion Paper.

LOOMES, G.C. (1989) 'Experimental Economics', Ch. 6 of J.D. Hey (ed.) *Current Issues in Microeconomics*, London: MacMillan.

PLOTT, C.R. (1982) 'Industrial Organization Theory and Experimental Economics', *Journal of Economic Literature* 20 pp. 1485–527.

PLOTT, C.R. (1989) 'An Updated Review of Industrial Organization Applications of Experimental Methods', in Schmalansee R. and Willig R.D. (eds), *Handbook of Industrial Organization,* Amsterdam: Elsevier, vol 2, pp. 1111–76.

PLOTT, C.R. and WILDE, L.R. (1982) 'Professional Diagnosis versus Self-Diagnosis: An Experimental Examination of Some Special Features of Markets with Uncertainty,' in V.L. Smith (ed.) *Research in Experimental Economics 2*, Greenwich: JAI Press.

REYNOLDS, M.R. (1988) 'Behavioural Models of Decision Making in Economics: An Exploratory Study in the Application of Dynamic Processing Methodology', University of York Doctoral Thesis.

ROTH, A.E. (1986) 'Laboratory Experimentation in Economics', *Economics and Philosophy* 2, pp. 245–73.

ROTH, A.E. (ed.) (1987) *Laboratory Experimentation in Economics: Six Points of View*, Cambridge University Press.

ROTH, A.E. (1988) 'Laboratory Experimentation in Economics: A Methodological Overview', *Economic Journal* 98, pp. 974–1031.

SELTEN, R. and STOECKER, R. (1986) 'End Behavior in Sequences of Finite Prisoner's Dilemma Supergames: A Learning Theory Approach', *Journal of Economic Behavior and Organization* 7, pp. 47–70.

TIROLE, J. (1988) *The Theory of Industrial Organization*, Cambridge, Mass.: MIT Press.

Part II

The Behaviour of Individual Firms and the Characteristics of Industrial Systems

4 On Imperfect Competition and Macroeconomic Analysis

Malcolm C. Sawyer

INTRODUCTION

Since the publication of the *General Theory* there has been the lurking idea that substantial unemployment lasting for a number of years is associated with the existence of imperfect competition. In the late 1930s ideas such as 'administered prices' (Means, 1935), full-cost pricing (Hall and Hitch, 1939) and the 'kinked demand' curve theory (Sweezy, 1939) were concerned in different ways with the notion that prices were sticky, and that this stickiness of prices arose in the context of imperfection competition. To some degree these works interacted with the perception that Keynesian economics involved the assumption of sticky prices. During the 1950s the use of IS–LM analysis based on fixed prices could be justified by reference to the idea that under imperfect competition prices tended to be sticky (in some rather undefined sense). Some aspects of the Clower-inspired re-appraisal of Keynesian economics also drew on the view that the source of sticky prices was the pricing policies under imperfect competition (see Malinvaud, 1977). Hicks's distinction between fixprice and flexiprice market has some correspondence with the dichotomy between imperfect competition and perfect competition when he postulated that '[t]here are markets where prices are set by producers; and for those markets, which include a large part of the markets for industrial products, the fixprice assumption makes good sense. But there are other markets, 'flexprice' or speculative markets, in which prices are still determined by supply and demand' (Hicks, 1974).[1] The work of Okun (1981) extended the argument into many areas of the economy that prices tended to be sticky in the face of demand changes.

There has been another strand which has been imperfect competition as an essential ingredient in any explanation of unemployment. One expression of this is given by Kaldor (1978) when he wrote that '[i]t is difficult to conceive how production in general can be limited with unutilised capacity

79

at the disposal of the representative firm as well as unemployed labour – unless conditions of some kind of oligopoly prevails'. Its recent manifestation has been largely due to Weitzman (1982) who contended that increasing returns with the associated imperfect competition was in a sense at the heart of unemployment. A number of papers in Worswick and Trevithick (1983) see the work of Weitzman as underpinning the analysis of Keynes: for example, '[w]e now have Weitzman's rigorous demonstration of what Keynes's intuition told him all along' (Thirlwall, 1983).

In this chapter we argue that the focus on the impact of price and output decisions made under imperfect competition on the output market as in some sense a 'cause' of unemployment is essentially incorrect. The basis of this argument is that the substitution of imperfect competition for perfect competition does not of itself generate equilibrium unemployment. The significance of imperfect competition is however seen to lie in other directions. First, imperfect competition and macroeconomic analysis are mutually supportive. The analysis of imperfect competition requires, for example, that the demand curve facing a firm or industry be positioned by reference to the general level of demand. Macroeconomic analysis requires some microeconomic underpinnings of which imperfect competition would appear to be a more realistic set than perfect competition. Second, the influence which industrial structure (especially the level of concentration) may have on the distribution of income (and thereby the level of aggregate demand) and on the rate of technical progress (with effects on investment demand and growth) is likely to be much more important. In particular, imperfect competition may generate levels of aggregate demand which are insufficient to support full employment. Third, the behaviour in disequilibrium is likely to be different under imperfect competition, compared with perfect competition, although this is not a topic which we explore in this chapter.

The chapter proceeds in the following way. In the next section a three-equation framework is set out which helps to generate the basic conclusion that the price–output decisions under imperfect competition do not generate unemployment of labour. This is followed by an interpretation of the temporary disequilibrium literature and of the idea that any constancy of price under imperfect competition prevents the attainment of full employment. Further sections consider the relationship between imperfect competition and macroeconomics, the importance of income distribution, investment and technical change for the level of employment, and the role of mistakes and expectations.

A FRAMEWORK OF ANALYSIS

The starting-point is the view that three building blocks are required, which cover price–output decisions of firms, wage–employment relationship based on labour market behaviour and an aggregate demand equation. Within each of those relationship a number of alternative equations reflecting different views can be considered. The price–output decisions of firms may arise from perfect competition or from imperfect competition. In either case, it is argued that a real wage–employment relationship is implied which has the appearance of a demand for labour but which is not in the conventional sense. The real wage–employment relationship from the labour market may be based on a supply of labour curve or may be derived from considerations of collective bargaining. The aggregate demand equation is based on a general view of savings and investment behaviour, but it will be seen that the crucial element is whether variables such as interest rates or price level appear in the aggregate demand equation.

The discussion of pricing and of the real wage–employment relationship is conducted at the level of either the firm or the industry. It will be assumed that there is no difficulty in moving from the industry level to the aggregate level, and that the nature of the relationship derived at the industry level also holds at the aggregate level. The major concern here is with the nature of the real wage–employment relationship (e.g. causal or non-causal) rather than its precise shape. Thus our argument is not materially affected if the particular relationship between real wage and employment derived at the firm or industry level is not preserved at the aggregate level.

The Output Markets

The profit-maximizing condition under perfect competition of price equal to marginal cost is rewritten as $(w/p) = mpl$ where w is money wage, p is price level and mpl the marginal productivity of labour, which is conventionally interpreted as a demand for labour function with the implied causation running from real wage to employment. But the interpretation used by Keynes was to focus on price equal to marginal cost aspect and treat it as a pricing equation. Hence for given money wage and level of output (arising from the level of effective demand), the marginal cost is determined which then sets the price. In the *General Theory*, Keynes maintained the negative relationship between real wage and employment ('real wages [are] inevitably rising in the same circumstances [of falling employment] on account of the increasing marginal return to a given capital equipment when output is diminished'), though later, under the impact of the empirical evidence of

Dunlop (1938) and Tarshis (1939) and the theoretical arguments of Kalecki (see Keynes, 1939), he had doubts. But the relevant point here is that the real wage–employment relationship arises from price decisions with price as (at this stage) the endogenous variable and money wage and employment as the exogenous variables. The level of employment is set by aggregate demand considerations, and variations in money wages are offset by corresponding variations in prices.

One strand of the *General Theory* can be interpreted as the idea that the product markets always clear whilst labour markets do not always do so. This is reflected in the assertion of Keynes that the marginal product of labour and the real wage would be equal (his Classical Postulate I which he accepted whilst rejecting Classical Postulate II that the real wage was equal to the marginal disutility of labour). The obverse of this, price equal to marginal cost, provides equilibrium in the goods market in the sense that (atomistic competitive) firms are maximizing profits and supply of output has adjusted to the level of demand. Further, the equality between aggregate demand and aggregate supply schedule to provide the point of effective demand is another reflection of this point.[2]

Theories of firms (varying from monopolistic competition through oligopoly to monopoly) have a similar structure in the sense that firms are portrayed as facing a demand curve, a production function and a set of input prices. Whatever the objectives of the firms, and whatever the industrial structure within which they operate, the firms can be portrayed as reaching a point price–output outcome. Variations in the level of demand facing the industry will generate different price–output outcomes. With *specified* variations in the level of demand, a curve which might suggest a 'supply' curve relating price and output can be mapped out. Further, and of particular relevance for this chapter, a relationship between the real wage and employment can also be mapped out. However, it is clear that the price–output relationship is not a supply curve in the conventional sense, nor is the real wage–employment relationship a demand-for-labour curve. In this chapter the emphasis is on the common features of imperfect competition, but three specific cases are examined in Appendix 1 to support the general conclusions. At the level of the industry, there is an equilibrium relationship between real product wage and employment such that variations in the level of aggregate demand map out that relationship. Aggregating across industries provides a relationship between the real wage and employment, which has the same status as the industry-level relationship. For the purposes of this chapter, the important element is the idea of a real wage–employment relationship based on price–output decisions made by producers. The shape of the relationship below is an inverted U-shape, but little said below depends on the precise shape.

A possible real wage–employment relationship is drawn in Fig. 4.1 as the *p*-curve. It has been labelled the *p*-curve because it can be also considered as a pricing equation (the interpretation here) but it is also a relationship between real wages and employment. Two features of that curve need to be highlighted. First, movements along the curve are generated by variations in the level of demand facing the industry. Movements along the curve could be made by the firms themselves but only at the expense of a departure from their objectives.

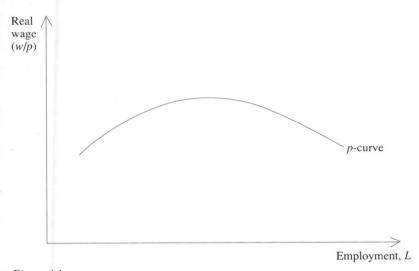

Figure 4.1

Second, there may well be sections of the curve which are positively sloped. This corresponds to the conclusion drawn by Weitzman (1982), and arises from the possibility of imperfect competition firms operating along the decreasing portion of their cost curves and/or the mark-up applied by the firms varying with the level of output (and employment).

The *p*-curve is for future reference written as:

$$w/p = f(L, w/m, X) \tag{1}$$

where w is money wage, p output price, L employment and m price of non-labour inputs. The variable X is used to label the factors which influence the firms' mark-up, and these could include the nature of the objectives of the firms, their market power, etc. As a shorthand these factors will be referred to as the 'degree of monopoly' (though it has a rather broader interpretation than the notion used by Kalecki).

The special case of constant average costs and mark-up corresponds to much (though not all) of the notions of price rigidity. In this case, the real wage–employment relation becomes horizontal. Since prices vary with costs, it is misleading to talk of fixed prices. Instead it would be preferable to use the distinction drawn by Kalecki (1971) between cost-determined and demand-determined prices.

The general case of imperfect competition can be seen as having three particular implications for macroeconomic analysis. First, it is clear that from the firms' behaviour the real wage–employment relationship can be positive or negative. Under imperfect competition, firms can operate subject to increasing or decreasing returns and the mark-up of price over (marginal or average) costs can vary with the level of output. The combination of those two features means that the real wage–employment relationship can be positive or negative.

Second, firms meet demand at the prices which they set. Hence there is *no* excess demand for output along the *p* curve as drawn in Fig. 4.1. In particular, even where price could be considered rigid, demand at the prevailing price is met by the producers. When the rigid price case is applied to perfect competition, the conclusion is drawn that there will be excess demand or supply, and that the complications of disequilibrium trading, quantity adjustment, etc., will set in. In the case of imperfect competition, this is *not* the case.

Third, there is a price adjuster under imperfect competition, operating rather like a Walrasian auctioneer. In the *tatonnement* process as envisaged by Walras, the auctioneer has the two key tasks of adjusting prices in response to excess demand and supply and to prevent disequilibrium trading. However, within each market firms are pictured by models of imperfect competition as operating in a similar manner. They adjust price to eliminate any excess demand and they do not trade out of equilibrium. The differences are that prices are adjusted in the interests of the firms and that there is not a single auctioneer who changes all prices.

Labour Market Considerations

The proposition that imperfect competition does not, through price and output decisions, generate unemployment can easily be seen as follows. In Fig. 4.2 three curves have been drawn. One is the *p*-curve from Fig. 4.1, and another is a corresponding curve drawn for perfect competition (and labelled

PC here). The relationship between the *PC* curve and the *p* curve is that the *PC* curve involves higher real wages (since the mark-up of price over costs is greater under imperfect competition than under perfect competition) and the slope of the *PC* curve is always negative. There may be, of course, circumstances (increasing returns to scale) where perfect competition is not viable and hence a comparison between perfect and imperfect competition could not be drawn. The *PC* curve shares one important property with the *p*-curve, namely, that movements along the curve requires variations in the level of aggregate demand. The third curve, labelled S_L, is the aggregate labour supply function relating total employment to the level of real wages.

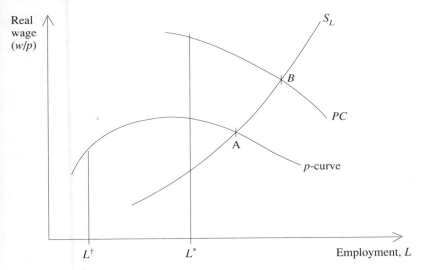

Figure 4.2

The status of points A and B in Fig. 4.2 are essentially the same even though one rises from imperfect competition and the other from perfect competition. They both involve equilibrium with full employment (defined as labour being on its supply curve). Both equilibrium positions face difficulties in being reached and in being sustained. These difficulties can be illustrated as follows. Suppose that employment was at L^*. Under perfect competition, assume that money wages began to fall in response to the excess supply of labour. With a constant level of aggregate demand in real terms, the level of employment remains unchanged and prices fall *pari passu* with wages, leaving real wages unchanged. The outcome under imperfect competition is essentially similar. If the *PC* and *p* curves are treated as demand-for-labour curves (which in our view would be incorrect but is a widely followed practice) and real wages assumed to move in the labour market according to excess demand and supply, then once again the outcome is similar. However, the difference does arise that there would be occasions when the real wage needs to rise in face of excess supply for equilibrium to be attained (e.g. starting at $L^\dagger$ in Fig. 4.2). Similarly, if there is not a mechanism in the labour market to bring about the required adjustment of real wages, then disequilibrium trade would occur with the usual well-known consequences.

The maintenance of full employment arises from consideration of whether the wages and profits generated at equilibrium (A, B) would themselves lead to a level of expenditure which would sustain that equilibrium. Writing Y as income, E as expenditure, W as wages and P as profits, then $Y = W + P$, but there is no particular reason to think that the consequent E (based on W and P) is equal to Y. More generally, any point on the p and PC curves may not be sustainable in this sense. This point enables us to see why the analyses of Ng (1986) and Weitzman (1982) are incomplete. Ng investigates the reactions of firms to a variety of exogenous changes (e.g. of aggregate demand, of costs) but does not impose the condition on his analysis that the assumed aggregate demand would be generated from the income arising from the price–output outcome.

Weitzman's approach suffers from a similar difficulty, though within his model it takes a different form. He parameterizes aggregate demand by labour income so that he in effect assumes that aggregate expenditure is equal to labour income. This is the classical savings function with no savings out of wages and with all profits being saved. It transpires that in his model (both in the short run and the long run) profits are zero, which arises from the (implicit) assumption of zero autonomous expenditure. Thus Weitzman's equilibrium position could be said to be sustainable by the assumption that all wages are spent and with the conclusion that there are no profits anyway. The details of this and other arguments are spelt out in Appendix 2.

This problem of sustainability can be assumed away by appeal to Say's Law of the form that supply sooner or later creates its own demand. Aggregate demand could adjust to support points such as A and B in Fig. 4.2, and if that were the case then the chapter could end at this point. However, when the view that '[c]ontemporary thought is still deeply steeped in the notion that if people do not spend their money in one way they will spend it in another' (Keynes, 1936) is not accepted, then it is necessary to consider the role of aggregate demand. However, before discussing aggregate demand, discussion of the labour market is completed by consideration of wage determination through collective bargaining.

The determination of wages through some form of collective bargaining can be treated in a number of different ways, and two are highlighted here. The p and PC curves can be considered as offers made by firms in terms of real wage–employment. Trade unions could then be seen to choose the point on the appropriate curve which best serves their interests. More sophisticated views of the bargaining process are clearly possible. But whatever the real wage–employment outcome (and however it is arrived at) the problem still remains that the chosen outcome may not be sustainable in terms of aggregate demand.

The other route is useful in linking with discussions over non-accelerating inflation rate of unemployment (NAIRU). A target real-wage approach to the outcome of bargaining over money wages is adopted, and the target money wage w^* of unions in their bargaining as the multiple of current money wages (w_{t-1}), expected prices (p^e_t) to actual prices (p_{t-1}) and an element which reflects movement towards target real wage (labelled RW), i.e.:

$$w^*_t = w_{t-1}.(p^e_t/p_{t-1})^d.(RW/w_{t-1}/p_{t-1})^a \qquad (2)$$

With allowance for the impact of unemployment on the achievement of this target, the following equation for money wage changes can be derived (for details see Sawyer, 1982a; 1982b):

$$\dot{w}_t = b_0 + d.\dot{p}^e_t + b_1.U_{t-1} + a.(lnRW - ln\ w_{t-1}/p_{t-1}) \qquad (3)$$

This equation has been derived from the idea of target real-wage bargaining, but contains the Phillips curve as a special case (where $a = 0$). It is assumed for simplicity that d is unity. It is helpful to derive a steady state equation in which expectations are fulfilled and real wages are constant which yields a real wage unemployment relationship of the form:

$$ln\ (w/p_{-1}) = c_0 + c_1.U + ln\ RW \qquad (4)$$

where $c_0 = a^{-1}.b_0$ and $c_1 = a^{-1}.b_1$.

The corresponding real-wage–employment relation (based for simplicity on a linear unemployment–employment relationship) is written as:

$$ln\ (w/p) = d_0 + d_1.L + ln\ RW \qquad (5)$$

Equation (5) is drawn in Fig. 4.3 as the w-curve. In the absence of any target real wage effect, a bargaining version of the Phillips curve is obtained with the w-curve vertical, and employment set on the labour market side and the real wage in the product market. The point C can be considered a NAIRU. The inflationary consequences are indicated on the diagram. Above the w-curve, real wages decline from collective bargaining considerations (so $\dot{w} < \dot{p}$) and conversely below the w-curve.[3] Above the p-curve, firms would wish to raise prices faster than wages, and again conversely below. It can then be seen that area Z is one of accelerating inflation, and area X of decelerating inflation. The areas S and T are the 'stable zones' with real wages moving towards C. However, this analysis is incomplete without some view of the determination of the level of employment.

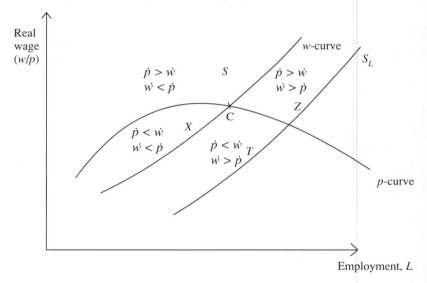

Figure 4.3

Whilst the specific construction differs, the interaction of the p-curve and w-curve shares some features with the analyses of Rowthorn (1977), Layard and Nickell (1985; 1986). It provides an analysis of a 'supply side' limit on employment level without invoking competitive market behaviour. However it has a major shortcoming, which arises from the nature of the p-curve. Different points on the p-curve correspond to different levels of aggregate demand, and the point C to a specific level of demand. There is no reason to think that the wages and profits corresponding to point C will generate the same level of aggregate demand as the firms initially faced. Thus from an aggregate demand point of view, point C need not be sustainable.

At a point such as A in Fig. 4.2, labour is on its supply curve, and it could be argued from the ideas embedded in Say's Law that a willingness to supply labour involves a willingness to spend the resulting income. Whatever the merits of that argument, it cannot be invoked in Fig. 4.3 since the w-curve is not the supply-of-labour curve.

Aggregate Demand

The equilibrium condition of savings equals investment is used as the basis for considering aggregate demand (ignoring the role of government and the foreign sector). The savings and investment functions used are intended to be rather general in the sense of including a range of views on savings and investment as a special cases. The savings function is taken as a Kaldorian one, i.e. $S = s_w .W + s_p .P$, where W is total wages and P total profits. Investment demand is taken to depend on profits, technological opportunities (TP), and interest rates (r), i.e. $I(Y, P, TP, r)$. Income (Y) is included as a proxy for capacity utilization (with capacity taken as fixed in the short run). Profits are included for a variety of reasons, e.g. as an indicator of rate of profit, of internal finance and linked with entrepreneurial optimism, which is the short run are all closely linked with the volume of profits. Technological opportunities are included to help with latter discussion but is held constant here. The rate of interest is included partly so that the Keynesian investment function is included as a special case, and partly for reasons which will be apparent later. The equilibrium condition expressed in real terms becomes:

$$s_w .W + s_p .P = I (Y, P, TP, r) \tag{6}$$

Since $W = (w/p).L$, $P = Y (L) - (w/p).L$, (6) can be regarded as an equation in (w/p) and L. The sign of the relationship between (w/p) and L is not certain, but we argue that a reasonable view would be that it takes the shape of the AD curve illustrated in Fig. 4.4. In the absence of differential savings propensities and of the impact of profits on investment, the line would simply be vertical.

Placing the aggregate demand and p-curves together as in Fig. 4.4 provides an equilibrium outcome which is sustainable in terms of aggregate demand. If the aggregate demand curve happens to pass through the equivalent of points A, B (Fig. 4.2) and C (Fig. 4.3) then there is a sustainable equilibrium outcome. However, at the level of generality used here, it is not possible to definitely conclude that there would be an intersection between the p-curve and the AD-curve. The greater the market power of firms

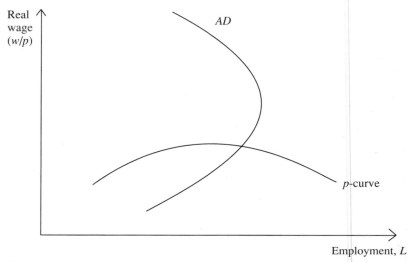

Figure 4.4

(higher 'degree of monopoly'), the lower would be the *p*-curve, and it is quite possible that there is no intersection between the two curves.[5]

The derivation of the *p*-curve above has been (implicitly) based on a constant number of firms. The analysis of Weitzman (1982) points to the importance of the long-run conditions where firms enter to bid away profits. As is shown in Appendix 2, the zero profits condition which Weitzman introduces as a long-run equilibrium condition is redundant in that it is already present in the short-run conditions. There are numerous possibilities concerning entry (e.g. some industries have free entry, others do not, some firms have lower costs than others), and here we intend to indicate the routes through which changes in the number of firms would have an influence. The first point to make is that in a macroeconomic model the volume of profits is determined by macroeconomic forces (Kalecki, 1971; Kaldor, 1955). Equation (6) is relevant here for it can be seen from there that the volume of profits will depend on propensities to save and to invest and the distribution of income.[6] Thus the volume of profits will be affected if any of those parameters are affected. As entry occurs, there will be extra investment to establish the new firms, but it is not clear how steady-state investment would be influenced by the number of firms. The aggregate demand curve may shift as entry occurs, since for a given real wage–employment combination, profits depend on fixed costs per firm, etc. The distribution of income may be influenced from the pricing side. An increase in the number of firms shifts the *p*-curve to the right (cf. multi-plant firms) but may also shift the *p*-curve downwards, as there is further pressure on profit margins. The rightward shift of the *p*-curve may (see Fig. 4.5) lead to a reduction in the real wage (when increasing returns to scale operate), leading to a contradiction of aggregate demand and a fall in employment (and a fall in profits arising from lower sales and higher unit costs).[7]

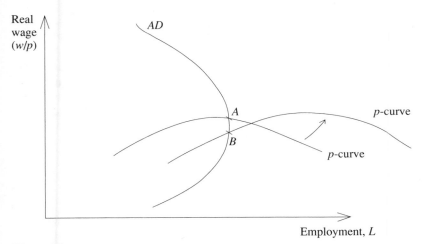

Figure 4.5

The effect of entry on real wages and employment is seen to depend on the nature of the aggregate demand equation combined with whether firms are typically operating subject to increasing or decreasing costs.

OVER-DETERMINACY

In the above framework of analysis there will be a problem of over-determinacy if all these equations (Equations (1), (5) and (6)) are used, since there appear to be only two endogenous variables (real wage and employment). It has been argued elsewhere (Sawyer, 1986) that different authors can be classified in terms of which equation they drop. Without rehearsing those arguments here, the following four points can be high-lighted. First, Keynes and Kalecki can be viewed as emphasizing the roles of the product market and of aggregate demand, and arguing that the labour market takes a subsidiary role.

Second, a Keynesian era could be identified with those periods of time when the labour force is unable to influence real wages, so that the level of employment in the economy is set by the interaction of aggregate demand and firms' pricing decisions (e.g. Equations. (1) and (6)). At times when the labour force has some but incomplete influence on real wages, then inflation would appear as the 'missing variable'. For example, in Equation. (3) above, if d is not equal to unity, then the rate of inflation would appear in Equation (5) and the rate of inflation would help to reconcile the price and wage setting side with the aggregate demand side. But when d equals unity, then the pace of inflation does not influence real wages (in equilibrium), and the use of inflation as an additional variable disappears.

Third, care must be taken in the interpretation of these equations. The status of the equation underlying the p-curve is one of association without any implied causation, and that movements along the p-curve require variations in the level of aggregate demand. The w-curve and AD-curve are equilibrium conditions, and again have no implied causation.

Fourth, the aggregate demand function may depend on variables such as interest rate, price level. The introduction of such variables, however, leaves the model segmented such that the 'supply side' of price and wage setting determines the level of employment and real wages. The level of aggregate demand is then seen to adjust to that level of employment and real wages through changes in interest rate, price level, etc. The mention of interest rates and the price level is not a matter of chance, but rather reflects much of the debate on the contribution of Keynes (e.g. Modigliani, 1944). In line with that debate we can now repeat the arguments as to why interest rates or price levels would be slow to adjust. For example, we could point to the insensitivity of investment to interest rates or to the lack of real balance effects on aggregate demand.[8]

The three equations ((1), (5) and (6)) have two endogenous variables on which attention has been focused, namely, the real wage and employment. However, there are many other variables involved which are sometimes treated as fixed, whether interest rates, price level, target real wage or 'degree of monopoly'. Giving priority to the 'supply side' over the 'demand side' is equivalent to saying that it is the 'demand side' variables such as interest rates, price level, which adjust, and the 'supply side' variables such as target real wage and 'degree of monopoly', which do not adjust.

THE REAPPRAISAL OF KEYNESIAN ECONOMICS LITERATURE

This particular literature may have at first sight little to do with the theme of this paper, since the market structure in that literature has been assumed to be perfectly competitive. Markets are characterized as operating without an auctioneer, leading to quantity rather than price adjustment. There are, however, two links with our theme. The first relates to the nature of the 'auctioneer' under imperfect competition. The idea of an auctioneer with specified functions was a device used by Walras to bring about equilibrium. Arrow(1959) raised the question of how prices adjust in a competitive market in the absence of an auctioneer when all agents are assumed to be price-takers. There have been a variety of attempts to introduce an element of price-making by economic agents whilst preserving the essence of competitive behaviour. An initial point is that all markets operate with a price adjuster, though not with the prevention of disequilibrium trading. But, in some markets, there are people who are not the ultimate buyers or sellers of the product concerned but who do act as price-setters (e.g. market makers on the London Stock Exchange, though they combine price-setting with some element of buying or selling).

The question is not whether there is a price-setter (for there always is) but rather who plays that role. It is our contention that Keynes saw that the arrangements for price-setting were different as between the product and labour markets, such that in the product market it was the sellers (producers) who set the price whilst in the labour market it was not solely the sellers, but could be the buyers alone or with some agreement amongst buyers and sellers. On that view of part of Keynes's approach, it would appear that Keynes's task would have been easier if he had assumed imperfect competition rather than perfect competition.[9] For simply the standard analysis of imperfect competition takes precisely that line so far as the product market is concerned, as seen above. Indeed in the product market it is generally accepted that the producers are the price-setters. The price-setters will have their own objectives, and this is clearly the case for imperfect competition. However, the usual models of imperfect competition also have that the firms set price and output jointly and the combination which is chosen lies on the demand curve (apart from mistakes, etc.).

The second is that out of this literature has arisen the fixprice/flexiprice distinction, with the view that fixed price arises from imperfect competition. Malinvaud (1977), for example, argues that '[t]he classical teaching, according to which prices quickly react to excess supplies or demand, is more and more inadequate for short-run macroeconomic analysis as we move into ever-higher degree of organization of society'. He proceeds to argue the '[t]he conclusion therefore emerges that short-term quantitative adjustments are much more apparent and influential than short-term price adjustments', and this conclusion is based on empirical evidence on cost-plus pricing of, for example, Godley and Nordhaus (1972). Hence, '[g]iven the short-run price rigidities that actually exist, the theory under consideration here is justified in assuming full price rigidity, i.e. in working with models in which prices and wage rates are exogenous. This is going to be a 'fix-price' theory according to the denomination proposed by J. Hicks'.

This reappraisal literature has, of course, portrayed quantity adjustment as much faster than price adjustment. There must be considerable doubt whether that would be an accurate portrayal of imperfect competition (and the arguments in this paper are based on price and quantity adjustment taking place at the same speed). Much will depend not so much on the individual structure *per se* but on the nature of the productive process involved. In those industries (which would surely cover the production of most goods, though not services) where production takes a significant time, it may well be argued that quantity adjustment would take a substantial period of time (say between 6 and 18 months) whereas prices can, if required, be adjusted very quickly. The point is that there may often be technical restrictions on the adjustment of output, whereas there are not such restrictions on price change. In the models of imperfect competition firms adjust output to satisfy the demand which they face (at the prices which they themselves set). This view can be justified on at least two lines. First, on average, firms have accurate perceptions of demand, and can plan ahead for their production. Second, much fluctuation of demand can be met by variations in stocks (though this would not apply to goods which are made to customer specifications).

CONSTANCY OF PRICES UNDER IMPERFECT COMPETITION

This discussion leads into a consideration of the so-called rigidity of price literature, beginning with Means (1935) (administered prices), Sweezy (1939) (kinked demand curve) leading up to Okun (1981). This literature is seen as seeking to explain rigidity of price but tending to forget that firms have chosen the price initially and choose to maintain the price. The distinction is made between constancy of price (i.e. prices do not change because of decisions made by the firms themselves) and rigidity of price (i.e. prices are not permitted to change by some external agency). Further, and of particular significance, firms are generally willing to supply at the chosen price whatever is demanded at that price.

An association has often been made between imperfect competition and inflexibility of price. However, within the imperfect competition approach, since firms are price-makers, when a constant price occurs it does so as a consequence of firms' own decisions, and is not externally imposed. It may be that infrequent price changes reflect the costs of making such changes or that the circumstances which influence prices remain unchanged. Thus there has always been an intrinsic difference between the inflexibility of prices under imperfect competition and the exogenously imposed rigid price which appears in much Keynesian and reappraisal of Keynesian economics literature.

However, the literature on pricing which supports the view that prices are unresponsive to demand has been cited in support of the assumption of rigid prices (see Malinvaud's statement quoted above). There are two difficulties with this argument. First, it relies on the distinction between fixprice and flexiprice, whereas the pricing literature in effect uses the demand-determined/cost-determined distinction. Clearly, in the estimation of most price-change equations, prices are not constant or fixed but rather vary with some combination of cost changes and demand, with much empirical evidence supporting the view that cost changes are much more important than demand (or demand changes). But it is a misnomer to call these fixed prices. Indeed, the implicit assumption in the estimation of quarterly price-change equations is that prices can be adjusted at least quarterly. But even if prices were held constant for some prolonged period of time (say, a number of years), the relevant question would still remain whether firms continued to meet the demand forthcoming at those prices.

Second, under cost-plus pricing formulations, any change in aggregate demand leads to *ceteris paribus* (mainly) quantity changes and not price changes; nevertheless it is not justified to make a direct translation from behaviour under imperfect competition to perfect competition. In the general model of imperfect competition sketched above, a fall in demand would lead to some combination of price changes (which could be a price increase, decrease or no change) and quantity changes, but the new price–quantity combination will lie on the demand curve facing the firm (mistakes, etc., apart) even if the price change is in fact no change. But under perfect competition, a fall in demand without price adjustment would lead to excess supply at the prevailing price; quantity adjusts to the minimum of demand and supply, with the firm forced off their supply curve.

There is, though, the question of the adjustment of the aggregate price level to generate a move back to full employment through the operation of a real balance effect. It can be argued that the combined effect of imperfect competition and collective bargaining is to considerably reduce the possibilities of downward movements of the price level. The practical relevance of this argument may be doubted in that in a world of credit money (see n.8) a fall in the price level may redistribute wealth between creditors and debtors, but it does not generate a rise in the real value of wealth. Further, there are legitimate doubts about the stability of the financial system in face of declining price level. It is anyway the case that a rise in the nominal money supply has the equivalent impact to a fall in the general price level, so that any general downward price rigidity arising from imperfect competition can be overcome in terms of impact on the level of aggregate demand.

This discussion so far has assumed that quantity adjustment presents no difficulties for the firm, which could be perhaps justified by the firms holding sufficient stocks to absorb variations in demand. The circumstances under which the firm would not be able to meet demand would be when capacity is insufficient or when stocks are inadequate. If, for reasons such as those advanced by Okun (1981), firms continue to maintain constant prices, then the view expressed above that supply adjusts to demand in the product markets would not hold. However, this would be a case of relatively high levels of demand, and chronic, if temporary, excess demand in the product markets. Casual observation suggests that chronic excess demand occurs rather rarely. The two examples often cited relate to rationing by some car producers in the post-war reconstruction era[10] and the rationing of UK customers by retail outlets faced by a shortage of sugar, etc., in 1973. Even if such behaviour were more widely observed, it would be associated with high levels of demand, at least relative to capacity, and with firms employing as much labour as they could. The association of such behaviour with unemployment would arise from an inadequacy of productive capacity rather than an insufficiency of aggregate demand. It may be that firms faced with an upsurge in demand which they perceive as temporary do not raise their prices (and conversely for a reduction in demand) for reasons of protecting consumer loyalty, reputations for fairness, etc. But so long as the firms meet demand at those prices, there continues to be no excess demand on the product market side.

However, some different considerations may come into play when goods and services are produced to order. A demand by an individual for, say, a house built to particular specifications cannot realistically be a demand for such a house at this instant, but rather has to be seen as a demand for such a house at some time in future (where the minimum time is set by the nature of production and to some degree by convention). In these circumstances, a producer can respond to a variation of demand by a combination of variations of price and the length of queue. However, this may suggest that the important differences between industries relate not so much to differences of industrial structure but rather to differences over length of production process and whether goods are sold from stocks or made to order.

There remains the case where firms do not change price because of their perceptions of the response of their rivals. One version of this is the kinked demand curve (Sweezy, 1939),[11] where each firm believes it would be unprofitable to change price because of the perceived response of a rivals' prices, though firms collectively would benefit from a price change. In particular, it is argued that neither cost nor demand changes would generate a price change. However, the crucial question in the context of macroeconomics is whether, at the unchanged prices, firms are prepared to meet the prevailing demand. If they are, then the economy remains one in which supply and demand are equated in the product markets.[12]

IMPERFECT COMPETITION AND AGGREGATE DEMAND

The concern of mainstream literature with the macroeconomic implications of imperfect competition have largely focused on price and (to a lesser extent) output decisions, and the flexibility or otherwise of prices (usually in the face of demand changes). In this section, it is argued that the tradition based on authors such as Kalecki, Steindl, indicates that imperfect competition does have macroeconomic implications. The argument concentrates on three aspects, namely, distribution of income, investment and technical change. This section makes no claim to originality, but is intended to draw attention to a neglected tradition and to stress some useful links between macroeconomics and industrial economics.

It can be seen by reference to Fig. 4.3 that when the labour market is unable to influence real wages then the level of employment depends on the position of the p-curve. In general, it would be expected that the mark-up of price over costs will be larger the greater the market power of firms. Thus the p-curve would shift downwards with a rise in market power, and the Kaleckian tradition would suggest that the AD curve is positively sloped. In that case, a rise in market power reduces the level of employment. The general point is that when aggregate demand is relevant, then market power influences the level of employment and unemployment. But when aggregate demand is taken as irrelevant, then the degree of market power influences the level of employment, but does not in itself generate unemployment, in that when the supply of labour curve is in place there is no unemployment.

Some tentative remarks can be made on the influence of industrial structure on the position of the AD curve. There is not a well-developed theory of investment under conditions of imperfect competition. It would be possible to argue informally as follows. The degree of competition between firms (rivalry) may influence investment, with more intense competition leading to more investment (*ceteris paribus*).[13] When investment is undertaken to secure lower costs and/or to permit the introduction of new products and processes, then the competitive pressures on firms will be seen as relevant for the investment decisions. The structure–conduct–performance paradigm would suggest that competition decreases as industrial concentration increases, but this is simply using competition in a structural sense. The Marxian view of competition would stress the rivalry between firms, which may be unrelated to the number of firms in an industry. It could be anticipated that the fiercer the rivalry between firms, the greater will be the rate of investment as firms seek to achieve lower costs through investment in new machinery.

The specification of the investment function, and in particular the role of profits, will depend on the development of the financial markets. When financial markets are undeveloped, the possibilities for external finance by firms are highly restricted. In such circumstances, it would be expected that internal finance (retained profits) would be an important influence on the level of investment. Savings out of wages and out of rentier income would have a depressant effect on aggregate demand without any compensating stimulating influence on investment. However, at the limit with savings only from profits and with investment constrained by the availability of internal finance, Say's Law is reinstated. This form of the classical savings function would appear more appropriate for the nineteenth century.[14] The late twentieth century is more appropriately characterized by a highly developed financial system, but one in which there is still a preference by firms for internal over external finance.

The influence of technical change on the pace of investment was crudely represented above by including a term *TP* in the investment function. An upward shift in *TP* leads to an outward shift of the *AD* curve, and a predicted rise in employment and output. There have been numerous studies within industrial economics literature on the relationship between industrial structure and the pace of technological change. Indeed, it can be argued that the relevance of industrial economics for levels of output and employment is much more substantial through the impact of industrial structure on technical change (and thereby investment and growth) than through the impact on price and output decisions.

THE COMPLEMENTARITY OF IMPERFECT COMPETITION AND MACROECONOMICS

A major part of the argument of Clower and others has been that '*either Walras' law is compatible with Keynesian economics, or Keynes had nothing fundamentally new to add to orthodox economy theory*' (Clower, 1965:

italics in original). The traditionally modelling of imperfect competition enters this debate through its general assumption that supply adjusts (through price and quantity changes) to demand, so there is a sense in which there is no excess demand in the product markets. Thus, from the application of Walras's Law (in the form of the sum of excess demand over all products and labour is zero), then the excess demand for labour as a whole will be zero.

There are some complications in considering Walras's Law in the context of imperfect competition, since the usual derivation of that law involves parametric prices, whereas under imperfect competition the producers set prices. The commodities labelled 1 through to m are those supplied by producers and demanded by households, whilst those labelled $m+1$ through to n are supplied by households to the producers. The prices of the former group are labelled p_i ($i = 1, \ldots, m$) and of the latter group w_j ($j = m + 1, \ldots, n$). The vector of ($p_1, p_2 \ldots, p_m$) is signified by p and that of ($w_{m+1} \ldots, w_n$) by w. A typical producer is faced with a demand function d_k (p, w), (k lying between 1 and m), and sets price p^*_k and intends to supply q^*_k where (p^*_k, q^*_k) lies on the perceived demand function. In the estimation of the demand function facing it, the firm will have to make assumptions about other prices. The analysis here proceeds on the basis that each firm correctly forecasts the prices charged by other producers and treats the price of inputs parametrically.

A profits function covering all producers is defined as:

$$P = \sum_{i=1}^{m} p^*_i \cdot q^*_i - \sum_{j=m+1}^{n} w_j \cdot d_j (p^*, w) \tag{7}$$

With the demand for each input depending on relative input prices and each firm's demands for inputs being consistent with the intended output.

Households receive income from the supply of inputs to producers and from (lump sum) profits. In the absence of financial assets, households are constrained to have expenditure equal to income, i.e.:

$$\sum_{i=1}^{m} p_i \cdot d_i (p, w) = \sum_{j=m+1}^{n} w_j \cdot s_j (p, w) + P \tag{8}$$

where the demand for goods and services and the supply of inputs depend on relative prices, and are considered notional in the sense of Clower. A particular case for Equation (8) is where the p_i's are those chosen by the producers (i.e. p^*_i). In that case, adding Equations (7) and (8) together yields:

$$\sum_i p^*_i . d_i = \sum_i p^*_i . q^*_i + \sum_j w_j . (s_j - d_j) \tag{9}$$

However the producers have acted to ensure that $d_i = q^*_i$, which leads to:

$$\sum_j w_j . (d_j (p^*, w) - s_j (p^*, w)) = 0 \tag{10}$$

In this approach, any failure of the input prices to be at the market-clearing level can lead to unemployment in the manner analysed by Clower and others. Specifically, with the short side of the market dominating, the use of inputs will be demand constrained for those inputs whose price is below the market-clearing level. Producers will then not be able to produce at the intended level. The sellers of inputs whose price is above the market-clearing level will of course find themselves demand constrained.

In this approach, the possibility of unemployment remains, but essentially arises from a lack of price adjustment in the input markets. In the particular case of a single type of input (homogenous labour), then the above argument would lead to the conclusion of zero excess demand for that input, i.e. there would be no unemployment. The general conclusion arises essentially from the idea that under imperfect competition there are agents who adjust price, namely the producers.

This line of argument suggests that imperfect competition is not a cause of unemployment (though it may be a cause of excess capacity). This conclusion is however drawn from an analysis of a non-monetary economy in which there is no mention of savings and investment. In an analysis where savings and investment are introduced, a rather different conclusion is drawn here, namely, that there is a degree of mutual support between the use of imperfect competition and the macroeconomic analysis of Kalecki and Keynes. In one direction, in analysing the decisions of a firm or industry, it is necessary to locate the position of the relevant demand curve(s), and an important variable in that location would be the level of aggregate demand.

In the other direction, in order to permit imperfect competition to be compatible with unemployment of labour, it is necessary to move away from the equivalent of a barter economy (on which the above derivation of Equation (10) was based) to a economy with financial assets.[15] This is essentially achieved when the aggregate demand curve is introduced, for although it is derived from the equality between savings and investment, it clearly recognizes that they could potentially differ (i.e. at points off the *AD* curve). Savings and investment can potentially differ from one another only in an economy with financial assets, for otherwise a decision to refrain from consumption still requires the acquisition of real goods and services. Without the possibility of a difference between savings and investment, any real wage–employment combination would be sustainable, and in particular the full employment combination would be.

The relationship between Keynesian economics and imperfect competition should not be seen as one in which the latter supports an assumption of rigidity of prices. Indeed, the relationship is seen as rather the reverse of that, namely, imperfect competition is more supportive of the notion that the product markets continuously clear (in that price–output combinations lie on the relevant demand curve), and hence that output prices adjust rapidly. Another and important implication of the use of imperfect competition refers to the interpretation of any relationship between real wage and employment derived from firm behaviour. It is clear that the real wage–employment relationship is not a demand function since the firms themselves are portrayed as setting both the real wage (via price decision) and employment level. This again fits in with the approach of Keynes in which aggregate demand leads to a particular combination of employment and real wage, such that a different employment–real wage combination would arise only if a different level of aggregate demand were established. It has been seen that the difference between imperfect competition and perfect competition is that the former permits both positive and negative associations between employment and real wage whereas the latter allows only a negative association.

EXPECTATIONS, MISTAKES AND ADJUSTMENT MECHANISMS

The equilibrium position derived from a consideration of wage and price behaviour would be consistent with 'rational' expectations in that all relevant expectations are fulfilled. Firms are assumed to know fully their demand and cost conditions. On the labour market side, suppliers of labour are assumed to know the real wage which they face or, in the case of collective bargaining, expectations on inflation are fulfilled. Further, any equilibrium including the aggregate demand equation also does not involve any element of expectations being unfulfilled. However, it must be noted that it is expectations on prices and output (i.e. short-term expectations) which are fulfilled. Long-term expectations are particularly relevant for investment decisions, and there is nothing in the model developed above which says whether or not these expectations are fulfilled.[16]

The other aspect of expectation formation which has been ignored above concerns the conjectures which a firm holds on the reactions of other firms to its own actions. The question of conjectures has generated a substantial literature but little by way of a consensus. But in many respects, the particular conjectures adopted by firms are not of fundamental importance here. Whatever the conjectures adopted by firms are, there will be an equilibrium outcome in terms of prices and output, given the level of demand and input prices which the firms face. The general relationship summarized in Equation (1) above is maintained, even though the specific shape of the relationship will depend on, *inter alia*, the conjectures adopted by the firms involved.

Suppose that firms generally mis-perceive the demand conditions which they face and over estimate demand. The resulting output will not all be sold, and stocks accumulate. In the first stage, income remains unchanged, but the evidence of rising stocks leads firms to reduce production (and perhaps to over-adjust to correct previous build-up of stocks) and move towards a level of prices and output consistent with the level of demand. A full model would, of course, be required to model expectations, etc., but if we were prepared to assume unchanging exogenous component of aggregate demand, it would seem reasonable to assume that prices and outputs will move towards the equilibrium outcome.

It could be argued that the equilibrium approach necessarily overlooks problems of co-ordination and ignores the roles of mistakes and business cycles. The co-ordination problem in the reappraisal of Keynesian economics literature could be seen to arise from the absence of an auctioneer, and the associated inability of unemployed workers to signal their willingness to both work and purchase. In discussing problems of co-ordination it is useful to distinguish two cases. First, a change in the composition of demand (at an unchanged overall level of demand) triggers off a deflationary spiral in the Clower-type approach. The short side of the market dominates, so that output falls in the market where demand has fallen but does not increase in the market where demand has risen. In the imperfect competition case, it has been argued that this would not be so, with price and output adjusting in both rising and falling demand markets. The representation of imperfect competition above does not permit this type of co-ordination difficulty, with supply adjusting upwards and downwards. There is the possibility, though, of capacity constraints, which may arise from a lack of capacity to provide full employment or from a level of demand which could only be satisfied by a level of employment in excess of full employment. The first case can be a source of unemployment but would not seem to be particularly associated with imperfect competition and is more likely to arise in the aftermath of destruction of capacity through war or through recession. The second case is clearly not one of unemployment.

Second, a change in the level of aggregate demand leads to a change in the level of output, with the relative size of the latter change depending on the price response. In the case the imperfect competition, it may be expected that the effect on prices may be rather small and can be 'perverse' (i.e. prices rise with a fall in aggregate demand). But the difference between perfect competition and imperfect competition is a quantitative one, not a qualitative one.

CONCLUSIONS

The supply side of the economy can be viewed as the determining factor for the level of economic activity, provided that one is prepared to assume that aggregate demand can, through changes in interest rates, price-level adjust to sustain any level of economic activity set on the supply side of the economy. However, that requires that interest rates, price level, etc., can bring about sufficient adjustments on the demand side, and that there are not adjustments on the supply side (say through changes in the degree of monopoly, the target real wage). Imperfect competition may, for well-known reasons, generate excess capacity, whereas perfect competition would not. However, in the labour market, it has been argued that the industrial structure does not make much difference, and in particular imperfect competition cannot be seen as a cause of unemployment (as a consequence of the price–output decisions).

The view taken here is that industrialized economies are characterized in an imperfectly competitive world, and the question of whether the economy would in some sense operate better under perfect competition is irrelevant since there is no prospect of moving the economy to a state of perfect competition. However, the question can be asked as to how industrial structure influences the macroeconomy. It has been argued above that the structure will have important implications for the distribution of income, investment and technical progress, all of which feeds into aggregate demand. The position of the aggregate demand curve is a particularly important element in the determination of the level of employment. This is not only a reassertion of the traditional Keynesian view on the role of aggregate demand but, as argued above, is a necessary accompaniment of imperfect competition (unless full employment is always to be assumed).

Much has been heard of the need for microeconomic foundations of macroeconomics, and the requirement that such foundations are based on 'rational' behaviour. The approach adopted in this chapter does not require any departure from maximizing behaviour (leaving aside whether such behaviour should be labelled 'rational'), though the approach does not require maximizing behaviour (with, for example, pricing and investment based on satisficing behaviour). When unemployment is seen as arising from aggregate demand failure, this is not a question of any absence of maximizing behaviour (since both savings and investment could be derived from maximizing considerations) but rather the mechanisms by which two sets of decisions (savings, investment) are reconciled. It should be further noted that the use of imperfect competition clearly requires a macro-economic foundation. In particular, the demand curve facing each firm has to be positioned by reference to the macroeconomic environment. Further, it has been argued that imperfect competition generally involves supply adjusted to demand, and to allow for the possibility of unemployment of labour requires some departure from Walras's Law. This departure was introduced through financial assets which permit savings and investment decisions to be separate from each other.[17]

Notes

1.   Hicks (1974) also argues that '[t]he major difference between the working of a fixprice market and that of a flexprice market now becomes apparent. In the fixprice market . . . actual stocks may be greater, or may be less than, desired stocks; in the flexprice market, on the other hand, actual stocks are always equal to desired stocks – when the stocks of the traders are taken into account.'
      An important feature of the fixprice theory is not that 'prices do not vary, but that the causes of their variation are outside the model. So we suspend the rule that price must change whenever there is an excess of supply or excess of demand.' However '[t]he fixprice commodities . . . are not to be supposed to have prices that are fixed, whatever happens; they are characterized, not by that, but by some degree of insulation from the pressures of supply and demand. If their costs of production rise, their prices may well rise; if their costs fall their prices may also fall, though perhaps very gradually.'
2.   This view of course runs counter to both the Clower–Leijonhufvud inspired reappraisal of Keynesian economics with its emphasis on failures of co-ordination and of both labour and product markets not usually clearing. It also runs counter to the perception of Keynes as invoking price rigidity. However: 'In contrast, Keynes' treatment of the labor demand function implies that the market for current output is clearing. The *General Theory* seems perfectly consistent on this point. Keynes implies throughout that prices, as contrasted with wages, adjust instantaneously, to bring the quantity demanded into line with the quantity supplied, the latter being fixed in the short run. Thus Leijonhufvud would seem to have no basis for his contention that Keynes generally reversed the Marshallian ranking of relative price and quantity adjustment speeds.' (Grossman, 1972) (See also Brothwell, 1975, and Chick, 1983.)

3. It may be more reasonable to assume that real wages would be constant or decline only slowly above the w-curve. In Equation (2) it has been assumed that money wages decline relatively to prices if the actual real wage is above the target real wage. It could be argued that the value of a should be zero if the actual is above the target real wage.

4. Suppressing TP and r for convenience, we have:

$$s_w.(w/p).L + s_p.(Y - (w/p).L) = I(Y, Y - (w/p).L)$$

with $Y = Y(L)$. The impact of a variation of (w/p) on L can be derived from:

$$s_w.\{d(w/p).L + (w/p).dL\} + s_p.\{Y'.dL - d(w/p).L - (w/p).dL\}) =$$
$$I_1.Y'.dL + I_2.\{Y'.dL - d(w/p).L - (w/p).dL\})$$

where Y' is first derivative of Y w.r.t. L, I_i first derivative of I with respect to the ith argument.

This yields:

$$d(w/p).L.\{s_w - s_p + I_2\} = dL.\{(I_1 + I_2).Y' - (w/p).(s_w - s_p + I_2)\}$$

It is not possible to unambiguous sign $dL/d(w/p)$, and indeed we may expect the sign to change as reflected in Figure 4.4. The term $(s_w - s_p + I_2)$ is taken as positive (and would be if no difference in savings propensities). The right-hand side would then have a positive and a negative component. At low levels of the real wage, the positive is taken to outweigh the negative, leaving an overall positive relationship between real wage and employment. But at high levels of the real wage, the relationship becomes a negative one. This line of argument has similarities with that of Sylos-Labini (1984) when he discussed the 'concept of the optimal rate of profit', where optimal is in terms of impact on the level of economic activity. The basic idea is that as real wages (relative to average productivity) and profits vary, there is a mixture of positive and negative effects on the level of aggregate demand.

5. McDonald (1985) uses a vintage model in which investment decisions are based on a fixed pay-off period, and concludes that there are plausible values of the profit margin for which there would be no solution for the equation investment equals savings. Further, 'the results are such that one would not be surprised if for some economies at certain times an empirically based investigation found that market power was a cause of aggregate demand deficiency.'

    Sylos-Labini (1984) argues that '[i]t might seem strange that an expansion of profits can be such as to prepare the ground for particularly severe crises. But it is so. The Great Depression which began with a collapse of the US economy in 1929 was proceeded, and in a sense 'caused' by, a period of an excessive expansion of profits.'

6. Linearizing Eqn (6) gives:

$$s_w.W + s_p.P = aP + bY + c$$

and taking $P/W = x$ then $Y/W = 1 + x$, we can solve for P as

$$P = c/\{(s_p - a) + s_w x - b(1 + x)\}$$

7. Weitzman (1982) assumes constant marginal cost of production so that the p curve is horizontal and its position is unaffected by the number of firms. However, because of increasing returns to scale, as more firms enter, average output falls, unit costs rise, but with marginal cost and price constant, profits per firm decline. Entry in Weitzman's model can only be properly discussed by making a modification to his model to introduce a non-zero component of autonomous demand (for otherwise, as shown in Appendix 2, profits are necessarily zero). The aggregate demand simply becomes profits equals autonomous component of aggregate demand. However as firms enter, average labour productivity declines, which causes the aggregate demand to shift to the right leaving real wages unchanged but employment increased.

8. The real balance effect can easily be dismissed in a world of credit money. 'The total real value . . . increases only to the extent to which money is backed by gold' (Kalecki, 1944).

9. Ohlin wrote that 'in this respect [assumption of perfect competition] as in other respects Keynes does not seem to me to have been sufficiently radical enough in freeing himself from the conventional assumptions. When reading his book [Keynes, 1936] one sometimes wonders whether he never discussed imperfect competition with Mrs. Robinson' (reproduced in Keynes, 1973): the reference to Mrs Robinson clearly relates to Robinson (1933) on imperfect competition.

10. 'For a long time after the war, for example, there were many goods, such as motor-cars, for which a huge pent-up demand existed, and which would have commanded an enormous price in a free market. Yet manufacturers, almost without exception, held prices down to what they considered a 'fair' and 'reasonable' level, well below the market or profit-maximising price' (Crosland, 1956).

11. The analysis of Hahn (1978) of such a case of firms not changing prices because of rivals' perceived responses is not relevant to our argument since he does '*not assume that the economy is intrinsically one of monopolistic competition*. The economy to be studied always has a Walrasian equilibrium. I shall show that it also has non-Walrasian equilibria' (italics in original).

12. The p-curve drawn in the Figures would become a little more complex. Over a range, neither demand nor cost changes would lead to a price change. For a change in the level of demand, this means that there is a horizontal section in the p-curve. For a change in costs arising from a relatively small wage change, price remains unchanged and the real wage changes in line with money wage change. For a large change in money wages, price would respond, leaving a much smaller change in real wages. For a modest change in non-wage costs, the p-curve would not shift.

13. A Jorgenson approach (which assumes, *inter alia*, malleable capital) would suggest that in comparison with perfect competition, monopoly would have a smaller capital stock alongside a smaller labour force and output, for the usual reason that monopolists restrict output when compared with perfectly competitive outcome.

14. Chick (1986) analyses the relationship between savings and investment in different eras as related to the development of the banking system. In particular, whether savings or investment is the active variable to which the other passively adapts is seen to vary depending on the nature of the financial system.

15. Clower argues that his analysis relates to monetary economy. However, Drazen (1980) argues that it is not money *per se* which creates the co-ordination problems but the 'uncoupling of transactions'. I almost said, in the text, 'a monetary economy' (rather than an economy with financial assets). However, in this argument it is not so much the existence of money, but the view that the intention to save does not inexorably lead to the purchase of real goods and services.

16. 'In his 1937 lecture notes, Keynes himself seems to place even greater relative emphasis on the effects of shifting long-term expectations by suggesting that the *General Theory*, if rewritten, should assume at the outset that short-period expectations were always fulfilled; and then have a subsequent chapter showing what difference it makes when short-period expectations are disappointed' (Hodgson, 1988, p. 218).

    For the theory of effective demand is substantially the same if we assume that short-period expectations are always fulfilled' (Keynes, 1973), and also '[n]ow Hawtrey, as it seems to me, mistakes this higgling process by which the equilibrium position is discovered for the much more fundamental forces which determine what the equilibrium position is' (Keynes, 1973).

17. I am grateful to Philip Arestis, Peter Reynolds, participants in seminars at the Universities of Kent and Stirling, and at the European Association for Research in Industrial Economics, Rotterdam, for comments on earlier versions of this chapter.

Appendix 1

(i) *Monopoly*

Let the demand facing a monopolist be $Q^d = (p/r)^{-k}D^b$ where p is the price of output of monopolist, r is an index of substitutes and D is a measure of real level of aggregate demand. The production function is taken for convenience as homothetic transformation of a Cobb–Douglas function so that $Q^s = f(L^c M^{1-c})$ where L is a measure of labour input, M of material input. The price of material input is m and wage of labour is w. The decision variables for the firm are taken as L and M, with p and Q derivable as a consequence of decisions on L and M. The relationship between L and M is given by:

$$M = ((1 - c) \ w/cm).L \tag{A1}$$

It is then possible to derive the equation for labour demand in terms of exogenous variables $(w, m, r$ and $D)$ as:

$$(k - 1/k).D^{b/k}.c.f'(X).f(X)^{-1/k}.((1 - c) \ w/cm)^{(1-c)} = (w/r) \tag{A2}$$

where $X = (L(1 - c)w/cm)^{1-c}$. There are numerous ways of expressing the employment decision which involves endogenous variables, and we require one which involves the real product wage, which is:

$$(k - 1/k).f'(X).c.((1 - c)w/cm)^{1-c} = w/p \qquad (A3)$$

The implied relationship between real product wage and labour employment in Eqn (A3) can be positive or negative, depending upon the sign of the second derivative of f. The relationship is illustrated in Fig. 4.1 with the curve labelled p-curve (drawn for a specific value of w/m).

It can be seen from Eqn (A2) that the employment (and behind that output) decision depends on price of substitutes (r) and the level of aggregate demand. But, in this example, the employment decision is uniquely linked with the real product wage of the firm.

There would be a complex aggregation problem to move from Eqn (A3) to the comparable aggregate relationship (summarized as Eqn (1) in the text). Apart from the non-linearities involved in Eqn (A3), there is also the complication of the interdependence of prices across industries. Informally we can argue as follows. For given real aggregate demand, money wages and input prices, consider an equilibrium set of output prices. Those output prices will then set workers' real wages as well as each firm's real product wage. At the same time as those prices are established, output and employment will also be established. The relationship between real wage and employment is then reflected in Eqn (1).

(ii)   *Oligopoly*

An oligopoly model along the lines of Cowling and Waterson (1976) which allows for some interdependence between firms' output decisions (in context of homogeneous product) would yield rather similar results. The equation of interest relates real product wage with employment level, and at the firm level this is:

$$(k - z)/k).f'(X).c.(w(1 - c)/mc)^{1-c} = w/p \qquad (A5)$$

where z is the perceived elasticity of total output with respect to firm's own output, and $X = L ((1 - c) w/cm)^{1-c}$ with L the firm's employment level. Aggregating across firms would yield a similar relationship at the industry level. The nature of the relationship between real wage and the level of economic activity is now complicated by possible variations in both k and z as the level of economic activity varies.

(iii)   *Sales revenue maximizing*

The firm seeks to maximize $S = p.q$ subject to minimum profit constraint A, and as is usual we assume that the constraint in binding. Thus the firm operates according to:

$$A = P = p.q - w.L - m.M \qquad (A6)$$

so that $p.q = w.L + m.M + A$. The cost-minimizing condition holds (so that $M = ((1 - c) w/cm).L$), so that we have:

$$(w/p) = c.f(X) - (Ac/p) \tag{A7}$$

where X is as defined above. The absolute output price here appears to influence the real wage, though this depends on the nature of the profits constraint, for if that constraint is set in real terms then the absolute price level disappears from Equation (A7).

Appendix 2

The purpose of this appendix is to present a detailed critique of Weitzman (1982) to back up the claims made in the text. The essence of the Weitzman model can be expressed in the following.

$$q = c(L - F) \tag{B1}$$

is the production function for the firm with q as output, L as labour employed (although note that factors not distinguished) and c, F are technological constants.

The demand curve for a firm's product is given by:

$$d(p) = a(1/p) + b(1/p).\{(1/p) - (1/\bar{p})\} \tag{B2}$$

where $a = (1 - u)Nw/m$, $b = (1 - u)Nw^2/Hv$ where u is rate of unemployment, N number of consumers (equal to number of workers), w money wage, m number of firms, H, v parameters of the demand conditions, p firm's own price and $\bar{p}$ price of rivals. The elasticity of demand for the firm (evaluated at $p = \bar{p}$, but the elasticity is calculated for a variation in p which is not followed by a variation in $\bar{p}$)

$$E = 1 + (b/ap) = 1 + wm/Hvp \tag{B3}$$

so that the elasticity of demand is independent of the level of demand. From the profit-maximizing condition that marginal cost is equal to marginal revenue, price can be derived as:

$$p = w/c(1 - Hv/cm) \tag{B4}$$

and for symmetric Nash equilibrium ($p = \bar{p}$) $d = a/p$ and then:

$$d = \{c(1 - u)N/m\}.\{1 - Hv/cm\} \tag{B5}$$

It can be noted from Eqn (B5) that the price and number of firms are positively related so that price would be lower under monopoly ($m = 1$) than under perfect competition. It will be seen below that within this model profits are always zero, and hence do not vary with the number of firms. It is argued that '[i]n the short run, the model treats as exogenously fixed: aggregate demand, the number of firms, and the nominal wage. Endogenously determined by profit maximization are: prices, output and employment.' This appears to be incorrect, for aggregate demand is treated as exogenous but is parameterized by u, and it can be easily calculated that aggregate demand is treated as $(1 - u)Nw$ (i.e. money labour income). However employment is treated as endogenous, which leads to $(1 - u)Nw$, and hence aggregate demand as being endogenous. From the firm's production function with demand satisfied by output $(d = q)$ we have $d = c(L - F)$ so that for the firm $L = (d/c) + F$. Total employment is (with m firms) $(md/c) + mF$ and this would be consistent with the initial employment level if $(1 - u)N = (md/c) + mF$. From Eqns (4) and (5):

$$m.p.d = (1 - u)Nw = mw.(d/c + F),\qquad\qquad\qquad\text{(B6)}$$

which slightly rewritten is:

$$p.d = w.(d/c + F)\qquad\qquad\qquad\text{(B7)}$$

This is precisely the zero profits condition equation (21) in Weitzman (1982) which is said to arise from free entry. But it is contained within the short-run (fixed number of firms) model. Indeed, it is merely a reflection of the well-known conclusion that when there are zero savings out of wages, profits are dependent expenditure out of profits (consumption or investment) (Kaldor, 1955), and so profits are zero because non-wage expenditure is zero. In effect, Weitzman assumed a classical savings function with zero savings out of wages and with all profits being saved.

There are in fact three independent equations in three endogenous variables (price, output and employment) (Eqns (B4), (B5) and (B6)) and in particular employment can be solved as:

$$(1 - u)N = m^2Fc/Hv\qquad\qquad\qquad\text{(B8)}$$

(and this is Weitzman's equation (22) rewritten as the solution for employment, rather than the number of firms). Since there are no profits even in the short run in this model, it is not in fact possible to treat the number of firms as endogenous. Whatever the number of firms there will be zero profits in this model, simply because there is zero non-wage expenditure.

From the absence of any autonomous component of aggregate demand, it follows that it is not possible to model the impact of an aggregate demand shock. Thus, the conclusion that '[t]he profit maximizing short term reaction to aggregate demand shocks is a pure quantity adjustment, which creates volatile pro-cyclical fluctuations of productivity and profits' (Weitzman, 1982)) cannot be sustained from the original model, though the modification given below does support that conclusion.

The simplest way of modifying this model is to introduce an autonomous component of aggregate demand, so that the demand function is modified to:

$$d(p) = a(1/p) + b(1/p).\{(1/p) - (1/\overline{p})\}\qquad\qquad\qquad\text{(B2')}$$

where now $a = \{(1 - u)Nw + Xw\}/m$, $b = \{(1 - u)Nw + Xw\}.w/Hv$ where X is the autonomous component of demand in real terms (measured in wage units). The elasticity of demand is the same as before and hence so will be the profit-maximizing price. So again $p = w/c[1 - Hv/cm]$, which gives the real wage:

$$w/p = c[1 - Hv/cm]\qquad\qquad\qquad\text{(B9)}$$

In symmetric equilibrium $d = a(1/p)$ where $a = Z/m$ (having put $Z = (1 - u)Nw + Xw$ for convenience)

Each firm is producing d using labour given by $c(L - F) = d$, hence employment is $mL = md/c + mF$ and then $(1 - u)N = mL = md/c + mF$ which is equal to $Z/cp + mF = (1 - u)Nw/cp + mF$. This is:

$$(1 - u)N = (1 - u)Nw/cp + mF \tag{B10}$$

The real wage is given by Equation (B9) and the level of employment by:

$$(1 - u)N = (cm/Hv) \, [mF + X(1 - Hv/cm)] \tag{B11}$$

It can be seen that a variation of autonomous demand would not affect the real wage but would generate changes in employment, etc. The profits in total are Xw, and hence profits per firm are Xw/m. The application of the zero profits condition would indicate the number of firms tending to infinity. However, it is more reasonable to think of firms continuing to enter provided that the rate of profit exceeds some minimum rate. To illustrate, suppose that a firm's capital requirement in real terms (wage units) is given by $K = h.L + i$ which is then equal to $h(1 - u)N/m + i$. The rate of profit is then given by $Xw/\{h(1 - u)N/m + i\}w$, and this would decline with the number of firms, and equating this with the minimum rate of profit would determine the number of firms. Substituting from Equation (11) would give $1/\{(hcmF/HvX) + (hc/Hv) - (h/m) + i\} = r_{min}$ and a quadratic equation for m (number of firms).

From Equation (B11), it can be seen that employment and number of firms are positively related, with the basic mechanism that the greater the number of firms, the lower employment per firm and the lower productivity. Hence more employees are required for a given level of output.

Bibliography

ARROW, K. (1959) 'Towards a Theory of Price Adjustment', in M. Abramovitsz (ed.) *The Allocation of Economic Resources*, California: Stanford University Press.

BROTHWELL, J.F. (1975) 'A Simple Keynesian Response to Leijonhufvud', *Bulletin of Economic Research* 27 pp. 3–21.

CHICK, V. (1983) *Macroeconomics After Keynes*, Deddington: Philip Allan.

CHICK, V. (1986) 'The Evolution of the Banking System and the Theory of Saving, Investment and Interest', *Economies et Societies*, Cahiers de l'ISMEA Serie Monnaie et Production, no. 3.

CLOWER, R. (1965), 'The Keynesian Counter-Revolution', in F. Hahn and F. Brechling (eds) *The Theory of Interest Rates* London: Macmillan.

COWLING, K. and WATERSON, M. (1976) 'Price–Cost Margin and Market Structure', *Economica* 43, pp. 267–74.

CROSLAND, C.A.R. (1956) *The Future of Socialism*, London: Jonathan Cape.

DRAZEN, A. (1980) 'Recent Developments in Macroeconomics Disequilibrium Theory', *Econometrica* 48, pp. 283–306.

DUNLOP, J. (1938) 'The Movement of Real and Money Wage Rates', *Economic Journal*, 48, pp. 413–34.

GODLEY, W. and NORDHAUS, W. (1972) 'Pricing in the Trade Cycle', *Economic Journal* 82 pp. 853–82.

GROSSMAN, H. (1972) 'Was Keynes a Keynesian?'*Journal of Economic Literature* 10, pp. 26–30.

HAHN, F. (1978) 'On Non-Walrasian Equilibria', *Review of Economic Studies* 45, pp. 1–17.

HALL, R. and HITCH, C. (1939) 'Price Theory and Business Behaviour', *Oxford Economic Papers* no. 2, pp. 12–33.

HICKS, J. (1974) *The Crisis in Keynesian Economics*, Oxford: Blackwell.

HODGSON, G. (1988) *Economics and Institutions*, Oxford: Polity Press.

KALDOR, N. (1955) 'Alternative Theories of Distribution', *Review of Economic Studies* 23, pp. 83–100.

KALDOR, N. (1978) *Further Essays on Economic Theory*, London: Duckworth.

KALECKI, M. (1939) *Essays in the Theory of Economic Fluctuations*, London: Allen and Unwin.

KALECKI, M. (1944) 'Professor Pigou on "The Classical Stationary State": A Comment', *Economic Journal*, 54, pp. 131–2.

KALECKI, M. (1971) *Selected Essays on the Dyamics of the Capitalist Economy*, Cambridge University Press.

KEYNES, J.M. (1936) *The General Theory of Employment, Interest and Money*, London: (Macmillan).

KEYNES, J.M. (1939) 'Relative Movements of Real Wages and Output', *Economic Journal* 49, pp. 34–51.

KEYNES, J.M. (1973) *The General Theory and After: Part II Defence and Development*, Collected Works, vol. 14, London: Macmilan.

LAYARD, R. and NICKELL, S. (1985) 'The Causes of British Unemployment', *National Institute Economic Review*, no. 110, pp. 62–85.

LAYARD, R. and NICKELL, S. (1986) 'Unemployment in Britain', *Economica* 53 (supplement), pp. S121–70.

MCDONALD, I. (1985) 'Market Power and Unemployment', *International Journal of Industrial Organisation* 3, pp. 21–35.

MALINVAUD, E. (1977) *The Theory of Unemployment Reconsidered* Oxford: Blackwell.

MEANS, G.C. (1935) 'Industrial Pricing and their Relative Flexibility' (US Senate Document 13, 74th Congress, 1st Session, Washington).

MODIGLIANI, F. (1944) 'Liquidity Preference and the Theory of Money', *Econometrica* 12, pp. 45–88.

NG, Y.K. (1986) *Meso-economics*, Brighton: Wheatsheaf.

OKUN, A. (1981) *Prices and Quantities: A Macroeconomic Analysis*, Oxford: Blackwell.

ROBINSON, J. (1933) *The Economics of Imperfect Competition*, London: Macmillan.

ROWTHORN, R. (1977) 'Conflict, Inflation and Money', *Cambridge Journal of Economicsa* 1, pp. 215–40.

SAWYER, M. (1982a) *Macro-economic in Question*, Brighton: Wheatsheaf.

SAWYER, M. (1982b) 'Collective Bargaining, Oligopoly and Macroeconomics', *Oxford Economic Papers* 34, pp. 428–48.

SAWYER, M. (1985) *Economics of Michal Kalecki*, London: Macmillan.

SAWYER, M. (1986) 'Conflict and Aggregate Demand in Post Keynesian Economics: The Problem of Over-Determinacy' (mimeo).

SWEEZY, P. (1939) 'Conditions of Demand under Oligopoly', *Journal of Political Economy* 47, pp. 568–73.

SYLOS-LABINI, P. (1984) 'On the Concept of the Optimum Rate of Profit' in *The Forces of Economic Growth and Decline*, Cambridge Mass.: MIT Press.

TARSHIS, L. (1939) 'Changes in Money and Real Wages', *Economic Journal* 49, pp. 150–154.

THIRLWALL, A.P. (1983) 'Comment' in Worswick and Trevithick (1983).

WEITZMAN, M. (1982) 'Increasing Returns and the Foundations of Unemployment Theory', *Economic Journal* 92, pp. 784–804.

WORSWICK, D. and TREVITHICK, J. (eds) (1983) *Keynes and the Modern World*, Cambridge University Press.

5 Flexibility and Industrial Organization Theory[1]

Alfredo Del Monte and Fabio Massimo Esposito

INTRODUCTION

The study of the determinants of intra-industry differences in firm size and organizational structure is a major field in industrial organization. Most industrial economists share the opinion that in the long run competition (selective mechanism) determines the success of only one organizational structure: the most efficient one. In the standard model of competitive equilibrium, production technology and market demand determine the size of the firms, all held to be identical.

Some researchers believe that these conclusions hold also when uncertainty and instability are considered. According to Chandler (1977; 1982) and Williamson (1975; 1985), among the possible structures of internal organization, the ones tending to predominate over time are those which ensure the minimization of production and transaction costs. This opinion seems to be shared also by a recent body of literature which has studied the current wave of transformations in the industrial system of capitalist countries.[2] According to the Flexible Specialization Model (FSM) (Piore and Sabel, 1984), a transition has been taking place from an industrial organization model dominated by large firms, based on the mass production of standardized goods and characterized by rigidity in its production system and socioeconomic structure, to a new model, which is more flexible and adaptable and also dominated by medium-sized firms and small units of production.[3] The FSM model links the notion of flexibility at system level with an industrial organization model dominated by small and medium-sized enterprises (SMES) and 'quasi-firms' (local units owned by large firms, but provided with wide powers of decisional autonomy).[4]

In contrast we believe that there are theoretical reasons why intra-industry differences in firm size and organizational structure are very diffuse and compatible with an equilibrium situation.[5]

The purpose of our chapter is to show that a fruitful way of approaching the problem of coexistence of heterogeneous firms and the relationship between industrial structure and uncertainty is through the study of *flexibility*, a characteristic that allows firms to adapt at low cost and quickly to variations in the environment. Mills and Schumann (1985) have shown that heterogeneous firms, having different degrees of Stiglerian flexibility, could coexist to accommodate demand fluctuations. In our paper we will show that there are different definitions of flexibility in relation to different ways of reacting to variations in the environment, and that the coexistence of heterogeneous firms can be seen as the result of different compromises between different aspects of flexibility.

In the first part of the chapter we analyse the relationship between the Stiglerian definition of flexibility and industrial structure, first by considering a monoproduct firm and then a multiproduct firm. In the second part of the chapter different concepts of flexibility will be examined.[6] It will be pointed out that the coexistence of different organizational structures equally fitted to respond to environmental changes represents a common characteristic of an economic system. Furthermore, it will be shown that the available empirical evidence does not corroborate the FSM hypothesis of an industrial system characterized by the increasing importance of small firms.

FLEXIBILITY AT THE LEVEL OF THE PLANT

Stiglerian Flexibility

Models dealing with firm flexibility differ according to the assumptions made about the information available to a firm, the decision-making process considered, and the nature of the decisions the firm is to make. This section and the next analyse the relationship between the degree of flexibility and environmental uncertainty or instability in the context of the traditional microeconomic theory of flexibility.

The theme of flexibility was first studied systematically by Stigler (1939), whose work was later formalized by many authors, including Marschak and Nelson (1962), Tisdell (1966), Mills (1984), and Mills and Schumann (1985). We shall refer to this body of work as the 'Stiglerian model'. In this literature, flexibility refers to those attributes of a production technology that accommodate greater output variation. Discussion of flexibility is carried out in terms of firms' cost curves.

With stationary demand, the firm in a competitive industry will choose the plant that minimizes the average total cost (statically efficient plant). This plant is 'adaptable' to produce output which varies from that corresponding to the minimum total average cost, q^o, but with a non-efficient technology (Stigler, 1939) that becomes less and less efficient as the distance from q^o increases. In contrast, flexible plants are those which 'permit to approximate the best technology for any output, at the cost of not being able to use the best technology for any output' (Stigler, 1939, p. 315).[7] Productivity in flexible plants is lower than in adaptable plants and costs increase more slowly, such that, within a certain range of outputs, adaptable plant production is cheaper than flexible plant production, while outside this range, flexible plant production becomes more convenient.

Following Stigler's definition, flexibility is greater when average total costs rise slowly around their minimum point and when marginal costs are gently inclined. A flexible plant holds a less convex ATC curve and a higher $\min ATC$ than an adaptable plant (Stigler, 1939, pp. 316–17), so that a trade-off exists between flexibility and static efficiency:

$$\frac{d^2\,ATC_A}{d\,q^2} < \frac{d^2\,ATC_B}{d\,q^2}$$

$$\min ATC_A > \min ATC_B \tag{1}$$

A = flexible plant
B = adaptable plant

The difference in $\min ATC$ can be viewed as the 'holding cost' for Stiglerian flexibility, while the convexity degree of the ATC curve measures the degree of flexibility.

A slightly different definition of flexibility has been given, with reference to a quadratic cost function, by Marschack and Nelson (1962): flexibility varies inversely with the curvature of total cost curves, and therefore it could be measured by the reciprocal of the second derivative of total cost. In the discussion which follows, we will use this definition.[8]

The choice between and adaptable plant and a flexible plant depends on several variables such as the technical characteristics of plants, the expectations on relevant variables, and the risk propensity of the entrepreneur. The greater the instability, interpreted as dispersion around the mean, the greater the likelihood that the firm will choose a more flexible plant. Stiglerian models analyse the relationship between the flexibility degree of the chosen plant and instability of demand, under the following hypotheses:

1. The firm knows the frequency distribution of expected demand.
2. Instability is measured by the variance of frequency distribution.
3. The firm is *risk-neutral* and maximizes expected profit $E(\pi)$.
4. The total cost function is quadratic.[9]

Under these assumptions, the models have found that a positive relation holds between plant flexibility and demand instability. An increase in demand instability will rise to a greater extent with the expected profit of the more flexible plant than that of the less flexible one. In the case of two plants with a different degree of flexibility there will be such a threshold that for any value of demand instability which is greater than that threshold, more flexible plant will be preferred. Furthermore, an inverse relation holds between flexibility and fixed costs (see below), which implies that smaller plants are likely to be more flexible than larger ones. A firm faced with greater price variability will prefer a higher degree of flexibility even at the expense of a loss in a static efficiency.

To which class of functions, other than quadratic functions, is it possible to extend the above results? Let us consider a perfectly competitive firm operating in a market with price uncertainty. The objective of the firm is to maximize expected profits. Firm profits are functions of p:

$$\pi = p \; q(p) - TC[\mathrm{q(p)}] \tag{2}$$

The mean of the frequency distribution of expected prices is p^*, and variance is $\mathrm{var}(p)$. Following Mills and Schumann we suppose that the firms can set their output level in each market period to equate marginal cost to price. The supply function for a competitive firm is $p = TC'(q)$ and $q^* = q^*(p)$ is the output that satisfies this condition.[10] We expand (2) in Taylor series around p^* and we consider only second order approximation:[11]

$$\pi = p^* \; q^* - TC(q^*) + q^*(p - p^*) + \\ (p - p^*)^2 \; [2 - TC_{qq}(q^*) \; q_p] \; q_p \tag{3}$$

from the rule of derivation of inverse function, we have:

$$d \; q/d \; p = 1/(d \; p/d \; q) = 1/(d \; MC/d \; q) = 1/TC_{qq}$$

and therefore:

$$\pi = p^* \; q^* - TC(q^*) + (p - p^*) \; q^* + [(p - p^*)^2/TC_{qq}(q^*)] \tag{4}$$

and taking expectation of (4):

$$E(\pi) = p^* \; q^* - TC(q^*) + [\mathrm{var}(p)/TC_{qq}(q^*)] \tag{5}$$

(5) represents a straight line. Since the second order condition for profit

maximization of a competitive firm is $TC_{qq} > 0$, the line always slopes upward: an higher value of var(p), the measure of demand instability, increases expected profits.

Let us consider two plants, and let plant A be more flexible than plant B: $TC_{A,qq} < TC_{B,qq}$ $\forall$, q. We call q_A^* and q_B^* the outputs that equalize marginal cost to price for the two cost functions. We wish to analyse how relative profitability changes with demand instability, through a consideration of the non-trivial case in which there is a trade-off between static efficiency and flexibility.

When we consider a general total cost function, different cases may arise (Fig. 5.1). The sufficient condition to get the intuitive result that the relative

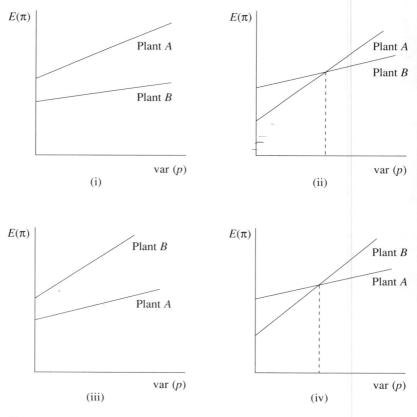

Figure 5.1

profitability of the more flexible plant will increase as demand instability increases is given by:

$$TC_{A,qq}(q_A^*) < TC_{B,qq}(q_B^*) \tag{6}$$

This condition always holds when we consider a quadratic cost function (the second derivative is constant). If total cost has a different functional form inequality (6) may not be satisfied.

From Equation (5) it appears that the relation between expected profitability and flexibility crucially depends on the characteristics of the second order derivatives of the total cost function. Specifically, we show that the relative size of the positive effect of demand instability on expected profits depends on the choice of the degree of plant flexibility. In what follows we discuss sufficient conditions for this result, in relation to three different hypotheses on the sign of the second derivatives of the total cost function. The less flexible plant will have an expected profit higher than the more flexible plant for a low value of var(p) and a lower for a high value of var(p) (Fig. 5.1(ii)) if:

1. When the second derivative of total cost function is constant, q_A^* and q_B^* must fall in the interval where $ATC_A > ATC_B$.
2. When second derivative is increasing, q_A^* and q_B^* must fall in the interval where both

$$ATC_A > ATC_B \text{ and } MC_B \leq MC_A \tag{7}$$

3. When second derivative is decreasing, q_A^* and q_B^* must fall in the interval where both

$$ATC_A > ATC_B \text{ and } MC_B \geq MC_A \tag{8}$$

If q_A^* and q_B^* fall in the interval where $ATC_A > ATC_B$ but out of the intervals given in condition (7) or (8) there are two possible cases:

(a) The less flexible plant will be chosen whatever the value of var(p).

(b) The less flexible plant is chosen for a low value of var(p) and the more flexible for an high value of var(p).

Outside the intervals given in the above conditions are the other possible cases indicated in Fig. 5.1.[12]

The above results show that the conditions necessary to have a positive relation between the relative expected profitability of the more flexible plant and demand instability are much more restrictive for a generic total cost function than for a quadratic total cost function.

In this context, the expected profit-maximization hypothesis is very important to establish a positive relation between uncertainty and flexibility. In fact, using Rothschild and Stiglitz's decision-making under uncertainty theory, it can be shown that a risk-averse firm maximizing $ECU(\pi)]$ will select a less flexible plant when uncertainty increases (Esposito, 1988). This result can be explained on the basis that a risk-averse firm gives a low weight to the higher expected profit which stems from the use of more flexible plant, and overvalues losses due to the rise of the minimum average total cost.

The intuitive result that the more flexible plant is more likely to be chosen when demand instability increases, therefore, is linked to the risk preferences of the firm and to specific technological characteristics of total cost function. Among the latter, the way in which flexibility is obtained is very important.

Mills and Schumann (1985) have investigated the relationship between flexibility, fixed costs, industry structure and fluctuating demand. They have proved the following propositions for the case of a competitive industry where demand fluctuates and technology for each firm is described by quadratic total costs:

1.   If competitive equilibrium supports technologically heterogeneous firms, the more flexible firms will have greater minimum average costs.
2.   There is an inverse relation between flexibility and fixed costs per unit of output (calculated at $\min ATC$ point).

These results allow the authors to say that smaller firms, defined as less capital-intensive firms, will be more flexible than larger ones, and that the effect of fluctuating demand is to allow the coexistence of small firms (more flexible and not static efficient) and large firms (static efficient but with a low degree of flexibility). Small firms achieve their greater flexibility by relying more on the use of variable factors of production.

These results obtained by Mills and Schumann give strong microeconomic foundations to the Flexible Specialization Model, which claims that the new industrial system will be dominated by small units.

However, while proposition (1) could be generalized to non-quadratic cost function (and, following Stigler, this must be always true, by definition of flexible firm), proposition (2) could not hold. The trade-off between static efficiency and flexibility could be reached with classes of total cost function for which there is a positive relationship between flexibility and fixed costs.[13] Therefore if competitive equilibrium supports technologically heterogeneous firms, the more flexible firms have greater minimum average costs, but they do not necessarily have the smaller fixed cost.

Some of the results found in the case of price-taker firms could be extended to non-competitive situations, assuming that demand is stochastic and the firm adjusts to variation in demand, choosing price and letting output be fixed by the market. Let price be fixed at p (because of an oligopolistic cartel, or a kinked demand curve, etc.), and that demand fluctuations are described by a frequency distribution with mean q^* and variance var (q).

Profit will be:

$$\pi = pq - TC(q) \tag{9}$$

To obtain a general expression for expected profit, we expand in Taylor's series around q^*:

$$\begin{aligned} \pi &= pq - TC(q) \\ &= (pq^* - TC(q^*)) + (p - MC(q^*))\,(q - q^*) + \\ &\quad - (1/2)\,TC_{qq}(q^*)\,(q - q^*)^2 \end{aligned} \tag{10}$$

and taking expectation of (10)

$$E(\pi) = pq^* - TC(q^*) - (1/2)\,\text{var}(q)\,TC_{pp}(q^*) \tag{11}$$

(11) represents a straight line where the independent variable is var(q). If TC is a quadratic cost curve, TC_{qq} is constant and positive, and (11) will slope downward. Expected profit will decrease as demand instability increases and the line corresponding to the more flexible plant will be the steeper one.

This result could be extended to a generic cost function. We assume such a class of cost curves that, given two plants, plant A is more flexible than plant B:

$$TC_{A,qq} < TC_{B,qq} \quad \forall q \tag{12}$$

Depending on where q^* falls, several cases may arise. If $ATC_A(q^*) > ATC_B(q^*)$, the more flexible plant has the smaller value of $\pi(q^*)$, so that the intercept decreases as flexibility increases. If q^* falls in the interval where TC is convex, $TC_{qq} > 0$, and the line is downward sloped. Therefore, from the inequality (12), the flexible plant will be preferred only for high values of

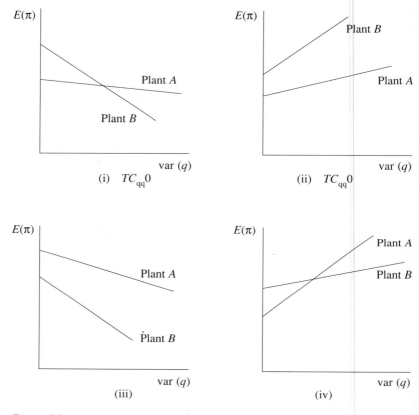

Figure 5.2

var(q) (Fig. 5.2(i)). If q^* falls in the interval where TC is concave, $TC_{qq}<0$, and the line is upward sloped. Therefore, from (12), the line for flexible plant would always lie below the other, and thus buying a flexible plant would never be profitable (Fig. 5.2(ii)).

If $ATC_A(q^*) < ATC_B(q^*)$, the flexible plant has greater profits. It will be always preferred when TC is convex (Fig. 5.2(iii)), while it will be preferred only for high values of var(q) if TC is concave (Fig. 5.2(iv)).

In the non-competitive case, therefore, the more flexible plant either is never chosen, or it is chosen only when demand instability is high. Such a situation as Fig. 5.1(iv) is ruled out.

Thus, heterogeneous firms can coexist in a non-competitive situation, too. The more flexible plant will have the greater minimum average total cost.[14]

It is clear from the above that demand fluctuations increase the probability of flexible technology being utilized. To the extent that greater flexibility is achieved by increased reliance on variable factors of production, and that the firm maximizes expected profit, Stiglerian flexibility can give strong microeconomic foundations to the Flexible Specialization Model. Stiglerian flexibility, however, is concerned with only one aspect of firm flexibility.

Flexibility and the Multiproduct Firm

Stiglerian flexibility refers to those attributes of a production technology that accommodate greater output variation. But in the 1970s and 1980s consumer demand became more diversified and unstable. It has become increasingly important for a firm to adjust its production to suit specialized demand.[15] Therefore the ability to shift from the production of a given output or a mix of outputs to another output or to a different mix of outputs cheaply and quickly becomes at least as important as the ability to change the total output at the lowest cost.

This section will give a formal definition of this kind of flexibility and it will discuss the link between different aspects of multiproduct flexibility. Most of the results of the preceding section are not applicable when multiproduct firm flexibility is concerned. In this case both the level of output (i.e. the scale of production) and the produced mix can be varied. In the case of the multiproduct firm it is impossible to obtain a clear relation between the degree of flexibility of a plant and the level of uncertainty, unless imposing restrictions on technology (that is, on the form of the cost function) and on output produced.

The multiproduct firm has been widely discussed in the works of Baumol, Panzar and Willig, who have inspired a large body of literature.[16] General equilibrium theory allows for the existence of multiple–output firms. Intuitively one might expect that a multiproduct firm will exist if, given an output vector $q = (q_1, \ldots, q_n)$, it is cheaper to produce q in a single multiproduct firm than in two or more specialized firms. This condition is fulfilled if multiproduct cost function $C(q)$ shows scope economies or transray convexity (Baumol, Panzar and Willig, 1982). We will use this model to extend the Stiglerian concept of flexibility both to the level and composition of output.

Although we cannot exclude the possibility that, for technological reasons, a plant which is more flexible with respect to the volume of production may be also more flexible than another one with respect to the product mix, in reality plants seem to exhibit a trade-off between volume flexibility and product-mix flexibility. Therefore, plants embodying different technologies may turn out to be more or less profitable, depending on the predicted and real combination of volume instability and mix instability.

Analogously to the case of a monoproduct firm, flexibility can be expressed in terms of the curvature of the total cost function of a multiproduct firm. In the case of the monoproduct firm, flexibility varies inversely with the curvature of total cost. In the case of a multiproduct plant we define flexibility at point q^* as the variation of the convexity of the total cost function $C(q)$ from the point q^* to every point q:

$$(q - q^*) [C_{ij}] (q - q^*)' \; \nleftrightarrow \; q \tag{14}$$

C_{ij} is the matrix of second derivatives of total cost function. When we extend (11) to all q^*, we get a definition of *total flexibility*.

We can say that a plant A is more flexible than a plant B at q^* if the variation in the convexity of the total cost curve of plant A from q^* to q is smaller. If this happens for all q and $q^* > 0$ we say that plant A has a higher total flexibility than plant B:

$$(q - q^*) [C^A_{ij} - C^B_{ij}] (q - q^*) < 0 \tag{15}$$

for all q^* and $q > 0$

The function C_A is more flexible than the function C_B if the matrix of the differences of second derivatives $[C^A_{ij} - C^B_{ij}]$ is negative definite for all q^*, $q > 0$.

The cost function of a multiproduct firm is sensitive to the composition as well as the scale of output. Total flexibility is the result of the interaction between mix and volume flexibility. As the firm changes its level of output and its product mix, cost will change in a quite different way, depending on the point q^* considered. It is possible that total costs exhibit both economies of scope and economies of scale at one level of output, but diseconomies of scale and economies of scope at a different level of output. It may happen, therefore, that for some q^* the inequality (15) is reversed.[17]

We can now define mix and output flexibility. Each vector q can be represented as:

$$q^* - q = tu \tag{16}$$

where $/t/$ is a scale parameter and $/u/$ is a versor. When $/u/$ is given, the composition of output is fixed and only the volume of production varies. When $/t/$ is given, the volume is held constant and mix varies. These flexibilities will be calculated, hinging on the concept of second directional derivative, that is analogous to the simple second derivatives of a function of a single variable.

Global output flexibility is calculated along a given ray u^o,[18] which identifies the given mix. We define a 'flexibility degree with respect to the global output' or 'ray flexibility', for a given mix, through a simple second derivative of $TC(q)$ with respect to $/t/$:

$$d^2 C(q(t))/d\ t^2 = \Sigma_i \Sigma_j\ C_{ij}(q(t))\ u_i^{\,o}\ u_j^{\,o} \quad i, j = 1, \ldots, n \quad (17)$$

The plant exhibiting the lower value of that derivative will be the most flexible plant. The plant A is more flexible than plant B if:

$$u^o\ [C^A_{ij} - C^B_{ij}]\ u^{o\prime} < 0 \quad (18)$$

This is a local definition, since what happens along a given ray could not occur along another.

Consider now mix flexibility. We are interested in how total costs change when the proportions in which $q_1, \ldots, q_n$ are produced are modified – assuming the volume $Q = \Sigma q_i$ to be constant, so that $/t/$ = constant. Let point q^* be on the hyperplane $h\ q^* = k$; take another point on the same hyperplane, along the u direction, i.e. a point $q = q^* + tu$, with $hq = h\ (q^* + tu) = k$, such that $hu = 0$. The second derivative along the direction u is defined by:

$$\Sigma_i \Sigma_j C_{ij}(q)\ u_i u_j \qquad \forall\ u \text{ for which } hu = 0 \quad (19)$$

Plant A is more flexible than plant B with regard to the product mix if it has the smaller second derivative through rays, *for a given scale*, or if:

$$u[C^A_{ij} - C^B_{ij}]\ u' < 0 \qquad \forall\ u \text{ for which } h\ u = 0 \quad (20)$$

We can call this flexibility 'transray flexibility'.

It is clear from (20) and (18) that ray flexibility and transray flexibility are particular cases of total flexibility as defined by (15). Without particular restrictions, ray flexibility does not imply transray flexibility.

A graphical representation for a two-goods function can help to clarify the difference between volume and mix flexibility. Suppose cost function has the form displayed in Fig. 5.3. Height measures total cost and the two "flat" and "horizontal" dimensions measure quantities of the two goods. Along Ob, Oc and Od rays, we can identify q_1 and q_2 values, which correspond to a given scale of production and also related costs (points $B, C,$

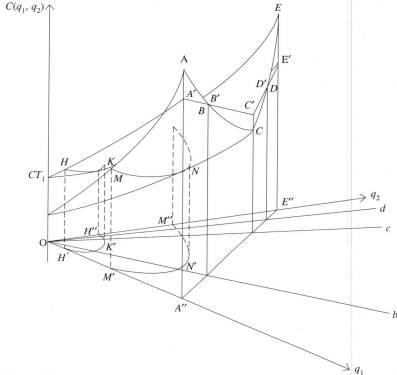

Figure 5.3

D). By repeating this construction for every ray at the same scale, a transray curve will be obtained (curve *ABCDE*). This construction has been repeated for another plant too, yielding the curve *A'B'C'D'E*, intersecting the *ABCDE* curve. The result of this construction is typically Stiglerian. There exists an optimal mix (*Oc* ray) allowing us to minimize total cost for that given scale. A plant with the *ABCDE* curve represents the better choice if that combination has to be produced at that scale. This plant shows lower costs for all rays included between *Ob* and *Od*. For the rays on the left of *Ob* and on the right of *Od*, in contrast, a plant with the curve *A'B'C'D'E'* shows lower costs. Since total cost varies more slowly, *A'B'C'D'E'* plant is the more flexible plant. We can reasonably suppose that the larger the fluctuations of product mix, it will become more profitable to adopt the more flexible plant, given a constant scale.

Fig. 5.3 might illustrate the difference between a plant dedicated to producing only along *Oc* ray and only at scale *t*, or only within (*t* − σ,

$t + \sigma$) interval, where σ is very small (Fordist plant) (plant B), and a plant using flexible automation (plant A). If the mix does not vary very much, dedicated machinery will be more efficient than flexibly automated machinery. Its costs, however, rise rapidly as the mix moves away from Oc ray, so that for high values of mix instability, it is likely that the flexibly automated plant will be adopted. This pattern occurs at t scale, but different patterns may occur at other volumes of production, so that while flexible plant might be always preferred at some scales, other volumes might always favour dedicated plants. A two-dimensional graphical representation of such problem is suitable.

Still using Fig. 5.3, let us determine all different goods combinations which can be produced with the same total cost. To do this we slice the two cost surfaces at the height CT_1. This slicing process generates, in the (C, q_1, q_2) space, two curves, one for plant A and one for plant B. The projections of such curves on the plane (q_1, q_2) are the curves $H'KH'$ and $M'N'M'$. These represent the combinations of goods capable of and being produced with the same level of total costs, CT_1 (isocosts). In the last case A will be preferred to the more flexible plant B because it allows more of both products to be produced for the same level of total cost. If we slice the two cost surfaces at a higher height different situations could happen.

In the simple case of a quadratic cost function for two goods, exhibiting U-shaped ray average total costs, transray convexity, economies of scope and increasing average incremental costs for each good, an increase in scale flexibility goes with an increase in mix flexibility (Esposito, 1988). In Fig. 5.4. we represent, on the plane $(q_1 q_2)$ the projections of the intersections of plans parallel to q_1, q_2 when the cost functions are quadratic. The two axes measure the quantities of products and the curves show different isocosts. The level of total cost is represented by the distance of the isocost from the origin. The further northeast a curve lies the greater is the cost associated with it. It can be seen that, at a 'low' scale, plant A will always be preferred to the more flexible plant B because it allows more of both products for the same level of total cost CT_1. For intermediate level of total cost (the isocosts are CT_2) we fall into a Stiglerian situation; when the mix is very different from that for which the plant was built and we have to specialize either in the production of q_1 or q_2 the more flexible plant is preferred as it allows more of both products for the same total cost, otherwise the less flexible plant is preferred. For high volume (the isocosts are CT_3) the more flexible plant will be always preferred. In addition, it seems that for quadratic cost functions a rise in flexibility enhances fixed costs. More precisely, this is the condition guaranteeing that cost functions will intersect. In the opposite case, flexible plant costs would always be lower.

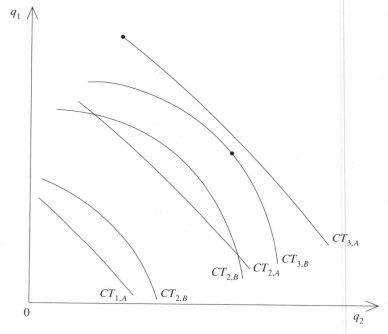

Figure 5.4

Without imposing further conditions, we are unable to say anything about the general relation between total flexibility, mix flexibility and volume flexibility, and about the link between flexibility and profitability in a situation of demand instability. In contrast with the monoproduct case where a trade-off between flexibility and static efficiency is a realistic hypothesis, such a trade-off is not always possible in the multiproduct firm.

There are at least three strategies that a multiproduct firm could choose to achieve a certain product mix. First, it could build a plant specifically dedicated to the production of the desired product mix, within a very narrow range of volumes. An example is the typical Fordist plant that is highly mechanized and with a relatively high level of working capital. It is able to minimize, in comparison to other strategies, the cost of producing the output at the planned level and composition.

The second strategy would be to build a plant capable of reaching a high flexibility both in the volume and in the mix. Such a plant would be endowed with flexible automation, which, with the help of microelectronics, would allow, in a very short time and with a relatively small cost, changes in output composition, customized production, and product innovation. The acquisition cost of such plants is higher than that of the first strategy, as they are more capital intensive.

In the third case, flexibility is achieved through choosing a 'network' organization based on tight and frequent relations with suppliers and buyers. If $q = (q_1, \ldots, q_n)$ represents a vector of outputs in a particular market, $C(q)$ represents the monetary value of both physical and organizational inputs that are required if q is produced by a single firm. In this case the cost function $C(q)$ would have to be characterized by lower capital requirements. Greater flexibility is achieved by increased reliance on variable factors of production, as in the model of Mills and Schumann, so that it is possible to apply 'Stiglerian flexibility' to the firms of the network. The characteristics of the cost function in this case are very dependent on the industrial environment: that is, the degree of development of the social division of labour.

The second strategy is characterized by a level of fixed costs higher than the two other strategies. Flexibility is reached through large investment. Here a positive relationship will exist between fixed cost and flexibility.

The first strategy is characterized by the lowest *ATC* of the expected production vector $E(q)$ and by fixed costs which are lower than those implied in the second strategy.

The third strategy is characterized by the lowest fixed costs, by high flexibility and an *ATC* of the expected production vector $E(q^*)$ higher than that implied by the first strategy.

No conclusion can be reached on the relation between the size of firms and flexibility. The first and the third (As the second and the third strategy) strategy represent different organizational structures and cannot be compared in terms of cost curves alone. The ability to innovate, to devise new products and services, and to deliver them in the shortest possible time are aspects of a different way of examining flexibility. Flexibility is the result not only of a 'technological choice', but also of an 'organizational choice'. We do not think that the above strategies refer to the same aspect of flexibility. Each strategy assumes a particular kind of evolution of the environment, such that the organizational structure selected is chosen to adapt to different environmental changes. For example, the third strategy, in contrast to the first one, will select one organizational structure which can carry out and implement frequent revisions of plans. The Stiglerian definition is concerned with the plant alone and is not able to deal with information, learning and adaptation. Therefore other definitions of flexibility concerning the whole firm as an organizational structure need to be considered.

FLEXIBILITY AT THE LEVEL OF THE FIRM

Different Aspects of Flexibility

A firm may achieve flexibility by a variety of means. It can buy an asset that increases its probability of adapting easily to unforeseen events.[20] It can simplify the product mix, or farm out certain tasks to sub-contractors who specialize in the activities which are not considered to be central. It can make increasing use of temporary or part-time workers. It can move towards just-in-time inventory control. It can decentralize decision-making within the firm in order to reduce the number of layers of management between the chief executive and front-line supervisors. It can increase co-operation with other firms to pursue collective goals, etc. These choices could imply selecting different machinery and organizational structures. Therefore, it is important to distinguish flexibility reached through organizational restructuring from that achieved by technical means. *Organizational flexibility* concerns the choice of the elements of organizational structure (the activities the firm undertakes in-house, the rules workers and managers have to follow in their work, etc.) which promote adaptation to the environment. *Production flexibility* concerns the degree in which the performances and the characteristics of a production system can be modified. Organizational and production flexibility will determine the ability of the firm to make effective and fitting changes in its structure at a limited cost and in a short time. Depending on the characteristics of the decisions to be taken, production and organizational flexibility play a different role in the firm's strategies.

Another fruitful distinction between different aspects of flexibility could be based on the Simon's (1960) analysis of the decision-making process. Simon distinguishes two main types of decisions, namely those which are *programmed* and those which are *not programmed*.[21] Decisions are programmed to the extent that they are repetitive and routinized, with a definite established procedure for handling them. Programmed decisions follow a detailed prescription that governs the sequence of responses of the firm to a complex task posed by the environment. Programmed decisions allow also routinized search procedures for new responses to the challenges posed by unforeseen events. In the case of programmed decisions it is possible to assume that the main alternative courses of action and their respective consequences could be described by an approximately known *decision tree*.

Decisions are non-programmed to the extent that they are novel, unstructured and consequential. Here, there are no specific procedures to deal with a problem, because it has not arisen before, because its precise nature and structure are elusive and complex, or because it is so important that it deserves a custom-tailored response.

We can distinguish two types of programmed decisions. When decisions do not take into account the future availability of new information, and when actions taken at one time are not changed in a future period when new information becomes available, these are single-stage decision problems, that is, static decision-making.[22]

Within this context, we can speak of static flexibility as the ability of the action chosen at the beginning to approximate the best result for each state of the world, at the cost of never being able to choose the best action. Static flexibility could be reached through an appropriate choice of the plant and increasing (decreasing) stock volume when demand decreases (increases), in order to keep the machinery utilization rate almost constant.[23] Stiglerian flexibility over the choice of a plant assumes that initial plans never change (plans inalterability hypothesis), and is a very good example of static flexibility. It reflects only the technological characteristics of a firm.

When the decision-maker has to make a sequence of decisions before a problem is resolved, we are in a dynamic decision-making context. At time t_1 new information is received and the decision-maker has to decide whether or not to change the initial action path. In making the decision between an existing and a new action, the crucial element is the switching cost. The decision-maker takes a decision on the basis of comparing discounted advantages of modifications with the cost of changing the plans, i.e., to switch from one action to another. The presence of a switching cost highlights the dynamic nature of flexibility. In general, a flexible action does not coincide with the best action (action that could be carried on in a situation of certainty). In addition, 'being flexible' has a cost, e.g. in terms of acquisition cost of machinery (holding cost).

We can compare the losses that a decision-maker would incur if his forecasts were not confirmed in the context of having to choose between the more flexible action and the 'best' action. In the former case, the extra costs are the 'holding cost' (missed profits or greater expenses) plus the switching cost; in the latter case the extra costs would amount to the switching cost (by definition, greater than that of flexible choice) plus the reduction in actual and expected profits in the new situation. Accordingly, a flexible action will be preferred to the 'best' action with respect to available information if the sum of 'expected' switching cost and the holding cost for the flexible action is lower than the possible loss caused by maintaining the 'best' action (see Hirschleifer and Riley, 1979, p. 1939).

Therefore the initial action should be chosen so that a small number of constraints may be imposed on the actions that will be undertaken in the following periods, in order to reduce switching costs. The change from initial action to other actions must be possible at a small cost. A decision with such qualities is characterized by *dynamic flexibility. One action is more flexible than another if the set of possible actions is wider and the cost to switch to another action is lower, after the initial decision has been made.* Dynamic flexibility expresses the ability of the firm to adapt itself to changes in the external world.

The notion of flexibility developed by Hart (1951) is an example of dynamic flexibility. His notion contains a simplified form of plans revision, and implies a Bayesian learning process.[24] In this model a positive relation between uncertainty and the flexibility degree of the chosen plant holds, if the firm maximizes both expected profit and expected utility of profit.

Dynamic decision-making and dynamic flexibility refer to situations where a decision tree can be built or predicted with good accuracy. But to deal with non-programmed decisions a broader notion of flexibility is needed, namely *structural* flexibility, which is defined as the firm's aptitude for facing up quickly, even through modifications of organization or production methods, to sudden and unexpected changes in the environment (Klein, 1988; Cohendet and Llerena, 1988).[25] It includes the ability (a passive one) to change production plans as a consequence of unexpected events or of the availability of new information (Hart flexibility), the ability to modify the organization of firm functions (purchases, R & D, production, marketing, etc.), and to enlarge the set of production and organizational techniques in order to shape the environment and its evolution. It determines the capability of a firm to invent, design, and develop possible courses of action for handling situations that are truly novel. In some senses, structural flexibility can be seen as the most important characteristic of innovative firms.

The different aspects of flexibility and organizational structure are strictly linked. An organizational structure that satisfies the requirements of a given aspect of flexibility does not necessarily satisfy others. For instance, flexibility could be attained, as we have seen above, by pursuing a strategy of outsourcing: that is, buying parts or whole products from other producers. If conditions are unstable, the traditional structure of vertical integration, in which virtually all critical parts are made in-house, could be better replaced with a network of small suppliers. A network structure of control, authority and communication is better adapted to instability conditions than a hierarchical structure of control, authority and communication (Burns, 1963). Such an organization can be flexible and efficient in a context in which many decisions are of the programmed type. Supplier relations can be routinized, and a close control over operations can be achieved.[26]

In a world characterized by a high level of instability other aspects of flexibility are also important. Network structures may not have the ability to devise new products and services and to compress the time needed to design and manufacture new products. If the turnover of new products is high, the relationship with suppliers cannot be routinized, and the quality and delivery of the new products could also suffer. A network firm would lose the capacity to design innovative products, and it could lose control over its operation.

Hierarchical structures could be of some advantage in coping with these problems, which concern structural flexibility. Investment in training and in flexible manufacturing systems, in reduction of the layers of management, in pushing down more authority in the organization, and creating smaller highly decentralized business units, as well as just-in-time systems, could allow a firm to manufacture critical parts in-house and still retain the ability to introduce new products in time and good quality.

Uncertainty in the external environment is composed of different elements (the level of global demand, the evolution of technology, the mix of products, etc.). Each of these might require specific organizational characteristics. Depending on the characteristics of the environment and its internal resources, a firm will choose an organizational form that compromises between different aspects of flexibility. For instance, on the one hand the recent trend in shortening the life of a product is tending to an organizational structure that satisfies structural flexibility, while on the other hand uncertainty concerning the level of capacity utilization tends to favour an organizational form that satisfies dynamic flexibility.

An interesting example of the coexistence of different organizational forms in one industry is that of the Italian textile industry. In Italy two different modes of organization coexist without either mode being hegemonic. The first is the integrated corporation which combines economies of scale in advertising and retailing, product differentiation and the international decentralization of production. The second, the network firm, is characterized by a very flexible organization composed of a number of small independent firms connected to the parent company, and concentrating production units and sub-contractors in only one area, while maximizing on investment abroad in the distribution stage.

A good example of the latter is Benetton. All its plants and sub-contractors are located in the Veneto. The distribution system is founded on an electronic network connecting sales agents, factories and the one warehouse, located in the Veneto, which rapidly distributes 50 million articles of clothing per annum worldwide. Another example, outside Italy, of an industry in which different organizational modes coexist, is the semiconductor industry, in which integrated Japanese firms face non-integrated American firms.

In other words, in any given time period, it is possible to have firms with different organizational forms which reflect different compromises between different aspects of flexibility: organizational structures which deploy different combination of a pure network structure and a pure hierarchical structure.

Organizational Flexibility and Flexible Specialization

In the preceding sections it has been shown that the notion of flexibility based on plants with different technological characteristics is not entirely suitable for understanding the complexity of real world situations. A more promising approach, as we have argued, is to consider the firm as organization and to investigate the flexibility of various kinds of organization. In a situation of high uncertainty and one in which new and unfamiliar problems and requirements continually arise, the number of unprogrammed decisions and the complexity of problems to be resolved increases. In such a situation, structural flexibility is the main determinant of the organizational structure of the firm. Some authors believe that structural flexibility is better satisfied, as we have already argued, by the network structure. This position has been taken by Sabel (1989), who builds on Aoki's (1984) work on the 'quasi-tree' structure of large Japanese firms.

Sabel sees the emergence in multinational firms of a structure characterized by operating units dedicated to making either only one product line or working for one customer. This new structure is based on vertical 'dis-integration'. All decisions are decentralized to the operating units, except high-level strategic decisions which remain with top management in the head firm. Workers and sub-contracting firms are considered as partners in production, possessing the power to reshape the product and the production process. Each operating unit is aid to build up its own network of suppliers, and establish long-term contracts with them. Operating units have stronger linkages with firms and suppliers which are spatially proximate, which promote transactions founded on mutual confidence and flexibility. Economies in transaction costs are obtained by releasing firms from the necessity to accurately specify the rights and duties of contracting parties as well as the very detailed rules of bureaucratic management. The creation, by each operating unit, of a production network based on spatial proximity and the large autonomy of these 'quasi-independent' branches, has created a structure where the management of industrial relations is more flexible and more adaptable to changing conditions than in other organizational forms. In the opinion of Sabel, small firms and operating units owned by the

'disintegrated' multinational firms will be dominant organizations in the approaching era of Flexible Specialization.
  Against this hypothesis can be raised the following objections:

1. It is not clear whether uncertainty implies a necessary tendency toward disintegration. Most analytical models developed to examine the effect of uncertainty on the firm's choice of organization – uncertainty in the supply of the upstream good (Arrow, 1975), fluctuations in exogenous excess demand of the intermediate products when price is inflexible (Green, 1986), random final goods demand with a Leontief production technology at the downstream stage (Carlton, 1979), and transaction costs theory (see Williamson, 1986) – support the hypothesis that uncertainty is one of the main reasons why a firm chooses to vertically integrate, even when there are no obvious technological advantages to be gained from integration. Without doubt, all the above models are too simple to account for the complexity and multiplicity of forces encouraging or opposing alternative forms of internal organization, and are therefore unable to invalidate the Flexible Specialization Model. However, they do weaken its arguments.

2. There is no reason to believe that 'disintegration' is the most efficient organizational form in conditions of uncertainty. Network and quasi-tree firms could be more dynamically flexible than the M-firm, but they are not necessarily more structurally flexible. The decentralization of risks and responsibilities which is peculiar to quasi-tree and network firms might duplicate effort, disallow a global view, and raise costs owing to weaker auditing of the operating units. It is therefore possible that other forms of organization may turn out to be at least as efficient as the 'disintegration' form. Without doubt, flexibility is an important part of the large firm's strategy, but there are many different forms of organization which can satisfy flexibility. The choice will depend on external conditions and the rigidity of the internal organization structure.

3. The FSM gives excessive weight to the process of decentralization of production within large firms and does not consider the process of concentration of R & D, testing, probing and prototype development in few geographic areas. The concentration and allocation of financial resources in the headquarters of large firms is still pertinent today, and implies a strengthening relationship between oligopolistic firms and their hierarchies of smaller firms.

4. Organizational form, it must be remembered, is a joint function of the level of technical progress and the nature of tasks posed by the environ-

ment. A significant change in these elements will determine modifications in the organizational structure, such as, for example, in the amount of centralization or decentralization that is desirable. Changes in social factors also could affect organizational structures, through their effect on the level of transaction costs.

Therefore it is possible that new developments may push firms towards more hierarchical structures. On the one hand, new information technology has increased the technical capacity to automate non-programmed decisions and therefore decreased the necessity of the decentralization. On the other hand, large firms have learnt to develop organizational routines and methods to deal with unstable conditions.

We believe that networked firms, as described by Sabel, are not the only organizational form capable of responding to unstable conditions. The necessity to deal with different aspects of flexibility could produce new hierarchical structures in which are incorporated characteristics of the network structure. Indeed, the main difference between present and past hierarchical organizational forms is the development, within a hierarchical structure, of lateral networks enabling communication and the flow of information and products. These lateral flows develop between sub-systems within the organization and between sub-systems of different organizations, along all the levels of the hierarchy. The spread of international and domestic multipartner agreements in recent years is an example of such lateral flows. The stages of product development, from initial R & D, design, prototype production and redesign, to assembly, stretch across domestic and international lines of co-operation. But, as many authors have shown, these collaborative agreements are also organized along hierarchical lines. A rapid rise in the number of agreements between firms is bringing about the formation of a worldwide corporate network, allowing firms to have permanent and even stronger control over innovation processes, finance, communications and production everywhere in the world. Such agreements can lead to a concentration of activities in specific areas, but they are also compatible with a dispersion of activities throughout the world, since the latter can be linked, controlled and managed by means of global electronic information networks.

A number of studies, in contrast to Sabel's view, have found a tendency towards increasing vertical integration in large firms (e.g. Cooke, 1988; Camagni, 1986; Perez, 1985). Production decentralization has often been found, but without the decentralization of control (Castells and Henderson, 1987, p. 7). This process is very clear in high-tech industries (Ernst, 1981; 1986; DeGeorge, 1985; Fishman 1982; Linvill, 1984). In the electronics industry, for example, multinational firms try to avoid possible crisis by establishing a permanent hegemony on technological standards for all products in all stages of the production process (Ernst, 1981; DeGeorge, 1985).

The decreasing importance of economies of scale is one of the reasons indicated by many authors behind the hegemonic emergence of small companies. In our opinion, it is impossible to find empirical evidence of this phenomenon. First, we have to remember the continuing validity of the general tendency to transform discontinuous production processes, which dominate many industries, into continuous ones. Flexible automation processes are managed by hierarchical and integrated control systems which transmit to microprocessors installed on machines a continuous flow of information concerning the order and manner in which different pieces should be processed. With respect to the products, the production process is discontinuous, but direct numerical control and advanced mechanical hardware, however, allow each machine to process sequences of pieces of different kinds without stoppage and to adjust or change tools when a different piece has to be produced. The flow of parts, therefore, is rendered continuous through the virtual elimination of set-up times. In a sense, it is the continuity of information flow that creates continuity in the production process. This continuity allows production costs to fall quite remarkably. Furthermore, CAD/CAM (computer-aided design, computer-aided manufacture) and computerized control can raise product quality and reduce waste. These methods are already in use in many industries, from cars to semiconductors and printed circuits. The cost of plant is much higher than in corresponding discontinuous process plants, and, consequently, high and relatively stable volumes are needed to recover these costs. In many cases, therefore, product differentiation becomes essential to take advantage of new technologies.

A second characteristic of these new processes is that the versatility of numerically controlled machinery has given birth to a complementarity between economies of scope and economies of scale (Bailey and Friedlander, 1982), since high volumes can be achieved by producing small batches of many different products. Furthermore, there is no need to apply flexible systems to all production stages: many components can be standardized through the use of CAD/CAM technologies, and thus differentiation applies to only a small range of parts. In other words, the final products which may appear to be very different from one another are, in fact, composed of a large range of identical parts. Standardization and differentiation are no longer incompatible, and large firms are now able to achieve the wide product-mix flexibility demanded in the marketplace.

This, of course, does not mean that new technologies do not leave any opportunities for small firms: the differentiation/standardization combination could promote the birth of small and medium-sized firms, to the extent that standardized parts might be produced by many small specialized suppliers. In this case, in fact, the cost of the capital required to enter industries utilizing such standardized parts would fall, along with barriers to entry, thus facilitating the birth of new firms. Lower entry barriers deriving from the existence of specialized producers of components forming a complex modular good is one of the reasons for the high birth rate registered in a number of areas of high industrial concentration (Del Monte, 1987a; 1987b).

CONCLUDING OBSERVATIONS

This chapter has reviewed the current theorizations of flexibility. The first part of the chapter analyzed whether the Flexible Specialization Model is consistent with the theory of flexibility at the level of the plant. We have shown that, unless very restrictive hypotheses are introduced, it is not possible to give an entirely positive answer to this question.

On the basis of our own and other authors' studies we can say that:

1. For a monoproduct firm, in competitive equilibrium, the relative profitability of the more flexible plants increases when instability or uncertainty increases. The opposite is true for a utility-maximizing firm.

2. For a multiproduct firm with a quadratic total cost function, a positive relation holds for a profit-maximizing firm only as far as output levels are concerned. With regard to the product mix, the nature of the relation depends on the given global output.

3. There is an inverse relation between Stiglerian flexibility and size (approximated by fixed costs level) in the case of the monoproduct firm and quadratic total cost function. In the case of the multiproduct firm, a positive relation seems to hold when total cost is quadratic.

4. When Hart flexibility is considered (i.e. when plan variation is considered), a positive relation between flexibility and uncertainty seems to hold for a monoproduct firm.

5. In an industry characterized by demand uncertainty, under equilibrium, it is possible for a range of flexible heterogeneous firms to coexist.

The second part of the chapter approached the question of flexibility through viewing the firm as a form of organization.

The first conclusion of the chapter is that a concept of flexibility which is different from the one traditionally assumed is necessary in order to understand the production and organization choices of a firm in conditions of uncertainty.

The second conclusion is that the complexity and multiplicity of forces favouring alternative types of plants and/or organizational modes make it very difficult to define an organizational structure with an 'optimal' degree of flexibility.

The third conclusion is that for given conditions in the external environment the coexistence of different organizational forms in one industry could be explained as the result of a variety of compromises between different aspects of flexibility.

We think that the study of how different organizational structures could coexist in an industry could be based on models of the firm which explain individual behaviour on the basis of a 'set of rules' established through a process involving trial and error, luck and creativity (Nelson and Winter, 1982, p. 453). These models are not based on the maximization principle, and they do not imply that each industry should evolve towards one 'opti-. mal' organizational form and technology. A firm's history will affect its organizational choice and this partly explains why different organizations and technologies coexist. At most, there will be a tendency to satisfy similar needs in different ways owing to different histories. This is why we believe that the persistence of different organization structures in the same industry can be seen as the result of different compromises between different aspects of flexibility.[27]

Viewed in this way, flexibility could have the same role as 'adaptation' in biology. In the same way as 'adaptability' is an essential condition for survival in a 'changing physical and natural environment', 'flexibility' is a means by which a single firm or a system of firms remain viable in a changing economic environment. Some biological models could be used to study interactions among individual or groups of firms with different flexibility. Intra-industry heterogeneity could be explained as an effect of different forms of adaptation to a given environment and/or as the effect of different degrees of flexibility.

For example, if we have two organizational modes – one more flexible and able to exploit all the niches of a market and one capable of exploiting only some of these niches – we could have a situation which in biology is called 'compensatory changes'. Consider herbivore species which occur in a given area, with one capable of subsisting on rice and bamboo and the other only on bamboo. If a famine of bamboo occurred, the first species might specialize in eating only rice, leaving bamboo to the other one, which thus would survive thanks to the flexibility of the first one. In the same way it is possible that in a changing economy less flexible firms or organizational modes survive by moving and expanding in market niches that are abandoned by more flexible firms seeking to exploit new opportunities. In this way we can explain the coexistence, in equilibrium, of firms with different degrees of flexibility, not as much as an effect of maximizing behaviour, but as an effect of adaptive behaviour. A promising direction of research could be the investigation, with the help of models used in ecology, of the dynamics of this equilibrium, in terms of the study of the conditions which must be satisfied for the coexistence of two (or more) competing organizational modes that display different degrees of flexibility.

Notes

1.   We are indebted to Piero Tani and Riccardo Martina for very helpful sugges-
      tions and criticisms. Hearty thanks to Ash Amin. Of course, opinions and
      errors are ours alone.
2.   Three schools have raised these issues with regard to economic systems:
      Neo-Schumpeterian Theories, Regulation Theory, and Flexible Specializa-
      tion Theory. Their main differences concern the identification of the features
      of the new industrial systems, and the implications of those changes for
      market structure.
      The *Neo-Schumpeterian School* (Perez, 1983; 1985; Freeman and Perez,
      1988) argues that every technology shows evidence of scale economies. The
      early development and diffusion of any new paradigm will then be carried
      out by small and medium-sized firms, but in the consolidation phase a
      dualistic system will emerge, including a stable and advanced sector of
      oligopolistic firms. For this reason, the maturity of Flexible Accumulation, i.e.
      the stage when the socio-institutional order and the technological paradigm
      become organic, is marked by an industrial structure based on large
      oligopolistic firms using flexible manufacturing systems (FMS).
      A second and related school of thought is the French *Regulation Theory*:
      it is more concerned with structural and macroeconomic changes rather than
      organizational or microeconomic questions (Boyer, 1988; Lipietz, 1987).
      The third school is the *Flexible Specialization Model* (Piore and Sabel, 1984).
3.   The FSM emphasizes that the 'unit of research' relevant to the understanding
      of industrial organization in the new regime of accumulation consists of
      those territorial systems showing a specific and high level of flexibility
      because of the co-operation among firms and also between firms and so-
      cioeconomic institutions. According to the FSM model the volatility of
      markets during the 1970s and 80s compelled firms to experiment with more
      flexible forms of organization, allowing quick changes of production. The
      distinctive mark of these new organizational forms is the combination of
      flexibility and specialization ('flexible specialization'). Vertical disintegra-
      tion and an independent process of development of small and medium-sized
      enterprises (SMES), encouraged by new technologies, are therefore shaping
      an industrial organization model found on SMES.
      Many large integrated firms have overcome the crisis of Fordist organiza-

tion through production decentralization and inter-firm 'networks'. Many production stages are carried out by small and medium-sized specialized firms which are permanently linked to the decentralizing firm, which is at the centre of the network. The increasing importance of networks of firms and the growth of independent and specialized SMES have enhanced the social division of labour, created agglomeration economies and brought about spatial concentration of industry.

4. The argument is the following: Flexibility is a distinctive characteristic of small units of production. In an uncertain world flexible and adaptable firms are more competitive, and since the world economy is characterized by increasing levels of uncertainty SMES and quasi-firms are therefore becoming increasingly important.

5. Intra-industry firm size heterogeneity can be attributed to many factors, for instance to technological diversity (Caves, 1980; and Porter, 1979), or to differences in managerial ability (Lucas, 1978; Oi, 1983; Jovanovic, 1982). The stochastic theory of the market structure shows that differences in size distribution could be the result of the law of luck (Simon and Bonini, 1958). Firm size heterogeneity may be the result of heterogeneity in firms attitude toward risk when the outcomes of each alternative choice are intrinsically or objectively probabilistic.

6. It will be shown that the concept of 'flexibility' which is implicit in the FSM refers to the capability of the industrial system (the firm) to adapt itself more easily (at lower cost) and more quickly to changes in the environment brought about by innovations, new tastes, new competitors, new economic and social relations, etc., and is different from that considered by the theory of flexibility developed in microeconomic theory.

7. In Stigler's opinion (1939, p. 316; 1952, p. 119), the most important ways of giving flexibility to a plant are: (*a*) the divisibility of fixed plant (many small machines instead of few large ones), in order to reduce variable costs for suboptimal outputs; (*b*) using a higher proportion of variable productive services, in order to reduce fixed costs. The first method is in use where the firm cannot forgo having large fixed plant (e.g. in the automobile industry), while the second one is employed where mechanization is not strictly necessary (e.g. in the 'sweatshop' industries).

8. The two definitions are different, unless restrictive hypotheses are introduced. For a quadratic cost curve, for instance, fixed costs should decrease when flexibility increases.

9. Mills and Schumann assume that firms in an industry can choose a production technology from a set of discrete options $i = 1, \ldots, k$ each with quadratic total costs.

$$TC_i = (1/2a_i)q_i^2 + b_i q_i + F_i$$

where $a_i b_i > 0$ are parameters and F_i represents fixed costs. The second derivatives of total costs and of average total costs are

$$TC_{i,qq} = 1/a_i$$
$$ATC_{qq} = 2F_i/q_i^3$$

The minimum level of average cost for a type i plant are

$$\min ATC = b_i + (2F_i/a_i)^{\frac{1}{2}}$$

The $/a_i/$ parameter is a measure of flexibility: an increase in $/a_i/$ means an increase in flexibility.

10. The supply curve coincides with the upward-sloping portion of the marginal cost curve as long as the price covers average variable cost.

11. We assume the total cost functions we encounter have a decreasing and relative negligible value of third, fourth, and n^{th} derivatives. If the cost function is quadratic all these derivatives are zero.

12. An interesting result emerges when $ATC_A < ATC_B$ and second derivatives are increasing. It is possible that less flexible plant could be preferred for high values of var(p), while more flexible plant for low values of var(p) (Fig. 5.1(iv)). When the total cost function is cubic this could happen when the more flexible plant has fixed costs which are higher than those of the less flexible plant. We emphasize that if we impose, according to the Stiglerian definition, that as flexibility increases the convexity of ATC decreases, this situation is ruled out.

13. This is the case for total cost functions of the type $TC = F + A\ q^b$, with $b > 1$.

14. This is true if we respect the spirit of the Stiglerian analysis of flexibility. Indeed, if we use the definition of flexibility in terms of second derivative of a generic TC function, the coexistence of heterogeneous firms does not imply, if we allow for demand instability, that the more flexible plant has the greater minimum average total cost.

Consider a situation in which the more flexible plant has greater fixed costs and a lower min ATC (this could happen when TC is cubic), and q^* falls where $ATC_A > ATC_B$, so that the more flexible plant has the lower intercept. If $TC_A'' < 0$ and $TC_B'' > 0$ in this interval, the line for A slopes upward, while the line for B downward, and they intersect. In this case too, the more flexible plant will be preferred only for high values of demand instability.

15. In many companies the average lot produced is lower than 100 pieces.

16. Literature on the multiproduct firm has been concerned with two issues: (1) The search for sufficient conditions for the existence of multiproduct firms (Sharkey, 1982; Panzar and Willig, 1981). (2) The definition of technological characteristics enabling the sub-additivity of the cost function. Colombo and Mariotti (1986) have proposed that one of the reasons for sub-additivity of flexibly automated plants is the virtual elimination of the idle times (due to set-up) of fund factors utilized for joint production processes.

17. The transray convex function proposed by Willig (1979)

$$C(\mathbf{q}) = F + [k_1(q_1)^a + k_2(q_2)^b]^m$$

$$0 \leqslant m \leqslant 1;\ am,\ bm \geqslant 1;\ k_1,\ k_2 > 0$$

does not fulfill inequality (15) without additional conditions on parameters.

18. Ray economies of scale are a straightforward extension of the concept of single product scale economies, and indicate the behaviour of costs as the

production levels of a given bundle of goods change.

19. Transray convexity condition assures that this derivative is positive. It represents the curvature of $C(q)$ with respect to all directions for a given volume Q.

20. When the labour force is considered to be an asset, we can say that an employer invests in flexibility if he trains his workers to adjust to changing technologies, as in Piore and Sabel's (1984) theory of flexibility.

21. Simon observes that these are not really distinct types, but a whole continuum with highly programmed decisions at one end of that continuum, and highly unprogrammed decisions at the other end.

22. At time t_0, in the case of single stage decision problems, a decision-maker faces n possible actions, whose outcome in t_1 will vary according to which of m possible states of the world will occur in t_1. In the face of it, it is only possible to make predictions about the possible state of the world in terms of probabilities. Given the outcomes matrix and provided that the probability of each state of the world can be assigned, the decision-maker selects one action at a single point of time. It is assumed that in t_1 it is not possible to shift from the action chosen at t_0 to a different one or/and that in the period between t_0 and t_1 further information will not become available.

23 Such a policy, followed in the 1960s and 70s cannot be maintained when there are high levels of market uncertainty and instability, because the amount of locked-up capital becomes uneconomic, as do the times of delivery to customers.

24. Consider a firm using a certain technology, represented by a given cost function. If at time t_0 it predicts that quantity $q^\wedge$ will be sold at time t_1, and new information indicating an increase in demand becomes available before t_1, the firm will revise its plans and make all the arrangements for increasing production (buying more materials and overtime labour, reprogramming production, setting up machinery, etc.) by using a certain amount of managerial services. The cost of varying plans and increasing production will be higher the nearer to t_1 the date when new information becomes available and the greater the required increase. For each date we may draw a cost curve, tangent at $q^\wedge$ to the curve representing the initial plan, and higher than it for all other quantities. That tangent cost curve represents the production cost for the quantity to be sold at t_1, when the message is received on that date and initial planned production was $q^\wedge$. A firm will be more flexible, the smaller the distance separating the plan curve and the revised plan curves. It can be demonstrated that as uncertainty increases, plants with a higher degree of flexibility improve their performances and become more profitable than other plants, if firms maximize expected profit. Building on Turnovsky (1973), a similar uncertainty–flexibility relation might hold also for a utility-maximizing firm.

25. The definition of 'dynamic flexibility' given by Klein (1988) is very similar to our definition of 'structural flexibility', but it concerns only two functions of the firm, namely R & D and production. Dynamic flexibility is defined as the capability of firms to make rapid adjustments to new circumstances in both R & D and production activities.

26. Dynamic flexibility requires a plant that can take advantage of unexpected opportunities (a plant that can be modified quickly and easily), instead of a

plant geared towards producing at the lowest possible cost at a given time (i.e. statically efficient). A dynamically flexible firm should abandon any attempt to minimize costs in each given time. Referring to the Japanese experience, Klein (1988) has claimed that dynamic flexibility involves plants which are smaller than statically efficient plants, since a large plant would prevent firms from cultivating that particular kind of atmosphere and organization which has allowed Japanese firms to reach and maintain their high level of competitiveness.

27. The existence of different organizational modes in different areas, on the other hand, could be seen as the result of not only differences in factor prices but also in the kind of prevailing uncertainty as well as the socioeconomic environment.

Bibliography

AMIN, A. and ROBINS, K. (1990) 'Industrial Districts and Regional Development: Limits and Possibilities', in G. Becattini, F. Pyke and W. Sergenberger (eds) *Industrial Districts in Italy*, Geneva: IILS. International Labour Office.

ANTONELLI, C. and LOCKE, R. (1988) 'International Competitiveness, Technological Change and Organizational Innovation: Strategy and Structure of the Italian Apparel Industry', paper presented to the conference on Managing the Globalization of Business, Capri, Italy, October.

AOKI, M. (1984) 'Innovative Adaptation through the Quasi Tree Structure: An Emerging Aspect of Japanese Entrepreneurship', *Zeitschrift fur Nationalökonomie* 4, pp. 25–35.

ARROW, K.J. (1975) Vertical Integration and Communication, *Bell Journal of Economics* 6, pp. 173–83.

BAILEY, E.E. and FRIEDLAENDER, A.F. (1982) 'Market Structure and Multiproduct Industries', *Journal of Economic Literature* 20, pp. 1024–48.

BAUMOL, W.J. (1977) 'On the Proper Cost Tests for a Natural Monopoly in a Multiproduct Industry', *American Economic Review* 67, pp. 809–22.

BAUMOL, W.J., PANZAR, J.C. and WILLIG R.D. (1982) *Contestable Markets and the Theory of Industry Structure* New York: Harcourt Brace Jovanovich.

BECATTINI, G. (ed.) (1987) *Mercato e Forze Locali: Il Distretto Industriale*, Bologna: Il Mulino.

BELLANDI, M. (1982) 'Il Distretto Industriale in A. Marshall', *L' Industria* 3, 3, pp. 355–75.

BOULDING, K. (1981) *Ecodynamics: a New Theory of Social Evolution*, Beverly Hills (California): Sage.

BOYER, R. (1988) 'Technical Change and the Theory of Regulation', in Dosi *et al.* (1988).

BURNS, T. (1963) 'Mechanistic and Organismic Structures', *New Society*, 31 January, pp. 17–20, reprinted in D.S. Pugh (ed.) *Organization Theory*, Penguin, 1971, pp. 43–55.

CAMAGNI, R. (1986) 'The Flexible Automation Trajectory: The Italian Case', paper presented to the International Conference on Innovation Diffusion', Venice, 17–21 March.

CARLTON, D.W. (1978) 'Market Behaviour with Demand Uncertainty and Price Inflexibility', *American Economic Review* 68, pp. 571–87.

CARLTON, D.W. (1979) 'Vertical Integration in Competitive Markets under Uncertainty', *Journal of Industrial Economics* 27, pp. 189–209.

CASTELLS, M. and HENDERSON, J. (1987) 'Techno-economic Restructuring, Sociopolitical Processes and Spatial Transformation: A Global Perspective', in *idem* (eds) *Global Restructuring and Territorial Development*, London: Sage.

CAVES, E. and PUGEL, T.A. (1980) 'Intraindustry Differences in Conduct and Performances: Viable Strategies', in *U.S. Manufacturing Industries*, New York University Press.

CHANDLER, A. (1977) *The Visible Hand: The Managerial Revolution in American Business*, Cambridge, Mass.: Harvard University Press.

CHANDLER, A. (1982) The M-form: Industrial Groups American Style, *European Economic Review* 19, pp. 3–23.

COHENDET, P. and LLERENA, P. (1988) 'Flexibilities, Complexity and Integration in Production Processes', in M. Ergas *et al.*, *Firm–environment Interaction in a Changing Production System – Theory, Behaviour and Trend: An International Overview*, Milan: F. Angeli.

COLOMBO, M.G. and MARIOTTI, S. (1985) *'Note Economiche sull'Automazione Flessibile'*, Dip. di Ingegneria – Area di Ricerca Economico-gestionale, Politecnico di Milano, November.

COLOMBO, M.G. and MARIOTTI, S. (1986) *Flexible Automation, Idle Times and Economies of Scope*, Dip. di Ingegneria – Area di Ricerca Economico-gestionale, Politecnico di Milano, May.

COOKE, P. (1988) 'Flexible Integration, Scope Economies and Strategic Alliances: Social and Spatial Mediations', *Society and Space* 6, 3, pp. 281–300.

DEGEORGE, F. (1985) 'Politiques Industrielles et Strategies des Enterprises dans le Jeu Concurrentiel International in Electronique: Pour une Voie Europeenne', *Memoire de Recherche*, December.

DEL MONTE, A. (1987a) *Nascita e Sviluppo di un Distretto Industriale High-Tech: Il Caso della Silicon Valley*, mimeo, Dipartimento di Scienze Economiche e Sociali, Università di Napoli.

DEL MONTE, A: (1987b) *Modelli di diffusione della imprenditorialità*, Bologna: Bulzoni.

DOSI, G. *et al.* (1988) *Technical Change and Economic Theory*, London: Pinter.

ERNST, D. (1981) *Restructuring World Industry in a Period of Crisis: the Role of Innovation*, UNIDO.

ERNST, D. (1986) 'Automation, Employment and the Third World: The Case of the Electronics Industry', in R. Gordon (ed.) *Microelectronics in Transition: Industrial Transformation and Social Change*, New Jersey: Ablex.

ESPOSITO, F.M. (1988) Il Problema della Flessibilità nella Teoria dell'Impresa, Degree Dissertation, Università di Napoli.

FISHMAN, K.D. (1982) *The Computer Establishment*, New York: McGraw-Hill.

FREEMAN, C and PEREZ, C. (1988) 'Structural Crises of Adjustment, Business Cycles and Investment Behaviour', in *Dosi et al.* (1988).

GORDON, D.M. (1988) 'The Global Economy: New Edifice or Crumbling Foundations?', *New Left Review* 168, pp. 24–64.

GREEN, J. (1986) 'Vertical Integration and Assurance of Markets', in Stiglitz and Matthewson (eds) (1986).

HART, A.G. (1951) *Anticipations, Uncertainty and Dynamic Planning*, New York: Mc Kelley.

HIRSCHLEIFER, J. (1978) 'Competition, Cooperation and Conflict in Economics and Biology', *American Economic Review*, 68, pp. 238–43.

HIRSCHLEIFER, J. and RILEY, J.G. (1979) 'The Analysis of Uncertainty and Information: An Expository Survey', *Journal of Economic Literature* 17, pp. 1375–421.

JOVANOVIC, B. (1982) 'Selection and Evolution of Industry' *Econometrica* 50, 3, May, pp. 649–70.

KLEIN, B. (1988) 'Luck, Necessity and Dynamic Flexibility', in H. Hanusch (ed.) *Evolutionary Economics – Applications of Schumpeter's Ideas*, Cambridge, Mass.: Cambridge University Press.

LEWONTIN, R.C. (1978) 'Adaptation', *Scientific American* 117, September.

LIPIETZ, A. (1987) 'La Regulation: Les Mots et les Choses', *Revue Economique* 5, pp. 1049–60.

LINVILL, J.G. (1984) *The Competitive Status of the U.S. Electronics Industry*, Washington D.C.: National Academy Press.

LUCAS, R.E. (1978) 'On the Size Distribution of Business Firms', *Bell Journal of Economics* 9, pp. 508–23.

MARIOTTI, S. (1982) *Efficienza e Struttura Economica: Il Caso del Tessile-Abbigliamento*, Milan: F. Angeli.

MARSCHAK, T. and NELSON, R. (1962) 'Flexibility, Uncertainty and Economic Theory', *Metroeconomica* 14, pp. 42–58.

MAYNARD SMITH, J. (1974) *Models in Ecology*, Cambridge University Press.

MILLS, D.E. (1984) 'Demand Fluctuations and Endogenous Firm Flexibility', *Journal of Industrial Economics* 33, pp. 55–71.

MILLS, D.E. and SCHUMANN, L. (1985) 'Industry Structure with Fluctuating Demand', *American Economic Review* 75, pp. 758–67.

NELSON, R.R. (1961) 'Uncertainty, Prediction and Competitive Equilibrium', *Quarterly Journal of Economics*, February, pp. 41–62.

NELSON, R. and WINTER, S. (1982) *An Evolutionary Theory of Economic Change*, Cambridge, Mass.: Harvard University Press.

OI, Y. (1983) 'Heterogeneous Firms and the Organization of Production', *Economic Inquiry* 21, April, pp. 147–71.

PANZAR, J. C. and WILLIG, R.D. (1981) 'Economies of Scope', *American Economic Review* 71, pp. 268–72.

PARACONE, C. and UBERTO, F. (1988) *Le Nuove Frontiere della Flessibilità Totale*, Roma: SIPI S.r.1.

PEREZ, C. (1983) 'Structural Change and Assimilation of New Technologies in the Economic and Social System', *Futures* 15, 5, pp. 357–75.

PEREZ, C. (1985) 'Microelectronics. Long Waves and World Structural Change: New Perspective for Developing Countries', *World Development* 13, 3, pp. 441–63.

PIORE, M. and SABEL, C.F. (1982) *The Second Industrial Divide: Possibilities for Prosperity*, New York: Basic Books.

PORTER, M.E. (1979) 'The Structure Within Industries and Companies' Performance', *Review of Economics and Statistics* 61, May, pp. 214–27.

ROTHSCHILD, M. and STIGLITZ, J.E. (1970) 'Increasing Risk, I: A Definition', *Journal of Economic Theory* 2, pp. 225–43.

ROTHSCHILD, M. and STIGLITZ, J.E. (1971) 'Increasing Risk, II: Its Economic Consequences', *Journal of Economic Theory* 3, pp. 66–84.

SABEL, C.F. (1989) 'Flexible Specialization and the Re-emergence of Regional Economies', in P. Hirst and J. Zeitlin (eds) *Reversing Industrial Decline? Industrial Structure and Policy in Britain and Her Competitors*, Oxford: Berg.

SCOTT, A.J. (1988) 'Flexible Production Systems and Regional Development: The Rise of New Industrial Spaces in North America and Western Europe', *International Journal of Urban and Regional Research* 12(2), pp. 171–85.

SCOTT, A.J. and STORPER, M. (eds) (1986) *Production, Work, Territory: the Geographical Anatomy of Industrial Capitalism*, Boston: Allen & Unwin.

SCOTT, A.J. and STORPER, M. (1987) 'High Technology Industry and Regional Development: A Theoretical Critique and Reconstruction', *International Social Science Journal* 112, pp. 215–32.

SHARKEY, W.W. (1983) *The Theory of Natural Monopoly*, Cambridge University Press.

SHESHINSKI, E. and DRÈZE, J. (1976) 'Demand Fluctuations, Capacity Utilization and Costs', *American Economic Review* 66, pp. 731–42.

SIMON, H.A. (1960) 'Decision Making and Organization Design', in *The New Science of Management Decision*, London Harper & Row, pp. 1–8 and pp. 35–50, reprinted in D.S. Pugh (ed.) *Organization Theory*, London: Penguin, 1971, pp. 189–212.

SIMON, H.A. (1979) 'From Substantive to Procedural Rationality', in F. Hahn and M. Hollis (eds) *Philosophy and Economic Theory*, Oxford University Press, pp. 65–86.

SIMON, H.A. and BONINI, C.P. (1959) 'The Size Distribution of Business Firms', *American Economic Review* 48, pp. 607–17.

STIGLER, G.J. (1939) 'Production and Distribution in the Short Run', *Journal of Political Economy* 47, 3, pp. 305–27.

STIGLER, G.J. (1952) *The Theory of Price*, New York: Macmillan.

STIGLITZ, J.F. and MATHEWSON, G.F. (eds) (1986) *New Developments in the Analysis of Market Structure*, New York: MacMillan.

TISDELL, C.A. (1966) *The Theory of Price Uncertainty, Production and Profit*, Princeton: Princeton University Press.

TURNOVSKY, S.J. (1973) 'Production Flexibility, Price Uncertainty and the Behaviour of the Competitive Firm', *International Economic Review* 14, (2), pp. 395–413.

WILLIAMSON, O. (1975) *Market and Hierarchies: Analysis and Antitrust Implications*, New York: Free Press.

WILLIAMSON, O. (1985) *The Economic Institutions of Capitalism*, New York: Free Press.

WILLIG, R.D. (1979): 'Multiproduct Technology and Market Structure', *American Economic Review* 69, 2, pp. 346–51.

6 Monopoly Capitalism Revisited

Keith Cowling

This paper seeks to update and extend the analysis contained in *Monopoly Capitalism*,[1] by considering research done since its publication. I will also consider some of the criticisms of the book which have been made. I will proceed by first identifying the central themes of the book and then pick up the topics which appear to merit some reassessment. These include rivalry and collusion, efficient bargaining, savings and corporate control, equilibrium v. anti-equilibrium and, lastly, the internationalization of production.

THE CENTRAL THEMES OF MONOPOLY CAPITALISM

Within the advanced industrial countries oligopoly is now pretty ubiquitous. Given the general presence of oligopoly we would expect some degree of market power to be a normal characteristic of the economy. (I shall return to this point in the section on rivalry and collusion.) Thus we would expect price to diverge from the competitive level and as a result we would have the beginnings of a theory of distribution. Assuming some degree of symmetry,[2] three factors jointly determine the share of profits under oligopoly: the degree of concentration of the industry, the degree of collusion and the industry elasticity of demand. To a considerable degree, each of these factors is under the control of the firms making up the oligopoly group. Thus firms within the same market may choose to merge their interests; as a result, those that remain may find it easier to collude, and they will have a greater incentive to do so; and, lastly, firms can create a greater dependency among their customers, and therefore a greater price inelasticity of demand, by appropriate investment in advertising and product differentiation activities.[3]

Over the past hundred years or so there has undoubtedly been a very substantial general increase in market concentration, and such an increase will tend to imply an increase in the share of profits, and therefore a reduction in the share of wages, due to the fact that we expect the degree of monopoly, or oligopoly, $(p - mc/p)$ to rise with concentration, assuming

148

profit-maximizing behaviour. This will come about directly (e.g. assuming Cournot behaviour), but also indirectly via the impact of concentration on the degree of collusion and on advertising and the degree of product differentiation. However, changes in concentration may have no effect if the degree of monopoly is effectively constrained by the existence of potential rivalry. This will generally be ruled out, either because of the existence of barriers to entry, or because of investment in excess capacity as a credible deterrent to entry, a theme we shall take up in the next section.

The process of concentration raises a further distributional issue. Much investment will be directed towards acquiring and maintaining dominant positions: that is, it will be devoted to distributional ends to be gained through market control. The competition for monopoly rents will itself create waste. Thus, given the degree of utilization of resources, a system which allows the generation of monopoly rents will result in a diversion of resources from expanding the output of the system towards the redistribution of that output. Excess capacity (to deter prospective entrants), and excessive advertising and product differentiation, through research and development, would be cases in point.[4]

I now wish to turn to the possible stagnationist tendencies which may be induced by the concentrating process we have identified. Whilst the *potential* clearly exists for an increase in the share of profits, putting on one side for the time being issues of trade union power and international competition, whether or not this is *realized* depends on the impact of the process itself on aggregate demand. The immediate impact would be a downward revision of planned investment in line with the planned reduction in the rate of output within those sectors where the degree of monopoly has increased. The reduction in aggregate investment, in the absence of compensating adjustments elsewhere, would lead to a reduction in the level of profits in the total system, which would lead to further cutbacks in investment, and so on. Compensating, upward adjustments in investment elsewhere may of course take place as a result of the underlying tendency for the potential share of profits to increase. However, such adjustments are likely to involve considerable lags, owing to the uncertainty surrounding profit expectations and the long gestation periods involved in new investment projects, coupled with the fact that the planned cutbacks in those sectors experiencing an increase in the degree of monopoly become unplanned cutbacks elsewhere.

Clearly any deficiency in investment could be made up by an increase in consumption out of the increased potential flow of profits, but this is unlikely to be fast enough, nor is it likely to be of the required extent, given that capitalists receive their income less frequently than workers, and also tend to have lower propensities to consume. Managerialism, reflected in rising intra-corporate consumption, could provide at least a partial antidote to such a realization crisis, but it contains its own contradictions. Although in aggregate, by tending to maintain demand, managerialism serves to maintain profits, it will be seen as something to be minimized by those (stockholders) interested in the flow of reported profits. Thus although the growth of giant firms operating in oligopolistic markets gives rise to a substantial growth in managerial discretion, with all the associated expenditure which that implies, such discretion will inevitably lead to measures to curtail it.

Other adjustments within the system are possible. Aggregate demand could be maintained via a growing net export surplus, but there is little reason to suggest that this is likely to follow a rise in the degree of monopoly within any particular economy, indeed just the reverse could happen, see Koo and Martin (1984). If the rise in the degree of monopoly is a general trend within the world industrial system as a whole then it is even less likely that a growing export surplus could be maintained over an extended period, since it would raise the issue of how the rest of the world's growing trade deficit was to be financed. Of course, if all else fails, governments could step in to manage aggregate demand in order to secure the full employment of resources. But clearly we cannot necessarily assume this sort of response. Maintaining full employment inevitably changes the balance of power between capital and labour, and the state will not usually be a disinterested observer of this process. Thus, given the unwillingness to intervene at certain conjunctures, a realization crisis remains a distinct possibility: not an inevitable outcome at any particular period of history, but nevertheless an almost inevitable consequence at some stage in the unravelling of the full implications of the oligopolistic system.

RIVALRY AND COLLUSION

Monopoly Capitalism included an attempt to reconcile close rivalry with collusive behaviour:

> rivalrous behaviour and collusion coexist and result from a high degree of concentration within a specific market. The closer the rivalry, the more immediate is the response to any attempt to secure an advantage, but the very immediacy of the expected response serves to maintain the degree of collusion – it makes a breakaway movement unprofitable (p. 12).

A lot of game-theoretic work since then has suggested that collusion is indeed not as fragile as many orthodox theorists had imagined it to be, but the results at first sight do not appear all that robust. However, experiments by Axelrod (1984) were rather revealing. Game theorists were asked to submit computer programs to play repeated 'Prisoner's Dilemma' games. The clear winner was very simple and familiar: tit for tat! You are nice to people until they are nasty; then you are nasty until they are nice again. Tit for tat elicits and rewards the co-operation of others and does this by offering co-operation, retaliating speedily to non-cooperation, but forgiving equally rapidly. This is the essence of the argument about rivalry and collusion. In addition some interesting recent psychological experimentation reveals that 'people have a tendency to cooperate until experience shows that those with whom they are interacting are taking advantage of them' (Dawes and Thaler, 1988). There is a norm of co-operation.

However, even if we are able to establish that collusion is not the fragile thing that many have assumed it to be, there remains the question of potential entry. *Monopoly Capitalism* relied, to some extent, on the Spence (1977) result that excess capacity would form a credible deterrent to entry, but Dixit (1980) had in turn shown that Spence's equilibrium was imperfect, in the Nash case. Subsequently Bulow *et. al.* (1985) and Kirman and Masson (1986) have rehabilitated much of the Spence position, but perhaps all these authors are missing the essence of the entry problem. We should think of the general concept of rivalry and collusion as a *potential*, as well as a reality. The real issue of entry, within a modern industrial economy, is when a corporation established in one market is considering invading another market dominated by another, where the *latter* is a *potential* rival in the *former's* market. It is this aspect of symmetry of rivalry which is lacking in the usual modelling of entry. This is an important omission because of the typical flexibility of the modern corporation, which allows it to move in any of a large number of directions, which in turn provides the basis for the generality of the symmetry assumption. The deterrent to entry is the immediacy of expected retaliation. This in turn is conditional on having the capacity to do so. This may take the form of plant and equipment but, more generally, it will comprise a strategic capability in terms of management, technology and marketing expertise. Of course as circumstances change so entry may take place: for example, as one market expands relative to another so the incentive to enter increases relative to the cost, but following our earlier discussion of rivalry and collusion we might expect the norm to be one of 'live and let live'. This would suggest that the norm would be one in which collusive outcomes within oligopoly groups would not be undermined by potential entry.

One last issue it is interesting to address in this section is the likely response of firms in oligopolistic markets to the onset of slump conditions. Can we expect price-cutting and a disintegration of collusive behaviour or a cementing of collusive arrangements in the face of common adversity? I conjectured (Cowling, 1982, p. 22, and Cowling, 1983) that the *initial* impact of a substantial fall in demand may cause an oligopoly group to fly apart. Each member of the group observes that its own sales have dropped and assumes that its rivals have been engaged in price-cutting, or similar market-share augmenting strategies. Each member therefore responds with similar strategies. However, if the explanation for the original observation was in fact a general slump in demand, this will gradually become more obvious to each member of the group. Faced with such mutual adversity we may anticipate that the group will tend to come together to attempt to solve its mutual problems. Thus the initial impact of a downturn in demand may well be a reduction in price–cost margins, but if the slump persists we can expect to see a recovery in margins as the degree of collusion within the oligopoly group increases. Evidence is now available to support this conjecture for the UK (Cowling, 1983), Norway (Berg, 1986) and the US (Bils, 1987).[5] Thus we can conclude that the coexistence of rivalry and collusion, a seemingly paradoxical state, is the general case, and, rather than being undermined by slump conditions, will actually be enhanced by the resulting presence of a greater degree of excess capacity.

SAVINGS AND CORPORATE CONTROL

I have argued earlier that monopolizing tendencies will eventually lead to a stagnation tendency. An alternative, and complementary, view has been offered by Christos Pitelis (1986). He argues that the process of capital accumulation inevitably leads to the increased socialization of capital. Initially this is achieved by the growth in discretionary shareholdings, but, at a later stage, compulsory shareholding associated with the 'pension funds revolution' takes the leading role.[6] In the case of Britain the growth of pension funds, coupled with the growth in corporate retained earnings, appears to have had a major impact in raising the ratio of aggregate savings to private disposable income. The net inflow in life assurance and pension funds increased, as a ratio to private disposable income, from 3.59 per cent in the decade 1954–63 to 4.44% per cent in 1964–73, and to 5.94 per cent in 1974–83, and corporate retained earnings increased in similar fashion from 12.41 per cent, to 13.08 per cent and finally to 15.75 per cent. But did this simply substitute for a *decline* in personal saving? In fact personal savings increased over the same period from 1.44 per cent, to 3.77 per cent, and finally to 5 per cent.[7] Econometric work has confirmed that personal savings *add on* to corporate savings rather than substituting for them, see Pitelis (1986). Thus Pitelis has unearthed an alternative source of a stagnationist tendency within an evolving advanced capitalist system: a declining propensity to consume related to the increasing socialization of capital. In the case of both the monopolization of product markets and socialization of capital origins of stagnation there is a clear demand-side rationale for firms to look abroad, either in terms of markets for the output of surplus capacity, or in terms of investment opportunities. In either case we may detect the origins, or the further development, of the transnational organization of production being related to demand-side developments within the advanced industrial countries. This provides a link through to a later section dealing with the internationalization of production.

EFFICIENT BARGAINING BETWEEN EMPLOYERS AND UNIONS?

Where competitive labour markets prevail our expectation is that wage share will be lower, the higher the degree of concentration. But can we expect trade union pressure for higher wages and better working conditions to mitigate, or reverse, this tendency? In *Monopoly Capitalism* I argued that with collective bargaining at industry level, or where individual bargains are rapidly transmitted throughout the industry, the impact on distribution would be limited.[8] In tightly organized, concentrated industries we can expect a high degree of collusion over wage fixing via multi-employer agreements or wage leadership, so that wage increases will be rapidly passed on as price increases. Thus while union pressure may secure higher wages, this is quite consistent with wage *share* remaining unchanged. Only where there is some hesitation on the firm's part, for example because of pessimistic expectations about the response of rivals, will distributional effects be significant.

But there is an alternative bargaining perspective which can imply that increases in union power will lead to inroads being made into the share of profits. We have assumed above that bargaining is simply over wages, but efficient bargaining may be expected to include both employment and wages. In such circumstances the contract curve could be of a shape, e.g. vertical or positively inclined, that implies increases in union power will be associated with a higher wage share, see e.g. McDonald and Solow (1981). In other words, rather than union power being focused purely on higher wages, which get transformed into higher prices, and therefore reduced employment, as the firm now picks the optimal lower level of output, the union is now simultaneously bargaining over the level of employment, and therefore implicitly the level of output.

Thus bargaining over wages *and* employment could indeed imply a redistribution arising from increased union power; but there is every reason to expect that employers will not acquiesce in such an approach to bargaining. Under plausible assumptions it can be concluded that the employer will set the bargaining agenda, and will restrict bargaining to wages alone, retaining sole discretion over the appropriate level of employment, see Dowrick (1988). The inclusion of jobs in the bargaining process is a matter of power as well as efficiency. This will be *generally* the case because the threat of job losses will serve to inhibit unions from pressing for higher wages. Thus the employer will continue to operate along the labour demand curve and wage increases will not lead generally to a redistribution between wages and profit. Of course we might expect to observe bargaining over jobs when (and where) workers are strong, but when they are strong (for example in times of low unemployment) they are less concerned about bargaining over jobs, since they can easily pick up alternatives; and when they are weak (for example in times of high unemployment) they are concerned about, but incapable of, bargaining over jobs. As Dowrick (1988) suggests, the bargaining advantage that accrues to the side setting the bargaining agenda may provide insight into why we should typically observe firms to be organized as capital hiring workers rather than as workers hiring capital.

Nevertheless, if it is generally true that unions cannot easily influence distribution, how do we explain some of the recent research that appears to suggest the opposite, for example, Freeman (1983) and Henley (1987)?

Firstly, unions can certainly reduce profitability and profit share if their actions result in an increase in the degree of excess capacity in the firm or industry. Secondly, in the case of overhead labour (for example, administrative, technical and clerical labour) wage/salary increases will not be passed on as price increases, so that distributional effects may be significant. Thirdly, in the short term an increase in wage will tend to increase wage share simply because time truncates the full response, and many of the studies which report this sort of effect are based on short-period observations. Lastly there *will* be cases where either the parameters of demand and cost functions, or the bargaining agenda, allow for union power to impact on distribution. I suspect the important dichotomy is between direct and overhead labour – in the former case union power will not have a significant impact, whereas in the latter case it will. Thus certain groups of workers, (the managerial and technological hierarchy) will find it possible to extract a share of the growing surplus accruing as a result of a monopolizing tendency, whereas other groups (direct production workers) will generally find it difficult.

EQUILIBRIUM V. ANTI-EQUILIBRIUM

The central issue in a critique of *Monopoly Capitalism* by Fine and Murfin (1984a; 1984b) relates to whether or not a general equilibrium perspective is most appropriate. On the supply side this arises in their critique of the (simple) aggregation procedures I use to define the average degree of monopoly, and on the demand side in their questioning of why the system tends to crisis in the first place.[9]

On the aggregation front they are concerned with the assumed independence of the industry elasticities of demand. If inter-industry cross-elasticities are indeed zero then they get implausible general equilibrium results, and with non-zero cross-elasticities the results are not so simple (i.e. industry price–cost margins will be circumscribed by the degree of inter-industry substitutability). The central issue is partial equilibrium versus general equilibrium.

Kalecki, the originator of the line of analysis developed in *Monopoly Capitalism*, had little use for general equilibrium concepts, and I feel much the same. Equilibrium concepts have a role in attempting to describe the system – but only a limited one. Where equilibrium concepts are introduced is within the structure of short-run oligopolistic output–price determination.

The system on the supply side is seen to be made up of blocs, each of which acts as if independent of the rest of the system, *in the short run*. Over time, as the rest of the system changes, so those changes feed into this short-run output – price setting behaviour. Non-zero cross-elasticities do not exist within this time period, although we expect them to exist in longer time periods. However, I do not assume any tendency to long-term equilibrium. 'The long run . . . is but a slowly changing component of a chain of short-period situations', as Kalecki would have it (Kalecki, 1971, p. 165). The dynamics of the system tend to move it away from equilibrium (see the later discussion of the demand side), but within it, at each point of time, the degree of monopoly will be determined within the oligopoly group in each bloc, and will remain largely undisturbed by forces outside that group, for example price, advertising and product changes taking place elsewhere in the system: an approximation, but perhaps a not unreasonable one.

Over time, the image is of a series of groups of oligopolists stabilizing themselves at price levels well in excess of marginal cost, but making strategic decisions to reinforce their position of market power. Thus power is maintained and indeed enhanced over time with the groups emerging as separate islands of decision-making, sheltered from outside competition by their own long-run strategies, described earlier as a process of potential tit for tat. Occasionally groups merge, expand their sphere of influence and raise their degree of monopoly. Thus distribution is determined by product market power which is cemented and enhanced over time. Market control is strategically developed. Clashes of interest *within* groups may lead to forms of non-price competition that eat into profits, but which also serve to maintain and enhance monopoly power. Elasticities within each bloc are endogenously determined via advertising and product policies.

This is the way I see the system: collusion and rivalry coexist. They should not be seen as alternatives! They should not be counterposed. This is also my reaction to Fine and Murfin's point about my 'one-sided view of the relationship between monopolisation and competition' (1984b, p. 139). They argue 'that monopoly and competition are inextricably connected . . . so that it is erroneous to construct a theory in which one varies in inverse proportion to the other' (1984b, p. 140). Exactly: rivalry and collusion coexist within tight, oligopolistic structures, as I tried to argue in the book.

On the demand side, Fine and Murfin ask: 'why is there a crisis in the first place which sows the seeds of deeper problems?' (1984b, p. 141). They seem to be working within the paradigm of Say's Law, whilst I am working with Anti-Say's Law. Say's Law requires that $I \equiv S$, regardless of the level of aggregate output; but only by chance will $I = S$ at some level of aggregate output. For Walras the aggregate investment function was *not independent* – demand for investment adjusted flexibly to fulfill the conditions of general equilibrium, see Morishima and Catephores (1985), and this is what Fine and Murfin wish to assume.[10] Entrepreneurs are the agents of equilibrium – they remove disequilibria and generate the conditions of Walrasian equilibrium. But since banks (or financial institutions more generally) can create credit, 'investment is determined by the size of investment plans and their quality' (Morishima and Catephores, 1985).[11] Thus investment is independent of savings: Anti-Say's Law prevails.

Specifically with regard to the investment function they argue that I exclude 'the element of coercion associated with the need to reduce costs and defend or extend market shares in competition with other capitals', (Fine and Murfin, 1984b, p. 142). This phenomenon may be present, but its necessity declines with monopolization and therefore it cannot resolve the crisis of demand precipitated by monopolization. The incentive for such investment or innovation remains, but it is muted by the existence of a tight oligopoly group, or by a dominant firm. Only with emerging asymmetries between firms will such activity tend to increase as a result of monopolization, and whilst these will always be present, they do not constitute the general norm. As Sylos-Labini (1962) has observed, the form of investment will also be affected. Because of the demand constraint, a concentrated economy will tend to favour labour-saving innovations; thus capital deepening is favoured over capital widening, which tends to imply rising unemployment. In turn this could weaken unions and prolong the crisis of demand.

I would conclude that general equilibrium simply does not relate to the institutions characterizing modern economies. Thus it does not seem useful to raise general equilibrium issues in a critique of an analysis of the present monopoly capitalist system.

THE INTERNATIONALIZATION OF PRODUCTION

I have painted a picture of prices rising in relation to marginal cost as markets have become more concentrated, but there remains the question of international competition. Although industrial concentration in all advanced industrial countries may be rising, its impact on price–cost margins may be nullified by rising import competition. Whether or not this is the case depends on who controls such trade. In contrast to the usual assumptions, imports are often under the direct control of the domestic oligopoly structure, via its own transnational base (including sub-contracting arrangements) or via agency and franchise agreements. The relationship between the degree of monopoly and the level of imports is a complicated one and the conventional wisdom that the degree of monopoly falls as imports rise can be very misleading. In some recent work, Neumann *et. al.* (1985, p. 17) conclude that, in the case of West Germany, 'collusiveness has not visibly decreased in spite of a substantial increase in foreign trade'. In the longer term it is possible to argue that the growth of intra-industry trade may *enhance* the degree of monopoly, rather than decrease it, by serving as a mechanism whereby dominant firms, with a domestic base plus transnational connections, may more easily squeeze out smaller and weaker domestic rivals. Thus free trade leads to the increasing dominance of the transnationals and can contribute to a higher level of concentration and degree of monopoly in each domestic market. For a formal derivation of the precise conditions see Sugden (1983).

Thus the growth of the transnational organization of production can have an impact on the distribution of income via product market effects, but this impact can also be supplemented via labour market effects working through a process of 'divide and rule' (Cowling and Sugden, 1987). The outcome of conflict between workers and employers depends on their relative bargaining power, and in its turn the bargaining power of workers depends very much on their ability to act collectively, and this is very difficult when people work in different countries. Whilst in principle it is possible for labour to overcome organizational difficulties, cultural factors pose more fundamental problems. This suggests that a firm may decide to produce in various countries so that it can face a divided workforce. Costs of different types of labour vary across countries and firms will take advantage of this, but costs also depend on the bargaining power of labour and its employers and this is endogenous to the firm's locational decisions. The growth of transnationalism gives added impetus to the redistribution from wages to profits via these labour market effects.

Having established that transnationalism can affect distribution, by bearing down on wages and raising price–cost margins, and having established earlier that redistributions favouring profits can lead to stagnationist tendencies, we can see that there can exist an indirect link between transnationalism and stagnation. This indirect link is in turn supplemented by more direct effects working from both the supply and demand side. On the supply side the combination of more-or-less unified international markets and giant international firms bestriding them provides a ready mechanism for the processes of deindustrialization to develop wherever the conditions for profitable accumulation are weakened. What we have witnessed is an increasing geographical flexibility of capitalist production which allows capital to escape organized labour. By making investment conditional on wage cuts, transnationals may also be able to gain the co-operation of the state in securing the appropriate environment in which wage costs will tend to be held down. On the demand side we now have a system where the effectiveness of demand management by the nation state is reduced because of the greater leakage induced by the transnational organization of production, thus reducing the incentive to adopt such measures, whilst at the same time the greater degree of integration of the international economy implies that stagnation tendencies in any one country will be more quickly transmitted to other countries, eventually leading to feedbacks on the originating country. An integrated world economy is produced, but without an overall planning mechanism. Thus, rather than having the stability which could result from international integration within a supra-national planning authority, we have the growing instability of international integration organized by individual transnational corporations. The most vivid example is the world financial system, with the resulting huge, short-term gyrations in exchange rates undermining the ability of industrial capitalism to plan its investment and production policies and make informed locational decisions. The central point is that the very flexibility of unregulated financial capital has induced this state of affairs where the efficiency of industrial capital is impaired.

CONCLUDING REMARKS

I have sought to update and extend the analysis of *Monopoly Capitalism*, and also respond to some criticisms. I conclude that the main thrust of the book remains intact and indeed is strengthened by research and observation completed since it was published. I would just wish to finish on a matter coming directly out of the last section. We are awash in a sea of professional comment which unreservedly recommends the free play of market forces at the international level. This is not simply a view advanced by the Right, but also by most Keynesian and liberal commentators. To my mind, simplistic economic arguments which once had substantial validity, and which of course retain some, are being pushed far too far by otherwise reasonable people, to the exclusion of other far more fundamental matters. The flowering of a multiplicity of cultures requires barriers to international forces: barriers not to people and ideas, but to capital. We need to nurture the roots of our society by establishing the autonomy of small communities, but, paradoxically, in a monopoly capitalist world, this requires state intervention to secure a level of aggregate demand consistent with full employment plus a strategic commitment to national industrial development. The aim of such a strategy is not to induce a stagnation in demand for the output of the rest of the world, but to establish conditions whereby a particular society can thrive and prosper. Dynamic, fully employed economies are not a threat to each other, but they cannot be established without some degree of isolation from world capitalist forces.

Notes

1. Cowling, K. (1982) *Monopoly Capitalism*, London: Macmillan.
2. The alternative, asymmetric, case of dominant firm(s) and competitive fringe I find descriptive of neither structure nor behaviour.
3. Pagoulatos and Sorenson (1986) have demonstrated that advertising expenditure is an important determinant of the inter-industry variation in the elasticity of demand, with high advertising expenditures implying low elasticities.
4. Wolff (1986) has attempted to identify the major components of such waste in the case of the US economy.
5. In the case of the work by Mark Bils the analysis only reveals a 'very counter cyclical mark-up'. However, the cycle is measured by *employment*, so that any *initial* change in mark-up due to a change in sales is probably missed. It remains the case that Bils provides strong evidence favouring a sharp increase in margins under slump conditions.
6. By 1985 pension fund assets in Britain had grown to £150 billion, which

represented 29 per cent of all business equity.

7. Of course there is much current discussion about the *falling* propensity to save. This is no doubt linked to the freeing-up, and indeed huge promotion, of the credit supplying industry. This is likely to have a one-off impact, rather than some continuing major effect on the underlying tendencies.

8. The exact outcomes will be dependent on the parameters of the demand and cost functions. For example, with constant elasticity of demand and constant short-run marginal cost, with labour as the sole component, it is easy to show that, in the case of wage-only bargaining, wage share will be unaffected by union power.

9. They also express concerns about my treatment, or non-treatment, of the dynamics of competition and exploitation within the sphere of production, but I don't see these as central issues. I could have included more on the process of competition, but I have already repeated comments on this, whilst I declared in the introduction that I was not really going to get embroiled in the matter of exploitation in the sphere of production. I see that as adding on to exploitation via the market and in distribution, and again I have discussed it briefly at various points: indeed I don't see exploitation within the sphere of distribution and production as being usefully divisible.

10. As Oskar Lange pointed out, Walrasian general equilibrium can only be interpreted in terms of a centrally planned economy (Lange, 1936).

11. Interestingly, Fine and Murfin make the point that I do not consider the role of credit. This is true in the case of private credit, and it can undoubtedly help in alleviating a short-run deficiency in aggregate demand, although increases in credit are usually observed to be correlated to rapid increases in real income. The longer-term impact is rather more problematic. For example, in the case of the United States a credit boom has apparently been required to move the economy towards full employment, but this has posed problems of fundamental imbalance in international trade. Of course the same is true with Keynesian-type reflation and exposes supply-side issues of monopoly capitalism, which are addressed in the final section.

References

AXELROD, R. (1984) *The Evolution of Cooperation*, New York: Basic Books.

BERG, A. (1986) 'Excess Capacity and the Degree of Collusion: Some Estimates for the Norwegian Manufacturing Sector'. *International Journal of Industrial Organisation*, pp. 99–108.

BILS, M. (1987) 'The Cyclical Behaviour of Marginal Cost and Price', *American Economic Review*, pp. 838–55.

BULOW, J., GEANAKOPLOS, J. and KLEMPERER, P. (1985) 'Holding Idle Capacity to Deter Entry', *Economic Journal*, pp. 178–97.

COWLING, K. (1982) *Monopoly Capitalism*, Macmillan: London.

COWLING, K. (1983) 'Excess Capacity and the Degree of Collusion: Oligopoly Behaviour in the Slump', *Manchester School*, December, pp. 341–59.

COWLING, K. and SUGDEN, R. (1987) *Transnational Monopoly Capitalism*, Brighton: Wheatsheaf.

DAWES, R. and THALER, R. (1988) 'Anomalies: Cooperation', *Journal of Economic Perspectives*, Summer, pp. 187–97.

DIXIT, A. (1980), 'The Role of Investment in Entry-Deterrence', *Economic Journal*, pp. 95–106.

DOWRICK, S. (1988) 'The Relative Profitability of Bargaining over Employment and/or Wages', Department of Economics, Australian National University, Working Paper no. 161.

FINE, B. and MURFIN, A. (1984a) *Macroeconomics and Monopoly Capitalism*, Brighton: Wheatsheaf.

FINE, B. and MURFIN, A. (1984b) 'The Political Economy of Monopoly and Competition', *International Journal of Industrial Organisation*, pp. 133–40.

FREEMAN, R. (1983) 'Unionism, Price–Cost Margins and the Returns to Capital', National Bureau of Economic Research Working Paper no. 1164.

HENLEY, A.G. (1987), 'Trade Unions, Market Concentration and Income Distribution in United States Manufacturing Industry', *International Journal of Industrial Organization*, pp. 193–210.

KALECKI, M. (1971) *Selected Essays on the Dynamics of the Capitalist Economy*, Cambridge University Press.

KIRMAN, A. and MASSON, R. (1986) 'Capacity Signals and Entry Deterrence', *International Journal of Industrial Organisation*, pp. 25–42.

KOO, A. and MARTIN, S. (1984), 'Market Structure and US Trade Flows', *International Journal of Industrial Organisation*, 173–98.

LANGE, O. (1936), 'On the Economic Theory of Socialism', *Review of Economic Studies*, pp. 53–71.

MCDONALD, I. and SOLOW, R. (1981) 'Wage Bargaining and Employment', *American Economic Review* 71, pp. 896–908.

MORISHIMA, M. and CATEPHORES, G. (1985) 'Anti-Say's Law versus Say's Law: A Change in Paradigm', University College, London, Discussion Paper no. 85–16.

NEUMANN, M., BOBEL, I. and HAID, A. (1985) 'Domestic Concentration, Foreign Trade and Economic Performance', *International Journal of Industrial Organisation*, pp. 1–20.

PAGOULATOS, E. and SORENSON, R. (1986) 'What Determines the Elasticity of Industry Demand', *International Journal of Industrial Organisation*, 237–50.

PITELIS, C. (1986) *Corporate Capital: Control, Ownership, Saving and Prices*, Cambridge University Press.

SPENCE, M. (1977), 'Entry, Investment and Oligopolistic Pricing', *Bell Journal of Economics*, Autumn.

SUGDEN, R. (1983), 'The Degree of Monopoly, International Trade and Transnational Corporations', *International Journal of Industrial Organisation*, pp. 165–88.

SYLOS-LABINI, P. (1962) *Oligopoly and Technical Progress*, Cambridge, Mass.: Harvard University Press.

WOLFF, E. (1986) *Growth, Accumulation and Unproductive Activity: An Analysis of the Post-War US Economy*, New York: Cambridge University Press.

7 Industrial Economics in Italy

Roberto Marchionatti and Francesco Silva

INTRODUCTION

In Italy, reflections on topics which can be attributed to industrial economics have often proceeded in directions different from the mainstream. The aim of this paper is to offer an overview of the most important Italian contributions in this field and to identify the reasons for these differences.

As is well known, from the immediate post-war years to the early 1970s, industrial economics (or industrial organization) developed around the two main paradigms: one from Harvard which developed the structure–conduct–performance paradigm, and one which concentrated on the behaviour of large managerial firms. These two approaches had basically the same problem, which was essentially how the discipline of efficiency can be imposed on markets, which are imperfect, and on firms, which structurally tend to enjoy extra profits or rents at the expense of consumers. This problem obviously arises whenever the markets for goods and capital are sufficiently large to enable the competitive mechanism to work efficiently. Such conditions, however, were not present in Italy in the immediate post-war years. It was generally accepted that the main bottlenecks in the Italian economy were caused by productive and organizational backwardness and by territorial imbalance, while the markets were still relatively small and poorly organized.

The result was that, in general, industrial economists (but not only they) concentrated on problems related to productive structure and to industrial growth. Attention was also directed to the crucial problem of how to eliminate the backwardness and the regional differences between North and South Italy, and the differences in the pattern of the sectoral activities with respect to the main industrial countries, and to France and Germany in particular. This was identified, together with the low productivity of labour, as the cause of Italian industry's relatively low level of competitiveness on international markets. This weakness was the source of constant concern as Italy is structurally an importer of raw materials, energy products and foodstuffs.

It was widely held among Italian industrial economists, at least up to the early 1980s, that such problems could not be solved by the market mechanism. That is to say, in Italy a generally negative opinion was dominant regarding the market's ability to allocate resources efficiently. This view, which emphasized the extension of market failures, was accompanied by strong political tension which has characterized the theoretical reflections of Italian economists and by a methodological approach which was profoundly influenced by historicism, in which realistic hypotheses were considered essential. The latter approach introduced a strong propensity to criticize orthodox theory, while on a practical level it led to active state intervention being given a determinant role.

Consequently, industrial policies of a structural kind, using incentives, transfers to firms and direct production by state firms, were the main measures adopted to eliminate backwardness. Italian industrial economists were therefore using theories and tools which were different from those which were central to the mainstream of economic thought.

Even when they considered classical theory such as the theory of oligopoly, as in the case of Sylos-Labini, they did so emphasizing the macroeconomic problems related to growth and employment in a modern economy where oligopoly is dominant, rather than the problem of the effects of competition on efficiency. In fact, Sylos-Labini says that the attempt to pass from the level of partial analysis to that of general analysis creates some problems for change in modern economies, and this represents the main aim of his books, and that those problems are 'perhaps' the only ones whose study make the job of an economist attractive and even fascinating.

The large firm is another important topic considered by Italian industrial economists. In fact, it is possible to say that the two fundamental topics of discussion in the 1970s were, on the one hand, industrial policy directed to solving structural problems in the Italian economy and, on the other hand, the phenomenon of the growth of large firms.

According to Momigliano, industrial economics is considered as a new tool which can be used to interpret reality characterized by rapid technological change, the logic of the large firm and the presence of state enterprises. He stresses that industrial policy which influences the conduct and the performances of firms and industries is crucially important. Thus, industrial economics covers the study of the management of firms, how they influence industrial structure and how government policy conditions this behaviour.

The existence (and growing diffusion) of small firms in Italy is to some extent difficult to fit into this dominant approach. Ever-increasing awareness of this problem has enabled economists to develop a rather original area of study, even though it is obviously not confined to the Italian situation.

Further, it has offered an alternative approach to the traditional structuralist method. As Giacomo Becattini, one of the main advocates of this critical approach, has said, the situational determinism of the structuralists should be replaced through typifying experience in field research, thus bringing together rigour and theoretical fantasy.

In the following paragraphs, the Italian contributions to industrial economics are presented under the headings of their main topics. As well as the headings which are quoted, industrial structure, growth, industrial policy, large and small firms are also considered in fields of study such as the analysis of imperfect markets and economics of innovation, where Italian contributions have not been so frequent, at least until recent years.

INDUSTRIAL POLICY

In the last few decades two ideas have been influencing Italian industrial economic thought and conditioning studies and proposals for industrial policy: the Italian economy is weak and backward when compared with the other main industrialized economies, and getting over this backwardness requires much more than the having faith in the invisible hand. The seeds of these ideas are contained in studies prepared just after the Second World War.

The Economic Commission which helped to prepare the Republican Constitution and later the parliamentary surveys into the problems of poverty and unemployment were the first documents to stress this state of backwardness in the Italian economy and to emphasize how urgent it was to promote a more rapid rate of industrial growth.[1] Since then two main positions have developed regarding the interpretation and policies to be implemented. On the one hand, there was the opinion of the liberal economists, including L. Einaudi, C. Bresciani Turroni and V. Lutz, who considered the market as the institutional means which could be entrusted with economic growth; on the other hand, there was the position of some young Keynesian economists including G. Fuà', G. Ruffolo, S. Steve, P. Sylos-Labini, some left-wing Catholics including P. Saraceno, F. Vito, E. Vanoni, S. Lombardini, and Marxists such as R. Morandi who attributed a primary role in the promotion of growth to the state. The latter approach prevailed then and continued to do so for at least the 30 years which followed.

This success, which depended on particular conditions in the cultural, economic and political history of Italy, had a twofold effect. From the point of view of economic policy, such a position meant that regulation and both direct and indirect state intervention in production of private goods and services were considered favourably. From the point of view of economic theory, only limited space was dedicated to more general questions, such as the working of the market and competition, which were at the heart of industrial economics in the Anglo-Saxon world.

The two main problems on which the debate focuses are the under-development of the South and the lack of competitiveness of the industrial sector.

The problem of the South, that is, the failure to modernize the institutions and the social and economic behaviour in the South has been a thorn in the side of Italian society since Union in 1861. Even now it represents a serious and complex economic and social problem.

The most important contributions made by economists in their attempts to understand the problem and to elaborate a policy of intervention were concentrated above all in the 1950s and 60s. The American intervention in providing aid for Italian economic reconstruction and the formation of the Mutual Security Agency immediately after the Second World War encouraged some economists including P. Rosenstein-Rodan, H. Chenery and A. Hirschman to study the problem of the South of Italy and to put forward policies for growth.

At that time the South represented one of the first cases of underdevelopment examined by economists. This experience contributed in suggesting to Rosenstein-Rodan (1961) the theory of the 'big push', according to which a minimum amount of investment is a necessary, though not sufficient, condition of success. Chenery (1955) developed the use of input/output tables to study the productive structure of a given area and to elaborate investment policies aimed at modifying it.

These ideas exerted a certain influence on policies for the South also through the formation and the research activities of SVIMEZ (Associazione per lo sviluppo dell'industria nel Mezzogiorno) a centre for research and studies into the problems of growth in the South, founded in 1946. It was for at least a decade a very important point of reference for Italian and foreign economists, and produced numerous influential Italian economists. The ideas most of this group shared were: (a) a more or less radical criticism of the neoclassical model; (b) doubts about the ability of the 'invisible hand' to resolve the problems of growth and unemployment in Italy; (c) a general support for Keynesian theory in macroeconomic policy and for state intervention in the promotion of growth in the South.

The economist who probably contributed most to the study of the problem of the South and above all to the decision of public policy adopted in the 1950s, was P. Saraceno.[2] In his opinion, the main aim of Italian society consisted in achieving a more rapid and more balanced growth between the

North and South. In the early 1950s there was a very high level of national unemployment, accompanied by excess capacity in the North and insufficient plant in the South. The policy proposed was structural and Keynesian in that it was to generate public expenditure demand for infrastructure and productive investment in the South.

However, private capital was scarce and, what is more, it was not very willingly invested in the South, not only because there was excess productive capacity there, but also because the financial market was itself myopic; the presence of external diseconomies in the South discouraged investment there. Therefore, Saraceno proposed the intervention of state-owned firms, as such firms could draw on public finance which could be added to resources raised on the capital market and had entrepreneurial expertise. These firms were founded with social aims but were not obliged to maximize profits.

In order to avoid the growth of state industry in the South at the expense of private industry in the North, some incentives were proposed which modified the profitability of the different firms' choices, above all for those in the private sector. In Saraceno's opinion, however, social benefits must be calculated beside private returns and this can be done through economic planning.

The policy for the South during the 1950s fitted in with some of these ideas. A public agency 'Cassa per il Mezzogiorno' was created in 1950 with the aim of co-ordinating the extraordinary intervention which was needed. In the 1950s the main form of expenditure was on infrastructure. The insufficiency of this kind of intervention led, in the late 1950s to the second part of the programme suggested by Saraceno being introduced: that is to say, incentives were offered, above all, to large firms, to encourage them to invest in the South. This was done by reducing the cost of capital and promoting investment by state-owned corporations, particularly in the steel, engineering and petrochemical sectors.

This policy gave rise to two lively economic debates. The first one concerned the nature of dualism and was started by the contribution to the neoclassical approach made by Bresciani Turroni and Lutz.[3]

According to Bresciani Turroni (1957) the Italian problem was the low level of saving and the availability of capital-intensive technology used by firms in the North to maintain competitiveness in foreign markets. The result was a low rate of growth and unemployment in the South. As the most efficient allocation of resources can be achieved through the market, the policy for the South can consist on the one hand in slowing down the increase in wages in the North, favouring profits and therefore savings, and, on the other hand, in public investment in infrastructure so as to reduce the external diseconomies present in the South.

However, he considers migration from the South to the more developed areas within the country and abroad as inevitable and permanent. In Lutz (1962) the North–South dualism was, instead, caused by the presence of higher wages in the North due to the increased bargaining power of the trade unions. This wage dualism, together with technology, as already indicated in the work of R. Eckaus, generated two different economies: the advanced North and the backward South with low levels of employment. Such dualism can be overcome by migration to the North which brings down wages and facilitates an increase in the per capita income in the South and therefore an extension of the local market.

Lutz's criticism of the policy adopted for the South is twofold: on the one hand, she stressed that enforced industrialization does not change the basic situation, that is to say, the greater efficiency of firms in the North; on the other hand, she stressed that the transfer of resources to the South stimulates consumption and therefore favours the more efficient firms in the North and not those in the South. These conclusions do not only disagree with those of Saraceno and therefore with the actual pattern of intervention in the South, but also with the opinion of most Italian economists.

According to L. Spaventa, the dualism, both territorial and in terms of wages, is due to the dominance of large capital-intensive firms operating in oligopolistic markets. In A. Graziani's opinion this dualism derives from the fact that there has been export-led growth which favoured firms with high levels of capital intensity (Spaventa, 1959; A. Graziani, 1969). It can generally be said that economists agree on the kind of policy which should be adopted for the South, in that they recommend a policy in which the state and in particular the state-owned corporations play a very active role. However, the kind of incentive offered is criticized and this has led to a second important debate being started.

The policy chosen by the economic authorities back in the 1950s was above all one of financial incentives, designed to reduce the cost of capital and favouring new firms, investment and therefore industrial employment. However, this kind of incentive stimulated capital-intensive investment in the South of Italy, mostly by large firms. Further, as the latter also had a greater power in getting these discretional incentives, the result was that small labour-intensive firms, which are important for the spread of industrialization and increased levels of employment, received very little help. It is suggested that such incentives favoured the creation of 'cathedrals in the desert', that is to say, capital-intensive activities and vertical integration such as in the steel industry, the petrochemical industry and assembly lines in the car industry. In fact, such plant not only failed to stimulate other activities but actually discouraged them by causing the level of wages to rise.

The criticism of this kind of incentive which was initiated with a paper by G. Ackley and L. Dini (1960) was continued, primarily, by A. Graziani and F. Momigliano and it led to the modification of the kind of incentives being offered. In particular, Momigliano (1964) showed that the incentives generated lower costs, but such gains were almost completely offset by the higher costs incurred owing to external diseconomies. This meant that vertically integrated investments with high capital intensity were favoured, in other words, investments which were less subject to external diseconomies.

Things have been changing in the last two decades: the South is less poor and industry has been developing in some limited areas. The South, however, is still the main economic and social problem in Italy, due to the high rate of unemployment (about 20 per cent), the weakness of the manufacturing structure and to widespread marginal and illegal activities. A parallel economy has been developed. In spite of this economists today pay less attention to such problems.

The conviction that today social and political conditions are binding constraints for economic development, on the one hand, and the limited success of the policy for the South, together with the success of the idea that it is better to rely on market forces than on mistaken intervention, on the other hand, have contributed to make economists put the problem of the South lower down on the agenda of their research. A deep-felt pessimism regarding the perspectives of industrialization and economic development of the South is now commonly shared by economists, together with the idea that Italian industry would gain from European integration more than from a policy devoting important sources to an effort to move industry to the South.

Industrial Structure and Competitiveness

The studies regarding manufacturing structure and competition concentrate into two main periods: the years which followed the end of the Second World War (reconstruction) and the years which came after the two oil shocks (industrial restructuring). These studies generally follow certain established lines which we will now try to summarize.

From the point of view of the tools, the most frequently used models in quantitative analysis are concerned with input–output and the neoclassical production function.

The input output model was originally introduced in the early studies into the Italian economy carried out by Chenery and his researchers (see Chenery *et al.*, 1953; Cao-Pinna, 1952) and was used widely in the 1960s to describe the productive structure and to examine North–South relations (Lunghini, 1959; V. Conti *et al.*, 1973; Pilloton, 1968). However, in the 1970s and 80s it was frequently used to make a detailed examination of the energy content of the industrial system, the effects of international integration and also deindustrialization (see e.g. Silvani, 1985; Siniscalco, 1987; Pasinetti, 1986). The use of aggregate production functions in the study of the productive system followed the work of E. Denison on the contribution of various factors to economic growth. The conclusion of these studies was that most of Italy's rapid economic development was due to one variable – residual technical progress (De Meo, 1967). The theoretical criticism of the aggregate production function by P. Garegnani and L. Pasinetti led to this analytical tool being shelved for some time. In the 1980s, however, the production function was brought out again to make econometric estimates of the effects of variations in the prices of inputs on their use in various industrial sectors; and it was concluded that Italian industry had quickly adapted to the new relative prices (Heimler and Milana, 1984).

Studies of industries, which at least up to the 1970s were very infrequent, are generally of a descriptive nature and concentrate, above all, on aspects of production and on foreign trade. It is seldom possible to speak of case studies carried out to verify hypotheses related to competitive processes or to other aspects of the industrial organization. From the point of view of motivation, the thread which links the researchers is the question of the ability of Italian industry to sustain overall growth and to produce a foreign trade surplus so as to offset the two large deficits caused by the imports of foodstuffs and raw materials including energy; such studies confirm the Italian industrial economists' prevailing interest in Italy's current economic problems. The 'debates' which followed not only involved researchers and those economists who were more directly involved in the decision process, but also became topics of wider concern.

Let us now examine in more detail the two main periods of flowering of studies in industrial organization.

The period of post-war reconstruction was dominated, from an industrial point of view by two problems: the need to build up an efficient basic industry (Sinigaglia, 1948), and to face foreign competition. Wages were much lower than in the other more-industrialized countries, but the level of productivity was much lower too. A moderate growth of wages was the first variable that could enable Italy to reach a stable competitive position. Technical progress incorporated in new investment was the second. In fact, economists constantly dedicated special attention to technical progress in the later decades (see e.g. Autori Vari, 1960; A Graziani, 1964; Pasinetti,

1959; Vicarelli, 1967).

Industrial growth in the 1950s and 60s raised a question which numerous studies have tried to answer: that is, whether the growth of production was sustained by exports or by internal demand. The former position is put forward authoritatively by A. Graziani and has become the most widely accepted (see A. Graziani, 1969; for the opposite point of view see Ciocca *et al.*, 1973). Foreign demand for consumer durables favoured scale economies and the fast growth of productivity. The rapid growth of these sectors stimulated other industries and facilitated the increase of wages in all these sectors, mainly concentrated in the North. It followed a pattern of a virtuous circle of productivity–wage–demand, but a vicious circle consisting of the widening industrial gap between the North and the South.

Strictly speaking not all these contributions can be considered studies in industrial economics. They are mainly concerned with problems of the economic system as a whole, in which industry has a very important role. Actually, it was in the 1970s that industrial economics was established as an autonomous field of economic policy. The origins of the discipline arose from a debate about the concept of 'industry', which began with the crisis which hit European industry and Italian industry in particular in the late 1970s. Some sectors (steel industry, petrochemicals and textile industry) had serious difficulties because of over-production and competition from the NICs. Other sectors had to face Japanese and/or US competition – in cars, electronics, advanced engineering, chemicals and fibres. Therefore, there was a problem of industrial restructuring, that is to say, it was necessary to reduce certain activities, to modify their organization and build up others. It was accepted both on a European level and an Italian level that a structural policy was necessary to achieve such changes (see e.g. OECD, 1976). In Italy measures were approved that envisaged sectoral intervention and for the first time a sectoral policy was mentioned. A permanent government commission was set up for industrial policy (CIPI) which promotes systematic studies into numerous sectors.

However, as the definition of sectors used for public policy is very broad, while sectors are more narrowly defined by firms it was quite reasonable to ask whether it was sensible to draw up policies based on such a broad definition of sector. Two approaches were confronting each other (Fornengo Pent, 1984). On the one hand, there are those who argue in favour of the sectoral policy and therefore selective state intervention. This approach argues that the state must play an active part in the control of the economy. Instead, on the other hand, there is the approach which places greater faith in the 'invisible hand'. This approach is favoured by those who wish to encourage horizontal intervention which benefits all firms' infrastructures, innovation policies, public-sponsored research, training and efficient financial markets. At that time, the former approach prevailed. Facts now show that the Italian state's selective 'rationality' very often brought negative results and therefore the latter approach has begun to gain support.

The restructuring of Italian industry is the result of macroeconomic policy – monetary policy, state transfers to the firms – more than sectoral policies, with a few exceptions, such as the steel industry and the chemical industry. This restructuring essentially consisted in large firms regaining their productivity and innovating capacity, but also in strengthening previous productive specialization. These results which differentiate the Italian experience from that of the other advanced industrial countries were the basis of a great deal of applied research in the 1980s as well as some new theoretical papers. The success of large firms has drawn renewed attention to their role in the economy, and this will be discussed in another section.

At the same time, the examination of the productive structure and of foreign trade produced a number of empirical studies whose results can be summarized as follows. Using Pavitt's classifications (1984) which have had a strong following in Italy, it has been shown that industry is highly specialized in the traditional and scale-intensive sectors, while it is despecialized in the science-based and specialized suppliers sectors. This productive structure is confirmed by the pattern found in exports (Pierelli, 1983). Exports have a large direct and indirect content of imports: in fact it can be seen that there was a strong increase in the imports of intermediate products and in the total value of those products. These data, which have often been interpreted as an indicator of the weakness of the position of Italy in world trade have led to a number of different lines of research.

The first line of research, and perhaps the most important, is based on the assumption that if Italy was going to get out of its precarious position in terms of trade balance it was necessary to build up a more innovative manufacturing sector, showing higher investment in R & D. Therefore an appropriate industrial policy which favoured such a development was needed. Consequently, in the 1980s there was growing attention of economists both on a theoretical and an applied level, into the economics of innovation and of R & D: two aspects which will be dealt with separately in another section.

The second line of research examines in more detail the implications of this productive specialization in Italy. Generally speaking, most empirical studies tend to show that the patterns of trade are more a consequence of structural factors connected with the international division of labour than to a specific weakness of the Italian industry.

From the point of view of exports, the main conclusion which was reached can be summarized as follows. The big increase in exports as a part of aggregate final demand was partly the specific success of Italian industry in the above-mentioned sectors, but it was also partly structural and common to all the industrialized countries owing to various factors including intra-industry trade. Another result is the direct relationship between the competitiveness of Italian exports and the R & D content (see, respectively, Onida (ed.), 1985, and Momigliano and Siniscalco, 1984). Considering imports, however, the strong increase in import-penetration both in investment goods and intermediary goods is to be interpreted generally as due, on the one hand, to the fact that Italian industry had moved a stage nearer to final production and this meant that imports of intermediate products increased (these points are considered in G. Conti and Vona, 1987; Coricelli and Galimberti, 1989; Milana (ed.) 1988).

In conclusion, it might be said that the good performance of the Italian industry in the 1980s has quite changed the attitude of Italian economists with respect to the original assumption of its weakness. After all, 40 years of weakness have produced a rather competitive industry, even though the Italian industrial structure, both in terms of sectors and of size of the firms, is quite different from that of the most developed economies and is more vulnerable to foreign competition.

THE ANALYSIS OF IMPERFECT COMPETITION

The origins of the analysis of imperfect competition are well known and can be traced back to the contribution which Sraffa made to the debate which took place in *The Economic Journal* between 1922 and 1930. His article 'The Laws of Returns under Competitive Conditions' of 1926, which is now considered a classic, is at the basis of industrial economics. A less famous but equally important paper in Italian had been published the previous year, and the 1926 article represented a partial summary (Sraffa, 1925; 1926). In the later article, after a 'destructive criticism', as Keynes wrote, of Marshall's theory of the value of competition, Sraffa proposed an analysis of competition based on Cournot's theory of monopoly. He emphasized the fact that the obstacles which break up the unity of the market are not of the nature of frictions, as is assumed in traditional theory, but are themselves active forces. They produce various effects, two of which were very important to the further development of market analysis: (*a*) the producer can deliberately affect the market prices and (*b*) every manufacturer produces in conditions of increasing returns. Sraffa's contributions, although not foreign to the origins of Italian thought,[5] influenced Anglo-Saxon thinking above all and did not have any significant influence in Italy in the pre-war years which followed.

In fact, during the period between the two wars in Italy, there were no important contributions to the theoretical analysis of imperfect competition. Interest was concentrated on the problem of the formation of cartels and trusts and their effects on competition as well as on the pertinent legislation. In 1934 Marshall's *Industry and Commerce* was published in Italian as was *Cartels, Groups and Trusts* by R. Liefmann. This line of thought was developed in Italy by F. Vito, who took up the approach set out in the work of Barone (1921). Further, Vito contributed to the spread of foreign contributions through his reviews of books on monopolistic competition and imperfect competition by Chamberlin and by Robinson; and he followed the works of Stackelberg in Germany and Mason in the USA as well as the discussion regarding the search for a definition of workable competition: lastly he studied the formation of prices in conditions of cartels using the empirical material available at that time (see e.g. Vito, 1930; 1954; 1967).

This line of research was also followed at the end of the Second World War in studies into competition and monopoly which the *Assemblea Costituente* promoted in order to estimate the extent of monopolies in the Italian economy. There was particular interest in monopoly at that time because it has been strengthened by the economic policy of Fascism. Then in the 1970s the research was continued with studies carried out by the Parliamentary Commission on the limits of competition and in the book by Prodi (1969) on take-overs and mergers as the main tools of restructuring in conditions of oligopolistic competition (see Camera dei Deputati, 1965, and Prodi, 1969; see also P. Bianchi, 1986).

In the post-war period the best-known international contribution on a theoretical level was certainty made by Sylos-Labini in his book on oligopoly published in 1957.[6]

In the first part of his book Sylos-Labini considers the problem of equilibrium in oligopolistic markets characterized by discontinuous productive processes. Previously the problem had been treated in two classic ways: (*a*) one relative to the analysis of duopoly and the Cournot–Stackelberg and Edgeworth solutions, and (*b*) the one which proposes a single solution based on the hypotheses of a kinked demand curve and the full-cost principle suggested by Hall and Hitch and Sweezy in 1939 and by Andrews in 1949.

Sylos-Labini criticized the method of conjectural variations[7] and took as the starting-point of his argument the approaches of the Oxford economists as well as Sweezy's. In Sylos-Labini's opinion, the Hall and Hitch solution was insufficient because, although it was more realistic than the marginalistic solution, the formal rigour leaves something to be desired: especially, the hypothesis of a kinked demand curve which claims that price, once it has been fixed at an acceptable level by all the entrepreneurs, tends to stay where it is. Sweezy, too, does not explain prices and current production: the combination of prices and production that will occur in reality depends on 'previous history', says the American economist. Sylos-Labini wonders whether it is possible to say more about 'previous history' and his proposal is to give, like Andrews and Bain, maximum importance in the determination of equilibrium price to the condition of entry for new firms (to the behaviour of potential competitors), an aspect to which economists had previously paid scarce attention.

Sylos-Labini assumes that the potential competitors, when they determine price in a concentrated oligopoly, behave as if the existing firms adopt a policy which is the most unfavourable to them: the entrant assumes that the established firms will maintain their output, and will reduce the price, in the face of potential entry. This assumption, which was defined by Modigliani (1958) as 'Sylos's Postulate' was central to the analysis of oligopoly in the 1960s and 70s.

Although the analysis of the formulation of price in an oligopolistic situation was an important contribution to industrial economics, the influence of Sylos-Labini among Italian economists was not only or mainly in gaining a better understanding of oligopoly but it was also, as we have already said, in making a proposal for an enquiry which aims at building a bridge between micro and macroeconomics and in which realism and historical factors are considered necessary elements in carrying out useful theoretical work.

However, although there were not many critical reflections and detailed studies into Sylos-Labini's model, a number were published in the years which followed. R. Bianchi (1974; 1980) made an important formal contribution. He developed a long-term equilibrium model in a homogeneous oligopolistic market where the productive technology available is characterized by marked discontinuity; and it enables the validity conditions of Sylos-Labini's approach to be defined in a static environment. The configuration of equilibrium which has to be determined is one in which there is a collusive group of dominant large firms. This group in its search for an optimum configuration must take into account the existing competing firms – smaller firms whose role is to satisfy marginal sections of demand – and potential competitors: 'fringe' firms and large firms. These large firms have to face a behaviour which is assumed to be one of total opposition.

In a later article, Bianchi discusses Modigliani's model and shows that the 'critical price' can assume different meanings, depending on the structural context within which it is formed. Other formal contributions on oligopoly were made by Sassu[8] and Acocella[9].

Together with his formal works, Sylos-Labini's model (as well as those originating in Oxford and the one proposed by Bain) was considered as the most relevant contribution to the theory of oligopoly made in those years, and in the words of Salvati (1967) taken together they are the most reasonable alternative theory proposed up to now. But Salvati does not deny that such alternatives 'are valid only in particular market conditions and with restrictive assumptions of behaviour, especially in a dynamic context.'

A similar opinion had been expressed by Guerci (1965) who argued that the theory of oligopoly should be used to interpret real problems by rigorously checking how close the hypotheses being studied approach real situations. Sylos-Labini's model is not suitable for all possible situations: specifically, Guerci showed how the theory of limit price ignored lateral entry, that is to say, the entry of firms that already operate in other branches of industry. Moreover, the discussion on entry is complicated when innovative processes are taken into account because, in fact, it is possible that established firms do not pursue many cost-reducing opportunities, and these opportunities are explored by new firms. Finally, when the dynamics of long-term demand is considered, assuming it has an increasing trend, the simple definition of limit price is not enough to keep new competitors out;[10] in fact, the attractiveness of conducting a limit price policy for firms depends on a complex set of factors. Guerci is also the author of one of the few studies carried out in Italy into the relationship between market structure and profitability. He is the author of the only study in the 1960s into the relationship between concentration and profit,[11] topic which has given rise to many empirical researches abroad. In an article dated 1970, using the annual reports of the 200 largest Italian firms, he studied the links between levels of profit, size of firms, concentration and risk in the Italian economy during the period 1964–8. The hypotheses of Baumol, Steindl and Sylos-Labini, which suggest that levels of profit and size go hand in hand, are not confirmed. In fact the correlation turns out to be in general hardly significant, similar to the 'classic' relationships between concentration and levels of profit. On the other hand the study does find a positive correlation between the level of profit and risk, measured as the variance of each firm's rate of profit around the average level for all firms.

In the 1980s the model concerning barriers to entry regained a more 'rationalistic' approach, and this was done especially by applying the theory of games to the problem of oligopoly.

The 'Sylos's Postulate' was abandoned and replaced with an advantage of first move rule. Various kinds of criticism of the original model proposed by Bain/Sylos/Modigliani have been put forward, many of which usually refer to the rationality of the behaviour of the established and potential players. Interest in these new approaches is recent and still limited.[12]

One of the applications of the theory of games worth mentioning is a study by Grillo and Cossutta (1986)[13] in which a model of oligopolistic competition is developed which excludes potential competitors when there is surplus productive capacity, and it is applied to the European car industry, where the problem is treated in the form of a game of negotiation as in Nash.

Bonanno has developed a model of strategic entry deterrence on the lines of Dixit[14] which is used to examine the effects of two forms of uncertainty: the possibility that potential entrants can find investments more attractive than entry, and one where the commitment of those present in the market may not be observed by the potential entrants. In another paper Bonanno and Vickers (1988)[15] examine the strategic motive for vertical separation in a duopoly model.

LARGE FIRMS, SMALL FIRMS AND INDUSTRIAL AREAS

Italian industry has always been characterized by a strong dualism regarding size of firms: a limited number of large firms which employ a small percentage of the total workforce in the industry operate alongside a vast population of small firms which absorb most of the labour force.[16]

Up to the late 1960s industry was concentrated in the so-called 'industrial triangle' (North-West Italy), and consisted mainly of large firms which were the engine of the so-called 'economic miracle'. There was already, at that time, a constant increase in the number of small firms but it was considered to be largely a transitory phenomenon due to the rapid growth which had left them space in the market. In fact, the average size of firms and market concentration were both expected to increase.

Instead, in the 1960s a twofold split appeared in the then established model of industrial organization, and it widened in the 1970s: (*a*) industrialization spread progressively beyond the 'triangle', entering other northern regions (Veneto, Emilia) and some regions in Central Italy (Tuscany, Umbria and Marche); (*b*) the emerging organizational model, chiefly but not only in these regions, is one of small or medium-sized firms. Sometimes they were dependent on large firms, while at other times they were autonomous, and often organized in complex systems. Part of this restructuring was a result of the crisis of large firms whose labour costs were too high and whose organization was too rigid. It was, however, partly due to the ability of the small firms to be more efficient, especially in terms of productivity. Economists did not recognize this new trend immediately because there was insufficient data and because the theoretical paradigm of the large firm was still dominant.

The phenomenon was first studied in the late 1970s, not only by industrial economists but also by regional economists, sociologists and historians. Interest in such an organizational model was not limited to Italian economists, nor was the model specifically Italian.[17]

In Italy, however, the good performances achieved by small firms (high profits and high exports) induced some economists to argue that these firms were the engine of industrial growth, considering the inefficiency of the large firms compared to the efficiency of many small firms. Such a conclusion seemed to ignore the fact that in an international economy where large firms were competing, the absence of large efficient national firms was an element of decided weakness.

During the last few years attention has again moved in favour of the large firms which have got over the very serious crisis of the 1970s and early 80s and have regained a central role in the industrial structure. It is recognized that large productive organizations are indispensable in the new international situation.

The attitude of emphasizing the importance of either large firms or small firms depending on their relative success has hindered a balanced and detailed analysis of the physiological coexistence of the two kinds of firms and has prevented their respective limits being carefully considered.[18] Behind this debate there are two different opinions regarding the origins of industrial organization: some emphasize the role of internal economies, captured by the organization of a large corporation, while others consider that external economies can be captured by informal co-ordination and co-operation among small productive units. Both of these two hypotheses tend to de-emphasize the role for the market for inputs or for outputs as the main instrument of governance of transactions and efficiency.

Let us examine the two positions separately.

The Large Firm

As has just been mentioned, economic studies into the problems of large firms in Italy can be divided into two phases. The first – the 1950s and the 60s – was very much influenced by the theories of the large corporations emerging at that time, especially by the contributions of E. Penrose and R. Marris on the one hand and H. Simon and J. March on the other. The reason for the success of the two theories is twofold.

Firstly, with the priority given in Italy to problems of growth with respect of those of efficiency, the models proposed by Penrose and Marris were considered to be more useful than in neoclassical ones. Secondly, an 'a priori' methodological judgement or prejudice quite widespread among Italian economists is very important. The idea was that it was better to have a model which described reality more accurately starting from realistic hypotheses. The above-mentioned models were considered more realistic and therefore more acceptable than the neoclassical one.

The objective of satisfying profits seems to be more realistic than that of maximizing profit. The existence of 'organizational slacks' and the use of a procedural rationality instead of a subjective rationality seems to be a more accurate description of the actual behaviour of a large firm.

There was another and more profound reason for the criticism of the neoclassical model. At the basis of neoclassical theory, there is the idea that the organization of the economy is achieved through private contractual relationships between subjects motivated by individual interests. The market is the main organization through which exchanges take place. The firm, an institution which has the responsibility of production, is a set of individuals contract – coordinated by a subject who is sometimes called entrepreneur and sometimes principal. Such contracts, however, are different from those stipulated on the market.

This kind of approach, which is called 'contractual', can be compared to the 'institutionalist' one which considers that firms have a public function: their choices involve wider interests than those of the contractual subject influencing the whole economy. The behaviour of the large firm cannot and must not be sacrificed to the private interests of the shareholders or of the managers: the large firm is a public institution, not a private concern. This approach is supported with small changes by authors such as A. Berle, G. Means and J. Commons in the United States and W. Rathenau in Germany. It implies that the control of firms cannot be left to the market, nor is it sufficient to have an antitrust policy. Other public institutions are necessary which control or some way have an influence on the choices made by large firms.

The studies into large firms in Italy, at least until very recently, were closer to the 'institutional' approach than the contractual one. Three kinds of contributions can be identified. The first closely follows the new ideas on the theory of the large firm. In the early 1950s S. Lombardini (see particularly Lombardini, 1954; 1971) elaborated an approach to the analysis of the large firm that in many ways anticipated the one developed by Marris. He considered the large firm as an organic entity which can grow on its own and is independent of the system. Later, at the beginning of the

1970s Lombardini developed a model of growth for markets in an economy where monopoly was widespread.

A further link with the theory of the large firm and in particular with Marris was through the work done by Filippi and Zanetti (1965; 1971). These two scholars began with an important, and in some ways pioneering, initiative of creating databanks which annually collected suitably revised annual reports of a large number of large firms. Using this information they checked the relationship between profit levels and the size of firms and found an inverse relationship between the two variables. They also examined the Marris relationship between growth and profitability. In the years which followed this initial work the usefulness of a temporal series of company data showed up when it was used to examine trends of behaviour and the results of large firms taken together. This data was used, for example, to study functions of investment, what determines productivity, the effects of the inflationary process on real and financial variables, the ways in which firms respond to changes in the prices of inputs, etc.

A second kind of contribution was made by F. Momigliano who, more than any of the others, tried to build a kind of general model of industrial organization in which the large private firm was given a central role.[19] He has a dualistic vision of the industrial structure. On the one hand, there are the large firms whose importance is destined to grow in time and which form the framework of industry, while on the other hand there are the small firms which exist and often prosper in niches of the market which the large firms leave them. The reason he expects large firms to increase their weight is twofold: the internationalization of markets which at that time was just beginning, leads to increased size, increased use of electronic technology and communication systems which enable firms to increase their area of hierarchic control without creating organizational diseconomies. He also argues that large firms are not only economic but also social and political institutions. Consequently sociological and juridical theories should be combined with the economic ones so as to build up a more complete theory of the firm. The control of large firms follows rules of rationality. However, this rationality

is achieved not through the search for an absolute abstract optimum but through a systematic search, facilitated by new methods of Operational Research, new methods of simulations with computer systems, better ways of finding relative solutions from among a high number of alternative concrete possibilities for a relative optimum in relation to what often appears from outside as a constellation of multiple objectives (Momigliano, 1975, p. 281).

Momigliano attributes an important role to large firms in the promotion of Italian growth and the rationality of the economic system. External factors, including particularly a very elastic supply of labour, have certainly favoured growth. However, as in the Penrose and Marris models, the growth of large firms generated their own demand and their own finance, while on the other hand the need to programme production flows led to an improved organization of the markets.

One problem is still to be solved and that is to make sure that the behaviour of the managers of large firms is in line with public interest. According to Momigliano, the solution to this problem is not the state-owned corporation. Italian experience suggests that it is not a guarantee of efficiency and that such firms grow following individual strategies, but not a national strategy defined by policy-makers (Momigliano, 1975). On the other hand, Momigliano, as most Italian economists with the exception of a meagre group of liberals, considers that an antitrust policy is 'liberal nostalgia' and is now out of date. The only solution for the control of industry that brings coherence to the choices of large firms, and is in keeping with the collective interest, appears to be through planning which has the power necessary to know and influence private choices.

The third more significant contribution on the theme of large firms is the one offered by Saraceno (1975) who built an interpretative model of the state-owned corporation. The system of state ownership in Italy was created in 1936 following a banking crisis and was extended after the Second World War.[20] It consists of three groups made up of three financial holdings owned and controlled by the state through majority shareholdings in a group of firms which are companies with a private juridical structure. Many of them with a minority private participation are quoted on the Stock Exchange. Therefore these firms do not have a single aim but two conflicting aims, this makes it more difficult and complicated to evaluate their results. This is because capital companies have profit as their objective and their performance is judged by the market, whilst companies which are controlled by the state can be assigned public aims such as public investment in the South or, in particular sectors, to defend employment, etc., and their performance is judged by politicians who in the final analysis are the real principals of such firms. According to Saraceno the pursuit of these two aims should not be the cause of confusion and inefficiency. The main aim of these firms should be exactly the same as that of the large private firm, and entrusting them with different aims would mean higher costs, that is to say improper charges. Once these costs have been valued, the public authority should transfer to these firms the financial resources necessary at no cost, the so-called 'dotation' funds, which would compensate firms for their improper charges. This raises a twofold problem: the owner, that is to say the politician, is concerned about the political results and therefore his managers do not have any incentive to ensure that the organization is run efficiently, while on the other hand it is seldom possible to measure the improper charges and therefore determine to what degree a certain result, measured in terms of rate of profit, is due to such charges or the inefficiency of the managers. In fact this confusion has been the cause of big losses for many years in the 1960s and 70s.

The decade 1975–85 was characterized by the scarce analytical interest shown by Italian economists in the theory of the firm. The new developments beginning with the papers by A. Alchian and H. Demsetz in 1972 were accepted much later. On the one hand, the good performances of the small firms attracted all the attention and on the other hand the crisis of the large firms shaded their image as leading actor in industrial development. The few studies regarding investment by large firms and their performance carried out by examining the data of their annual reports are exceptions (see Zanetti, 1976; Filippi, 1983). More recently, the generally unexpected recovery of large firms has brought them back into the limelight perhaps more than ever before and not only for economists.

The economic studies which this new-found interest has stimulated are characterized by a rather descriptive approach. The common aim is that of describing the various aspects of the new phenomena of success and growth of large firms.

Lines of study which had been almost totally absent from economic debate, for example the external growth of the firm, the relationship between the stock exchange and large firms and investment abroad began to be examined.[21] The study of the firms' behaviour that led to the reversal of the negative performance encouraged industrial economists and scholars of management sciences to collaborate and compare results. Such contacts had been almost completely nonexistent previously. A body of literature was built up of both old and new case histories of large firms. Studies, which were particularly influenced by the ideas of M. Porter and by O. Williamson, were carried out into the strategies and the organization of large firms. A rather original development in this field is offered by the examination of a structure which is typical of large firms in Italy: that is to say, firms organized in groups where control lies in the hands of a family (in particular, see Brioschi *et al.*, 1988). Finally, many studies were dedicated to a type of behaviour which was fairly diffuse in Italian firms, namely, agreements and joint ventures. The theoretical approach of these studies was a typically transaction costs approach (Mariti and Smiley, 1983).

Small Firms

Studies regarding small firms, their relationships with large firms and their organization within a system are one of the most interesting contributions of industrial economics in Italy. For many reasons these studies were not stimulated by the wish to create an analytical framework on which to build new theoretical models or to use existing models and check them out by elaborating the data available. The first reason was the lack of models, for only recently did economic theory begin to produce models of industrial organization; however, they were mainly concerned with problems of static efficiency in large firms. Secondly, the available systematic data which can be used for the study of small firms were limited in Italy. Consequently, it was inevitable that researchers turned to carrying out surveys into specific situations of single industries or geographic areas. Thirdly, the aim of the research into this topic was generally to describe 'what was happening' in the economic and social ambient which surrounded the researcher and much less frequently was it to build up a theory that could be used generally. Last but not least it must be said that this kind of research attracted scholars who shared a methodological approach that favoured the 'esprit de finesse' instead of the 'esprit de geometrie'. In other words the more fruitful approach of study was considered to be the one that kept the phenomenon being studied as a whole and relied on intuition and theoretical eclecticism to consider the economic variables and what they can influence. This method was preferred to the analytical one that classifies reality into its various variables so as to build a general theory model concerning these single variables. Case studies were the natural result of such an approach.

The study of small firms was not generally directed to the question of how small firms can coexist with large firms in a competitive world: with few exceptions Italian industrial economists did not focus attention on competition.[22] The study of small firms instead was directed towards another classical problem of industrial organization, the question as to why such a large percentage of transactions was not governed internally by a few large firms nor by the market but by intermediate forms which linked the firms and the market (federations) and so co-ordinated the activities of many small firms (see e.g. Mariotti and Cainarca, 1986; Dei Ottati, 1987).

Mariti (1980) proposes four theoretical models which can be used to answer this question. The first model is the one which adopts the transaction costs proposed by O. Williamson and successively the theory of incomplete contracts. This became the most frequent theoretical reference. The second is the heterodox theory of production proposed by N. Georgescu-Roegen which can, above all, be used to interpret the phenomenon of vertical integration involving a number of elementary productive units (see particularly Tani, 1987). The Georgescu-Roegen model gained a following in Italy which it did not have elsewhere. This was because of the fairly widespread belief that the neoclassical model was inadequate as a tool to understand actual economic phenomena. The third economic model is Smith's theory of the extension of the market and its effects on vertical integration of firms. The most frequent references are to papers presented by A. Young and G. Stigler on the relationships between the size of the market and of the firm. The fourth is the much used concept of industrial districts elaborated by A. Marshall which shows how a system of firms situated in certain areas and co-ordinated by non-hierarchical relations can generate external economies not for the single firm but for the whole system.

The analysis of these facts brought to light the following characteristics regarding small firms and the inputs market to which they accede:

1. Small firms with a labour force of between 20 and 99[23] generally cannot be considered to be 'marginal' and they possess productive technology which cannot be classified as backward;[24]
2. Small firms specialize in activities with low economies of scale or where such savings are of little importance and where demand is highly variable and differentiated;
3. Small firms are generally part of a system of complex productive transactions with both large and small firms and this relationship is governed neither by the market nor by a hierarchy;
4. Small firms enjoy particularly favourable conditions in the labour market: lower wages, more favourable industrial relations;[25] but less favourable financial conditions: interest rates are higher and there is limited access to credit.

Three main kinds of organizational patterns were identified for small firms. The first which was, above all, a characteristic of the 1970s and the areas where there are large firms is known as 'productive decentralization'. The greater rigidity of the labour force and its higher cost obliged large firms to buy services, products and parts of products from small firms instead of making or providing them internally. The latter, in fact, produced goods at lower cost for the reasons already mentioned (see Wellisz, 1957; Contini and Revelli, 1986). Small firms are suppliers to large firms and they are often dependent on them, in other words, they are subject to 'lock-in' effects (see Brusco, 1982; see also Enrietti, 1983).

The second, known as 'flexible specialization', concerns firms which produce mainly for the market, that is to say they are not suppliers to one or a few large firms. Their efficiency depends on specialization or productive flexibility, in other words, on the existence of situations in which mass production is inefficient (see particularly Barca and Magnani, 1985; Brusco, 1986). In the case of specialization, there are single-product firms whose costs are lower because there are learning economies linked to highly specialized work on a small scale. In the case of flexibility, the advantage derives from the firm's ability to adapt production to frequent quality changes, thanks to the simplicity of organization and to the use of flexible plants. The relatively wide-ranging effort dedicated to studying such technological aspects was a particular characteristic of industrial economics in Italy. The initial hypothesis was designed to show that the technological flexibility of small firms was a factor which gave small firms an advantage over large ones. More recent surveys, however, indicate that large firms too have regained their flexibility and economies of scale are again an advantage (see Cainarca *et al.*, 1989).

The third organizational model is the one of 'industrial areas'. In each area there are few vertically integrated firms and most of them carry out one or a few phases (intermediate or final) of the complete production process. The rigid division of labour between the firms generates economies of specialization. What is more, the production function of each small firm is more elastic than that of a large firm, and as more than one firm is specialized in the same phase of production the overall productive structure can rapidly change, so giving to the system great elasticity to satisfy fluctuations in demand. Further, the parallel presence of numerous firms provides the group with greater overall flexibility, that is to say the ability to differentiate the product without incurring high costs. The relationships between firms which are in the same productive phase, be it intermediate or final, are characterized by a strong competitive spirit. However, there are very close contractual links generated by the frequency of tied transactions with other firms which are upstream or downstream in the productive process. Usually these ties are not for very long periods of time and they are not hierarchical. The nature of these contrasts is determined within a social ambience that permits a flow of information between the firms about reciprocal capacity and reliability; in other words, reputation is created and consequently the use of external institutions in arbitration is less frequent and transaction costs are lower. This is the second advantage of this organizational model, together with high elasticity and flexibility of production. The constant relationship, both as competitors and as suppliers, between firms generates a third advantage, that is an intense flow of information about processes and markets, and this means there is a more rapid diffusion of innovations and an impulse to competitive processes. Finally, a further advantage of this organizational model concerns labour costs; for generally in the labour market there are conditions which provide firms with low-cost mobility of labour and moderate levels of income. This exogenous situation is generated by a social environment where there is a supply of skilled labour and where there is a prevailing attitude which can be described as follows: 'when you work you do so without cheating yourself or others', that is to say, there is a low propensity of opportunism (or the possibility of opportunism).

Given certain exogenous conditions regarding technology, demand and the labour market, such an environment improves the efficiency of a certain kind of organization based not on a hierarchical order but on formal and informal relationships which contain elements of competition and of co-operation. This kind of ambience generates internal economies from which the single firm can benefit. The limit to this sort of organization is the lack of a single planning centre which can offer services regarding production and sales. This gap is often filled by institutions set up by a number of firms or by relying on public institutions created to act in the interest of the specific areas.[26]

The various organizational models of small firms are to be found in different forms all over Italy because of the different territorial distribution of the various industries and different cultural traditions. This pattern of growth, above all in the so-called Third Italy[27] is said to be characterized by 'urbanized countryside' or in other words the distribution of factories in all parts of the country so that they are not concentrated around certain large urban centres, where large firms prevail.

ECONOMICS OF INNOVATION

Studies regarding the economics of innovation were, to a certain extent at least, stimulated by the researches on an aggregate level carried out by A. Graziani and De Meo into the growth of industrial production and into the contribution of capital and labour inputs to economic growth in Italy during the 1950s and early 60s.[28] They showed that Italian industry had improved productivity at an high average annual rate, above all in Northern and Central Italy, which was exceptional even when compared to international levels. These studies raised the twofold question of which factors the actual increase in productivity should be attributed to, and which processes determine technical progress.

The first problem was considered in terms of a macroeconomic approach to economic growth: De Meo's thesis, according to which growth was to be attributed essentially to autonomous technical progress, was most criticized. The second problem – what are the determinants of technical progress? – led to the question about innovation.[29] The hypotheses of the analysis were derived from Schumpeter, an author whose influence in Italy was not insignificant because his ideas were spread by some of the most important Italian economists of the immediate post-war period: Graziani, Napoleoni, and Sylos-Labini (who was one of Schumpeter's students at Harvard). Momigliano (1975) took up the debate on the contribution of Schumpeter and the 'Schumpeterian' Hypothesis. His specific contribution in the 1970s looks essentially at two factors: the role and the activities of R & D in large firms, and innovation policy. Momigliano assumed that the protagonist of innovation was no longer the Schumpeterian entrepreneur but 'the ability to forecast and plan the large firm'; the R & D laboratory and managerial technostructure: 'The technostructure innovates, . . . because it is necessary and it is possible to ensure a continuous flow of innovations so as to create and condition new demand and in this way successfully manage competition in oligopolistic markets'.

Thus, Momigliano carries out his investigation under the headings of organizational theory and decisional models, the way in which innovations are planned and the criteria on the basis of which they are directed and adopted. Momigliano also states that a public policy in R & D is necessary because of technological delays and market failures.[30]

The role of the diffusion of innovation in creating technological advantage was recognized rather late in international economic literature. The first study carried out in Italy into the characteristics of the process of the diffusion of innovations was made by Prodi (1970) who, through the empirical analysis of a number of cases, focused attention on the singular situation of notable capacity to absorb innovations rapidly and the weakness of autonomous innovation which characterized industrial growth in Italy up to the threshold of the 1970s.

Since the mid-1970s there has been notable progress at an international level in the empirical description and the conceptualization of the sources, characteristics and direction of technical change as well as the study of competition between potential innovators. In Italy the most important stimuli have come from some reflections on evolution theory by Nelson and Winter and on the exogenous conception of technological change put forward by Freeman, and more recently by the work of Rosenberg and David.[31]

Among the numerous studies that have been developed along such lines there have been many dedicated to the characteristics of innovative processes in certain industries and in relation to certain kinds of technology. Various studies can be mentioned here, e.g. those into microelectronics carried out by Dosi (1984) and Malerba (1985) as well as the ones by Cainarca, Colombo and Mariotti (1987) on the diffusion of flexible automation and studies on the diffusion of new information technologies by Antonelli (1985; 1988 (ed.)).

From the point of view of the conceptualization of innovative processes, Amendola (1984; Amendola and Gaffard, 1988) and Dosi and Egidi (1987) consider innovation as a process of generation of new skills and the solution of problems. Amendola has criticized the traditional image of innovation as a linear process without feedback and separate from production which is achieved through the adoption of new machines and products, which had previously been conceived. He suggests that the innovative process is brought about in one sequential analytical scheme in which its development takes place in the production process; in this way the essence of production becomes the specialized research for the most suitable ingredients with which to solve a problem.

Dosi and Egidi suggest that innovation is a procedure through which the innovator, when successful, solves a particular set of problems more efficiently, and hence, through the resulting routines, reduces complexity and procedural uncertainty: 'The main activity of each agent . . . will try to find . . . new and . . . deterministic procedures of control . . . The permanent gap between the efficiency of the currently existing information and knowledge defines the uncertain domain of Schumpeterian innovative behaviours'.

This activity of solving problems, however, implies the development of models and procedures. Dosi (1982; 1984) introduces the concept of a technological paradigm. This technological paradigm is a pattern for the solution of technoeconomic problems, for example semiconductors, the chemistry of synthesis, or the internal combustion engine. Dosi shows that technical change in microelectronics can be represented by an exponential trajectory (a concept also taken up by Nelson and Winter) of the improvement in the relations between the 'density of the electronic chips, speed of computation, and cost per bit of information'.

An attempt was made to incorporate the new characteristics of the innovative ambience in a model built up by Silverberg, Dosi and Orsenigo (1988) that investigates the nature of diffusion processes in an environment characterized by technological diversity and the different behaviour of the economic agents, uncertainty, learning and disequilibrium dynamics.

A Schumpeterian hypothesis that has never received due support is the one which proposes a positive relationship between profitability and innovation. Antonelli (1989) has re-examined such a relationship on the basis of a sample of Italian firms, and has found that empirical data does not confirm the Schumpeterian hypothesis that a direct relationship exists between the two variables; while there is an inverse relationship according to which losses appear to stimulate innovative efforts, following a failure inducement pattern of R & D expenditure; a relationship which can also be found in March and Simon.

An important question in the study of technological change is the one concerning the measurement of inventive and innovative activities. The indicators which are most commonly used to do this are the statistics on the resources destined for R & D and those on the registration of patents. On the basis of a study into the diffusion of innovation in Italian industry, a recent paper (Archibugi *et al.*, 1987) explored the degree to which such indicators are representative of innovative activity. The findings suggest that they reflect the phenomenon of the intensity of innovation quite faithfully, although there are significant differences between sectors. The indicators quoted in fact ignore technical change resulting from the application in one sector of innovations derived from other sectors: a typical example being the textile industry in which most innovations come from suppliers of equipment and materials. Antonelli (1986) has used the international diffusion of innovative processes as a measure of technological change and it turns out to be the most important factor in explaining the flows of international trade and competitiveness in a non science-based sector such as textiles.

CONCLUSIONS

The overview of the Italian contribution has enabled us to explain and clarify the discussion of the assumptions made regarding the lines of research followed by Italian industrial economists and in these short concluding remarks an attempt is made to point out some other implications.

The originality of the Italian contribution which in the 1970s was at different levels has been emphasized at various stages. Firstly, the breadth of vision with which some of the topics, such as small firms, relationships between industrial structure and competitiveness in the economic system as well as the implications of structural industrial policy have been considered, and the reasons why such factors were given such importance are to be found above all in the uniqueness of the socioeconomic conditions and the growth model that characterized the Italian economy during those years.

Secondly, the originality is apparent in the methodological approach and in the range of questions which Italian economists ask. Here it can be seen how the Italian approach to industrial economics has been strongly influenced by historicism, and how the need for realism has prevailed over the use of a formal respectful approach. Further, it can be noted how political and ideological projects were strongly represented as underlying factors in the formulation of the economic problems.

This originality has also meant a progressive loss of direction and undoubted delay when compared to the development of the discipline elsewhere.

As is well known, since the 1970s industrial economics in the United States and particularly in Great Britain has undergone such radical changes with respect to the dominant Harvardian approach that the expression a 'new industrial economics' has been coined. From a methodological point of view, these new approaches have made increasing use of microeconomic tools and models of imperfect competition. They have also adapted notions from the theory of games so as to replace static analysis with one which embodies the dynamics of industrial structures, and often hypotheses that economic agents operate in conditions of incomplete information have been used. It has therefore been fundamental to abandon simple generalizations. On a theoretical level, aspects which are crucial to the old industrial economics, such as the importance of economies of scale in determining the degree of concentration and the role of barriers to entry, have undergone a profound revision, too.

In this way the analysis of the causes, the nature and the affects of competitive behaviour as assumed in the Harvardian approach, which had tried to avoid being put into the context of a precise microeconomic model, is radically reviewed and criticized.

In Italy these new approaches had an echo, at first limited and considerably delayed in their effect, chiefly because, as has been mentioned earlier, the classic Harvardian approach was only partially accepted in our country. The turning-point, if that is what it can be called, was in the 1980s, and it was due as much to its own theoretical limits (as in the Mason–Bain approach) as to the crisis of the political aims that had influenced it up to that time; thus the model of industrial economics which was dominant in the 1970s has tended to become obsolete.

Except for the neo-Marshallian approach, which, as has been said above, is very much alive on a theoretical level in Italy and internationally, there has been a growing convergence towards the mainstream analysis, thanks to the increased presence of many young Italian economists at British and American universities. The contribution of Italian researchers within this area, however, is still modest if measured in terms of articles published in international journals, but it is growing.

It is hoped that this trend is not a question of a dogmatic convergence but active participation. However it should be remembered that the importance of institutional and cultural factors should be not ignored in the elaboration of models, since focusing attention on such points represents, perhaps, the most important contribution made by the Italian reflections on Industrial Economics in the 1960s and 70s.

Notes

1. These problems and relative discussions are described in A. Graziani (ed.) (1972). See also Grindrod (1955).
2. The great influence of Saraceno both in the elaboration of policies and ideas went beyond the problem of the South, and it is the fruit of a very special combination of circumstances, experience and contacts. His academic training and work was not typical of an economist: he was scholar and university teacher of banking and business administration, but also had a detailed and personal knowledge of the workings of corporations, having worked before the Second World War for IRI (Istituto per la Ricostruzione Industriale). This state-owned corporation, together with the Bank of Italy, was for decades one of the main places for industrial and financial management training, as well as being one of the main centres for the elaboration of ideas and projects that were eventually to influence economic and industrial policy. He was encouraged to study and take part in a wide range social and economic activities by Vanoni, an economist and politician of notable influence on the Catholic left and ideologically a critic of liberal policies. Saraceno himself became an influential exponent of this political faction, contributing among other things to the elaboration of policies for the South and the general economic policy of the 1960s, a time when the alliance between the Catholics and the Socialists led to increased state intervention in the economy and in particular in industry.
3. This British economist contributed much with his writings and with his frequent visits to Italy, above all to the Bank of Italy, to the development of economic thought particularly on the question of economic growth and monetary policy. Although her views did not gain much following at the time, she certainly helped to stimulate a higher level of economic analysis.
4. Among the main recent contributions on this topic see Del Monte and Giannola (1978); Siracusano *et al.* (1986); Sylos-Labini (1985); Sarcinelli (1989).
5. In particular there were the contributions made by Barone in 1984 on the unacceptability of the supply curve in conditions of increasing costs and Amoroso's pro-Cournotian position against Edgeworth. See Barone (1894), Amoroso (1921), Edgeworth (1922).
6. Sylos-Labini (1957): a preliminary edition was published in 1956 for limited circulation.
7. He argues 'there is no limit to the conjectural variations. The solutions are infinite', a disconcerting situation whose problems, from the point of view of the theory of value, had been pointed out by Napoleoni (1956). There are almost no contributions following the Cournot–Edgeworth approach, a

significant exception being the contribution by Contini (1968), in which the author examines the possible alternatives to price discrimination in a closed model of bilateral monopoly *à la* Edgeworth.

8. Sassu (1978) applied Bianchi's model to the problem of the adoption and diffusion of innovation.

9. Acocella (1979) proposed a dynamic model of oligopoly in which he analysed the conditions regulating the existence and the stability of equilibrium for a dominant group of oligopolistic firms which have two control variables: price and R & D expenditure.

10. Gaskins (1971), using the theory of optimal control to examine a situation in which the demand function is increasing over time, concludes that the optimal price equilibrium is higher than the price limit.

11. Guerci (1970). In the 1970s another study about the same topic was by Valcamonici (1977). Studies into concentration were more numerous and we can mention Battara (1965), Boni and Gros-Pietro (1967) and more recently Arrighetti (1989).

12. Two important reviews and reflections on recent trends in oligopoly theory can be found in Delbono (1987) and Delbono and Scarpa (1988).

13. The results of the model show that in conditions of uncertainty and surplus capacity it is possible to find a strictly positive probability of there being a price war between producers, or in other words each firm follows an aggressive policy aimed at eliminating some of the other competitors in the market.

14. Bonanno (1988). In the model it is shown that 'even very small probabilities of no entry and of failure to observe commitment may be sufficient to eliminate the attractiveness of actions aimed at deterring entry' (p. 361).

15. It is shown that vertical separation, in conjunction with an appropriate contract between manufacturer and retailer, can be a profitable strategic move which works by inducing the rival firm to act in a more friendly manner.

16. The first inquiry into dimensional dualism, based on the data of the industrial census is to be found in Bruni (1961).

17. The small firms' new role in industrial organization in the 1970s and 80s is examined above all in Piore and Sabel (1984). The authors emphasize the importance of specialization to the success of small firms in some countries including Italy, Japan and partly in Germany.

18. As S. Wellisz wrote as early as 1957, when referring to Italian industry, 'the relation between large and small business is one of cooperation beneficial to both sides as well as one of competition' (Wellisz, 1957, p. 122).

19. The beginnings of autonomous development in industrial economics in Italy can be traced in Momigliano. Just as Saraceno, he brings together the activities of studying and teaching and a very active participation at a practical level in a large private company – Olivetti. He also worked as economic consultant to the government. It is possible to understand, therefore, his assiduous attempt to bring theory and company practices together, and in this way make private choice coherent with public policy through continual communication between the two levels of policy-making. This author's main ideas on the theme of large firms and market forms are gathered in Momigliano (1975).

20. In that year the first group IRI was created. The other two groups ENI (Ente

Nazionale Idrocarburi) and EFIM (Ente per il Finanziamento dell'Industria Meccaniceo) were created after the Second World War and at the same time the government body which oversees them, the Ministero delle Partecipazioni Statali.

21. A collection of comments on this theme as well as an examination of the results of Italian firms can be found in Banca d'Italia (1988); particularly on internationalization of the firms see R & P (Ricerche & Progetti) (1988).

22. An interesting exception in this field of study regarding small firms is offered in the researches of Contini and Revelli (1986) on the birth and death of firms. Using longitudinal data supplied by INPS (Istituto Nazionale per la Previdenza Sociale) relative to certain limited variables for a universe of Italian firms and a greater number of accounting variables for a wide sample of firms, Contini established that: (*a*) in the case of small firms the greater the number of entries, the greater is the selection; (*b*) survival is influenced by organizational and productive choices that require entrepreneurial ability; (*c*) selection does not mean, at least in the medium term, a levelling of profit margins. See in particular Contini (1984).

23. Firms with fewer than 20 employees often have craft characteristics and benefit from laws which regulate industrial relations and this means that their labour costs are lower than those of larger firms.

24. In the 1970s and up to the middle of the 1980s, small firms invested much more in machinery than large firms. See Barca (1988).

25. It should be remembered that in the 1970s industrial relations were characterized by bitter conflict, above all in large firms.

26. For information regarding industrial districts see Bagnasco (1988); Becattini (ed.) (1987); Brusco (1982), Fuà and Zacchia (eds) (1983); Garofoli (1987).

27. This term generally refers to that part of the country outside the industrial triangle and Southern Italy: in other words, North-East and Central Italy.

28. De Meo (1965); the already quoted Graziani (1964) and Vicarelli (1967).

29. This transfer of interest to the determinants of technical progress was also induced by the criticism, already mentioned, of the aggregate production function by the so-called neo-Ricardians.

30. The organization and effects of policies to encourage applied research, innovation and technological modernization in the Italian industrial economy was the subject of continual study in the works of Momigliano. For the most recent work see Momigliano (ed.) (1986).

31. It should be noted that other theoretical approaches such as the game-theoretic approach to the problem of the relationship between market structure and innovation have not given rise to many original contributions: the only exceptions being of the very recent paper by Delbono (1989) and Delbono and Denicolò (1989).

Bibliography

ACKLEY, G. and DINI, L. (1960) 'Agevolazioni Fiscali e Creditizie per lo Sviluppo dell'Italia Meridionale', *Moneta e Credito*, March. xiii pp. 25–52.

ACOCELLA, N. (1979) 'L' Equilibrio Oligoplistico in un Contesto Dinamico',

Note Economiche xii pp. 3–29.

AMENDOLA, M. (1984) 'Productive Transformations and Economic Theory', *Quarterly Review*, Banca Nazionale del Lavoro, vi 151 pp. 351–366.

AMENDOLA, M. and GAFFARD, J.L. (1988) *The Innovative Choice: An Economic Analysis of the Dynamics of Technology*, New York: Basil Blackwell.

AMOROSO, L. (1921) *Lezioni di Economia Matematica*, Bologna: Zanichelli.

ANTONELLI, C. (1985) 'The Diffusion of an Organizational Innovation. International Data Telecommunications and Multinational Industrial Firms', *International Journal of Industrial Organisation* 3, pp. 109–118.

ANTONELLI, C. (1986) 'The International Diffusion of Process Innovations and the Neo-technology of International Trade', *Economic Notes*, no. 1, pp. 60–83.

ANTONELLI, C. (ed.) (1988) *Information Technology and Industrial Change: The Italian Case*, Boston: Klumer Academic Publisher.

ANTONELLI, C. (1989) 'A Failure-Inducement Model of R & D Expenditure. Italian Evidence from the Early 1980's', *Journal of Economic Behaviour and Organization* xii, pp. 159–80.

ARCHIBUGI, D. CESARATTO, S. and SIRILLI, G. (1987) 'Attività Innovativa, R & S e Brevetti: Un Analisi dei Risultati dell' Indagine CNR–ISTAT sulla Diffusione dell' Innovazione', *L' Industria*. Rivista di economia e politica industriale, no 4, pp. 497–514.

ARRIGHETTI, A. (1989) 'Forme di Mercato e Dinamica della Concentrazione Industriale in Italia', in Padoan *et al.* (eds), *Concorrenza e Concentrazione nell' Industria Italiana*, Bologna: il Mulino.

AUTORI VARI (1960) *Il Progresso Tecnico e la Societa' Italiana*, Milano: Giuffrè.

BAGNASCO, A. (1988) *La Costruzione Sociale del Mercato*, Bologna: il Mulimo.

BALLONI, V. (1978) *Origini, Sviluppo e Maturità dell'Industria degli Elettrodomestici*, Bologna: il Mulino.

BANCA D'ITALIA (1988) 'Ristrutturazione Economica e Finanziaria delle Imprese', a special issue of *Contributi all' Analisi Economica*, Roma: Banco d'Italia.

BARBETTA, G.P. and SILVA, F. (eds) (1989) *Transformazioni Strutturali delle Imprese Italiane*, Bologna: il Mulino.

BARCA, F. and MAGNANI, M. (1989) 'L'Industria tra Capitale e Lavoro', Bologna: Il Mulimo.

BARCA, F. (1988) 'La Dicotomia dell'Industria Italiana: Le Strategie delle Piccole e delle Grandi Imprese in un Quidicennio di Sviluppo Economico', Roma: Banca d'Italia.

BARONE, E. (1894) 'Sul Trattamento di Questioni Dinamiche', *Giornale degli Economisti* ix, pp. 407–35.

BARONE, E. (1921) 'Les Syndacats (Cartelles et Trusts)', *Revue de Metaphysique et de Morale* (Italian edition, *La Nuova Collana degli Economisti* 9, Torino: UTET 1934).

BATTARA, P. (1965) 'La Concentrazione Industriale', in *Atti della Commissione Parlamentare di Inchiesta sui Limiti Posti alla Concorrenza*, Roma.

BECATTINI, G. (1979) 'Dal Settore Industriale al Distretto Industriale', *Rivista di Economia e Politica Industriale* i, pp. 7–21.

BECATTINI, G. (ed.) (1987) *Mercato e Forze Locali: Il Distretto Industriale*, Bologna: il Mulino.

BIANCHI, P. (1984) *Divisione del Lavoro e Ristrutturazione Industriale*, Bologna: il Mulino.

BIANCHI, P. (1986) 'Nuova concorrenza dinamica e potere di mercato', *L'Industria* vi, pp. 65–104.

BIANCHI, R. (1974) 'Economie di Scala e Barriere all' Entrata. Un Modello di Oligopolio', *Note Economiche* no. 4, pp. 95–134.

BIANCHI, R. (1980) 'Modigliani, Sylos Labini e Bain: Vent'Anni Dopo', *Note Economiche* no. 1, pp. 3–35.

BONANNO, G. (1988) 'Entry Deterrence with Uncertain Entry and Uncertain Observibility of Commitment', *International Journal of Industrial Organisation* no. 6, pp. 351–62.

BONANNO, G. and VICKERS, J. (1988) 'Vertical Separation', *Journal of Industrial Economics* no. 3, pp. 257–65.

BONI, M. and GROS-PIETRO, G.M. (1967) *La Concentrazione Industriale in Italia*, Milano: F. Angeli.

BRESCIANI TURRONI, C. (1950), 'The Problem of Depressed Areas and the Financing of their Economic Development', *Review of Economic Conditions of Italy*, iii, pp. 167–78.

BRIOSCHI, F. BUZZACCHI, L. and COLOMBO, M. (1988) 'La Raccolta di Capitale di Rischio nei Gruppi Industriali Italiani e la Separazione tra Possesso e Controllo', in IRS (1988).

BRUNI, L. (1961) 'Aspetti Strutturali delle Industrie Italiane', *Studi SVIMEZ*, Milano.

BRUSCO, S. (1975) 'Organizzazione del Lavoro e Decentramento Produttivo nel Settore Metalmeccanico', in FLM (Federazione Lavoratori Metalmeccanici) Bergamo (ed.), *Sindacato e Piccola Industria*, Bari: Laterza.

BRUSCO, S. (1982) 'The Emilian Model: Productive Decentralization and Social Integration', *Cambridge Journal of Economics* no. 6 pp. 167–84.

CAINARCA, G.C., COLOMBO, M.G. and MARIOTTI, S. (1987), 'Innovazione e Diffusione; Il Caso dell'Automazione Flessibile', *L' Industria*. Rivista di economia e politica industriale.

CAINARCA, G., COLOMBO, M. and MARIOTTI, S. (1989), 'Sentieri di Automazione ed Evoluzione della Struttura Industriale', in Barbetta and Silva (eds) (1989).

CAMERA DEI DEPUTATI (1965) 'Atti della Commissione Parlamentare di Inchiesta sui Limiti Posti dalla Concorrenza nel Campo Economico', Roma.

CAO-PINNA, V. (1952) 'La Costruzione del Bilancio Analitico dell'Economia Italiana per il 1950', *L'Industria* 4, pp. 527–546.

CARLI, G. (ed.) (1977) *Sviluppo Economico e Struttura Finanziaria in Italia*, Bologna: il Mulino.

CHAMBERLIN, E.H. (ed.) (1954) *Monopoly and Competition and their Regulation*, London: Macmillan.

CHENERY, H. (1955) 'Il Compito dell'Industrializzazione nello sviluppo dell'Italia Meridionale', *L'Industria* 3, pp. 378–408.

CHENERY, H., CLARK, P. and CAO-PINNA, V. (1953) 'The Structure and Growth of the Italian Economy', Rome: USA, MSA Special Mission to Italy for Economic Cooperation.

CIOCCA, P., FILOSA, R. and REY, G. (1973) 'Integrazione e Sviluppo dell'Economia Italiana nell'Ultimo Ventennio: Un Riesame Critico', *Contributi alla Ricerca Scientifica*, Rome: Banca di'Italia.

CONTI, G. and VONA, S. (1987) 'Struttura Produttiva, Modello di Specializzazione e Vincolo Estero: Un Commento', *L'Industria* 3, pp. 383–402.

CONTI, V., LANCIOTTI, G. and TRESOLDI, C (1973) 'Struttura ed Evoluzione della Domanda e dell'Offerta nell'Industria Manifatturiera Attreverso le Matrici delle Interdipendenze Settoriali', *Contributi alla Ricerca Economica*, Rome: Banca d'Italia.

CONTINI, B. (1968) 'Note in Tema di Monopolio Bilaterale e Discriminazione dei Prezzi', *Giornale degli Economisti* 1, pp. 86–101.

CONTINI, B. (1984), 'Dimensioni d'Impresa, Divisione del Lavoro e Ampiezza del Mercato', *Moneta e Credito* 148 pp. 417–37.

CONTINI, B. and REVELLI, R. (1986) 'Natalità e Mortalità delle Imprese Italiane: Risultati Preliminari e Nuove Prospettive di Ricerca', *L'Industria* 2 pp. 185–235.

CORICELLI, F. and GALIMBERTI, I. (1989) '*Il Commercio Intra-Industriale di Beni Intermedi dell'Italia degli anni '80'*, in Barbetta and Silva (eds) (1989).

DEI OTTATI, G. (1987) 'Il Mercato Comunitario', in G. Becattini (ed.) (1987).

DELBONO, F. (1987) 'Barriere all' Entrata: dal Prezzo Limite agli Investimenti Strategici', *Note Economiche* 2, pp. 38–54.

DELBONO, F. (1989) 'Market Leadership with a Sequence of History Dependent Patent Races', *Journal of Industrial Economics*, xxxviii, pp. 95–101.

DELBONO, F. and SCARPA, C. (1988) 'La determinazione della Struttura di Mercato in Recenti Modelli di Oligopolio: Competizione nei Prezzi e nella Qualita', *Note Economiche*, 1, pp. 48–76.

DELBONO, F. and DENICOLO, V. (1989) 'Asymmetric Equilibria in a Dynamic Model of R & D', *Economic Notes* 2, pp. 192–209.

DEL MONTE, A. and GIANNOLA, A. (1978) *Il Mezzogiorno nell'Economia Italiana*, Bologna: il Mulino.

DE MEO, G. (1965) *Produttività e Distribuzione del Reddito in Italia nel periodo 1951–1963*, Roma: ISTAT.

DE MEO, G. (1967) *Redditi e Produttivita' in Italia* (1951–1966), Roma: ISTAT.

DIXIT, A. (1982) 'Recent Developments in Oligopoly Theory', *American Economic Review*, Papers and Proceedings, 72, pp. 12–17.

DOSI, G. (1982) 'Technological Paradigms and Technological Trajectories: A Suggested Interpretation of the Determinants and Directions of Technological Change', *Research Policy* xi, 3, pp. 147–62.

DOSI, G. (1984) *Technical Change and Industrial Transformation*, London: Macmillan.

DOSI, G. and EGIDI, M. (1987) 'Substantive and Procedural Uncertainty. An Exploration of Economic Behaviours in Complex and Changing Environments', SPRU, Discussion Papers, University of Sussex.

EDGEWORTH, F.Y. (1922) 'The Mathematical Economics of Prof. Amoroso', *Economic Journal*, xxxii, pp. 400–7.

ENRIETTI, A. (1983) 'Industria Automobilistica: La Quasi–integrazione Verticale come Modello Interpretativo dei Rapporti tra le Imprese', *Economia e Politica Industriale*, 38 pp. 39–69.

FILIPPI, E. (1983) 'Imprese e Inflazione; Considerazioni Sulla Politica Industriale nell' Ultimo Decennio', *L' Industria* 3, pp. 347–69.

FILIPPI, E. and ZANETTI, G. (1965) *Finanza e Sviluppo della Grande Industria in Italia*, Milano: F. Angeli.

FILIPPI, E. and ZANETTI, G. (1971) 'Exogenous and Endogenous Factors in the Growth of the Firm,' in Marris and Wood (eds) (1971).

FORNENGO PENT, G. (1984) *Il Problema della Ristrutturazione Industriale: La Soluzione Italiana*, Milano: F. Angeli.

FUÀ, G and ZACCHIA, C. (eds) (1983) *Industrializzazione Senza Fratture*, Bologna: Il Mulino.

GAROFOLI, G. (1987) 'Il Modello Territoriale di Sviluppo degli anni '70 e '80', *Note Economiche* 1, pp. 156–75.

GASKINS, D.W. (1971) In 'Dynamic Limit Pricing: Optimal Pricing Under Threat of Entry', *Journal of Economic Theory* 3, pp. 306–322.

GOBBO, F. (1974), *L'Industria Italiana della Carta: Un Oligopolio Imperfetto*, Bologna: Il Mulino.

GRAZIANI, A. (1964) *Sviluppo del Mezzogiorno e produttività delle risorse*, Napoli: ESI.

GRAZIANI, A. (1969) *Lo Sviluppo di un'Economia Aperta*, Napoli: ESI.

GRAZIANI, A. (ed.) (1972) *L'Economia Italiana: 1945–1970*, Bologna: Il Mulino.

GRILLO, M. and COSSUTTA, D. (1986) 'Excess Capacity, Sunk Costs and Collusion: A Non-cooperative Bargaining Game. Some Considerations on the European Car Industry', *International Journal of Industrial Organisation* IV, pp. 251–70.

GRILLO, M. and SILVA, F. (1989) *Impresa, Concorrenza e Organizzazione*, Roma: NIS.

GRINDROD, M. (1955) *The Rebuilding of Italy: Politics and Economics, 1945–1955*, London: Royal Institute.

GUERCI, C.M. (1965) 'Concezioni Astratte e Criteri Empirici di Comportamento negli Studi Contemporanei sull'Oligopolio', *Giornale degli Economisti* 2, pp. 780–821.

GUERCI, C.M. (1970) 'Tassi di Profitto e Strutture di Mercato nell' Industria Italiana', *L'Industria*, Rivista di Economia Politica, 4, pp. 503–29.

HEIMLER, A. and MILANA, C. (1984) *'Prezzi Relativi, Ristrutturazione e Produttivita'*, Bologna: Il Mulino.

IRS (1988) *Rapporto sul Mercato Azionario*, Milano: 24 Ore-il Sole.

KUENNE, R.E. (ed.) (1967) *Monopolistic Competition Theory. Studies in Impact. Essays in Honour of E.H. Chamberlin*, New York: John Wiley & Sons.

LOMBARDINI, S. (1954) 'Monopoly and Rigidities in the Economic System', in Chamberlin (ed.) (1954).

LOMBARDINI, S. (1971) 'Modern Monopoly and Economic Development', in Marris and Woods (eds) (1971).

LUNGHINI, G. (1965) 'La Struttura del Sistema Economico Italiano', *L'Industria* 2, pp. 237–58.

LUTZ, V. (1962) *Italy, a Study in Economic Development*, Oxford University Press.

MALERBA, F. (1985), *The Semiconductor Business: The Economics of Rapid Growth and Decline*, Madison: University of Wisconsin Press.

MARCHIONATTI, R. (1986) 'Riflessioni suile Teorie del Mercato Capitalistico: Dal Dibattito degli Anni Venti all'Economia Industriale', *Economia e Politica Industriale* 50, pp. 177–204.

MARIOTTI, S. and CAINARCA, G. (1986) 'The Evolution of Transaction Governance in Textile-Clothing Industry', *Journal of Economic Behaviour and Organization* 4, pp. 351–74.

MARITI, P. (1974) 'Processo Competitivo e Aspetti Dinamici in un'Industria a Forte Domanda Estera', *L'Industria* 7, pp. 53–99.

MARITI, P. (1980) *Sui Rapporti tra Imprese in una Economia Industriale Moderna*, Milano: F. Angeli.

MARITI, P. and SMILEY, R. (1983) 'Co-operative Agreements and the Organization of Industry', *Journal of Industrial Economics*, 4, pp. 437–451.

MARRIS, R. and WOODS, A. (1971) *The Corporate Economy*, London: Macmillan.

MILANA, C. (ed.) (1988) *Ristrutturazione e Produttivita' nei Paesi Industriali*, Bologna: Il Mulino.

MODIGLIANI, F. (1958) 'New Developments on the Oligopoly Front', *Journal of Political Economy*, 31, pp. 437–51.

MARCH, J. and SIMON, H. (1958), *Organizations*, New York: John Wiley & Son.

MOMIGLIANO, F. (1964) 'Effetti degli Incentivi Diretti nelle Convenienze allo Insediamento Industriale', Roma: Ministero del Bilancio.

MOMIGLIANO, F. (1975) *Economia Industriale e Teoria dell' Impresa*, Bologna: Il Mulino.

MOMIGLIANO, F. (ed.) (1986) *Le Leggi della Politica Industriale in Italia*, Bologna: Il Mulino.

MOMIGLIANO, F. and SINISCALCO, D. (1984) 'Specializzazione Internazionale, Technologia e Carattestiche dell'Offerta', *Moneta e Credito* xxxvii, pp. 121–66.

NAPOLEONI, C. (1956) 'Concorrenza Monopolistica' and 'Oligopolio', in *Dizionario di Economia Politica*, Milano: Comunità.

OECD (1976) *Policies for Promoting Industrial Adaptation*, Paris.

ONIDA, F. (ed.) (1985) *Innovazione, Competitivita' e Vincolo Energetico*, Bologna: Il Mulino.

PASINETTI, L. (1959) 'On Concepts and Measures of Changes in Productivity', *Review of Economics and Statistics* xli, pp. 270–87.

PASINETTI, L. (1986) *Mutamenti Strutturali del Sistema Produttivo*, Bologna: Il Mulino.

PAVITT, K. (1984) 'Sectorial Patterns of Technical Change: Towards a Taxonomy and a Theory', *Research Policy* 13, pp. 343–73.

PIERELLI, F. (1983) 'I Mutamenti nella Struttura degli Scambi Mondiali e la Posizione Italiana', in *Contributi alla Ricerca Economica*, no. 16, Banca d'Italia.

PIORE, M. SABEL, C. (1984) *The Second Industrial Divide*, New York: Basic Books.

PILLOTON, F. (1968) 'Effetti Moltiplicativi degli Investimenti della Cassa per il Mezzogiorno nel Periodo 1951–55', in SVIMEZ, *Il Mezzogiorno nelle Ricerche della SVIMEZ*, Milano.

PRODI, R. (1969) *Concorrenza Dinamica e Potere di Mercato*, Milano: F. Angeli.

PRODI, R. (1970) *La Diffusione delle Innovazioni nell' Industria Italiana*, Bologna: Il Mulino.

R & P (1988), *L'Italia Multinazionale: L'Internazionalizzazione dell'Industria Italiana*, Milano: 240re-il Sole.

ROSENSTEIN-RODAN, P. (1961) 'Notes in the Theory of the "Big – Push"', in H. Hellis (ed.), *Economic Development for Latin America*, New York: St. Martin's Press.

SALVATI, M. (1967) *Una Critica alle Teorie dell'Impresa*, Roma: ed. dell'Ateneo.

SARACENO, P. (1975) *Il Sistema delle Imprese a Partecipazioni Statali nell' Esperienza Italiana*, Milano: Giuffri.

SARCINELLI, M. (1989) 'Mezzogiorno e Mercato Unico Europeo: Complementarietà o Conflitto di Obiettivi?', *Moneta e credito* xlii, pp. 129–161.

SASSU, A. (1978) 'Diffusione delle Innovazioni Tecnologiche e Oligopolio',

Giornale degli Economisti xxxvii, pp. 363–80.

SILVANI, M. (1985) 'Dipendenza Energetica, Struttura Produttiva e Composizione del Commercio Estero', in Onida (ed.) (1985).

SILVERBERG, G. DOSI, G. and ORSENIGO, L. (1988) 'Innovation, Diversity and Diffusion: A Self-Organization Model', *Economic Journal* 98, pp. 1032–54.

SINIGAGLIA, O. (1948) 'The Future of the Italian Iron and Steel Industry', *BNL Quarterly Review* I, pp. 240–5.

SINISCALCO, D. (1987) 'Alcune Conseguenze Macroeconomiche della Crescente Integrazione Internazionale del Sistema Produttivo Italiano', *L'Industria* 3, pp. 337–58.

SIRACUSANO, F, TRESOLDI, C. and ZEN, G. (1986) 'Domanda di Lavoro e Trasformazione dell'Economia del Mezzogiorno', in Temi di Discussione no. 83 Banca d'Italia, Rome.

SPAVENTA, L. (1959) 'Dualism in Economic Growth', *BNL Quarterly Review*, xii, pp. 387–434.

SRAFFA, P. (1925) 'Sulle Relazioni Tra Costo e Quantita Prodotta', *Annali di Economia*, vol. 2, Torino, pp. 277–328.

SRAFFA, P. (1926) 'The Laws of Returns under Competitive Conditions', *Economic Journal* xxxvi, pp. 535–50.

SYLOS-LABINI, P. (1957) 'Oligopolio e Progresso Tecnico', Turin (English edition, '*Oligopoly and Technical Progress*', Cambridge, Mass.: Harvard University Press, 1962.

SYLOS-LABINI, P. (1985) 'L'Evoluzione dell'Economia del Mezzogiorno negli Ultimi Trentanni' in Temi di Discussione no. 46, Banca d'Italia, Roma.

TANI, P. (1987) 'La Decomponibilità del Processo Produttivo', in Becattini (ed.) (1987).

VALCAMONICI, R. (1977) '*Struttura di Mercato, Accumulazione e Produttività del Lavoro nell'Industria Manifatturiera Italiana 1951–1971*', in Carli (ed.) (1977).

VICARELLI, F. (1967) 'La Funzione di Produzione ad Elasticità di Sostituzione Costante e la Stima del Tasso di Progresso Tecnico', *Rivista di Politica Economia* 2, pp. 975–1060.

VITO, F. (1930), *I Sindacati Industriali*, Cartelli e Gruppi, Milan.

VITO, F. (1954) 'Monopoly and Competition in Italy', in Chamberlin (1954).

VITO, F. (1967), 'Monopolistic Competition and Italian Economic Thought', in Kuenne (1967).

WELLISZ, S. (1957) 'The Coexistence of Large and Small Firms. A Study of Italian Mechanical Industry', *Quarterly Journal of Economics* lxxi, pp. 116–31.

ZANETTI, G. (1976) Le Motivazioni all' Investimento nella Grande Impresa, Bologna: Il Mulino.

Part III

The Theory of the Firm and Industrial Organizaton

8 Collaborative Strategies of Firms: Theory and Evidence

Neil Kay

In recent years the proliferation of collaborative arrangements between firms has stimulated much academic study into the phenomenon. The evolution of joint venture activity has attracted a great deal of interest with research joint ventures receiving particular attention. There are now a number of databases providing evidence as to patterns of corporate activity in this area.

In this chapter we shall provide a broad survey of the literature in this area before looking at evidence from studies and databases. Firstly, we shall look at general issues and problems relating to collaborative arrangements and joint venture activity, with special reference to high technology industry (e.g. Casson; Caves; Martin; Teece; Teece and Pisano). Secondly, we shall consider the specific problem of co-operative R & D and research joint ventures (e.g. Jacquemin; Dasgupta; Jacquemin and Spinoit; Katz; Bozeman *et al.* Ordover and Baumol; Ordover and Willig; Ouchi and Bolton; Reynolds as Snapp; Scott). In addition, patterns of collaborative activity behaviour will be analyzed with reference to a number of existing databases.

We shall also consider two sets of empirical questions drawing on two recent papers. Firstly, what transactional and organizational issues influence current patterns of joint venture activity in high technology industries? (Kay, Robe and Zagnoli). Secondly, what impact will the completion of the EC's internal market (1992) have on collaborative activity wihtin the EC? (Kay). On this latter question the 1985 White Paper from the Commission and the subsequent Cecchini Report both argue that 1992 will facilitate and encourage cross-frontier industrial collaboration within the EC. We argue that 1992 will reduce both the need for cross-frontier collaboration to gain market access and the willingness to collaborate with firms that are increasingly likely to be potential rivals, especially in the high technology industries. Consequently, the direct effect of 1992 will be to reduce the level of cross-frontier joint venture activity relative to other strategic options such as mergers, acquisitions and exporting.

COLLABORATIVE STRATEGIES OF FIRMS: THEORY AND EVIDENCE

The nature of collaborative activity between firms has recently received much attention in both the economics and managerial literature. While the managerial literature has noted and analysed cooperation between firms for some time, it is an area which has been relatively neglected in economics until very recently.

In this chapter we shall argue that there is generally a remarkable difference in emphasis between the two literatures as far as the efficiency implications of collaborative activity between firms is concerned. The economic literature tends to focus on the ability of collaborative activity such as joint ventures to avoid wasteful duplication of activity, encourage spread of knowledge at low cost, facilitate appropriability, provide devices to deal with free riders, and spread risks. When compared with the alternative of independent competing firms, the ability of cooperative ventures to internalize and synchronize control over economic activity appears to offer significant opportunities for dealing with traditional market failure problems in this literature. The major efficiency problems in the economics literature are anti-competitive implications of cooperation and collusion. By way of contrast, the managerial literature is characterized by persistent concern with contractual and administrative costs of collaboration, as well as appropriability problems created by such arrangements. Rather than solving efficiency problems, this literature generally views them as high-cost options and basically to be treated as devices of last resort. In the following sections we argue that the economics literature must recognize and deal with the efficiency implications of the managerial literatures general treatment of collaborative arrangements as problematic and costly devices to be used only when there is no reasonable alternative.

There are immediately a number of qualifying statements to be made about the above generalisations. Firstly, to some extent the differences may reflect differences in perspective rather than belief; for example the managerial literature's concern with generation of competitive (monopoly?) advantage may be 'wrong-side economics' from the point of view of the economics literature. Secondly, some economists do explicitly recognize issues raised by the managerial literature and incorporate discussion of them in their writings (e.g. Jacquemin, 1988; Teece, 1986). Thirdly, in developing economic explanations of collaborative activity consistent with their being treated as devices of last resort as in the managerial literature, we have found that the most likely explanations have actually been anticipated in the economic literature (e.g. Berg and Friedman, 1977 and 1978;

Mariti and Smiley, 1983). Fourthly, collaborative arrangements are typically a much more varied and heterogeneous bunch than the strategic alternatives of mergers and arm's length transactions. For example, US R & D consortia and technology–marketing alliances between Japanese and US firms may both be classified as collaborative activity. There is obviously a danger of comparing fish with fowl, a problem which exists even within the literatures.

However, even allowing for these qualifications, there remain strong differences between the respective literatures which invite comment and speculation. Therefore, in Section 1, we shall first of all summarize the economic literature's approach to the problem of collaborative activity (in particular joint ventures) before contrasting this with the managerial literatures perspective in Section 2. In Section 3 we first consider joint ventures (henceforth JV) as a form of economic organization before considering possible motives for JV activity in Section 4. In this section we take the managerial literature as our starting-point.

In Sections 5 and 6 we consider empirical evidence in the light of arguments developed in Section 4 concerning the nature of JVs. Section 5 is based on Kay, Robe and Zagnoli (1987) and is concerned with determinants of the nature and characteristics of JV activity. Section 6 is based on Kay (1989) and is a critical examination of the European Commission's and the Cecchini Report's claim that collaborative activity will be fostered by the 1992 programme. This is considered in the light of the previous arguments and the available evidence.

The conclusion of the paper is that conventional economic explanations based on mainstream economic foundations (including neoclassical, decision and game-theoretic sources) tend to neglect important features and behavioural characteristics of collaborative activity. In one sense at least we make a plea for a step backward; there is little point in building normative and policy-oriented analysis of JV activity until we can explain such basic issues as the apparent rapid escalation of collaborative activity in recent years, the apparently high failure role of JVs, and the short-lived nature of most agreements.

We also suggest that alternative perspectives and frameworks are consistent with the explanations developed here. However, for ease of exposition we do not refer to these throughout the chapter, not least because of the variety of approaches that may contribute to understanding in this area. Issues (and implied approaches) discussed below include contracting and exchange problems (transaction costs approach), structuring of hierarchies (organization theory), the firm as a non-decomposable system (system theory), appropriability problems (property rights literature) and the development and growth of firms (evolutionary theory). As we shall see, each of these five concepts will be of relevance in our analysis of collaborative activity. That so many issues may be of significance should not be regarded as surprising in dealing with a complex phenomenon which encompasses so many aspects of competition and co-operation, firm and market, organization and exchange. Our objective here is not to try to provide clear-cut answers drawing upon these sources, but merely to signpost interesting opportunities for future research.

1.   ECONOMIC ANALYSIS OF COLLABORATIVE ACTIVITY

Collaborative and co-operative activity are generally used as generic terms to describe a wide variety of firm and market relations, including minority shareholding, licensing, certain buyer–supplier relationships, consortia, franchising and JVs. Some of these terms may themselves be used in a variety of ways. In this chapter we shall focus on the particular phenomenon of JV, a particular form of collaborative activity which has aroused a great deal of interest in recent years. JVs are usually defined as involving:

> the creation of either a separate legal undertaking or at least some recognisable joint committee or association clearly identifiable as separate from its founders; the transfer by the founders of personnel and assets (often including intellectual property rights) to the new undertaking; and the allocation to the new undertaking of responsibility for carrying out a particular function or functions decided upoon by its founders (Goyder, 1988, p. 174).

The subsequent discussion here relates most strongly to JVs, though some of it may also be of relevance to collaborative activity in general.

When compared to arm's length transaction between two firms (e.g. a licensing agreement), a JV has obvious advantages in certain circumstances. These advantages parallel the internalization advantages that may be provided by in-house operation (e.g. through merger) and have been extensively discussed in the transaction cost and multinational enterprise literature (e.g. Williamson, 1985; Caves, 1982). Benefits include opportunities to improve monitoring and control of ventures, adaptability of decision-making, and avoidance of duplication of activity.

However, it is important to bear in mind during the following discussion that JVs are not only an alternative to arm's length agreements, but also to single ownership options such as green field start-ups, mergers, and single parent venture buy-outs. It is not sufficient to compare JVs to arm's length alternatives, it has to be shown why they also superior to single ownership alternatives, especially since single ownership alternatives such as merger are the traditional (and indeed obvious) way to internalize control over co-operative opportunity between two firms.

First, however, in 1.1 to 1.4 we shall summarize some general perspectives in the economics literature on this phenomenon.

1.1 Joint Ventures may be a Low Cost Form of Economic Organization

In one sense, this is implicitly assumed by many studies of JVs and R & D JVs in so far as analysis of costs tend to emphasize research and production costs rather than costs of organization. In this respect management and organization of JVs is effectively treated as a free good. Some economic analyses of JVs that discuss organization costs concentrate on features that may mitigate organizational problems. For example, Casson (1987, p. 134) argues that it is easy to overstate the risk of conflict in the case of JVs. He suggests that JVs may benefit from a co-operative 'mystique' that may beneficially influence managerial behaviour. Abstinence from day-to-day interference will be observed by sensible parents and they should encourage the joint subsidiary's managers to develop loyalty to the venture itself. Thus, in Casson's view, the avoidance of managerial conflict may only marginally influence the choice between JV and do-it-yourself strategies.

Similarly, Buckley (1988, pp. 139–41) argues that it is possible to analyse some ventures using conventional economic analysis in certain circumstances as devices by which parties can demonstrate mutual forbearance (i.e. refrain from cheating each other) and build up trust. Beamish and Banks (1987) also argue that forbearance in JVs may reduce transaction costs associated with opportunistic behaviour, small numbers bargaining problems are also reduced if forbearance is practised, and pooling of information reduces uncertainty. Thus, Williamson's (1975) transaction cost problems associated with opportunism, small numbers and uncertainty may be handled in a JV in Beamish and Banks' view. Some writers (e.g. Reynolds and Snapp, 1986) also argue the related point that free riding can be dealt with more easily when transactions are internalized within a JV.

Slightly anticipating later discussion, I have to admit to some reservations regarding the above argument. In some respects such discussion sails close to tautology by suggesting that the transaction costs of a JV will not be a problem if transaction costs are not a problem. One manifestation of opportunism could be that partners convincingly communicate forbearance and trustworthiness while practising the reverse. In a variant of Arrow's paradox of the demand for information, it should be generally difficult or impossible to ascertain potential partners intent *ex ante*, or indeed in some cases *ex post*.[2]

1.2   Joint Ventures may Encourage Dissemination of Knowledge without Threatening its Appropriability

Katz (1986, p. 528) argues that 'a cooperative R & D agreement may serve as a mechanism that internalises the externalities created by spillovers while continuing the efficient sharing of information. This information is accomplished by having firms commit to payments before the R & D is conducted and, hence, before any spillovers can occur'.

The literature on research JVs generally emphasizes this possibility (e.g. Dasgupta, 1988, p. 11; Bozeman *et al.*, 1986, pp. 264–5; Ordover and Baumol, 1988, p. 27; Stoneman and Vickers, 1988, p. X; Scott, 1988; Reynolds and Snapp, 1986, p. 141; Ouchi and Boulton, 1988). In principle the argument could be extended to cover knowledge spillovers in JVs generally.

However, whether a JV contract is generally an effective method for ensuring appropriability is questionable. Again, by their very nature, spillovers may be difficult or impossible to anticipate *ex ante*, and even *ex post* it may be impossible to evaluate what level or type of spillovers partners have obtained from a specific venture. There may be no market price for such externalities even in a JV. In the case of tacit or uncodified knowledge embodied in human skills and experience, appropriability problems may even be increased through demonstration effects associated with a JV: 'tacit knowledge by definition is difficult to articulate, and so transfer is hard unless those who possess the know-how in question can demonstrate it to others' (Teece, 1986, p. 287). We shall discuss these possibilities further in subsequent sections.

1.3   Joint Ventures may Spread Risks and Provide Access to Capital

'Cooperative R & D . . . may allow risk sharing among firms, which can be important to managers and, thus, to stockholders . . . [and also] an agreement may provide means by which firms can pool their resources to obtain sufficient capital to finance large R & D projects if capital markets are imperfect' (Katz, 1986, p. 529). Reynolds and Snapp (1986) support this as a possible objective of co-operative R & D.

However it is not immediately clear why these financial functions could not be better supported by dedicated financial institutions with a competitive advantage in risk-bearing and capital-raising functions. Such solutions would also reduce appropriability problems and difficulties associated with co-operative arrangements involving competitors. It may be true that technological closeness of JV partners may improve the ability to monitor each other's contribution and performance, but it still seems unlikely that financial motives alone could provide a central justification for JVs.

1.4 Joint Ventures can Reduce Duplication of R & D Activity

Avoidance of wasteful duplication of R & D projects by adopting a co-operative solution is a frequently cited advantage of research JVs (Dasgupta, 1988, p. 10; Ordover and Baumol, 1988, p. 27; Ordover and Willig, 1985, p. 316; Stoneman and Vickers, 1988, p. X; Reynolds and Snapp, 1986, p. 141). Again the argument can be extended naturally to provide an explanation for JV activity in general.

It is true that JVs may provide a superior solution to wasteful duplication in certain cases. However, this still does not explain why JVs should be preferred to single ownership alternatives. For example, rather than haggle over the JV contract, and have to cope with a dual control managerial system and associated appropriability problems, a more obvious and efficient solution might be for one partner to buy out the other as soon as the JV subsidiary is set up. Since this frequently happens eventually anyway, an immediate single ownership solution could economize on transaction and organization costs associated with JV control.

1.5 Joint Ventures may have Anti-Competitive Implications

To set against the gains in efficiency identified in the points above, there may be anti-competitive implications (Ordover and Willig, 1985, p. 317; Katz, 1986, pp. 529, 541; Martin, 1988; Stoneman and Vickers, 1988, p. X; Bresnahan and Salop, 1986; Reynolds and Snapp, 1986; Vickers, 1985). Most obviously collaboration in the J.V. can lead to collusion in the subsequent product market.

There is no doubt that such collusion is a possibility. More recently there have also been suggestions that management may pursue JVs as part of a strategy of making their companies bid-proof: an omelette of JVs may be difficult for an acquirer to unscramble. Without denying such possibilities it will be argued in the next section that JVs are more costly than is generally allowed for in the economics literature. If collusion is an objective of a JV, it is a very expensive blunt instrument for this purpose. It might seem reasonable to expect that thoughtful and creative managements could develop more subtle methods to collude.

2.   MANAGERIAL LITERATURE ON JOINT VENTURES

Not surprisingly, the managerial literature tends to disregard the anti-competitive implications of JVs discussed in 1.5 above. Since the creation of competitive advantage may be interpreted as the establishment of monopoly power in some context, the managerial perspective provides recipes for the generation of monopoly, in contradistinction to the economics literature's concern with control of monopoly effects. These perspectives are not necessarily irreconcilable, especially if the managerial literature is viewed from a Schumpeterian perspective. However they are clearly different in this respect.

While the difference of emphasis is understandable in the case of anti-competitive implications, there is also a considerable difference between the two literatures in terms of their respective interpretations of the efficiency implications of JV as a form of economic organization. The economic literature is generally sanguine as regards the ability of JVs to deal with transaction and organizational problems, while the managerial literature consistently reports severe difficulties in this context. Their analyses may be divided into two main categories, contractual and administrative problems. We will illustrate the points with the use of Fig. 8.1 below.

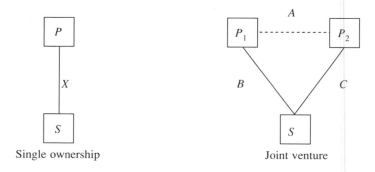

Single ownership   Joint venture

Figure 8.1   Single ownership and joint venture alternatives

2.1   Contractual Problems of JV

There are a number of transaction costs typically associated with setting up and maintaining a JV, as indicated by the dotted relationship A between the two parents (P_1 and P_2) of subsidiary S in Fig. 8.1 above. Firstly, search for a satisfactory partner may be a non-trivial task, especially if there are cultural and attitudinal differences between potential collaborators (Renard, 1985, pp. 42–3). Secondly, negotiation of the JV can be a costly and time-consuming business. Renard (1985, pp. 44–5) identifies 12 rules for effective negotiation; sample rules include step-by-step negotiation and testing the water with trial collaboration. Collectively, systematic application of these rules would ensure that JV negotiation is costly. While firms do economize on the application of the rules, Renard points out that such skimping increases the likelihood of JV failure. Thirdly, appropriability problems are still identified as severe problems in this literature as far as intangible assets are concerned. Two Harvard Business Review articles (Reich and Mankin, 1986, and Hamel *et al.* 1989) are typical of this literature in that they look at recent collaborative arrangements and argue that appropriating partners' intangible assets, such as technological and organizational knowledge, may be an objective of collaboration. Such externalities have no effective market price (Roehl and Truitt, 1987) and may impair the effectiveness of JVs, inhibit their formation, or result in costly defences to limit leakage of such competitive advantage through JV (Hamel *et al.*, 1989). As Roehl and Truitt (1987, p. 87) point out, relationships bear little resemblance to the 'calm ordered environments often envisaged by the academic ideal based on total trust and shared objectives'. Hamel *et al.*'s (1989) analysis is based on the fact that partners will selfishly try to get as much as possible out of the venture – hopefully without sacrificing their own competitive advantage.

2.2 Administrative Costs of JV Dual Control

This is represented in Fig. 8.1 by the dual line of control, B from P_1 and C from P_2 controlling subsidiary S. In a sense the organizational complications of this system of control relative to outright single ownership is self evident; if it is preferable generally to be the servant of two masters, why are most hierarchies organized on the inverted-V principle? In fact, ambiguity, confusion and conflict is reasonably expected from dual control of a JV. This is confirmed in the managerial literature (e.g. Renard, 1985, p. 46; Lyles, 1987, p. 79; Perlmutter and Keenan, 1986; Killing, 1982; Schaan, 1988). It would be surprising if it were otherwise. For our purposes it is sufficient to note that administrative costs arising from JV dual control are likely to be greater than for the single ownership option in Fig. 8.1.

A point that merits emphasis in this context is that JVs are an extremely complex form of hierarchy. As Fig. 8.1 indicates, it is not appropriate to regard it as a partial or compromise structure located on some intermediate point on some market–hierarchy spectrum. Compared to the outright control or single ownership option it is a more sophisticated and complex administrative structure. We discuss the implications of this further in Section 3.

2.3   Costs of JV versus Single Ownership Options

In addition to the above references, useful analyses are also contained in a variety of articles in special issues of the *Columbia Journal of World Business* (Summers of 1986 and 1987) devoted to JVs and collaborative activity. A difficulty is that this literature is more dependent on informal evidence, anecdotes and case studies than is the economic literature; systematic evidence is difficult to find in this literature. However, many of the issues analysed are difficult to analyse in formal terms, and such studies are often making the best of a difficult job.

It is sufficient for our purposes if this analysis helps to demonstrate a simple point: JVs are typically contractually and administratively more expensive than single ownership alternatives. Either feature should be sufficient to give single ownership a cost advantage over a JV; together they raise the fundamental question as to why such costly forms of economic organization should evolve at all. Mergers, green field start-ups or JV partner buy-outs would all appear to be simpler and cheaper alternatives in general. In a sense, the economic literature has gone too far too quickly; rather than focus on the efficiency gains and competitive losses inherent in JVs, we need to develop explanations as to why they develop in the first place. We develop this theme in the next section.

3   JOINT VENTURES AS ECONOMIC ORGANIZATION

The previous section has raised an interesting puzzle that has tended to be glossed over in economic analysis of JVs: if JVs are relatively expensive forms of economic organization, why do single ownership alternatives such as merger, green field start-up or single parent buy-out not evolve instead? In fact many JVs are reported as having failed to achieve their objectives, or eventually convert into some form of single ownership; contractual and administrative problems of JVs are frequently cited as the reasons for failure or conversion to single ownership.[3] However, we need to develop explanations as to why management would rationally choose a JV option, unless we are willing to entertain theories based on irrational managerial behaviour.

In Kay, Robe and Zagnoli (1987) we suggest how it may be possible to analyse JVs in this respect.[4] Firstly, if we analyse JVs in contractual and administrative cost terms as above, it becomes clear that is is generally misleading to see them as a hybrid or compromise form of economic organization, lying on some hypothetical spectrum between market exchange at one end and full-scale internalization or hierarchy at the other. It is true that JVs contain both market exchange and hierarchical elements (relation A and B/C respectively in Fig. 8.1). However, it is a simple step from suggesting that JV is a compromise intermediate or hybrid form of economic organization in markets and hierarchies terms to arguing that JVs may trade off some features of market exchange in exchange for hierarchical features (or vice versa, depending on which end of the spectrum one starts at). For example, Jacquemin and Spinoit (1985) argue that 'cooperative agreements are an alternative to either arms-length markets or integration within the firm under a single administrative structure. Its choice could, therefore, indicate that it is perceived as a less costly or more effective way than the alternatives of either in-house development, merger or normal market transactions' (p. 10). Jacquemin and Spinoit then argue that the contractual aspect of JVs gives flexibility that may not be obtainable through full scale in-house developments or mergers, while binding together competitors within a JV facilitates appropriability of R & D and overcomes problems of free riding associated with a pure market solution (pp. 10–11).

We believe that it is misleading to regard JVs as a potentially less costly form of economic organization integrating advantages from the market and hierarchy elements of its structure. As Fig. 8.1 indicates, JVs are a more complex form of hierarchy than single ownership. Relative to the single ownership option, JVs do not trade off hierarchy for market elements: they generally *exacerbate* hierarchical problems rather than reduce them, as is confirmed by the managerial literature discussed above. In fairness to Jacquemin and Spinoit it should be pointed out that they also recognize such problems of co-operative arrangements in the case of R & D agreements, citing complex hierarchy, contracting and appropriability problems in particular (pp. 12–14) (see also Jacquemin, 1988). In short, JVs generally add market *and* organization costs relative to single ownership alternatives; it is not an 'intermediate' form of economic organization regarded in market and hierarchic terms.

Consistent with this, JVs are generally treated as a device of last resort as evidenced by the managerial literature. It appears that choice of economic organization in this context is lexicographic: JVs are adopted when there is no reasonable alternative. In fact this is a circumstance which is generally recognized in the case of compulsory partnerships, e.g. Third World countries erecting barriers to green field start-ups or take-over by foreign firms, and encouraging JVs with local firms. However in Kay, Robe and Zagnoli (1987) we argue that once JVs are generally regarded as more costly than alternatives, analysing them as devices of last resort is the natural perspective to adopt.

This prompts an obvious question: if JVs are generally more costly than alternatives, surely they would only be adopted in special (and potentially inefficient) circumstances, e.g. forced partnerships by foreign governments? In the next section we shall in fact argue that they may be a rational response by firms even in the absence of forced partnerships.

4. MOTIVES FOR JOINT VENTURES

In a series of papers, David Teece (1986; 1987;[5] 1989) has argued that collaborative arrangements to exploit technological innovation may be based around exploitation of complementary assets supplied by the respective parents. This is consistent with observed patterns of resource provision by parents: for example, one parent may supply technology and the other marketing expertise, or parents may augment each other's technological skills with their own technological expertise. Complementarity is a recurrent theme in the managerial literature, and is also recognized in the economics literature (e.g. Ordover and Willig, p. 316).

However, this raises a further question as far as the choice of JV rather than single ownership alternatives like merger are concerned. While mergers are devices by which complementary assets can be integrated, they may also be utilized to integrate substitute assets (horizontal merger) and unrelated assets (conglomerate merger). Why should JVs be limited to cases involving complementary assets?

Conglomerate JVs are ruled out by definition; after all, if JVs' parents are presumed to be providing real technical and marketing resources as well as simply financial backing, parents will be inevitably related to the subsidiary. More interestingly, our analysis above suggests why purely horizontal JVs are unlikely: if all a partnership offers are substitute assets, then firms could more easily and cheaply go it alone. Teece's emphasis on the role of complementary assets appears justified in the context of JVs. We can therefore refine the question at the end of the last section into: why should JVs be utilized to exploit complementary assets if they are generally more expensive than single ownership alternatives? We suggest some circumstances consistent with such choices.

4.1 Joint Ventures Involving Complex Systems

Understandably the basic unit of analysis in the economic literature has been the JV itself. The establishment and operation of the JV is treated as the basic building block of analysis in analogous fashion to the focus on product markets in traditional neoclassical theory.

In Kay (1979; 1982) it was argued that focusing on the systemic properties of firms could help generate analysis and insights not possible with the traditional reductionist perspective of neoclassical theory. Such a perspective may also be helpful in the case of JVs. Rather than look at the implications of JVs in isolation, it may be helpful to place them in the context of the corporate system.

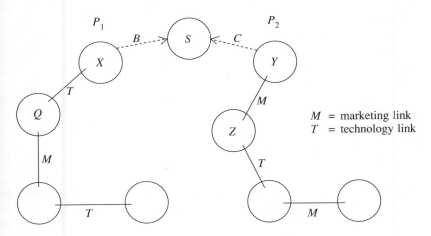

Figure 8.2   JV involving two diversified firms

Fig. 8.2 is adapted from Kay, Robe and Zagnoli (1987). P_1 and P_2 are presumed to be large diversified firms, operating four divisions each with intra-firm marketing (M) or technological (T) links with other divisions. Now suppose P_1 could contribute technological resources and P_2 marketing resources to a venture S that could commercially exploit these complementary assets; what alternative forms of economic organization exist to integrate these assets?

B may be taken as P_1's technological and C as P_1's marketing resources in Fig. 8.1. As implied in the discussion of Fig. 8.1, a JV between X and Y in Fig. 8.2 would be a complex and cumbersome choice, contractually and organizationally.

However, consider the choices facing the respective firms in the above case. The assets are complements, not substitutes, and so the firms may require each other's co-operation to pursue the venture; green field start-ups may be infeasible if complementary assets are difficult or costly to replicate (e.g. in the case of such assets as innovation, reputation, established distribution channels, and so on).

Single ownership could be achieved if one parent was to buy out the other, e.g. if P_2 was to purchase the relevant technological assets from P_1, or P_1 was to purchase the necessary marketing resources from P_2. Sale of X to P_2 or Y to P_1 is the most obvious solution. However, such trades could have substantial externalities in the form of sacrificed synergies or economies of scale that both divisions presently contribute to within their firms, as indicated by the respective M and T links. Consequently, single parent buy-out may be precluded because of these negative externalities.

Outright merger of the two firms may also be impracticable. In this case there may be further substantial negative external effects (relative to the JV) in the form of considerably enlarged and complex organization, $P_1 + P_2$. In the context of the limited co-operation gains represented by X and Y's potential venture, outright merger could be described as akin to using a sledgehammer to crack a nut (Kay, Robe and Zagnoli, 1987). Again the gains from single ownership and control of S must be set the potential diseconomies of co-ordinating the significantly larger and more complex system. The point is recognized in Mariti and Smiley (1983):

> mergers involve the combination of whole firms with numerous uncertainties about the ability of the parts to function smoothly together, and the resulting difficulties of the merger may overwhelm the cost reducing benefits of larger volume in one or several individual products. Co-operative agreements, on the other hand . . . [reduce costs] without the uncertainties and difficulties of full scale mergers (pp. 444–5).

Berg and Friedman (1977 p. 1332) also point out that full-scale merger may be inefficient or too costly to arrange 'due to inappropriate meshing of product lines'.

As a consequence, JV may be turned to as the form of economic organization that internalizes control (albeit expensively) without incurring the negative effects external to the JV associated with single parent buy-out or outright merger. In other words, even though JV may be the most expensive form of economic organization considered at the local level of the venture itself, once system-wide effects are recognized it may be a relatively cheap way of pursuing the venture, looked at from the level of the firm itself.

Two important points can be made regarding the implications of this argument. Firstly, it opens up the prospect of linking the evidence of managerial literature to a theory of rational choice as far as JV activity is concerned. As long as system-wide effects are ignored, it is necessasry to presume that JVs are a relatively low-cost forms of economic organization *at the level of the venture itself*, and so characterized by such features as forbearance, mutual trust, and success in dealing with appropriability problems – features which may certainly be present in some JVs, but which are not generally observed in the managerial literature. Once system-wide firm level effects are recognized, the existence of severe contractual and administrative problems within the JV itself can still be reconciled with its being chosen over single ownership alternatives.

Secondly, it allows for a rational answer to Mariti and Smiley's question: 'if cooperative agreements do allow reduction in costs, why were they not in use as much 15 years ago as they are today?' (1983, p. 447).[6] They suggest that either increased competition (resulting from decreases in market growth) has forced firms to adopt cost minimization, or that previous conditions of market growth had diverted attention to management of the demand side at the expense of cost-side considerations.

While both of these considerations may contribute to the formation of collaborative agreements, there is a further explanation consistent with choice of least-cost option over the whole period and not just the latter part. Consider divisions X and Y in Fig. 8.2 above. Suppose some years previously they had been independent firms in their own right and that a process of internal growth and/or acquisition had later created P_1 and P_2. How would venture opportunity S have been treated in those early days?

The most obvious solution is the single ownership solution, say through X and Y merging or one acquiring the other. The absence of adverse system-wide effects associated with ventures involving large diversified firms (e.g. P_1 and P_2) clears the way for the simple traditional single ownership solution. It is only when firms grow in size and diversity (e.g. to P_1 and P_2) that system-wide effects result in collaborative agreements such as JVs evolving as the least-cost solution, at the level of the firm if not the venture.

What is attractive about this explanation is that it sees JVs as a natural consequence of the evolution of firms and industries. System-wide effects from single ownership solutions to the integration of complementary assets are likely to increase as firms grow in scale and diversity. Scale of firm relative to size of venture opportunity is itself sufficient to generate the adverse system-wide effects discussed above, but the effects are likely to be exacerbated if the growth strategy involves diversification. Thus the growth of firms naturally leads to the evolution of JVs, and may be consistent with profit-oriented strategies throughout.

4.2   Other Possible Motives for JVs as devices of Last Resort

We have argued that explanations for the evolution of JVs should accommodate the general observation in the managerial literature that JVs are generally more costly than alternative forms of economic organization, at least over the region of the venture itself. System-wide effects discussed in Section 4.1 above help provide one explanation consistent with this observation. Others are discussed in Kay, Robe and Zagnoli (1987) and we briefly summarize them here:

1. **Concentrated markets**: Single-ownership alternatives may attract the attention of antitrust authorities if monopoly power is a consequence. Further, even if the venture itself does not have direct anti-competitive implications, merger could have other system-wide anti-competitive effects, e.g. in Fig. 8.2, Q and Z may be direct competitors. JV may be the only way to integrate complementary assets of X and Y without compromising competition and attracting the attention of the antitrust authorities. Berg and Friedman (1978) argue that JVs between firms in the same industry are generally safer than merger in this respect. It is worth noting that this stimulus to JV would be a natural consequence of growth and evolution at firm level, just as in 4.1 above. In this case, however, the effect of growth on incentives to conduct a JV is through the intermediate effect on market concentration.

2. **Disincentive effects**: Single ownership options such as a buy-out of the other partner or a merger may have undesirable outcomes from the perspective of either or both parents.[7] For example, independence may itself be an objective (Berg and Friedman, 1977, p. 1332), or merger may deaden innovativeness by incorporating creative systems within larger bureaucracies unfamiliar with their needs and characteristics.[8] Again, these effects may be strengthened by growth effects at firm level in so far as they may be related to the degree of scale and diversity of an innovator's potential partner. In short, even though JV may be expensive, it may be the only way to achieve the desired outcome. This contrasts with much of the economics literature which fixes the desired outcome and then considers alternative means for achieving it, e.g. in races to be first to patent. Form of economic organization may affect outcome as well as cost.

3. **Forced partnership**: This is a widely discussed reason for adopting JVs and little needs to be added here.[9] Again it is consistent with JVs being a high-cost alternative to single ownership; if JV is the only option permitted, then potential cost of alternative forms is irrelevant.

It is worth emphasizing that all the above possible explanations are consistent with JVs being the highest-cost form of economic organization over the region of the venture itself. Complex system, concentrated markets, and disincentive effects explanations point out that single ownership alternatives may have undesirable system – (firm-) wide effects, the disincentive effects explanation identifies outcomes as being potentially adversely affected by single ownership, while JV may be the only game in town in the case of forced partnership. Apart from the forced partnership, each explanation is strengthened by systemic effects arising from growth and diversification on the part of at least one of the potential partners. They are entirely consistent with the managerial literature's emphasis on JV as costly devices of last resort. There is no need to follow the common route adopted in the economics literature and presume that JVs may be lower cost alternatives over the region of the venture itself, if free riding and appropriability problems can be dealt with, and partners co-operate in a spirit of trust, forbearance and mutual harmony. In a sense it is a relief to know that the old, familiar self-seeking self-interested economic man can still be found in collaborative arrangements, even though it may be disappointing that the existence of such arrangements does not necessarily imply the existence of a nobler version of *homo sapiens*.

It is also noteworthy that each of these explanations has been previously alluded to in the economics literature (e.g. Berg and Friedman, 1977; 1978; and Mariti and Smiley, 1983). Yet there has been no real evidence of attempts to develop them into anything other than casual *ad hoc* explanations, and their potential relevance has not been recognized by most current analyses in the economics literature. Indeed, as long as the evidence of the managerial literature is ignored, there is little pressure to invoke such explanations. It is only when the increasing use of JVs has to be reconciled with their observed costliness that the potential significance of such explanations becomes apparent.

In Sections 5 and 6 we shall consider empirical evidence on JVs and the extent to which it is generally consistent with this perspective of JV as a costly device of last resort.

5. PATTERNS OF JV ACTIVITY

From our preceding discussion, potential determinants of JV activity of direct interest to us include size and diversification of firms, and degree of market concentration. We consider here available evidence in this respect and the implications of other empirical findings of relevance.

S.V. Berg and P. Friedman, in their 1978 survey of JVs in American industry confirm that if any co-operation between two firms in the same industry attracts antitrust attention, 'there is evidence that horizontal JVs are viewed as safer than full horizontal mergers'. Their explanation of the fact that sixty-two per cent of the JVs by basic chemical firms from 1966 to 1973 were horizontal while only thirty eight per cent of the mergers were horizontal (Berg and Friedman, 1978, p. 30). This tends to be consistent both with arguments that concentration will tend to encourage JV activity, as well as exploitation of complementary assets between firms in the same industry. In a 1976 article, J. Pfeffer and P. Nowak had contested that JV should receive a less stringent treatment than mergers on the part of antitrust authorities. Finding the proportion of horizontal parent-pairings to be positively correlated with child industry concentration, they concluded that corporate JVs tend to be anti-competitive instruments. It was clear for them that the numerical importance of JV in concentrated markets was an evidence of their use to secure monopoly advantages. In fact, Berg and Friedman (1978, p. 164) argue that it is firm size rather than concentration which determines the extent and incidence of JV activity, the concentration measures providing a positive correlation with JV activity only because of a link through the size of firms in an industry.[10] Predominance of JVs in concentrated markets should not allow for an interpretation of JV as being mainly used to enhance market power, and interpretation frequently given but rejected by Berg and Friedman (1979, p. 18), after a rate-of-return analysis of JV.

That size is the most important single factor for JV creation is also claimed by S.E. Boyle, whose early study of JVs having at least one parent among the 'Fortune 500' showed that joint subsidiary participation increases as the size of firm increases. For example, firms classified among the 100 largest manufacturing corporations were identified as parent corporations in 42 per cent of the cases, whereas the 100 smaller firms on the list appeared as parents in only 4 per cent of the cases. (Boyle, 1968, p. 85). Also, 'the larger the company, the more likely it is to be involved in many joint subsidiaries' (p. 92), a result which is consistent with our size argument, but also with the diversification one: the larger the firm, the more likely it is to be diversified. More empirical studies are needed here, especially from the point of view of separating out effects of size and diversification, and also with respect to the role of the M-Form in stimulating JV activity.

That JVs are not used as transitional, intermediary structures preceding merger is evidenced by Berg and Friedman's (1978) study of the cases of termination of chemical JVs between 1924 and 1969. In 50 cases of termination studied, only 2 were due to a parent merging into the other. In the

48 remaining cases, those which were not due to financial failure (20 cases) or an antitrust settlement (4 cases), were the result of a purchase by one parent (22 cases), by a third party (4 cases) or the result of a merger of the JV into another JV by same parents. So there seems to be a tendency for JVs to be transformed into some other organizational form after a few years of operation, but *not* to be a step towards *merger* of the parents.

Simultaneously, Berg and Friedman (1979) notice the relatively short lives of JVs, but stress the fact that the absorption of the JV by one parent does not necessarily mean that the JV failed (p. 10). If JVs are not without risks, 'some terminations reflect not the "financial failure" of the JV, but rather the advent of new areas of investment of higher potential returns for at least one of the parents' (p. 30).

Therefore it does appear that the evidence is consistent with JVs evolving as firms grow and diversify (as we would expect from our earlier analysis), though the relationship in concentrated markets appears more complex. The last two sets of empirical results are also of relevance as far as our interpretation of JVs as a device of last resort are concerned. Firstly, it is natural to think of JV as a stepping stone to merger as long as it is thought of as an intermediate form between market and hierarchy. That it is not a stepping stone is consistent with its being a device of last resort. Secondly, with respect to short life of ventures, there is natural corollary to the earlier argument that increase in size of firms may generate significant system-wide effects relative to the venture itself: diminishing the scale of the venture itself, relative to a given size of firm, might reduce the incentive to merge to exploit limited venture opportunities. Consequently, JV may appear as the natural solution to short-lived minor opportunities; while short life may reflect failure, it may also reflect a bias towards choosing JV in these cases.

6. 1992 AND INDUSTRIAL CO-OPERATION

The Commission of the European Communities (CEC) in its 1985 White Paper (CEC, 1985) and the background research programme sponsored by the Commission (Cecchini, 1988; European Economy, 1988) argue that 1992 and the completion of the EC's internal market will encourage collaborative activity between firms. We critically evaluate this projection in the light of our previous discussion of JVs as a measure of last resort. Firstly, the White Paper makes industrial co-operation within the EC a major objective of the 1992 programme.

The removal of internal boundaries and the establishment of free movement of goods and capital and the freedom to provide services are clearly fundamental to the creation of the internal market. Nevertheless, Community action must go further and create an environment or conditions likely to favour the development of cooperation between undertakings. (CEC, 1985, p. 34).

It argues that the barriers to industrial co-operation will be reduced by the 1992 programme, and that industrial co-operation will consequently increase:

in spite of the progress made in creating such an environment, cooperation between undertakings of different Member States is still hampered by excessive legal, fiscal and administrative problems, to which are added occasional obstacles which are more a reflection of different mental attitudes and habits. The absence of a Community legal framework for cross-border activities by enterprises and for cooperation between enterprises of different Member States has led – if only for psychological reasons – to numerous potential joint projects failing to get off the ground. As and when the internal market is developed further, enterprises incorporated in the form of companies or firms will become more and more involved in all manner of intra-Community operations, resulting in an ever-increasing number of links with associated enterprises, creditors and other parties outside the country in which the registered office is located. (CEC, 1985, pp. 34–6).

The conclusions of the research work sponsored by the commission to investigate the economics of 1992 are consistent with the White Paper in these respects. Cecchini (1988) and European Economy (1988, March), the summary reports of this research programme, also see increasing business co-operation in R & D as a major consequence of the 1992 programme.

Europe-wide standards . . . are an essential level both for prising open national market and then welding them together through technological alliances. Of great importance to such alliances are EC-Sponsored R & D programmes like ESPRIT which, way beyond their monetary significance, are a crucial focus for fusing cross-frontier innovation and business. (Cecchini, 1988, p. 89)

Market integration brings with it a number of factors giving European firms the chance to regain technological leadership . . . (including) the rapid development of cross-frontier business cooperation for R & D. (Cecchini, 1988, p. 75)

The Commission's research programme on 1992 endorses this view, identifying a number of regulatory and political obstacles to co-operation in Europe, many of which would be removed or reduced by the 1992 programme (European Economy, 1988, pp. 136–7). Both Cecchini (pp. 87–8) and European Economy (1988) identify what they call a 'paradox' in the existing patterns of co-operative behaviour on the part of EC firms.

> The paradox which emerges is that cooperation with Community partners has so far been less frequent than cooperation with partners in non-member countries. The total number of joint ventures set up has remained very stable; in 1985/6, Community operations still lagged behind (24.7% of the total) by comparison with domestic operations (42%) and international operations (33%) . . . But European cooperation could grow substantially as a result of the removal of some of these barriers. (European Economy, 1988, p. 137)

For our purposes, the important question here is how the 1992 programme will affect collaborative behaviour between firms. There are two relevant points here. Firstly, the more open a market, the more likely it is that firms will be able to compete satisfactorily on their own without the need for local partners; the general lowering of fences and the processes of harmonization and mutual recognition make exporting and unilateral control (through in-house expansion or mergers and acquisitions) increasingly attractive options. Secondly, the more open a market, the greater the possibility that potential collaborators are also potential competitors. Consequently, firms may be increasingly reluctant to enter into co-operative agreements which give away their technological knowledge. Thus, completing the internal market should enhance intra-EC trade and/or mergers and acquisitions, but inhibit JV activity. In short, both the *need* and the *willingness* to conduct co-operative agreements with other EC partners should diminish as a direct consequence of the completion of the internal market. *These arguments derive directly from our earlier interpretation of JVs as a costly device of last resort.*

This is a radically different pattern from that predicted by the White Paper and the Cecchini Report. Below we look at empirical evidence on various aspects of corporate behaviour from this alternative perspective.

(1) A recent INSEAD survey of trends in international collaborative agreement (Morris and Hergert, 1987) bases its analysis on the INSEAD database. This database is compiled from public announcements of 839 collaborative agreements reported in *The Economist* and *The*

Financial Times over the period 1975 to 1986. Consistent with Cecchini's 'paradox', EC firms were more likely to choose non-EC partners than EC partners. However, what is particularly striking is that although 47.2 per cent of all collaborative agreements reported in the INSEAD database involved at least one US partner, only 8.4 per cent of agreements involved solely US partners. Thus, Cecchini's 'paradox' holds even more strongly from the perspective of the US despite – or rather because of – its status as a completed market: US firms tend not to seek other US collaborative partners.

It is possible that there is an unavoidable bias in the data-set; to the extent that the *Economist* and *Financial Times* are more likely to report collaborative arrangements involving European firms, some collaborative arrangements involving only non-EC firms might be overlooked. However, even if this were the case, it is notable there were marginally more US–Japanese collaborative agreements reported than US–US agreements, despite geographic, cultural and other barriers to US–Japanese co-operation.

Also of relevance is that most US–US cooperative ventures were for joint product development only, while the majority of co-operative agreements in the database overall involved production and/or marketing elements. Thus, within this completed market, it appears relatively easier for US firms to forge JVs that might have pre-competitive elements than those closer to the market end. Even so, it is noteworthy that, for product development co-operative ventures involving US firms, the database reports more than twice as many agreements with EC partners US with other US firms, suggesting that it is easier to form such agreements across trading blocs, rather than within them.[11] To the extent that the United States is a completed market to be taken as a model for 1992, these patterns are significant, striking, and generally consistent with our expectations.

(2)   The Cecchini 'paradox' is that 'international cooperative link ups between E.C. partner firms have up to now proved less frequent than those with a non-E.C. participant. The scope for correcting this balance is considerable once the barriers come down' (Cecchini, p. 88). The explanation developed above resolves this paradox. To the extent that intra-EC trade is already more open than trade with non-EC countries, we would expect to find strategic barriers to intra-EC JVs. There is no inconsistency – or paradox – in observing high levels of intra-EC trade coexisting with relatively low levels of intra-EC co-operative agreements. It is what we would expect from the alternative

perspective developed above.

(3) Turning now to the likely effects of 1992 itself, we might expect the first effects of the programme to be observable now. The White Paper was published in June 1985. Allowing for corporate moves in mergers and JVs already in train to work through, as well as for other lags in reformation of corporate strategy, the 1986–7 reporting period would be the first full-time period during which the impact of the 1992 programme could be observed.

In fact, Commission figures on JVs involving firms from different EC countries fell from 24.7 per cent of all JVs involving EC firms in 1985–6, to 17.8 per cent in 1986–7. By way of contrast, there was a substantial rise in the number of JVs between EC and non-EC firms, rising from 33.3 per cent in 1985–6 to 50 per cent of the total in 1986–7 (CEC 1988). The Cecchini 'paradox' appears to be strengthening, though of course these patterns are quite consistent with what we would expect if firms were redrawing their corporate strategies in the light of the competitive implications of the 1992 programme. Were the 1992 programme also to contain convincing proposals for reduction of trade barriers between the EC and non-EC countries, we would not have expected to have found such proliferation of JV activity between EC and non EC firms. If this is a sustainable trend it may signal firms' disbelief in EC assurances that EC external trade policy will not move the bloc towards 'Fortress Europe'. The report on competition policy does comment that 'an analysis of the main motives cited for joint ventures involving non-EC companies showed that marketing or marketing and production appeared very frequently: This could reflect the desire of American and Japanese companies to co-operate with Community partners to spread risks or bypass trade policy measures' (CEC 1988, p. 237).

(4) While the figures on JV activity overall are consistent with our expectations, the pattern is even more striking in the critical high-technology sectors (chemicals, electrical, mechanical, and computers). In these four sectors, Community-level JVs represented only 8.8 per cent of the total involving EC firms in 1986–7, while those involving a non-EC partner represented 61.4 per cent of the total (CEC, 1988). These figures are consistent with other studies of collaborative agreements involving EC firms in the knowledge intensive industries. A LAREA CEREM study of 497 agreements in the aerospace, biotechnology, information technology and materials industries be-

tween 1980 and 1985 found that only one quarter of agreements involving EC firms were with other EC firms, while a FOR (Futuro Organizzazione Risorse) study of 468 agreements involving EC firms in the aerospace, information technology, scientific instrumentation and pharmaceutical industries from 1982 to 1985 found that only 29 per cent of agreements were with other EC firms (Mytelka and Delapierre, 1987). Further, while the overall level of all JV activity involving EC firms (national, community and international) was about the same as 1985–6 in those sectors, the share of Community-level JVs in 1986–7 fell from 24.1 per cent of the total in 1985–6, while the number of JVs involving a non-EC partner in 1986–7 increased from a previous share of 35.2 per cent in 1985–6 (CEC, 1988).

Both the low share of Community-level JVs compared to EC–non-EC level JVs in the high-technology sectors, and the switch away from Community-level JVs in those sectors in 1986–7, is consistent with what we would expect of a relatively open market which is becoming progressively more open. Cecchini's 'paradox' holds even more forcefully and dramatically when these sectors are isolated. However, if firms are reluctant to enter into collaborative agreements that may give away technological advantages to potential rivals, we would expect our predicted patterns of behaviour to hold even more strongly in the high technology sectors – as, in fact, they do. A corollary is that the existence of trade barriers may facilitate JVs involving research and development, while lowering trade barriers may diminish the sensitive R & D content of such activity; consistent with this, the Competition Policy Report found that only 19 per cent of JVs recorded in 1985–7 involved at least some R & D content, compared with 26 per cent in 1985–6 (CEC, 1988a, pp. 236–7).

(5)   The other side of the 1992 coin is the likely effect on direct competition intra-EC: that is in terms of intra-EC trade, mergers and acquisitions, as substitute strategies to JVs. The direct effects of the 1992 programme would be to encourage a switch from bilateral JV strategy to unilateral action, cross-frontier, intra-EC.

Unilateral action may be reflected in intra-EC exporting or merger activity, so it would be important to consider both patterns together to obtain an accurate future of this aspect of the effects of the 1992 programme. However, we shall look particularly at merger activity since this is an important issue in its own right as well as an indicator of the competitive effects of the 1992 programme.

Merger activity at Community level showed a small increase from

22.9 per cent of total mergers involving EC firms in 1985–6 to 24.8 per cent in 1986–7 (CEC, 1988). It is also noteworthy that the competition policy report found that research and development reasons for merger in 1986–7 had increased in frequency. The report suggests: 'This could reflect the strategy of firms seeking to achieve technology transfer without the risks of cooperation' (CEC, 1988, p. 236). However, the report does not explain why this motive should suddenly increase in frequency in 1986–7. In fact, both increase in merger activity at EC level and the increased desire to internalize R & D within corporate boundaries are to be expected as a consequence of the 1992 programme. The increased R & D motive neatly complements the other finding above, that R & D diminished as a motive for JV in 1986–7.

(6) So far we have followed Cecchini by analysing the *absolute* incidence of JVs and mergers in different markets. However, we can consolidate our argument by analysing JVs and mergers as options and analysing their frequency relative to each other as markets move towards completion.

We may regard the degree of market completion as progressively increasing from EC–non–EC through Community to national level operations. We would similarly expect to find firms increasingly preferring the merger to the JV route as the degree of market completion increases.

For each of the four years covered in CEC, 1988 (i.e. 1983–4 to 1986–7), the ratio of mergers to JVs increases from EC–non–EC through Community to national level operations. Thus, for 1986–7 there were over seven times as many mergers as JVs within national markets of EC member countries, while EC–non–EC JVs were more than twice as frequent as mergers. This illustrates the point that it helps to look at corporate strategies together, and the evidence is consistent with strong *relative* switches away from JVs to mergers as the degree of market completion increases.

While the figures on mergers and JVs for 1986–7 must be regarded as weak signals relating to one year only, the major conclusion we are left with after examining all these studies or databases is that they generally support what we would expect to find from moves towards completing the internal market. That is, the incidence of JVs should be directly related to the existence of trade barriers, not inversely as Cecchini believes. These effects should be more marked in the high technology industries. R & D collaboration should diminish as a consequence of the moves towards completion of the market. Increasingly, merger and exporting should be preferred to JV strategies within the completed market.

One further possible implication of the above discussion is that post-1992 intra-EC motives for collaboration may increasingly feature potentially anti-competitive elements such as market-sharing as defensive responses to sharpened competition. However, we have no direct evidence on this possible effect.

In addition, Cecchini does recognize that 'links with non-EC participants are also very useful for European competitiveness and might be more used as a platform for attacking world markets (as well as the non-EC partner's penetration of Community markets)' (Cecchini, 1988, p. 88). Ironically, however, it is in the context of *world* markets that JVs between EC firms are likely to be more sustainable; in this context JV and technological collaboration especially may be seen as a non zero-sum game by participants. However, the 1992 programme is about changing the rules for competition within the EC, not markets outside it; if global markets present collaborative opportunities post-1992 for EC firms these should exist independently of the 1992 programme. As far as the most likely pattern of competitive behaviour post-1992 is concerned, we would expect that successful moves towards completion of the internal market would result in a series of strategic alliances being formed between EC and non-EC firms to compete within the completed market. A symptom of the *success* of moves towards completion of the market would be rapid decline in EC-level JVs.

7. CONCLUDING COMMENTS

In this paper we have not attempted to match the degree of formalization and rigour of the standard economics literature on collaborative activity. We have traded off rigour and precision for a broad-based approach in an attempt to explain general patterns of collaborative behaviour, such as the relatively recent proliferation of JV activity, and the likely impact of completing an internal market on collaborative arrangements between firms.

Therefore the paper should not be analysed or tested against a precise model-building standard, but should hopefully be seen as signposting promising areas of analysis. However, it should be acknowledged that the paper does have a subversive intent in so far as the signposts tend to point away from mainstream economic theorising. For example, once contractual problems are recognized, the transaction cost literature[12] is of obvious relevance. Appropriability problems suggest we should draw upon the property rights literature.[13] The role of organization and hierarchy suggests that research into organizational decision-making may be of relevance.[14] Our emphasis on the growth and development of corporations draws upon insights offered by the evolutionary theorists[15] while the concept of the firm as a non-decomposable system is a development of system-theoretic concepts.[16] The role of systems concepts and problems of decision-making under uncertainty are recurring themes in this paper, and these literatures have directed, suggested or influenced their use here.

Collaborative strategies of firms have been a useful test-bed for comparing the mainstream perspectives of conventional theory with some alternative interpretations and frameworks. As well as pursuing further theory development and empirical testing, it could be useful to conduct dialogues between researchers in this area to explore the extent to which differences in analysis are a reflection more of emphasis than belief; for example, while we have argued that Buckley and Casson's concepts of forbearance, altruism and mutual trust are unlikely to describe collaborative activity in general, nonetheless there may be special cases where such attitudes are rational (e.g. mutual dependence of partners having made JV-specific commitments, or repetitious transactions). Also, both these authors recognize the role of obstacles to mergers in encouraging collaborative activity.[17] To what extent there actually exist irreconcilable differences is unclear, and should be one avenue for further consideration.

However, our major conclusion is quite simple. Looking at the firm as an integrated system in which participants may be faced with severe and intractable information problems is a helpful and potentially productive perspective. It helps account for the managerial literature's treatment of JVs as measures of last resort only, while indicating a variety of theoretical frameworks that could be drawn on for future analysis in this area.

Notes

1. This is an activity which is to be generally encouraged in view of the public good nature of this commodity.
2. The process of internalization itself may not eliminate problems of monitoring of opportunistic behaviour, especially if firms are trying to appropriate such intangible assets as tacit technical knowledge and organizational methods of their partners.
3. Analyses which indicate that JVs are characterized by high failure rates include Killing, 1982, p. 120, and Gomes-Cassieres, 1987, p. 97. It should be

pointed out, however, that many of these studies implicitly assume that failure is indicated by short life or absence of accounting profits. However, if JVs are characterized by objectives other than profit or high levels of externalities, this may be too simplistic a view of failure.

4.   The discussion here and in Section 4 draws on this paper.
5.   With G. Pisano.
6.   However, Mariti and Smiley caution that it is difficult to identify trends in this case, the absence of reliable data being a complicating factor.
7.   In an unpublished paper, Michael Dietrich has pointed out that transactions may involve demand-side effects as well as supply or cost side implications.
8.   Size mismatch is cited as a common problem in merger and integration studies in the managerial literature. For an early study of this problem, see Kitching, 1967.
9.   Much of the literature on joint venture activity in Third World literature reports forced partnerships.
10. See Berg and Friedman, 1980, p. 164. Although Berg and Friedman's empirical findings concerning the size-of-firm effect are consistent with JVs being adopted as a device of last resort, their explanation for the relationship is quite different. Device of last resort explanations here depend on size of firm, increasing barriers to merger alternatives; Berg and Friedman instead argue that size of firm generates capital economies to fund JVs and enables the larger firm to engage in multiple JVs.

     However, 'device of last resort' explanation here is preferred in so far as it is simpler, parsimonious, and consistent with a wider range of observed phenomena.
11. As well as strategic barriers to JV activity erected by the completed market, strong US antitrust policy may also have helped to discourage JV formation.
12. For example, see Williamson, 1975 and 1985. However, for problems in the existing transaction cost approach, see Kay (forthcoming).
13. For example, see Alchian (1977).
14. See March and Shapira (1982) for a stimulating coverage of some recent work in this area.
15. See especially, Nelson and Winter (1982).
16. For work in this vein, see Kay, 1979 and 1982.
17. For example, see Buckley (1988), p. 140.

Bibliography

ALCHIAN, A.A. (1977) *Economic Forces at Work*, Indianapolis: Liberty Press.

BEAMISH, P.W. and BANKS, J.C. (1987) 'Equity Joint Ventures and the Multinational Enterprise', *Journal of International Business Studies*, Summer, pp. 1–16.

BERG, S.V. and FRIEDMAN, P. (1977) 'Joint Ventures, Competition and Technological Complementarities: Evidence from Chemicals', *Southern Economic Journal* 43, pp. 1330–7.

BERG, S.V. and FRIEDMAN, P. (1978) 'Joint Ventures in American Industry: An Overview', *Mergers and Acquisitions*, Summer, 28–41.

BERG, S.V. and FRIEDMAN, P. (1979) 'Joint Ventures in American Industry: Managerial Policy and Public Implications', *Mergers and Acquisitions*, Autumn, pp. 9–17, and Winter, pp. 18–29.

BERG, S.V. and FRIEDMAN, P. (1980) 'Causes and Effects of Joint Venture Activity: Knowledge Acquisition vs Parent Horizontality', *Antitrust Bulletin* 25, 14–3–68.

BOYLE, S.E. (1968): An Estimate of the Number and Size Distribution of Domestic Joint Subsidiaries, *Antitrust Law and Economic Review*, Spring, pp. 81–92.

BOZEMAN, B., LINK, A. and ZARDKOOHI, A. (1988) 'An Economic Analysis of R & D Joint Ventures', *Managerial and Decision Economics* 7, 263–6.

BRESNAHAN, T.F. and SALOP, B.R. (1986) 'Quantifying the Competitive Effects of Production Joint Ventures', *International Journal of Industrial Organisation* 4, pp. 155–75.

BUCKLEY, P.J. (1988) 'Organisational Forms and Multinational Companies', in S. Thompson, and M. Wright, (eds) *International Organisation, Efficiency and Profit*, Oxford: Philip Allan, pp. 127–68.

CASSON, M. (1987) 'Contractual Arrangement for Technology Transfer: New Evidence from Business History', in *The Firm and the Market*, Oxford: Blackwell, 121–52.

CAVES, R.E. (1982) *Multinational Enterprise and Economic Analysis*, Cambridge University Press.

CEC (1985) *Completing the Internal Market: White Paper from the Commission to the European Council*, Luxembourg.

CEC (Commission of the European Communities) (1988) *Seventeenth Report on Competition Policy*, Brussels/Luxembourg.

CECCHINI, P. (1988) *1992 : The European Challenge*, Aldershot: Wildwood House.

DASGUPTA, P. (1988) 'The Welfare Economics of Knowledge Production', *Oxford Review of Economic Policy* 4, pp. 1–12.

EUROPEAN ECONOMY (1988) 'The Economics of 1992', no. 35, March.

GOYDER, D.G. (1988) *EEC Competition Law*, Oxford: Clarendon Press.

GOMES-CASSIERES, B. (1987) 'Joint Venture Instability, Is it a Problem?' *Columbia Journal of World Business*, Summer, pp. 97–102.

HAMEL, G., DOZ, Y.L. and PRAHALAD, C.K. (1989) 'Collaborate with your Competitors – And Win', *Harvard Business Review*, Jan–Feb, pp. 133–9.

JACQUEMIN, A. and SPINOIT, B. (1985) 'Economic and Legal Aspects of Cooperative Research : A European View', Centre for European Policy Studies Working Paper, Brussels.

JACQUEMIN, A. (1988) 'Cooperative Agreements in R & D and European Antitrust Policy', *European Economic Review* pp. 32, 551–60.

KATZ, M.L. (1986) 'An Analysis of Cooperative Research and Development', *Rand Journal of Economics* 17, pp. 527–43.

KAY, N.M. (1979) *The Innovating Firm*, London: Macmillan.

KAY, N.M. (1982) *The Evolving Firm*, London: Macmillan.

KAY, N.M. (1989) 'Corporate Strategy, Technological Change and 1992', *Working Paper of the Standing Commission on the Scottish Economy*, Glasgow.

KAY, N.M. (forthcoming) 'Markets, false hierarchies, and the evolution of the modern corporation', *Journal of Economic Behaviour and Organisation*.

KAY, N.M., ROBE, J-P. and ZAGNOLI, P. (1987) 'An Approach to the Analysis of Joint Ventures', European University Institute, Working Paper, Florence.

KILLING, J.P. (1982) 'How to Make a Global Joint Venture Work', *Harvard Business Review*, May–Jun, pp. 120–7.

KITCHING, H. (1967): Why Do Mergers Miscarry, *Harvard Business Review*, 45, pp. 84–101.

LYLES, M.A. (1987) 'Common Mistakes of Joint Venture Experienced Firms', *Columbia Journal of World Business*, Summer, 79–84.

MARCH, J.G. and SHAPIRA, Z. (1982) 'Behavioural Decision Theory and Organisational Decision Theory', in G.R. Ungson, and D.R. Braunstein, *Decision-making: An Interdisciplinary Perspective*, Boston: Kent Publishing.

MARITI, P. and SMILEY, R.M. (1983) 'Cooperative Agreements and the Organisation of Industry', *Journal of Industrial Economics* 31, pp. 437–51.

MARTIN, S. (1988) 'Joint Ventures and Market Performance in Oligopoly? Unpublished paper, European University Institute, Florence.

MORRIS, D. and HERGERT, M. (1987) 'Trends in International Collaborative Agreements', *Columbia Journal of World Business*, Summer, pp. 15–21.

MYTELKA, L.K and DELAPIERRE, M. (1987) 'The Alliance Strategies of European Firms and the Role of ESPRIT', *Journal of Common Market Studies* 26, pp. 231–53.

NELSON, R. and WINTER, S. (1982) *An Evolutionary Theory of Economic Change*, Cambridge, Mass.: Harvard University Press.

ORDOVER, J. and BAUMOL, W. (1988) 'Antitrust Policy and High Technology Industries', *Oxford Review of Economic Policy* 4, pp. 13–34.

ORDOVER, J.A. and WILLIG, R.D. (1985) 'Antitrust for High Technology Industries: Assessing Research Joint Ventures and Mergers', *Journal of Law and Economics* 28, pp. 311–33.

OUCHI, W.C. and BOLTON, M.K. (1988) 'The Logic of Joint Research and Development', *California Management Review*, Spring, pp. 9–33.

PERLMUTTER, H.V. and KEENAN, D.A. (1986) 'Cooperate to Compete Globally', *Harvard Business*, Mar–Apr, Review, pp. 136–52.

PFEFFER, J. and NOWAK, P. (1986) : Patterns of Joint Activity: Implications for Antitrust Policy: *Antitrust Bulletin*, xxi, pp. 315–39.

REICH, R.B. and MANKIN, E.D. (1986) 'Joint Ventures with Japan are Giving Away Our Future', *Harvard Business Review*, Mar–Apr, pp. 78–86.

RENARD, P. (1985) 'Joint Ventures – The Keys to Success and Some Cautions', *European Management Journal* 3, pp. 39–47.

REYNOLDS, R.J. and SNAPP, B.R. (1986) *International Journal of Industrial Organisation* 4, pp. 141–53.

ROEHL, T.W. and TRUITT, J.F. (1987) 'Stormy Open Marriages are Better: Evidence from U.S., Japanese and French Cooperative Ventures in Commercial Aircraft', *Columbia Journal of World Business*, Summer, pp. 87–95.

SCHAAN, J-L. (1988) 'How to Control a Joint Venture even as a Minority Partner', *Journal of General Management* 14, pp. 4–16.

SCOTT, J.T. (1988) 'Diversification versus Cooperation in R & D Investment', *Managerial and Decision Economics* 9, pp. 173–86.

STONEMAN, P. and VICKERS, J. (1988) 'The Assessment : The Economics of Technology Policy', *Oxford Review of Economic Policy* 4, pp. i–xvi.

TEECE, D.J. (1986) 'Profiting from Technological Innovation: Implications for Integration, Collaboration, Licensing and Public Policy', *Research Policy* 15, pp. 285–305.

TEECE, D.J. (1989) 'Competition and Cooperation in Technology Strategy', Berkeley, California, University of California Working Paper.

TEECE, D.J. and PISANO, G. (1987) 'Collaborative Arrangements and Technology Strategy, Berkeley, California: University of California Working Paper.

VICKERS, J. (1985) 'Pre-emptive Patenting, Joint Ventures, and the Persistence of Oligopoly', *International Journal of Industrial Organisation* 3, pp. 261–73.

WILLIAMSON, O.E. (1975) *Markets and Hierarchies*, New York: Free Press.

WILLIAMSON, O.E. (1985) *The Economic Institutions of Capitalism*, New York: Free Press.

9 The Multinational Firm and the Theory of Industrial Organization[1]

Nicola Acocella

1. INTRODUCTION

The theory of foreign direct investment (henceforth referred to as FDI) is of relatively recent origin. It was first put forward in 1960 by Stephen Hymer in his PhD thesis at Massachusetts Institute of Technology (MIT) (Hymer, 1976). Before that time, the various international capital movements were not distinguished from one another, since they were all explained in terms of differentials in interest rates between the various countries. However, this theory was at odds with certain facts and trends, already clearly identifiable at the end of the 1950s, which were to characterize the next two decades. In particular, there were : the local financing of the foreign subsidiaries of American enterprises, and the simultaneous onset of portfolio investment from European countries in the United States and of FDI from the USA in Europe. These factors made it extremely difficult to accept a single, unified explanation of all these different capital flows. The predominance of FDI in some industries, and at the same time the existence of crossed FDI in a particular industry, were further factors which underlined the need for a specific hypothesis to explain the phenomenon of FDI and induced researchers to seek the hypothesis in the field of industrial organization and outside balance of payments theory.

In 1960, Hymer had referred to two factors in order to explain why a firm based in one particular country might decide to extend its productive activities beyond the frontiers of that country and thus transform itself into a multinational enterprise (MNE). Hymer's two factors were as follows:

1. The possession of certain 'advantages' – in the field of technology, marketing, management, etc. – which it would not be profitable for the firm to hand over to foreign operators.
2. The need to remove oligopolistic competition.

The first of these two factors leads to the concept of the MNE as an institution capable of increasing efficiency; the second as an institution provided with power, that is, able to bring influence to bear on the behaviour of rival operators in such a way as to overcome competition.

Some authors (see Kindleberger, 1984) have maintained that the very extensive literature on the determinants of FDI that has appeared since 1960 has done little more than ponder over and, at times, bring into better focus, concepts already to be found in Hymer. The opinion expressed in the present paper is somewhat different. With regard to the first of the factors considered by Hymer, further in-depth work has been done and there have been significant transformations, in parallel with developments in the theory of the firm and industrial organization (the internalization of markets approach and that of transaction costs). Conversely, traces of the second of the factors indicated by Hymer have been progressively lost in FDI theories, notwithstanding the fact that further significant contributions which have appeared in recent years have stressed the need for a strategic approach to the theory of the firm and of industrial organization. We agree that, taken as a whole and in relation to the initial stage of the phenomenon, Hymer's analysis provided an excellent departure point for the development of a general theory of FDI and MNE, precisely because it included both factors of efficiency and considerations of strategy and power.

One of the arguments put forward in the present paper is that the elimination of the latter considerations dangerously undermines FDI theory. This theory has gained in depth with regard to the explanation in terms of efficiency, but has lost in terms of the extent of coverage, with important consequences both at the level of methodology and at that of the direct interpretation of reality. Section 2 first briefly recapitulates the main theories within the efficiency paradigm (the eclectic theory and the transaction cost approach, or TCA), and then makes a critical examination of the eclectic theory. Section 3 discusses the limitations of the other theory directed at efficiency, namely TCA. Section 4 discusses the reasons for the progressive abandonment of the strategic approach (SA) within the theory of MNE, in contrast to the renewed interest in the problems of strategy within the theory of the firm and industrial organization. Section 5 puts forward some elements for the formulation of a more general theory of FDI and MNE.

2. MULTINATIONALS AND EFFICIENCY: THE LIMITATIONS OF THE ECLECTIC THEORY

Let us briefly outline the eclectic theory (Dunning, 1981). This serves to explain the choice between FDI and alternative international operations (basically exports, on the one hand, and licensing and similar operations on the other), by establishing three different and necessary conditions, all in terms of efficiency:

1. The possession of ownership advantages (OAs) with regard to firms of other nationalities in serving particular markets, as originally suggested by Hymer (1976) and Kindleberger (1969);
2. The existence of localization advantages (LAs) in foreign countries, which makes it profitable for the enterprise to utilize these advantages through FDI rather than through exports;
3. The existence of internationalization advantages (IAs), as suggested by Buckley and Casson (1976) and by Williamson (1981), Teece (1981) and others. IAs guarantee direct exploitation of ownership advantages instead of their sale or leasing to foreign firms.

It must be clearly stated in the first place that all three of these conditions tend to characterize FDI as a vehicle for efficiency.

In fact, with regard to the first condition, OAs are considered to be a true factor of production (Hymer, 1970, p. 78). Only firms which have high performance by virtue of the OAs held can compete successfully with foreign companies. On the other hand, there will probably be a spillover of these advantages into the host countries. Certainly, those economists who consider OAs to be a necessary condition for FDI are well aware that they arise as a product of oligopolistic rivalry. Nevertheless, since, in the theory in question, OAs are considered as given, consideration of the behaviour of the enterprises in the perspective of strategy or power is dropped. The existence of localization advantages then ensures that the enterprise will grow along lines which tend to equalize factor prices, thus once again guaranteeing efficiency.

In the next section we will see that the third condition also ensures efficiency. The attempt by some scholars to include strategic factors within the sphere of internalization advantages is debatable.

If we pass on to the consideration of the logical coherence of the eclectic theory,[2] then the double requirement of OAs and IAs seems unjustified. In fact, from the viewpoint of its proponents, internalization theory is *self-sufficient*, that is to say, it is capable on its own of accounting for FDI. This theory aims to explain the reason why an enterprise grows and, in particular, why it becomes a multinational, thus giving rise to the creation of internal rather than external markets for the sale of finished goods, component parts, patents and the like.

It would certainly be possible to do without the OA concept (Casson, 1984), all the more so if it is considered that every enterprise, by the very fact of its existence (i.e. because it is on the market), must obviously have some features which distinguish it from its competitors and which can be considered as giving it an edge over them.

To place emphasis on the existence of OAs would, therefore, be a truism (Acocella, 1985; Teece, 1986). By saying that a firm, in order to become multinational, should posses some OAs, one would simply be saying that there should be a firm on the market. At most, it might be important to know those characteristics of enterprises which, in specific historical and geographical circumstances, constitute factors of success. And these are, precisely, contingent. The maintenance of the OA category as a necessary condition would be at odds with foreign direct investment by enterprises which are relatively backward in technology, marketing and management. Such cases are common in both developed and developing countries and this is an important fact in so far as it shows, for example, that success factors are not necessarily bound up with technological progress, though in some cases this can be an important factor in competitiveness.[3] On the other hand, the geographical and sectoral pattern of a country's FDI is linked with the character of the success factors which predominate in that country.[4] In Hymer and Kindleberger, arguments were used to support the introduction of the OA concept into FDI theory based on the existence of costs and risks connected with operating at a distance in different social and economic contexts (see Hymer, 1976, pp. 38–41; Kindleberger, 1969, p. 12).

Proponents of IAs point out, however, that the concept of specific OAs cannot be applied in the same way to firms that have already acquired a multinational status as it is to enterprises about to become multinational. 'The whole concept . . . must therefore be questioned . . . The concept is artificially attenuated at the point where the firms crosses national boundaries'. (Buckley, 1985, p. 4). In fact, it is the very act of internalization through FDI that may bring advantages to the enterprise such as to enable it to meet any costs and risks that may arise in connection with its initial expansion abroad (Acocella, 1975). Further advantages of FDI will emerge within the framework of a strategic approach (see Section 4).

In reality, the concept of OA – apart from being insufficient (as the eclectic theory states) – is not even necessary in order to explain FDI. The following sections will show that the other two conditions of the eclectic theory are also unnecessary.

3. MULTINATIONALS AND EFFICIENCY: THE TRANSACTION COST APPROACH

As is well known, the TCA considers MNEs to be a special case of multi-division or multi-stage firms, which are created wherever markets are internalized across national boundaries. There are two strands to the TCA: the British one (see Buckley and Casson, 1976) and the American one (Williamson, 1975; Teece, 1981), both stemming from Coasian roots. The limitations of TCA can be discussed under four headings: the first three concern both national and multinational enterprises, whereas the fourth refers more specifically to the latter type of enterprise.

The first limitation to this approach derives, in our opinion, from the nature of the analysis, which is of a micro-microeconomic nature and one of partial equilibrium. The choice between external or internal transactions or other contractual forms takes place – operator by operator and, for each operator, transaction by transaction – in terms of the minimization of costs in a given environment, while each operator's choice has no repercussions on those of the others.

In particular, technology and demand are given (on this point see also Turvani, 1987, p. 42), which implies that a considerably large part of the options that the operators are effectively faced with, when choosing between internal and external markets is deliberately excluded from the corpus of the TCA. The problem of interest – according to the theory under examination – is not that of what to produce, or how to produce it, or how to boost demand, or what are the reactions of competitors to the firm's decisions, etc., but merely whether the transaction arising from a given act of production should take place on the (external) market or inside an alternative institution, the enterprise. Now, every scholar is acknowledged to be free to choose the simplifying hypothesis required for his analysis. However, if the hypothesis of a given technology and demand were interpreted as a simplifying hypothesis, the partial nature of the TCA would be recognized as something which not all its supporters seem willing to do.[4] In addition, as already stated, the repercussions that an operator's choice has on other operators are not considered. We shall return to this point shortly, when we discuss the static aspect of the TCA.

The second point of criticism of the TCA refers to the specification of the exact content of the costs of external transactions, on the one hand, and the costs of bureaucratic organizations (or of intermediate institutional forms) on the other. This point has been the subject of recent developments (see, for example, Casson, 1985a). In fact (and this will be made much clearer in Section 4), the choice between one type of transaction and another not only depends on its costs, but also on its advantages.

This might be a pure question of semantics, if transaction costs were thought of as *net transaction* costs. However, since, on the one hand, it is rare to find detailed accounts of transaction costs, and, on the other, no one states in the literature – at least to our knowledge – that *net* transaction costs are to be considered, perhaps this clarification was worth making. In fact, it is not simply a question of semantics. To speak in terms of advantages expected from one or other types of transaction leads one to consider those connected with strategic behaviour, as will be more clearly seen in Section 4.

Buckley and Casson (see Buckley and Casson, 1976; Casson, 1984; Buckley, 1985) are the only authors trying to include consideration of market power in the sphere of factors which exert an influence on the internalization of markets. They consider, above all, the possibility of an enterprise internalizing: (*a*) the market for an intermediate good in order to bring about price discrimination, which would be impossible on the external market; (*b*) the market for an intermediate or final good where there exists 'bilateral concentration' of market power, with the possibility of uncertain or unstable contractual situations (see Buckley and Casson, 1976, pp. 37–8). Up to this point, the situations are those already considered by Hymer and Kindleberger. But, in their most recent works, the authors we are dealing with tend to expand the strategic factors incorporated in the internalization advantages. Casson (1984, p. 6), for example, maintains that internalization can concern 'markets in price commitments and production commitments', which can be used also for purposes of collusion.

Nevertheless, such markets do not invariably exist, nor can they be defined in reality. Oligopolistic collusion and rivalry can take on a wide variety of forms, so strategic FDI cannot always be looked upon as an instrument of market internalization. However, if internalization costs and advantages were defined in broader terms, it would still be necessary to tackle the strategic aspects of FDI through a dynamic – and not a static – analysis. These clarifications apart, we nevertheless consider the greater openness of the 'British branch' of the TCA to the characteristic problems of the SA to be of interest.

Once the costs and advantages of internalization have been specified, the factors or variables on which they depend must be precisely stated. Otherwise, having abstained from making falsifiable statements, there would be the risk of judging everything which exists in reality as rational (efficient). All in all, an answer should be given to the question: what does the advantage of internalizing transactions depend on? The reason is that the statement that internalization is due to the existence of transaction costs higher than those of administrative 'management' is insufficient. In other words, the conditions must be identified by which an abstract type of organization (market or enterprises at both ends of the range) will be replaced by another (Buckley, 1985, p. 18; and, in similar terms, Teece, 1985, p. 236). In this case, too, there have been only very few attempts. Teece (1983 and 1986) has connected the net costs of internal governance to an index of know-how complexity, in the case of horizontally integrated MNEs, and an index of asset specificity, in the case of vertically integrated MNEs. This is clearly the case of a very partial approach, even if an interesting one.

In a study which is more articulated as far as the nature of transaction costs is concerned, but limited to the choice between international cartels and MNEs, Casson (1985b) indicates the determinants of this choice in the following factors: degree of product homogeneity, returns to scale, the static or dynamic character of the technology, the general capacity for innovation, and the risk of expropriation of foreign assets. It is an interesting and indeed convincing attempt, if it is limited to a static or comparative static analysis, as the TCA usually does.

This leads us to the third limitation of the TCA. The problem is that this type of analysis (static or comparative static analysis) masks a basic defect of the TCA: transaction costs are considered to have been brought about by objective market 'imperfections' and the active role taken by the enterprises in this respect is ignored. Now, only within the framework of a comparative static analysis can it be reasonable to consider technology and the degree of product homogeneity as given. Doubtless, if these elements are given, there will be a certain degree of preference for internal markets over external ones or any other sort of contractual solution. Yet the fact is that the choice of technology and the choice of product quality constitute important instrumental variables for the firm.

Within the context of the TCA there are some scholars who recognize that the enterprise is not simply an organization brought into being to respond to objective imperfections, but an institution that plays its part in creating them (see Buckley, 1985, p. 10, and Calvet, 1981, p. 56), not least through the choices of technology and product quality. However, Calvet claims that: 'It is the limitation of markets *per se* which enables us to understand the emergence of hierarchies in general and of multinational hierarchies in particular.'

The fallacy of this reasoning is clear: if the enterprise creates imperfections, the terms of the choice (between imperfect markets and enterprise) are influenced by the choice itself. In a static analysis, the outcome would amount to circular reasoning, which can only be escaped from by denying or ignoring the enterprise's role in creating imperfections. In a dynamic analysis, admission of the influence of a firm over its environment is the presupposition of a strategic behaviour: in other words, an operator chooses between market and enterprise while thinking of the opportunity offered by one of the terms of the immediate choice (internalization of the markets), so as to exert a positive influence on his own subsequent choices and a negative one on the choices of other operators (competitors or others).

To summarize the critical remarks so far made, microeconomic analysis of partial equilibria, failure to consider all the advantages of the various institutions, and the static nature of the reference framework are among the main shortcomings of the TCA which seem hard to overcome if one remains within the limits of that approach. In our opinion, they preclude an analysis of the relations between the enterprise and other operators which are important for the very purpose of understanding all the terms of choice between markets and internal transactions. In particular, it seems necesssary for this purpose to introduce concepts such as power, strategy, etc., which involve reference to a different analytical framework, to be discussed in Sections 4 and 5.

As already stated, the fourth point of criticism of the TCA concerns the more specific aspects of MNEs and, in some ways, follows on from the previous remarks: underestimation of the role of technology and demand prevents the appraisal of the aspects of their diversity at international level. This, together with the hypothesis according to which no operator exerts his influence on the choice of others, causes the strategic elements of FDI to be overlooked. This has particularly serious consequences as to the possibilities of understanding the conduct of MNEs *vis-à-vis* segmented national markets for products and factors. We shall come back to this point in the following section.

4.   STRATEGIC ELEMENTS IN THE MULTINATIONALIZATION PROCESS

In this section we intend to discuss, first of all, the reasons put forward in support of strategic factors present in the initial formulation of Hymer and Kindleberger's theory of FDI. We shall then examine the strategic elements which should be included in a theory of MNE and FDI.

In the introduction we have already mentioned the fact that the strategic element contained in the initial formulation of the FDI theory had been gradually eliminated from the dominant analysis. The most recent contributions on the subject appeared in fact in the mid-1970s, in the very period in which the theory of internalization was put forward.[5]

A justification of the abandonment of the SA is provided by Calvet (1981, p. 47). Of his numerous arguments, two seem to us to be of outstanding importance. The second one is shared by Teece.

As to the first, Calvet (1981, p. 55) remarked that if the impossibility for markets to operate efficiently were taken for granted because of the existence of monopolistic power – as Hymer and Kindleberger tended to assume – then no institutional choice would be necessary, since the need to retain market power would decide the form that the international operation would assume, i.e. it would lead, as the only possible result, to FDI. According to Calvet, on the contrary, the form of such an operation cannot be established *a priori*, even in an oligopolistic context, until its object and the environment in which it takes place have been specified. We entirely agree with this observation: the oligopolistic nature of the enterprise considered may have led to too easy an acceptance of the idea that the 'natural' form of an international operation is FDI. The TCA has certainly added some appropriate words of caution regarding this point. There is now, however, a risk of the pendulum swinging too far in the opposite direction, and of the TCA purely and simply replacing the strategic element in the industrial organization approach, instead of adding analytical elements.

Conversely, another argument put forward by Calvet (1981, p. 48) and also by Teece (1985, pp. 234–61) seems not to be valid. According to these authors, Hymer and Kindleberger's reference paradigm is a fictitious market, devoid of frictions. The presence of imperfections and MNEs, which are the product and cause, in their turn, of these imperfections, would thus justify a policy which opposes the MNEs themselves. However, according to Calvet and Teece, this would only come about if the choice were between the MNEs and a perfect market and not between the MNEs and a realistically imperfect market.

We agree on the fact that Hymer and Kindleberger's starting-point (and at times also their reference-point) is a perfect market. Nevertheless, both Hymer[6] and Kindleberger (1969, pp. 187–92) are very careful to stress the point that the MNE, apart from being an organization endowed with power (and, in particular, a creator of imperfections), is an institution which tends to increase efficiency in realistic situations of market imperfection.[7]

If the industrial organization approach tended to emphasize both poles of the MNE's dual nature, omission of any reference to the strategic aspect in the current MNE literature does not constitute a return to a balanced position from an extreme one, but rather an outright mutilation of an important aspect of the FDI theory. This mutilation of the strategic aspect and its replacement by the TCA may possibly be interpreted as an attempt to specify the terms of the option between FDI and alternative international operations from the point of view of efficiency. But this would require knowledge not only of the advantages, but also of the costs ensuing from the reduction of the phenomenon of multinationalization to mere factors of efficiency.

Some proponents of the eclectic theory or paradigm maintain that the strategic (or 'ideosyncratic') aspect of the firm's behaviour could be incorporated in their framework, even if in a rather uncomfortable way, but no more so than if 'one was attempting a formalized theory of the uninational firm' (Dunning, 1988, p. 7). The existence in the real world of strategic behaviour is not denied by the TCA. Indeed the possibility of opportunistic behaviour[8] on the part of other operators is crucial to the decision to internalize transactions. But opportunistic or strategic considerations play no part in the choice between the home market and the foreign market as far as the enterprise faced with the alternative is concerned: e.g. the possibility stemming from horizontal or vertical integration for the enhancement of its market power, for the reduction of the competitor's level of information and for directing credible threats towards potential new entrants is not taken into account.

In other words, the consideration of opportunism, devoid of its aspects of power concerning the enterprise itself, proves to be a veritable mutilation of the analytical apparatus and of the field to be investigated. This seems all the more worrying in the presence of important developments that have come about in recent years in the theory of the firm and industrial organization as far as strategic behaviour is concerned.

In order to understand its importance for the purpose of the present argument, I shall try to define the meaning of the term 'strategy' in detail. This may be described as an operator's conscious action aimed at acquiring or increasing power *vis-à-vis* other operators, even to the extent of sacrificing present profits (or satisfactions). Strategic behaviour, in the first place, is a manifestation of power, i.e. ability to influence the behaviour of other operators – rival enterprises, workers, governments, etc. – in favour of the operator concerned. In addition, the outcomes of strategic behaviour are usually inefficient: as we shall see, collusion and the erection of barriers to entry may result in social 'waste', in the form of advertising, excess capacity, etc. Appraisal of efficiency should be made in a dynamic context, but this would be problematic at the present stage of theoretical knowledge.

The possibility of adopting a strategic behaviour has various implications for competitors. Above all, these concern the entry of new firms into the market, which can be effectively prevented by resorting to numerous instruments (Encaoua *et al.*, 1986; Geroski and Jacquemin, 1984; Jacquemin, 1987). It is important for us to highlight the fact that some of these instruments can have an effect on the very size of the enterprise, which the TCA claims to explain in exclusive terms. In particular, we refer to the creation of excess capacity as a 'credible threat' to potential entrants into the market (Spence, 1977; Dixit, 1979; and Dixit, 1980). The spread of new products, brands and sales points is also important as a pre-emptive move.

Certainly, the need for restricting the entry of new rivals, a focal point in oligopolistic theory, does not play a similar role in the MNE theory. Nevertheless, it should not be neglected. In fact, it has probably been of particular importance since the latter half of the 1950s and throughout the following decade, when the United States FDI was boosted by the prospect of the growing European markets, not least because of the creation of the EEC. It seems to have become important, once again, in view of the creation of the European Single Market in 1993. Now, as then, foreign investments are justified as a pre-emptive move.[9]

More generally, MNEs have distinctive features which strengthen their opportunities for adopting strategic behaviour *vis-à-vis* their rivals. Since they are engaged in various markets, not only from the aspect of the type of product – as a national enterprise might be – but also geographically, they have a more extensive set of information, better capacity for understanding different situations, and greater power of response.[10]

The strategics discussed so far were all directed at the firm's competitors. However the position of the MNE needs also to be considered with regard to other operators, specifically governments and workers and their organizations.

A further reason for the strategic behaviour of MNEs lies in the different conditions an enterprise is exposed to in various countries on account of the different national economic policies. The aims of these strategies may be the following: reduction of tax or tariff burdens, gaining of credit, taxation and tariff incentives, access to protected markets and the elimination of restrictions. In general, the instruments available to the multinational firms are more incisive than those used for the same purposes by national firms. In this respect, it is worth pointing out that, apart from transfer prices, the threat of transferring certain assets abroad is much more credible – and therefore effective – if it is made by a firm already operating in an international context.[11]

The national character assumed by workers' trade unions and, in any case, the specific national character of labour markets can, moreover, contribute to locational choices and the division of labour between the production facilities sited in the various countries (ILO, 1976; Greer and Shearer, 1981; and Sugden, 1985).

5. SUMMARY AND ELEMENTS FOR A MORE GENERAL FRAMEWORK FOR THE ANALYSIS OF DIRECT INVESTMENT AND THE MULTINATIONAL ENTERPRISE

The first part of this section provides a summary of some of the points dealt with in previous sections. Contrary to predictions made at the end of the 1970s (Dunning, 1979, p. vii), the theory of FDI and of MNE has still not reached the stage of maturity. In fact, an explanatory hypothesis which is sufficiently comprehensive to be accepted by a large majority of economists is still not available. Basically, there are three main theories: the eclectic theory, the TCA – in both its American and British versions – and finally a strategic approach, which is, however, confined to a minority of economists, mostly of a 'radical' persuasion. The large number of approaches certainly mirrors a variety of actual situations and behaviour, and also of theoretical frameworks and value judgements.

None of the theories seems to be entirely satisfactory in itself, not even the eclectic theory, which attempts to encompass the internalization theory. There are essentially two reasons for considering the second and third of these theories unsatisfactory: the first reason refers only to the eclectic theory, the second both to the eclectic theory and to the TCA.

First of all, criticism must be levelled at the eclectic theory with regard to its lack of logical coherence. In fact OAs are not a necessary condition for FDI, even in the extreme situation of an enterprise about to become a multinational. Casson is right to maintain that IAs are sufficient *on their own* to explain FDI. By laying down a double necessary condition – the existence of both IAs and OAs – when the former are undoubtedly a sufficient condition in themselves, the eclectic theory is logically inconsistent. However, the elements included in the concept of OAs are not without practical significance. If conceived as features of the enterprise – also linked to those of their countries of origin – these elements can guide the analysis on the one hand towards an understanding of FDI typologies and, on the other, of those characteristics which most readily induce enterprises – against a given historical background – to become multinational, or which facilitate their success abroad (on this latter point, see Casson, 1984, pp. 7–8).

Conversely, hardly anyone questions factors of location. Indeed, once again, it is not a problem of necessary factors, but of elements that help to determine the advantage of making FDIs, rather than alternative international operations (exports or some intermediate form).

As a second line of criticism, in the eclectic theory there are no references whatsoever to strategic factors that will induce an enterprise to become international through FDI. The place that these factors occupied in the original formulation of the FDI theory has been taken by the internalization factors. Those scholars who introduced the internalization factors must undoubtedly be given the merit of having filled a gap. In fact, the industrial organization approach had often considered FDI to be the 'natural' form of international operation by an oligopolistic enterprise, or else it was thought sufficient to consider it an operation undoubtedly justified by the oligopolistic nature of the firm which carried it out. From this viewpoint, consideration of internalization factors makes it clear above all that the forms of international operations are manifold. It also makes the choice between these forms endogenous. At this level, unquestionably, progress has thus been made. However, the costs of this operation are equally clear, particularly because of the expulsion of strategic factors, as shown in the previous sections.

In our opinion, on the contrary, these factors can and must assume a key role in the explanation of FDI and MNE. However, we cannot absorb strategic factors into the sphere of transaction costs, as the 'British branch' of the TCA seems to be attempting to do.

Also in that version of the TCA – still more in that of Williamson and others – failure to consider (explicit) strategic factors leads to a static levelling-out of the theory of the firm. In the case of the 'American branch', the enterprise appears to be nothing more than the sedimentation of internalized transactions on the basis of objective elements. Consequently, it appears in some respects similar to that bloodless neoclassical creature that Coase (1937) and other progenitors of the neo-institutional approach wished to exorcise. The drawback of such an approach is, *inter alia*, that of having a theory of the firm (or of the MNE) capable, fundamentally, of explaining the firm's organizational structure, whereas it is also of interest to have a theory of the firm's conduct and performance.

From another aspect, the risk is of remaining confined to a subset of Jacquemin's matrix (1987, p. 157), which considers two levels of the enterprise's action (production and organization) and two orders of motivation (the search for efficiency and the search for strategic commitment). The TCA would give expression to the efficiency motive in relation to organizational problems, but would neglect problems of production and the search for strategic commitment.

We wish to make it clear, above all, that the problem that concerns us – i.e. the need to explain the existence of the MNE – lies precisely at the intersection between the two action subsets considered by Jacquemin. In fact, FDI is, at one and the same time, a decision regarding production (the choice of producing abroad) and an organizational decision (it is the enterprise under consideration, not others, that produces abroad). At the level of efficiency, both location factors (which are an expression of productive efficiency) and internalization factors (which indicate organization efficiency) concur in the decision to engage in FDI.

But the same production/organization problem needs to be tackled in terms of strategy. Strategic factors influence production (for example, in order to erect barriers against foreign rivals, a commitment may be necessary in the form of excess capacity). The same factors also influence organizational aspects (the advantages of having full ownership of a subsidiary or of setting up a joint venture, a cartel, etc.). Thus a MNE comes

Table 9.1   Main factors in company choices

Actions	Motives	
	Efficiency	*Strategy*
Production (what, how much and when to produce)	*Technico-economic factors* (Product and factor prices; economies of scale and scope, etc.)	*Strategic-productive factors* (Costs and advantages of price strategies; costs and advantages of commitments and threats)
Production-organization (where to produce and who produces)	*Location factors* (International differentials of factor prices, economies of scale, transport costs, etc.)	*Strategic-locational factors* (Costs of foreignness, benefits to the product of a local production image; influence of FDI on industrial relations: influence of FDI on the relationships with competitors.
	Internalization factors (Transaction costs at an international level)	*Strategic-organizational factors* (Costs and advantages of FDI, non-equity agreements, etc., at world level, as instruments of co-operation/conflict)
Organization (choice of institutions)	*Internalization factors* (Transaction costs)	*Strategic-organizational factors* (Costs and advantages of various forms of co-operation/conflict)

into being at the intersection of production and organizational choices, on one side, and criteria of efficiency and strategy, on the other side.

In order to understand the determinants of FDI, it is therefore necessary to take *simultaneous* account of factors of location and internalization, as well as of strategic-productive and strategic-organizational factors. Any one of these factors will justify the existence of FDIs, provided that there are no contrary indications from either of the others.

We are now in a position to reformulate Jacquemin's matrix in such a way as to include the problem typical of FDI and the MNE (see Table 9.1). The relevant factors for an explanation of the actions (productive, productive-organizational and organizational), indicated in the rows, can be read off, according to the different motivations, in column 2 (efficiency) and column 3 (strategy).

FDI, which, as we have stated, is to be considered as an action of a productive-organizational nature, can be explained with reference to motives of both efficiency and strategy. Within the sphere of the former, the location factors must be considered simultaneously with those of internalization. If the motives are strategic, then both the strategic-productive and the strategic-organizational factors must be taken into account. As already stated, each of the factors mentioned is sufficient in itself to explain the existence of FDI; however, it is clear that one has to give an overall assessment of all the factors, as in every act of management.

One of the advantages of this approach lies in the fact that the factors which go to explain the decision to invest abroad are of the same nature as those which explain other decisions and the outcome of these decisions, both for firms in general and for MNEs.

Certainly, the theory of the MNE would appear in this way to be much more complex and less clear-cut than is the case with the TCA. However, it could also be more productive. We would thus have a new, less restricted kind of eclectic theory and one that would be more consistent. Polychromy, which has its aesthetic satisfactions, is not seen in that way from the standpoint of scientific methodology. But no matter! The MNE theory, which has at times contributed to the theory of the firm, is always affected by it. And the theory of the firm is at present very far from being a monolith.

Notes

1. I should like to thank John Cantwell and Francesca Sanna Randaccio for their helpful comments regarding earlier drafts of this paper.
2. In the last few years some advocates of the eclectic theory have tended to regard it as a paradigm or framework instead, considering it inappropriate to search for a general theory in a field where there are not only many different facts to explain but also various conflicting ideological standpoints and theoretical perspectives (Dunning, 1988; Cantwell, 1989).
3. Let us suppose that in one country (let's say Japan) there are a number of firms in a particular industry possessing different technological skills while having more or less the same management and marketing abilities. According to the eclectic theory one would expect that the firms that were leaders on a technological ground would be the leading foreign investor(s). This is not necessarily so, because in some circumstances the relatively backward firms would have a greater incentive to invest abroad, whether they had advantage over some foreign competitors or not.
4. For Italy, see Acocella (1985). For developing countries, see Lall (1983) and Wells (1983). For example, Williamson only fleetingly concedes the importance of technological factors in determining the size of enterprises (Williamson, 1985, chap. 4). Among the few supporters of the TCA who recognize its partial character is Buckley (1985, p. 101).
5. Among the very few exceptions, see Franko (1977); Graham (1978); Newfarmer (1979); and Vernon (1979). In more recent years, however, see Sugden (1985) and Cowling and Sugden (1987), Yu and Ito (1988).
6. In reality, Hymer's position is one of considerable variety and evolution. In his PhD thesis he devotes little space to the aspect of power; the paper in which he tackles this subject in depth appeared five years later (Hymer, 1965). His last writings (in particular, see Hymer, 1970, and Hymer, 1971) place more and more emphasis on the oligopolistic nature of the MNE. Nevertheless, the dual nature of the MNE is still clearly stressed in 1970 (see Hymer, 1970, in particular p. 443).

    The work in which Hymer introduces the dual nature of FDI in a more precise and reasoned way is a little-known one of 1968 (see Hymer, 1968). On the side of efficiency, Hymer for the first time makes explicit reference to Coase (1937) to explain the replacement of imperfect markets by enterprises (Hymer, 1968, pp. 951–4), whereas in his PhD thesis he underlined the superior nature of the enterprise *vis-à-vis* imperfect markets, without referring to any previous analyses of the matter. On the side of power he explicitly states that the enterprise not only reacts to the environment, but can at the same time modify it (Hymer, 1968, pp. 955–60) and that the expectation of increasing profits through collusion may be a sufficient determinant for FDI (Hymer, 1968, pp. 970–1).
7. The differences between Hymer's and Kindleberger's positions are stressed by Sanna Randaccio, 1984.
8. Opportunism, or strategic behaviour, is defined as the shrewd pursuit of egoistic aims (see Williamson, 1975, p. 26; and 1986, p. 129).
9. The TCA might, in this case, suggest an explanation in terms of the higher costs that an enterprise outside the Common Market (or the 'Single' Market) would have to bear. This explanation is insufficient, because it does not

provide a reason for decisions taken by an enterprise to locate inside the Common (or the 'Single') Market *before* the latter comes into operation. This means that there is always a strategic element, which tends, for instance, to avoid the consolidation of positions of power by the enterprise inside the Common Market. The effects of erecting tariff barriers in terms of strategic behaviour are examined in A. Smith, 1987, and A. Jacquemin, 1989.

10.   See Cowling and Sugden (1987, pp. 49–50), who refer for this last point to the literature on multi-market enterprises (especially Edwards, 1979; Bulow, Geanakoplos and Klemperer, 1985; Scott, 1982; and Feinberg, 1985).

11.   As to the strategic behaviour of multinationals towards governments, see, among others: Stopford and Wells, 1972; Streeten, 1976; Doz, 1980; and Grosse, 1980).

Bibliography

ACOCELLA, N. (1975) *Imprese Multinazionali e Investimenti Diretti, le Cause dello Sviluppo*, Milano: Giuffrè.

ACOCELLA, N. (ed.) (1985) *Le Multinazionali Italiane*, Bologna: Il Mulino.

ALIBER, R.Z. (1970) 'A Theory of Direct Foreign Investment', in C.P. Kindleberger (ed.) *The International Firm*, Cambridge, Mass.: MIT Press.

BUCKLEY, P.J. (1985) 'A Critical View of the Theory of the Multinational Enterprise', in P.J. Buckley and M. Casson, *The Economic Theory of Multinational Enterprise*, New York: St Martins Press.

BUCKLEY, P.J. and CASSON, M. (1976) *The Future of the Multinational Enterprise*, London: Macmillan.

BULOW, J.I., GEANAKOPLOS, J.D. and KLEMPERER, P.D. (1985) 'Multimarket Oligopoly: Strategic Substitutes and Complements', *Journal of Political Economy* 93.

CALVET, A.L. (1981) 'A Synthesis of Foreign Direct Investment Theories and Theories of Multinational Firm', *Journal of International Business Studies* 12, pp. 43–60.

CANTWELL, J. (1989) 'Teorie dell' Internalizzazione della Produzione', in N. Acocella, and R. Schiattarella (eds) *Teorie dell'Internazionalizzazione e Realtà Italiana* (an English version is also available as: 'Theories of International Production', *University of Reading DP in International Investment and Business Studies*, no. 122, 1988).

CASSON, M. (1984) 'General Theories of Multinational Enterprise: A Critical Examination', University of Reading DP in International Investment and Business Studies, no. 77.

CASSON, M. (1985a) 'Transaction Costs and the Theory of the Multinational Enterprise', in P.J. Buckley, and Casson, M., *The Economic Theory of Multinational Enterprise*, New York: St Martins Press.

CASSON, M. (1985b) 'Multinational Monopolies and International Cartels', in P.J. Buckley, and M. Casson, *The Economic Theory of Multinational Enterprise*, New York: St Martins Press.

COASE, R. (1937) 'The Nature of the Firm', *Economica*, November, reprinted in K.E. Boulding and K.E. Stigler (eds) *Readings in Price Theory*, Homewood:

Richard D. Irwin, 1952.

COWLING, K. and SUGDEN, R. (1987) *Transnational Monopoly Capitalism*, Brighton: Wheatsheaf.

DIXIT, A. (1979) 'A Model of Duopoly Suggesting a Theory of Entry Barriers', *Bell Journal of Economics* 10, pp. 20–32.

DIXIT, A. (1980) 'The Role of Investment in Entry Deterrence', *Economic Journal*, 90, pp. 95–106.

DOZ, Y.L. (1980) 'Strategic Management in Multinational Companies', *Sloan Management Review*, Winter 21, pp. 27–46.

DUNNING, J.H. (1979) 'Foreword' to N. Hood and S. Young, *The Economics of Multinational Enterprise*, London: Longman.

DUNNING, J.H. (1981) *International Production and Multinational Enterprise*, London: Allen & Unwin.

DUNNING, J.H. (1988) 'The Eclectic Paradigm of International Production An Update and Reply to its Critics', *Journal of International Business Studies*, Spring, 19, pp. 1–31.

ENCAOUA, D., GEROSKI, P. and JACQUEMIN, A. (1986) 'Strategic Competition and the Persistence of Dominant Firms: A Survey', in J. Stiglitz and G.F. Mathewson (eds) *New Developments in the Analysis of Market Structure*, Cambridge, Mass.: MIT Press.

EDWARDS, C.D. (1979) 'The Multimarket Enterprise and Economic Power', *Journal of Economic Issues* 13, pp. 285–301.

FEINBERG, R.M. (1985) '"Sales-at-Risk": A Test of the Mutual Forbearance Theory of Conglomerate Behaviour', *Journal of Business*, vol. 58, pp. 225–41.

FRANKO, L.G. (1977) 'European Multinational Enterprises in the Integration Process', in G.V. Curzon (ed.) *The Multinational Corporation in a Hostile World*, London: MacMillan.

GEROSKI, P. and JACQUEMIN, A. (1984) 'Dominant Firms and Their Alleged Decline', *International Journal of Industrial Organization*, 2, pp. 1–27.

GRAHAM, E.M. (1978) 'Transatlantic Investment by Multinational Firms: A Rivalistic Phenomenon?', *Journal of Post-Keynesian Economics* 1 no. 1, pp. 82–9.

GREER, C.R. and SHEARER, J.C. (1981) 'Do Foreign-owned US Firms Practice Unconventional Labour Relations?', *Monthly Labour Review* 104, pp. 44–8.

GROSSE, R.E. (1980) *Foreign Investment Codes and Location of Direct Investment*, New York: Praeger.

HYMER, S.H. (1965) 'Direct Foreign Investment and International Oligopoly', Mimeo.

HYMER, S.H. (1968) 'La Grande Corporation Multinationale', *Revue Economigue*, no. 6.

HYMER, S.H. (1970) 'The Efficiency (Contradictions) of the Multinational Corporation', *American Economic Review*, 60, pp. 441–8.

HYMER, S.H. (1971) 'The Multinational Corporation and the Law of Uneven Development', in J.R. Bhagwati, (ed.) *Economics and World Order*, New York: World Law Fund.

HYMER, S.H. (1976) *The International Operations of National Firms*, Lexington: Lexington Books, (reproduction of his PhD thesis, 1960).

ILO (International Labour Organization) (1976) *Multinationals in Western Europe: The Industrial Relations Experience*, Geneva.

JACQUEMIN, A. (1987) *The New Industrial Organization, Market Forces and Strategic Behaviour*, Oxford: Clarendon Press.

JACQUEMIN, A. (1989) 'Il Comportamento Strategico Internazionale e Multinazionale', in N. Acocella and R. Schiattarella (eds) *Teorie dell'Internazionalizzazione e Realtà Italiana*, Napoli: Liguori.

KINDLEBERGER, C.P. (1969) *American Business Abroad*, New Haven: Yale University Press.

KINDLEBERGER, C.P. (1984) *Multinational Excursions*, Cambridge, Mass.: MIT Press.

KOJIMA, K. (1978) *Direct Foreign Investment: A Japanese Model of Multinational Business Operations*, London: Croom Helm.

LALL, S. (1983) *The New Multinationals. The Spread of Third World Enterprises*, New York: Wiley and Sons.

NEWFARMER, R. (1979) 'Oligopolistic Tactics to Control Markets and the Growth of TNCs in Brazil's Electrical Industry', *Journal of Develoment Studies*, April, 15, pp. 108–40.

OZAWA, T. (1979) *Multinationalism, Japanese Style: The Political Economy of Outward Dependency*, Princeton, NJ: Princeton University Press.

RAGAZZI, G. (1973) 'Theories of the Determinants of Direct Foreign Investment', *IMF Staff Papers*, July.

SANNA RANDACCIO, F. (1984) 'The Current State of Research on the Theory of Multinational Enterprise', EUI Colloquium Papers on 'The Early Phase of Multinational Enterprise in Germany, France and Italy, Florence, 17–19 October.

SCOTT, J.T. (1982) 'Multimarket Contact and Economic Performance', *Review of Economics and Statistics* 64, pp. 368–75.

SMITH, A. (1987) 'Strategic Investment, Multinational Corporations and Trade Policy', *European Economic Review* 31, pp. 89–96.

SPENCE, M. (1977) 'Entry Capacity, Investment and Oligopoly Pricing', *Bell Journal of Economics*, 8, pp. 534–44.

STOPFORD, J.M. and WELLS, L.T. (1972) *Managing the Multinational Enterprise*, New York: Basic Books.

STREETEN, P. (1976) 'Bargaining with Multinationals', *World Development*, 4, pp. 225–9.

SUGDEN, R. (1985) 'Why Transnational Corporations?', mimeo.

TEECE, D.J. (1981) 'Multinational Enterprise: Market Failure and Market Power Consideration', *Sloan Management Review*, 22, pp. 3–17.

TEECE, D.J. (1983) 'Technological and Organizational Factors in the Theory of Multinational Enterprise', in M. Casson (ed.) *The Growth of International Business*, London: Allen & Unwin.

TEECE, D.J. (1985) 'Multinational Enterprise, Internal Governance and Industrial Organization', *American Economic Review*, May, 75, pp. 233–8.

TEECE, D.J. (1986) 'Transaction Cost Economics and the Multinational Enterprise. An Assessment', *Journal of Economic Behaviour and Organization* 7, pp. 21–45.

TURVANI, M. (1987) 'Introduzione', in Williamson O.E., *Le istituzioni economiche del capitalismo*, Milano: Angeli.

VERNON, R. (1979) 'The Product Cycle Hypothesis in the New International Environment', *Oxford Bulletin of Economics and Statistics*, November, 41, pp. 255–67.

WELLS, L.T. (1983) *Third World Multinationals*, Cambridge, Mass.: MIT Press.

WILLIAMSON, O.E. (1975) *Markets and Hierarchies, Analysis and Antitrust Implications*, New York: The Free Press.

WILLIAMSON, O.E. (1981) 'The Modern Corporation: Origins, Evolution, Attributes', *Journal of Economic Literature*, November; reproduced in Williamson, 1985, as chap. 11.

WILLIAMSON, O.E. (1985) *The Economic Institutions of Capitalism. Firms, Markets, Relational Contracting*, New York: The Free Press. Ital. trans., *Le istituzioni del capitalismo*, Milano: Angeli, 1987.

YU, C.M. and ITO, K. (1988) 'Oligopolistic Reaction and Foreign Direct Investment: The Case of the U.S. Tire and Textiles Industries', *Journal of International Business Studies*, Fall, 19, pp. 447–60.

10 The Behaviour of Risk-Averse Firms in a Duopolistic Market[1]

Riccardo Martina

INTRODUCTION

The study of the determinants of the behaviour and scale of business firms is one of the most pervasive and fascinating research topics in the field of industrial economics. As Schmalensee put it in a recent survey article (1988), it represents, nowadays as in the past, one of the main topical *foci* which define the discipline. Several studies, often supported by a large body of empirical research, have proposed different explanations of size inequality and seller concentration. Among these, as Tirole (1989) argues, the ones which stressed the link between basic market conditions, such as technology and consumer preferences (Scherer, 1980), and the scale of the firms, have played a crucial role in the development of both the theoretical and empirical literature. According to these studies, economies of scale (or scope) would be 'the most obvious candidates' to explain such empirical regularities as 'the high rank correlations of manufacturing industries' concentration levels between industrialised nations' (Schmalensee, 1988, p. 653). However, as Tirole puts it (1989, pp. 20–1), it can be argued that this 'technological view' does not provide a satisfactory theory of firm size. In a decentralized market economy, with negligible transaction costs, firms could duplicate their activities, operating sub-divisions as quasi-firms, in order to overcome the limits to their size imposed by increasing average cost curves. On the other hand, firms could decide to exploit technological advantages 'through contracting with separate entities' (Tirole, p. 20).

Industrial organization theorists have tried to overcome these and other weaknesses of the traditional approach, proposing several new lines of research aimed to provide a more insightful description of the firm's conduct and of the evolution of industrial structures. These approaches, which differ on several aspects, share the common perspective of aiming to provide a systematic analysis of the effects on the behaviour of the firm and, as a consequence, on the market structure, of different market failures. Among these, uncertainty plays a relevant role in determining that wide range of behavioural patterns that, under given circumstances, economic agents (firms) appear to possess.

It is far from surprising, therefore, that a large body of literature on market structure has been focused, in recent years, on the effects of an introduction of uncertainty on the working of perfectly and imperfectly competitive markets. Following the seminal contributions of Sandmo (1971) and Leland (1972), a number of papers have pursued, within this framework, an original line of research aimed at analysing the effects of uncertainty on the structure of imperfectly competitive markets with risk-averse firms. This recent literature, as will be discussed below, has achieved a number of interesting results, thus contributing to the definition of a complete taxonomy of the relationships between the structural parameters of the models, which include the risk preferences of firms, their behavioral patterns, their size and the level of concentration in the market. Some of these results, however, have been derived in the context of models characterized by fairly stringent assumptions; while successive attempts to test their robustness in a more general framework have only been partially carried out (Martina, 1989).

In this chapter a further step towards a general analysis of the behaviour of risk-averse firms in a duopolistic market is proposed. Following the approach proposed by Diamond and Stiglitz (1974), the paper analyzes, in the context of a duopoly model where the only restriction on firms' preferences is given by the assumption of concavity of the utility functions, the effects on the output decisions of two rival firms of an increase in the degree of risk aversion of one of the players. Our findings will confirm those presented by Horowitz (1987) for the case of a duopoly model with constantly risk-averse firms.

The paper is organized as follows: Section 1 discusses the results achieved by the literature, stressing the existing trade-off between the generality of the assumptions and the weaknesses of the conclusions. Section 2 introduces the model and presents the analysis of the effects of a Diamond–Stiglitz increase in risk aversion on the output decisions of firms. Section 3, finally, suggests some future developments of this line of research.

1. THE LITERATURE ON THE BEHAVIOUR OF RISK-AVERSE FIRMS IN DUOPOLISTIC MARKETS

The study of the behaviour of risk-averse agents under uncertainty can be regarded as one of the major fields of research in economic theory in the past four decades. Since the seminal work by Tobin and Arrow on the relation between liquidity preference and risk aversion, a large number of contributions (reviewed among others, in Hey, 1979; Hirshleifer and Riley, 1979; Lippman and McCall, 1981) have investigated the robustness of several theoretical predictions of the 'certainty' literature when economic agents display a risk-averse attitude. Owing to the recognized success of the research, undertaken by Sandmo, Leland and others, on the behaviour of a risk-averse firm in competitive and monopolistic markets, and to the more recent interest on the effects of risk aversion on the industry equilibrium (Appelbaum and Katz, 1986; Ishii, 1989) a promising research programme has started on the behaviour of risk-averse firms in oligopolistic markets, aimed to provide a link between this body of literature and the traditional approach to the oligopoly problem.[2]

As in all market situations where the outcome depends on the strategic behaviour of the players, uncertainty is inherent to the oligopoly problem; as Hey (1979, p. 144) puts it, 'take away the uncertainty from duopoly, or from oligopoly, and one takes away the whole subject: uncertainty is the very essence of the problem'. In a standard oligopoly model, uncertainty, for each player, is in the way the rivals are going to react to his own decisions; as such, uncertainty can be properly labelled as 'endogenous' (Pacheco *et al.*, 1988), since it emerges from the interaction of the players.

However, the agents' decision-making processes can be influenced by uncertainty in other relevant ways; given a market model for the players, uncertainty can take the form of one or more random variables whose realized values cannot be affected by the actions of the agents.[3] In this context, characterized by 'exogenous' uncertainty, agents face a more difficult task in determining their maximizing strategies. On one side, in fact, their decisions will depend on their rivals' actions; on the other, they will depend on their subjective probability distributions of the random variables. The agents' decisions and, as a consequence, the market outcome, will therefore be influenced by the joint effects of strategic policies and attitudes towards risk.

As for the first, the simple conjectural variation model provide a useful framework in order to analyse the effects of different 'degrees of collusion' on the behaviour of firms; in much the same spirit, a static duopoly model with risk-averse firms can provide a manageable framework in order to carry out some tentative analysis of the effects of risk attitudes on the decisions of oligopolistic firms. The papers reviewed in this section, although with some relevant differences, share this common approach.

Before presenting the main results of this literature, it is interesting to examine shortly how these papers deal with the problem of modelling the strategic behaviour of economic agents under conditions of 'exogenous' uncertainty. Agents, in these models, are assumed to be expected-utility maximizers; in the context of a static duopolistic game, with quantity-setting firms, the solution to the maximization problem leads the firms to make a simultaneous, once-for-all, output announcement which will depend on the parameters of the market model, on their attitudes towards risk and on the probability distribution of the random variable. This approach, which follows very closely Sandmo's analysis of the behaviour of a risk-averse competitive firm under uncertain demand, clearly rests on the transformation of a game of uncertainty into a game of certainty (see Resmusen, 1989, pp. 52–3).

In this context, the pay-offs of the players become dependent on Nature's moves, since they are defined on the basis of the expected values of the agents, and therefore on their subjective probability distributions. The framework thus defined allows them to focus attention on the relation between attitudes towards risk and agents' decisions.

The papers on duopoly models to be discussed are essentially devoted to this issue. Recently, Horowitz (1987), Martina (1989), Pacheco et al. (1988) have studied the effects of uncertain demand on the strategic behaviour of risk-averse duopolistic firms producing an homogeneous good, using different assumptions on the preference structure of the firms. In particular, in Horowitz's paper the preferences of the risk-averse duopolists are repre-sented by a constant absolute risk-averse function; in Martina's paper, the only restriction imposed on the utility functions of the firms is that of concavity, while in Pacheco *et al.* firms are assumed to maximize the dif-ference between the expectation and the variance of profits.

As expected, the results presented in these papers show the existence of a trade-off between the generality of the assumptions and the neatness of the results. In Horowitz, for instance, the author succeeds in presenting some interesting comparative static results, avoiding any cumbersome al-gebra. In his paper, after having examined the effects on the output decisions of the firms of a variation of the parameters of the demand and the cost functions, confirming the result of the certainty literature,[4] Horowitz in-vestigates the effects on the production levels of firms of a variation in the degree of risk aversion. The author finds that an increase of the degree of risk aversion of, say, firm *i* will unambiguously lead to a reduction of the output produced by firm *i* and to an increase in the output produced by its rival, firm *j*, therefore proving that the equilibrium outcome of the strategic game is crucially affected by the risk attitudes of the players.

Horowitz, Pacheco *et al.* make a specific hypothesis on the preferences of the firms: the authors assume that the duopolists maximize a quadratic utility function given by the difference between expected profits and their variance, with 'the latter being multiplied by a parameter measuring the rate at which the firm trades-off (expected) profits for risk – thus defining the degree of risk aversion of the firm' (Pacheco *et al.*, p. 2). Adopting this fairly special framework, the authors are able to prove that a mean preserving increase in the variability of the aggregate demand induces a reduction in the output of at least one of the two producers, and has an overall effect of reducing the total quantity supplied in the market. On the contrary, a spread-preserving increase in the total demand induces a positive reaction in the producers; as a result, total output obviously will increase.

Finally, as Horowitz, Pacheco and others prove, an increase in the degree of risk aversion of each firm has a negative effect on its own and on total output, while inducing a positive reaction on the rival production decision. The analysis of the effects of an increase in the degree of riskiness of the distribution of the random variable has been developed also by Martina (1989) in the context of a model with a general class of concave utility function. In this framework, the author finds that while the total output produced in the market will unambiguously be reduced, a risk-averse producer could react to an introduction in risk increasing his market share depending on his relative size (i.e. on his technology and on his attitude toward risk).

Even if the results presented in these papers appear to please the economic intuition and, more important, to confirm the results established in the 'certainty' literature and those found in the studies on the behaviour of a competitive firm under uncertainty, there is a peculiar aspect which emerges from these analyses, which is worthy of emphasis. In the class of models we have been discussing, agents' actions are essentially determined by two elements whose direct influence cannot be possibly disentangled: firms behave, in the mean time, as risk-averse agents and as strategic players.

As risk-averse agents they will act, as in the traditional analysis of the perfectly competitive firm faced with demand–price uncertainty, 'to avoid the low (or negative)-margin, high output prospect, even if it means missing some high-output, high profit opportunities' (Horowitz (1987), p. 249).

As strategic players, on the other hand, they will try, whenever possible, as the traditional analysis of the static duopoly game shows, to exploit profit opportunities which could derive from the reduction in the production of one of the players (see, on this point, for example, Marrelli and Martina, 1988). In order to do that, a duopolistic risk-averse firm could prefer to increase its production, even in the face of an introduction in uncertainty; the reason being that the reduction in output of the rival causes an increase in the marginal revenue of the firm, thus eliciting an increase in its output announcement.

As can be easily recognized, it is the very nature of the problem – risk-averse attitudes combined with strategic behaviour – to generate, in some circumstances, counter-intuitive results.

3. THE EFFECTS OF AN INCREASE IN THE DEGREE OF RISK AVERSION

The effects of an increase in the degree of risk aversion on the decision variable of an economic agent have been thoroughly studied by Diamond and Stiglitz in their 1974 paper. The authors propose to consider a family of utility functions, indexed by a parameter ρ which measures the degree of risk aversion. Following Diamond and Stiglitz's approach, an increase of ρ will denote an increase in the degree of risk aversion if and only if:

$$\frac{\partial}{\partial \rho} R = \frac{\partial}{\partial \rho} (-\frac{U_{\Pi\Pi}}{U_{\Pi}}) > 0$$

where R denotes the Arrow–Pratt measure of absolute risk-aversion and the subscripts respectively the first and second derivatives of the utility function with respect to its argument π, the profit function.

Let us now examine the effects of an increase of the degree of risk aversion on the output decisions of two rival firms. The framework of the analysis is given by the standard duopoly model with quantity setting agents. Firms, indexed by 1 and 2, operate in a market with either uncertain demand or uncertain technology (a parameter of the market model of the firm is a random variable) and take their output decisions solving an expected utility maximization problem. Output levels are announced simultaneously by the firms and the market price is determined, as in the Cournot model, by the equality of the demand function and the total supply announced by the firms. It is assumed that the form of the cost functions and of the market demand function guarantee the existence and the uniqueness of the equilibrium. The analysis aims to examine how the output decisions of the two duopolists are affected by a variation in the degree of risk aversion of one of the two firms: namely, we study how an increase, say, in the risk preferences of one of the two competitors influences his own output decision and that of his rival. It will be shown that an increase in the degree of risk aversion of duopolist 1, say, will have opposite effects on the output decisions of the two firms: namely, it will induce a reduction in the output announced by firm 1 and an increase in the output announced by firm 2.

This result is similar to that presented by Horowitz in his 1987 paper, where the author analysed the behaviour of a pair of constant absolute risk-averse duopolists; the analysis presented below can therefore be regarded as a generalization of Horowitz's findings to a broader class of utility functions.

The expected utility maximization problem of the two firms can be written as:

$$\max F = E_\alpha \, U[\Pi^1 \, (q_1, q_2, \alpha), \rho_1] \tag{1}$$

$$\max G = E_\beta \, U[\Pi^2 \, (q_1, q_2, \beta), \rho_2] \tag{2}$$

where α and β are the random variables in the firms' market model and ρ_i the parameter measuring the degree of risk-aversion of firm i. In this context, it could well be the case that $\alpha = \beta$, e.g. the random variable is the intercept of the market demand function. The first order conditions of the profit maximization problem are given by:

$$F_{q_1} = E_\alpha[U_\pi(q_1, q_2, \rho_1) \, \Pi_{q_1}] = 0 \tag{3}$$

$$G_{q_2} = E_\beta[U_\pi(q_1, q_2, \rho_2) \, \Pi_{q_2}] = 0 \tag{4}$$

at $q_1^* \, q_2^*$

We can now proceed to study how variations in the risk preferences of, say, firm 1 influences the producer's output decisions. By differentiation of the first order conditions, we get:

$$\begin{bmatrix} F_{q_1 q_1} & F_{q_1 q_2} \\ G_{q_2 q_1} & G_{q_2 q_2} \end{bmatrix} \begin{bmatrix} \partial q_1^*/\partial \rho_1 \\ \partial q_2^*/\partial \rho_1 \end{bmatrix} = - \begin{bmatrix} F_{q_1 \rho_1} \\ 0 \end{bmatrix} \tag{5}$$

where, in order to ensure the existence and the uniqueness of equilibrium, we assume that: (1) $F_{q_1 q_1}, G_{q_2 q_2} < 0$, and (2) the determinant D of the second order derivatives is positive. From (5), we get:

$$\partial q_1^*/\partial \rho_1 = - (F_{q_1 \rho_1} \quad G_{q_2 q_2}) \, / \, D \tag{6}$$

$$\partial q_2^*/\partial \rho_1 = (F_{q_1 \rho_1} \quad G_{q_2 q_1}) \, / \, D \tag{7}$$

which imply that $\partial q_1^*/\partial \rho_1$ will have the same sign of $F_{q_1 \rho_1}$, whereas $\partial q_2^*/\partial \rho_1$ will have a sign opposite to that of $F_{q_1 \rho_1}$, if $G_{q_2 q_1} < 0$ (i.e. if the reaction functions are downward sloping). In order to sign the expression $F_{q_1 \rho_1}$, it is first necessary to specify the effect of the random variable on the profit function. Let us assume that Π_α is positive, as it would occur if the random variable were the intercept of the linear market demand function.

We proceed now to evaluate the expression $F_{q_1 \rho_1}$:

$$F_{q_1 \rho_1} = \int_0^\infty U_{\pi \rho_1} \ [\Pi^1(q_1, q_2, \alpha), \rho_1] \ \Pi^1_{q_1} \ dF(\alpha) \tag{8}$$

Recalling that, if ρ_1 parametrizes risk aversion:

$$\frac{\partial}{\partial \rho_1} (-U_{\pi\pi}/U_\pi) > 0 \text{ or } \frac{\partial}{\partial \pi} (U_{\pi\rho_1}/U_\pi) < 0$$

we can rearrange (8), to have:

$$F_{q_1 \rho_1} = \int_0^\infty \frac{U_{\pi\rho_1}(\Pi^1, \rho_1)}{U_\pi \ (\Pi^1, \rho_1)} \ U_\pi \ \Pi^1_{q_1} \ dF(\alpha) \tag{9}$$

Let us assume now, that $\Pi_{q_1 \alpha} > 0$ (i.e. the effect of an infinitesimal change of the random variable on the marginal profit is positive), and that:

$$\exists \ \alpha^*, \text{ such that } \Pi^1_{q_1} \geq 0 \ \forall \ \alpha \geq \alpha^* \tag{10}$$
$$\Pi^1_{q_1} < 0 \ \forall \ \alpha < \alpha^*$$

which implies that in our analysis the random variable α can take values which make the marginal profit function negative.
Recalling that, from First Order Conditions, $E(U_\pi, \Pi_{q_1})=0$, we can multiply

it by the constant $\left. \dfrac{U_{\pi\rho_1} \ (\Pi^1, \rho_1)}{U_\pi \ (\Pi^1, \rho_1)} \right|_{\alpha^*}$ to get:

$$\int_0^\infty \frac{U_{\pi\rho_1}[\Pi^1(q_1, q_2, \alpha^*), \rho_1]}{U_\pi[\Pi^1(q_1, q_2, \alpha^*), \rho_1]} \ U_\pi \ \Pi_{q_1} \ dF(\alpha) = 0 \tag{11}$$

Subtracting this expression from (9), we get:

$$F_{q_1 \rho_1} = \int_0^\infty \left[\frac{U_{\pi \rho_1}}{U_\pi} - \frac{U_{\pi \rho_1}}{U_\pi} \alpha^* \right] U_\pi \, \Pi_{q_1}^1 \quad dF(\alpha) \tag{12}$$

Since, by assumption, $\Pi_\alpha > 0$, $\Pi_{q\alpha} > 0$, we can write that

$$\text{for } \alpha \geqslant \alpha^*, \quad \frac{U_{\pi \rho_1}}{U_\pi}\bigg|_\alpha - \frac{U_{\pi \rho_1}}{U_\pi}\bigg|_{\alpha^*} < 0 \tag{i}$$

since,

$$\frac{\partial}{\partial \alpha} \frac{U_{\pi \rho_1}}{U_\pi} = \frac{\partial}{\partial \pi} \frac{U_{\pi \rho_1}}{U_\pi} \frac{\partial \pi}{\partial \alpha} < 0,$$

Recalling, from assumption (10), that $\Pi_{q_1} \geqslant 0$, it follows that the integral (11) has a negative sign.

$$\text{for } \alpha < \alpha^*, \quad \frac{U_{\pi \rho_1}}{U_\pi}\bigg|_\alpha - \frac{U_{\pi \rho_1}}{U_\pi}\bigg|_{\alpha^*} > 0 \tag{ii}$$

As for (i), recall that, by assumption (10), $\Pi_{q_1} < 0$; it follows that the integral (11) has a negative sign. Therefore, under the hypothesis that $\pi_\alpha \geqslant 0$ and $\pi_{q_1 \alpha} \geqslant 0$,

$F_{q_1 \rho_1} < 0$, which in turn implies that:

$$\partial q_1^* / \partial \rho_1 < 0, \ \partial q_2^* / \partial \rho_1 > 0$$

namely, that an increase in the degree of risk aversion of firm 1 causes a reduction of its output and an increase of the output produced by its rival. Given the structure of the problem, it is clear that the same conclusion would be achieved under the assumption of a negative effect of the random variable on the profit function and on the marginal profit function.

4.   CONCLUSIONS

As Horowitz puts it in the concluding remarks of his 1987 paper, 'the fact that a competitor's risk preferences can affect another's output decisions in an unambiguous fashion is interesting but not especially earth shattering'. The extension of the Horowitz result to a model with general utility functions proposed here does not dismiss this claim. However, as we argued at length above, the results achieved by the research in this field have to be correctly regarded as small building blocks towards a more general theory of the strategic behaviour of risk-averse firms (agents) operating in imperfectly competitive markets. In this context, the finding that intensity of risk aversion affects the output decisions of firms, and therefore their sizes, suggests the existence of possible explanations of the size inequality of firms different from the traditional, 'technological', ones.

This result, coupled with those related to the effects on the output decisions of risk-averse managers of an introduction in uncertainty, confirms that, even in the framework of a simple static duopoly model, the introduction of uncertainty can provide a number of insights on the working of the markets. As such, this line of research appears to be extremely fruitful of new interesting results on relevant aspects of both industrial organization and of public policy. An immediate step towards them appears to be an extension to a world of imperfectly competitive markets of the literature on incentive schemes; in this context, the assumption of different attitudes towards risk of different agents, as managers and stock-owners, seems likely to offer new stimulus to the research on the effects of uncertainty on the size of firms and on the structure of the markets.

Notes

1. Financial contribution from the Consiglio Nazionale delle Ricerche (NATO-CNR Junior Fellowship) is gratefully acknowledged. I wish to thank M. Marrelli for helpful suggestions in revising earlier versions of this work. I am grateful to V. Dardanoni for allowing me to draw on jointly authored material and for his comments on this chapter.

2. The assumption of the risk-averse attitudes of firms has been often subjected to several criticisms. It was Sandmo (1971) who argued, for instance, that the idea of representing the behaviour of the firm through a Von Neumann-Morgenstern utility function had to be regarded as a 'strong assumption'. On the contrary, Leland (1972) provides arguments to support the plausibility of this hypothesis.

3. As Pacheco *et al.* noted (p. 1), Friedman (1983) argues that the problem of the effects of 'exogenous uncertainty' can be of great interest for the study of the oligopoly problem: 'One wonders whether introducing uncertainty merely means that everything carries through after being restated in expected value terms or whether fundamental changes in behaviour result. . . . It is probably necessary to introduce intrinsic uncertainty in the model' (p. 135).

4.   Martina (1989) proves the robustness of these results for the case of duopolistic firms with concave utility functions.

Bibliography

APPELBAUM, E. and KATZ, E. (1986) 'Measures of Risk Aversion and Comparative Statics of Industry Equilibrium', *American Economic Review* 76, pp. 524–9.

DIAMOND, P.A. and STIGLITZ, J.E. (1974) 'Increases in Risk and Risk-Aversion', *Journal of Economic Theory* 8, pp. 337–60.

DIXIT, A.K. (1986) 'Comparative Statics for Oligopoly', *International Economic Review* 27, pp. 107–22.

FRIEDMAN, J.W. (1983) *Oligopoly Theory*, Cambridge University Press.

FRIEDMAN, J.W. (1986) *'Game Theory with Applications to Economics*, New York: Oxford University Press.

HEY, J.D. (1979) *Uncertainty in Microeconomics,* Oxford: Martin Robertson.

HIRSHLEIFER, J. and RILEY, J.C. (1979) 'The Analytics of Uncertainty and Information: An Expository Survey', *Journal of Economic Literature* 17, pp. 1375–421.

HOROWITZ, I. (1987) 'Regression Estimated Parameters, Market Demand and Quasi-Cournot Behaviour', *International Journal of Industrial Organization* 5, pp. 247–52.

ISHII, Y. (1977) 'On the Theory of the Competitive Firm under Price Uncertainty: A Note', *American Economic Review* 67, pp. 768–9.

ISHII, Y. (1989) 'Measures of Risk-Aversion and Comparative Statics of Industry Equilibrium: Correction', *American Economic Review* 79, pp. 285–6.

LELAND, H.E. (1972) 'The Theory of the Firm Facing Uncertain Demand', *American Economic Review* 62, pp. 278–91.

LIPPMAN, S.A. and McCALL, J.J. (1981) 'The Economics of Uncertainty: Selected Topics and Probabilitic Methods', in K.J. Arrow and M.D. Intriligator (eds) *Handbook of Mathematical Economics,* Amsterdam: North Holland.

MARRELLI, M. and MARTINA, R. (1988) 'Tax Evasion and Strategic Behaviour of the Firms', *Journal of Public Economics* 37, pp. 55–69.

MARTINA, R. (1989) 'A Duopoly Model with Risk-Averse Firms', *Studi Economici* 38, pp. 3–23.

PACHECO, P., PEREE, E. and TORRES, F.S. (1988) 'Duopoly under Demand Uncertainty', European University Institute Working Paper, no. 88/358.

RASMUSEN, E. (1989) *An Introduction to Game Theory*, Oxford: Basil Blackwell.

ROTHSCHILD, M. and STIGLITZ, J.E. (1970) 'Increasing Risk, I: A Definition', *Journal of Economic Theory* 2, pp. 225–43.

ROTHSCHILD, M. and STIGLITZ, J.E. (1971) 'Increasing Risk II: Its Economic Consequences', *Journal of Economic Theory* 3, pp. 66–84.

SANDMO, A. (1971) 'On the Theory of the Competitive Firm under Price Uncertainty', *American Economic Review* 61, pp. 65–73.

SCHERER, F. (1980) *Industrial Market Structure and Economic Performance*, 2nd edn, Chicago: Rand-McNally.

SCHMALENSEE, R. (1988) 'Industrial Economics: An Overview', *Economic Journal* 98, pp. 643–81.
TIROLE, J. (1989) *The Theory of Industrial Organization*, Cambridge, Mass.: MIT Press.

Part IV

Technical Progress and Market Structures

11 Technological Change and Market Structure: The Diffusion Dimension

Paul Stoneman

INTRODUCTION

I have been asked to discuss technological change and market structure. This might lead to expectations of a chapter on research and development spending, its relation to firm size and concentration and Schumpeterian hypotheses. If so, then I am afraid expectations will be disappointed. I will only be referring to R & D *en passant*. Instead I will be concentrating on the use of new technology, or technological diffusion, rather than its generation. There are several reasons for this. First, I feel that the R & D literature has been pretty well surveyed and explored elsewhere. Secondly, I am much more interested in diffusion than R & D and much more attuned to what is happening in the diffusion field. Third, and most importantly, I tend to feel that diffusion is the poor relation in the technological change literature. It has merited much less attention than R &D, although in reality it is only as diffusion proceeds and as new technologies are used that such new technologies have their impact and their benefits are realized. Finally, I do not actually know of a large body of work that relates diffusion to market structure, and thus exploring this particular issue is more exciting than looking once again at R & D.

For the purposes of this chapter I will take market structure as shorthand for the size distribution of firms. Clearly there are many dimensions of market structure that this does not cover, e.g. barriers to entry, but as a focal point this definition is useful. Throughout the chapter I will use 'concentration' as synonymous with market structure.

Throughout the chapter I have in mind an economy that can be represented by a capital goods supplying sector and a capital goods using sector that provides final products. New technologies embodied in capital goods are assumed to come from the capital goods sector, are used in the capital-using sector and are here called process innovations. New consumer products are assumed to originate in the capital goods using sector and are called product innovations.

With this conception of the economy, market structure will refer to the size distribution of firms in the capital goods producing and the capital goods using sectors. The relation between diffusion and market structure is thus a relation between diffusion and the size distributions of firms in the two sectors. It goes almost without saying, that the relation between diffusion and market structure is a two-way relationship: market structure affects diffusion patterns, and diffusion patterns affect market structure. It is the same in the R & D literature. However, by looking at diffusion we can gain an extra dimension that is more dynamic than we are used to. If diffusion affects market structure, then at different stages of the diffusion process we may expect to see different market structures in the industry into which the new technology is being diffused. We may thus wish to explore the relation between the diffusion path and the path of market structure.

~   The chapter begins with the investigation of a very simple probit diffusion model, concentrating on process innovations, in which the supply of the new technology being diffused simply accommodates the demand for that technology, and in which market structure of the using industry is not affected by diffusion. Next we introduce the supply side by concentrating again on a new process technology, and again assuming that the using industry market structure is not affected by diffusion. Thirdly, we once more assume an accommodating supply industry, but allow now that diffusion does affect market structure of the using industry and see what patterns emerge. Finally, we look at the importance of the product/process distinction, and some aspects of the inter-firm/intra-firm distinction.

Throughout the paper we implicitly characterize the diffusion process by the speed of diffusion and the asymptote of the usage curve (the satiation level). We are thus interested in how market structure interacts with the final level of use of the new technology and the rate at which that final level is approached.

MARKET STRUCTURE AND THE DIFFUSION OF A NEW PROCESS TECHNOLOGY IN A DEMAND-BASED PROBIT MODEL

Davies (1979) finds, assuming other determining factors fixed, that the rate of diffusion of a new process technology is, empirically, negatively related to the number of firms (N) in the using industry and the variance of the log of firm size (σ_x^2) in that industry. Although most concentration measures can be considered as weighted functions of N and σ_x^2, until the weights are specified it is not possible to say whether, from these results, diffusion speed increases or decreases with concentration. Davies' results were derived from a probit framework. Romeo (1977), working in an epidemic/logistic framework, found a positive coefficient on σ_x^2, but it is not really possible to explain that finding with any degree of precision in a logistic framework.

In Davies' (1979) probit framework the findings are not too difficult to rationalize. It is assumed that there is a new process technology that a firm may acquire by acquisition of one (and only one) unit of a new capital good at price p_t in time t. The returns to ownership (R) vary with firm size (S), positively, say $R = \gamma S$. Let S be distributed according to the cumulative density function $F(S)$. Then a firm will acquire in time t if p_t, the cost of acquiring the technology in time t, is such that

$$p_t \leqslant R = \gamma S \tag{1}$$

or if $S \geqslant \dfrac{P_t}{\gamma}$ $\tag{2}$

The number of owners at time t (M_t) is then

$$M_t = N(1 - F(\frac{p_t}{\gamma})) \tag{3}$$

Take a very simple distribution for $F(S)$, say the logistic distribution, then

$$F(S) = \frac{1}{1 + \exp[-(S - \alpha)/\beta]} \tag{4}$$

where   mean $(S) = \alpha$
and   var $(S) = \beta^2\pi^2/3$

From (3) and (4)

$$\log_e (\frac{M}{N - M}) = \frac{\alpha}{\beta} - \frac{p_t}{\beta} \tag{5}$$

Thus for a given price, p_t, we see that

$$\frac{\partial M}{\partial N} = \frac{M}{N} > 0 \tag{6}$$

$$\frac{\partial M}{\partial \alpha} = \frac{1}{\beta} \cdot \frac{M}{M(N-M)} > 0 \tag{7}$$

$$\text{and } \frac{\partial M}{\partial \beta} = \frac{1}{\beta} \left(-\log \left(\frac{M}{N-M} \right) \right) \tag{8}$$

If $\frac{M}{N-M} < 1$, $\log \left(\frac{M}{N-M} \right) < 0$. Thus if $M < \frac{1}{2} N$, $\frac{dM}{d\beta} > 0$ and if

$M > \frac{1}{2} N$, $\frac{dM}{d\beta} < 0$. Given these results an increase in N increases use, but

the elasticity of M with respect to N is unity. An increase in the mean of firm size, α, also increases use. An increase in the variance of firm size, β, increases use for $M < \frac{1}{2} N$, and decreases use for $M > \frac{1}{2} N$.

The results, obviously, do not match the empirical results of Davies but one may see the way that they are generated from a simple model.

As far as diffusion models go, this is very simple. By making the return a function of firm size, it gives a direct link between diffusion and the firm-size distribution. However, this is not essential. One may specify some other dimension across which firms differ and define the $F(\ )$ distribution as a distribution of 'reservation prices' instead. If one can then argue that the mean and/or variance of these reservation prices is related to some measure of market structure one can get a similar result. We will not, however, pursue that here.

One problem with such probit models as these is the technique choice rule $p_t < R$. In a world where p_t is falling, as it must to drive the diffusion (if R does not increase with t), this may be an inappropriate rule. It states that the technology is adopted at the first date it is profitable to adopt. However the actual rule should be that adoption occurs at that date when it is *most* profitable to adopt. This rule will involve the potential buyers expectations on p_t. If buyers are myopic then $p_t < R$ is the rule that results. However in the absence of myopia, the expectation of p_t will enter the decision rule. To fully explore this, however, we need to add a supply side.

THE SUPPLY SIDE

In a series of papers with Norman Ireland (e.g. Ireland and Stoneman (1986)), I have explored diffusion models of the probit type in which a supply side is explicitly incorporated. We will concentrate on that detailed in Ireland and Stoneman (1986).

As before, buyers only purchase one unit of a new capital good. We index buyers in decreasing order of the service flow, such that a buyer with index x obtains a constant flow of services $g(x)$ per period of ownership and $g_x < 0$. For the xth ranked buyer, two conditions have to be satisfied for adoption in time t.

$$-p(t) + \frac{g(x)}{r} \geq 0 \text{ (profitability condition)} \tag{9}$$

$$-D\hat{p}(t) + rp(t) - g(x) \leq 0 \text{ (arbitrage condition)} \tag{10}$$

where $D\hat{p}(t)$ is a continuous time representation of the buyers expectation of the change in price between t and $t + dt$. (We use the D operator to represent a derivative with respect to time.) Under myopia $D\hat{p}(t) = 0$, and thus the xth indexed buyer will acquire at the first t when $rp(t) = g(x)$. Under perfect foresight, the only other case considered, $D\hat{p}(t) = Dp(t)$, and given, as is the case, $Dp(t) < 0$, the arbitrage condition dominates the profitability condition and (18) defines the dynamic demand for the technology. We note that as buyers only ever buy one unit, the rank x of the marginal buyer in time t equals the number of acquirers to time t.

On the supply side we assume n quantity setting, identical firms, each maximizing its expected profit given the behaviour of the other $(n - 1)$ firms. We assume that while production takes place unit cost $c(t)$ falls until some time t, after which it increases, i.e.

$$Dc(t) \underset{>}{\overset{<}{=}} 0 \text{ as } \hat{t} \underset{>}{\overset{<}{=}} t$$

It is then shown that on the optimal profit-maximizing path, the two trajectories under myopia and perfect foresight can be characterized by:

Myopia

$$rp = g(x) = rc - Dc + \frac{n-1}{n} \cdot Q \frac{g_x}{r} \tag{11m}$$

$$g(x_1) = rc(t_1) \tag{12m}$$

Perfect foresight

$$-Dp + rp = g(x) = rc - Dc - \frac{xg_x}{n} \tag{11pf}$$

$$g(x_1) = rc(t_1) - \frac{x_1}{n} \cdot g_{x_1} \qquad (12\text{pf})$$

where $Q = Dx$, and t_1 is the terminal diffusion date.

The first point to make is that as $n \to \infty$ (11pf) and (12pf) tend to (11m) and (12m) with $n = 1$, i.e. the perfect foresight path for a large number of producers approaches the myopia path with a single supplier. The logic of this result is that, as n increases, the supplying industries becomes nearer to being competitive. Then all profits from the adoption of the new technology goes to the users, who choose a rate of take-up to maximize total rents – thus emulating the choice of the single monopoly supplier with myopic buyers.

For $2 \leqslant n \leqslant \infty$ on the perfect foresight path, (11pf) and (12pf) indicate that at t_1, $Dc = 0$ and thus $t_1 = \hat{t}$. Thus the terminal date is unaffected by n, and is still t. From (12pf) a sufficient condition for $x(t)$, $t \leqslant \hat{t}$ to increase with n is that $d(xg(x))/dx > 0$, and $d^2(xg(x))/dx^2 < 0$. This condition is analogous to that of positive but declining marginal revenue in a static market and we will assume that it holds. Then a greater number of suppliers implies increased usage for all t due to the lower price trajectory of the most competitive environment, and we can state:

Proposition 1: Multiple suppliers and buyers' perfect foresight yields an open loop equilibrium with sales until $\hat{t}$ and higher sales at any point in time the greater the number of suppliers. As the number of suppliers becomes infinite the perfect foresight path approaches the path under myopia with one supplier.

Under myopia with multiple suppliers, we have from (11m) that for all $t < t_1$, $rc - Dc = g(x) - (n-1) Qg_x/rn$, whereas with a single supplier $rc - Dc = g(x)$. Given $g_x < 0$, x will be greater for all $t < t_1$ with a greater number of suppliers. One solution to (11m) and (12m) has $Dc = 0$ and $Q = 0$ at t_1, which implies $t_1 = \hat{t}$. Although other solutions to (11m) and (12m) which involve $Dc < 0$ and $Q > 0$ at t_1 (and thus $t_1 < \hat{t}$) are possible, we cannot consider any t_1 thus generated as a valid terminal point since such a solution would not constitute an open loop equilibrium. The reason for this is that any one firm would then take other firms' production to end at t_1 and would conjecture additional profits for itself by remaining in production at t_1 and waiting for cost savings to generate further profitable sales. As all firms would have similar conjectures, an open loop equilibrium can only be characterized by production continuing until $\hat{t}$ after which no further cost reductions are possible. We can thus state:

Proposition 2: Multiple suppliers and buyers' myopia yield an open loop equilibrium where accumulated sales are greater at any time before $\hat{t}$ than in the case of a single supplier.

We may thus state that a more competitive market structure in the supply industry encourages greater use of the new technology. However in Ireland and Stoneman (1986) we also point out that within the confines of the model, the welfare optimal diffusion path is the path that would be generated by a monopolist supplier facing myopic buyers. As we have stated, the same path is generated by a supplying industry facing buyers with perfect foresight as $n \to \infty$. As n increases diffusion speeds up and we may thus state that an increase in n is welfare improving if buyers have perfect foresight but will produce too rapid diffusion if buyers are myopic.

This result and the model, however, take the existence of the technology as predetermined. As we have indicated, the profits of the suppliers will depend on the foresight of buyers and the number of suppliers. As n increases, suppliers' profits decrease and profits are also lower under perfect foresight. These profits (or the expectation of them) represent the incentive to develop the technology in the first place. In a further paper with Norman Ireland discussed in Stoneman (1987), we consider this complication, basically arguing that given free entry into R & D for developing new technologies, n will be endogenous, as well as the nature of the technology to be diffused. Moreover we point out there that the effectiveness of the patent system will be an important factor determining n and thus the number of suppliers of the new technology and the diffusion path.

ANOTHER LOOK AT THE DEMAND SIDE: FEEDBACK FROM USE TO PROFIT GAINS

Thus far we have modelled the demand side as if the gain to any individual adopter is independent of the number of adopters to date. A more Schumpeterian assumption would relate the gain from adoption to the extent of adoption so far. This is the basis of Reinganum's (1981) model. In essence, assume that apart from adoption dates, all adopters are the same. Let a firm using the new technology make profit $\prod_1(M, N)$, and a firm using old technology make profit $\prod_0(M, N)$ where M is the number of adopters and N the number of firms in the industry. Reinganum *assumes* that

$$\Delta\pi(M, N) \equiv \pi_1 (M, N) - \pi_0(M, N)$$

decreases with M. With an adoption rule that a firm adopts if $p_t < \Delta\pi (M_t, N)$, one may then trace out a diffusion path as p_t falls over time. As would be obvious, if $\Delta\pi$ is not a monotonic function of time, the model is much more difficult to operate. Moreover Fudenberg and Tirole (1985) have criticized Reinganum for not considering pre-emption and Quirmbach (1986) has also criticized the Reinganum model.

Rather than pursue these criticisms we will, on the altar of simplicity, look them straight in the eye and pass on to consider a simple model that will contain the essence of the argument. This model is based on that used in Waterson and Stoneman (1985). Consider an industry with N firms of whom at any time M_t are the users of the new technology. The new technology yields production costs c_1, the old technology cost c_0, $c_0 > c_1$. There is a linear demand curve

$$z = a - bQ , \qquad a, b > 0 \tag{13}$$

where $\quad Q = \sum_i q_i \qquad i = 1 \dots N$

and z = industry price, q_i = output of firm i.

Ignoring fixed costs, users of both types of technology maximize profits

$$\pi_i = (a - bQ)q_i - c_k q_i \qquad k = 0, 1 \tag{14}$$

assuming Cournot conjectures. This yields

$$q_0(M, N - M) = \frac{a - (M + 1) c_0 + M c_1}{b(N + 1)} \tag{15}$$

$$q_1(M, N - M) = \frac{a + (N - M)c_0 - (N + 1 - M) c_1}{b(N + 1)} \tag{16}$$

as the output of old and new technology firms. We assume that c_1 is not low enough to drive $q_0(M, N)$ negative.

Then

$$q_1 - q_0 = \frac{c_0 - c_1}{b} \tag{17}$$

and

$$Q = M q_1 + (N - M) q_0 \tag{18}$$

We will assume that adopters are completely myopic and consider that the profit gain at the date of adoption will last forever. With this assumption we may look at the per period profit gain without the complication of integrating over time.

Then

$$\pi_1 - \pi_0 = [a - bQ] [q_1 - q_0] - c_1 q_1 + c_0 q_0$$

$$= \frac{a}{b} (c_0 - c_1) - \frac{M}{b} (c_0 - c_1)^2 - N q_0 (c_0 - c_1)$$

$$= \frac{c_1(c_0 - c_1)}{b} - c_1 q_0 + c_0 q_0 \tag{19}$$

As M increases the profit gain from adoption decreases, for

$$\frac{d(\pi_1 - \pi_0)}{dM} = \frac{-1}{b} (c_0 - c_1)^2 (\frac{2}{N + 1}) < 0. \tag{20}$$

Looking at the effect of market structure

$$\frac{d(\pi_1 - \pi_0)}{dN} = - q_0(c_0 - c_1) + \frac{dq_0}{dN} (1 - N) (c_0 - c_1). \tag{21}$$

Given $\dfrac{dq_0}{dN} = - \dfrac{q_0}{N + 1},$

$$\frac{d(\pi_1 - \pi_0)}{dN} = (c_0 - c_1) (q_0) (\frac{-2}{N + 1}) < 0. \tag{22}$$

Thus in this simple framework the profit gain from adoption decreases with N. With this result, for a given cost of acquiring the new technology, M_t will be lower as N is higher.

This is not however the main reason for analysing this model. I am more interested in using it to explore how market structure of the using industry will vary as diffusion proceeds. Basically if M is zero (all firms use old technology) and all are assumed the same, concentration as measured by CR_k would be k/N. As diffusion proceeds however, q_0 and q_1 change and thus so would measured market structure.

Now we may state that

$$CR_k = \frac{Mq_1 + (k - M)\, q_0}{Mq_1 + (N - M)\, q_0} \quad \text{for } k \geq M \tag{23}$$

and $CR_k = \dfrac{kq_1}{Mq_1 + (N - M)\, q_0} \quad \text{for } k < M \leq N.$ (24)

For $k \geq M$

$$CR_k = \frac{\dfrac{M(c_0 - c_1)}{b} + kq_0}{\dfrac{M(c_0 - c_1)}{b} + Nq_0} \tag{25}$$

and $\dfrac{dCR_k}{dM} > 0.$

For $k < M$

$$CR_k = \frac{kq_0 + k\, \dfrac{c_0 - c_1}{b}}{\dfrac{M(c_0 - c_1)}{b} + Nq_0} \tag{26}$$

and

$$\text{sign } \frac{dCR_k}{dM} = \text{sign } \left[\frac{(c_0 - c_1)^2}{b^2} \left(\frac{k\,(-1 - M)}{N + 1} \right) - \frac{kq_0(c_0 - c_1)}{b} \right] \tag{27}$$

$$= \text{negative.}$$

Thus for $k \geq M$, CR_k increases with M, for $k < M$, CR_k decreases with M. The actual signs themselves are not important. The critical issue is that measured concentration changes as diffusion proceeds. Market structure results from the diffusion process, but more importantly, an observation on market structure at a moment in time is just one point on a path of market structure, and this one point may not be a true guide to the structure of that industry.

CONCLUDING REMARKS

We have explored the relation between diffusion and market structure in several modelling frameworks. There is no consistent set of findings from these models but it is too early in this analysis to expect consistency. Perhaps of more interest here is to conclude by considering two other issues: intra-firm diffusion and product differentiation, this latter being an essential part of any study of the diffusion of product innovations.

The above discussion has concentrated on diffusion across firms and assumed that firms only ever buy one unit of the new technology. Relaxing this assumption raises questions on how market structure will affect the rate at which new technology is adopted within the firm. This is not an issue that appears to have been much discussed in the literature, but should be amenable to analysis.

In a recent paper, Stoneman (1990) I have looked at diffusion in a model of horizontal product differentiation. In that paper I suggest that if brands are controlled by different oligopolists rather than a single brand monopolist then the diffusion will be affected by this. In particular I suggest that there will be an end game under oligopoly, and diffusion under oligopoly will be more extensive than under monopoly. For most of the diffusion path however, the differences in market structure will have no effect. These are, however, conjectures, and represent and avenue for future research.

References

DAVIES, S. (1979) *The Diffusion of Process Innovations*, Cambridge University Press.

FUDENBERG, D. and TIROLE, J. (1985), 'Preemption and Rent Equalizaiton in the Adoption of New Technology', *Review of Economic Studies* 52, pp. 383–401.

IRELAND, N. and STONEMAN, P. (1986), 'Technological Diffusion, Expectations and Welfare', *Oxford Economic Papers* 38, pp. 283–304.

QUIRMBACH, H. (1986), 'The Diffusion of New Technology and the Market for an Innovation', *Rand Journal of Economics* 17, no. 1, Spring, pp. 33–47.

REINGANUM, J. (1981), 'Market Structure and the Diffusion of New Technology', *Bell Journal of Economics* 12, pp. 618–24.

ROMEO, A. (1977) 'The Rate of Imitation of a Capital Embodied Process Innovation', *Economica* 44, pp. 63–9.

STONEMAN, P. (1987) *The Economic Analysis of Technology Policy*, Oxford University Press.

STONEMAN, P. (1990), 'Technological Diffusion, Horizontal Product Differentiation and Adaptation Costs', *Economica*, 57, pp. 49–62.

WATERSON, M. and STONEMAN, P. (1985) 'Employment, Technological Diffusion and Oligopoly', *International Journal of Industrial Organisation*, September 3, pp. 327–44.

12 Inventive Activity and Risk Aversion[1]

Damiano Silipo

INTRODUCTION

There is a large amount of evidence showing that the discovery of a new good or a new technique is the result of luck as well as of the rational pursuing of a specific aim (see Jewkes *et al.*, 1969, p. 356). Sometimes the pursuing of a specific aim leads to findings in different fields as a by-product of the R & D activity (Nelson, 1959). Indeed the very essence of R & D activity is the uncertainty about the nature of discovery and the amount of expenditure necessary to achieve the discovery.

In this paper we analyse the inventive process leading to the production of a new good or a new technique. We consider the effects of the manager's attitude to risk on the rate and allocation of R & D expenditure over time. Given the stochastic nature of R & D, in order to obtain more robust results, we perform simulations on the model. Simulations are carried out for both the contractual and non-contractual cost case of the projects.

The random factors as well as the deliberate seeking characterizing the inventive process have been pointed out (among others) by Arrow (1970). This chapter models the nature of production of knowledge along this line. The approach followed in modelling the characteristics of the innovative process stresses the *selective*, (finalized in quite precise directions) and *cumulative* (in the acquisition of knowledge) nature of R & D activity pointed out by alternative explanations of technical change (Alchian, 1950; Nelson and Winter, 1982, p. 414; Rosenberg, 1976; Pavitt, 1979; for a recent review of these theories see Dosi, 1988). In contrast to this last, we claim that the approach undertaken in the present paper can be adopted to explain more general aspects of the innovative process than the particular problems involved.

On the other hand, the literature on the incentive to invent under uncertainty stresses the role of exogenous variables (market structure, degree of competition on R & D, etc.) on the rate and direction of inventive activity (see Arrow, 1962, pp. 609–25; Dasgupta and Stiglitz, 1980; Bhattacharya and Mookhrjee, 1986).

Moreover the optimal allocation of R & D expenditure has been considered for a given degree of risk aversion (Aldrich and Morton, 1975; Cyert *et al.* 1978; Deshmukh and Chikte, 1977).

In this paper we analyse the rate and allocation of R & D expenditure through time for different degrees of risk aversion when the manager pursues a specific aim and the outcome of research is stochastic. In this respect this paper provides further insight into the forces affecting inventive activity.

THE SETTING

We consider a situation in which the firm's R & D laboratory searches for a new good or a new method of production. We envisage a good or technique made of a certain number of components, the number of which is known, but the identity is not. The set of all possible components is, however, known, and so the research involves working through the components until the correct ones are found.

The research of the right components takes place by carrying out experiments. An experiment consists in performing a combination of components; so the set of combinations made with the known components contains combinations with no correct elements, combinations with some elements correct, and the combination with all the elements correct. By performing experiments the researcher try to infer the right elements entering in the combination. The discovery is achieved when the correct combination is achieved.[2] At any time the probability of succeeding in a R & D project depends on the line of enquiry undertaken as well as on the amount of expenditure devoted to the project. We express this proposition formally as follows

$$p_t = p_t \, (s_t, \, n_t, \, m_t) \tag{1}$$

where p_t denotes the probability of succeeding in a R & D project in period t, which depends on the amount of expenditure devoted to the project in the same period, s_t, on the number of elements which at the beginning of period t have still to be discovered, n_t, and the number of elements that have not yet been eliminated, m_t.[3] These two parameters define the information structure of the firm. The values of n_t and m_t depend on the particular lines of enquiry undertaken previously. Moreover, we assume the information arising from the experiments is deterministic: i.e. the researcher is able to recognize if in the combination there are correct elements and which ones *are* the correct elements.[4]

At the beginning of the research the manager is assumed to be endowed with a prior probability distribution on the set of the possible combinations characterizing the discovery. Let us assume there is no prior information about the likelihood of the possible combinations. So the prior probability distribution is uniform, and the information gathered comes only from the experiments' results. The researcher updates the prior probability distribution by sequentially performing experiments. On the other hand, the path of discovery depends also on the adopted decision function by which the previous experiments' results are processed. A possible decision function could be to consider next all the combinations that contain correct elements, and then choose, within this set, the experiments to perform. Since we assumed a uniform prior probability distribution, in each and every period the choice between the remaining elements is made randomly. So the discovery is the result of luck as well as of a rational choice.

Another possible decision function consists in performing combinations that do not contain the elements already discovered. Once an element has been found, it is possible to get to the discovery faster by considering 'entirely new' combinations, since in this case the probability of eliminating elements and hence discovering the right elements is higher than when combinations with the elements already discovered are performed. The stopping probability by adopting the latter decision function is in fact stochastically dominated by the former decision function.

In the design of the simulations we adopt the decision function which is stochastically dominating. However, the above argument is not a formal proof that the adopted decision function is the best.[5]

With the above assumptions we analyse the manager's optimal amount and allocation of R & D expenditure in the project in terms of the optimal number of experiments and their optimal allocation through time.

Using simulations we can evaluate the optimal allocation of experiments through time in a sequential and in a predetermined decision-making framework. In the predetermined approach all the decisions are made at the outset. The researcher considers alternative sequences of experiments until the truth is discovered. For each sequence he evaluates all the possible paths of discovery, and then he computes the stopping probability and the corresponding expected profits. The optimal strategy is the sequence of experiments that maximizes the expected profits over all the possible sequences. (see Raiffa, 1970). In the next period no choice of acts has to be made. The researcher carries out the decisions undertaken in the first period. In the predetermined approach the experiments' results are then evaluated *ex ante*.

On the contrary, in the sequential approach the decisions are taken sequentially through time. In each period the optimal number of experiments is determined according to the previous period's experiments results. At the outset the researcher evaluates each possible result in the last period of his temporal horizon and by backward induction he decides the optimal number of experiments to perform in each period. According to the effective results of the experiments he restates his calculations. The researcher proceeds in a similar way until the discovery is achieved.

The predetermined and the sequential approach can be adopted to analyse the R & D expenditure for different kinds of projects. If the nature of the project requires making decisions in the project until its completion (e.g. the aircraft industry), the predetermined approach is more appropriate. On the other hand, if the nature of the project does not require undertaking the decisions once and for all (e.g. the chemical industry), then the sequential approach is more appropriate.

In the simulations we consider both cases. For each case both the risk-neutral and the risk-averse behaviour is analysed.

Before presenting the results of the simulations with respect to the 'technology of information' we should point out that we adopt simulation techniques because of the stochastic nature of the model and the difficulties of handling the analytical solution, which do not allow us to get unambiguous results.

THE PRODUCTION FUNCTION OF INFORMATION

In the first set of simulations[6] we evaluate the relationship between the probability of succeeding in the project and the amount of expenditure devoted to it. This relation can be considered in a static and a dynamic approach. In the former the probability of succeeding is evaluated in relation to the amount of expenditure devoted to the project (or, alternatively, the number of experiments performed) in a given period of time. On the contrary, in the latter the experiments are performed through time and so the researcher can learn from the previous experiments' results.

We performed the simulations for several conditions on the initial values of the parameters. For the particular case of $n_t = 2$ and $m_t = 7$, and with the simplifying assumption that only the combination of two elements are considered, we present the result of the simulations for the static case in Fig. 12.1.

The probability of discovering the truth in a specific time t, as a function of the number of experiments performed in that period, increases more than proportionally for the first experiments and then increases less than proportionally. The economic explanation of the present conclusion can be found

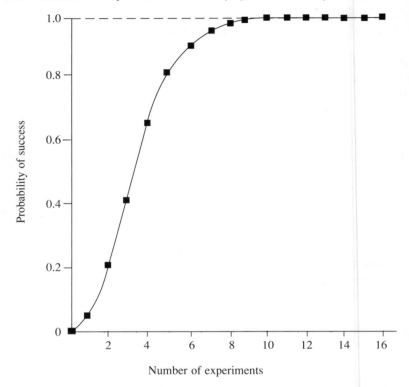

Figure 12.1

in disorganizational economies when the R & D laboratories exceed certain dimensions. It can be shown that this relationship is independent of the particular values of the parameters. The initial conditions about n_t and m_t affect the amount of expenditure which is required to achieve the discovery, not the functional form of the stopping probability. The bigger are the values of n_t and m_t the higher is the amount of expenditure required to obtain the discovery. However the random factors entering into the discovery process should be pointed out.

We should stress that the relation shown in Fig. 12.1 is a static one. So the experiments are performed simultaneously and there is no possibility of learning from the experiments' results. On the contrary, in a intertemporal context it is possible to take account of the previous experiments' results in the decision-making process. The stopping probability for the above example when one experiment at a time is performed is shown in Fig. 12.2.

The results of the simulation show that 3 experiments may be required to

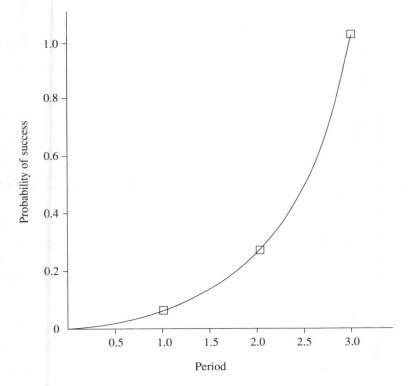

Figure 12.2

achieve the discovery when the experiments are performed sequentially; whereas in the simultaneous case to get to the discovery at least 16 experiments may be necessary.

We denote the difference in the number of experiments to obtain the discovery in the sequential and the simultaneous case as the gains from learning. On the other hand, we should stress the cost connected with performing the experiments sequentially. In the latter case it takes longer to achieve the discovery than in the case of simultaneous performing of the experiments, given the same amount of available resources. In other words, in the discovery process there is a trade-off between the timing of discovery and the amount of resources necessary to achieve the discovery. Increasing R & D levels of expenditure in the first periods of the research increases the probability of achieving the discovery sooner; in the mean time it reduces the possibility of learning from the experiments' results. So the intertemporal allocation of experiments depends on the manager's attitudes towards the learning process which takes place in the discovery process.

With the next set of simulations we evaluate, within the present framework, the rate and allocation of experiments through time of a maximizing expected profit manager under different assumptions on the nature of the R & D projects and risk-aversion behaviour.

R & D EXPENDITURE ALLOCATION IN A PREDETERMINED FRAMEWORK

In this section we address the question of the R & D activity in relation to different degrees of risk aversion. We assume the manager maximizes the expected utility of profits:

$$\max_{s_t} EU(\Pi) = \max_{s_t} EU \; [p_1(s_1, n_1, m_1) \, R - s_1 +$$

$$\sum_{t=2}^{r} \int_0^{n_t} \int_0^{m_t} V_t(n_t, m_t) f(n_t, m_t, s_{t-1}) \, dn_t \, dm_t] \qquad (2)$$

$$t = 1. \ldots , r$$

where U is the manager's utility function, R is the per period patent profit rate, s_t is the expenditure in the project, V_t is the maximum value function in period t, r is the manager's temporal horizon and $f(n_t, m_t, s_{t-1})$ is the joint density function of n_t and m_t for given values of s_{t-1}. As evaluated from period $t-1$ the values n_t and m_t are random variables of the amount of expenditure in period $t-1$; they can vary between the values of these parameters at the beginning of the research and zero, the common value assumed from the parameters when the truth has been discovered.[7] We assume the cost function is linear.

Adopting a dynamic programming framework, we find by backward induction the optimal allocation in the other periods in terms of the possibility of discovering the truth in the last period of his intertemporal horizon (see Bellman, 1957). Let us consider the optimal rate and allocation of experiments for a risk-neutral and a risk-averse manager. In the former the utility function U in (2) is linear; in the latter U is a concave function of profits.

First we investigated whether a risk-averse manager spends less on the project than a risk-neutral manager and how they differently allocate experiments through time. In order to compare the two cases of risk-aversion behaviour we run the simulations under similar conditions.

For some initial values of n_t and m_t the results on the optimal allocation of experiments are presented in Table 12.1.

Table 12.1

	Risk-neutral manager	Risk-averse manager ($r_{AP} = .001$)	Risk-averse manager ($r_{AP} = .1$)
Optimal number of experiments ($n_t = 2$, $m_t = 7$)	4 1 1	4 1 1	3 1 1
Optimal number of experiments ($n_t = 2$, $m_t = 12$)	6 2 1	6 2 1	4 2 1

After a large number of runs and for a wide range of iterations we found unambiguously that the more risk averse the manager is, the less he invests in R & D.

The results for the predetermined case are given in Table 12.1, assuming the discount rate $\alpha = .90$ and the per period patent rate $R = 5$. If the initial conditions are $n_t = 2$ and $m_t = 7$ the optimal strategy for a risk-averse manager is to perform four experiments in period one, one experiment in period two and one experiment in the third period. So three periods may be necessary to achieve the discovery. For a risk-averse manager with the Arrow–Pratt index of absolute risk-aversion $r_{AP} = 0.1$ (for an analysis of the risk-aversion indexes see Hey, 1979) the optimal strategy is to perform three experiments in period one, one experiment in period two and one combination in period three. So we can conclude that the risk-averse manager spends less in the R & D project than a risk-neutral one. Moreover, the more risk-averse the manager is, the less is the level of expenditure in the R & D project.

We found that this result is general and does not depend on the initial conditions or the particular values of the parameters. However, we should point out that the results of the simulations are of uncertain generality. They depend on the particular combinations picked up in the simulation process, which make random the nature of the results even if we performed a large number of iterations.

From Table 12.1 it can be noticed that the decrease in the number of experiments for the risk-averse manager takes place in the earlier stages of the research, suggesting that a risk-averse manager is less 'impatient' than the risk-neutral one, preferring to have a relatively higher level of expenditure in the later stages, when some results have came out from which he can consequently learn. So we should expect that a risk-loving manager spends more on the project and has a relatively higher level of expenditure in the earlier stages of the research.

We considered then the effects of changes in some parameters on the manager's behaviour. Specifically, we investigated how the optimal allocation of experiments changes consequently to a change in the discount rate and the per period patent rate. The results show a positive relationship between the level of expenditure in R & D and an increase in the discount rate. In the particular case of $n_t = 2$ and $m_t = 7$ the optimal allocation of experiments for some values of the discount rate are presented below:

Table 12.2

Per period patent rate ($\alpha = .90$)	$R = 1$	$R = 5$	$R = 10$	$R = 15$	$R = 20$
Risk-neutral manger	2 1 1	4 1 1	5 1 1	6 1 1	6 2 1
Risk-averse manager ($r_{AP} = .01$)	1 1 1	4 1 1	5 1 1	6 1 1	6 1 1
Risk-averse manager ($r_{AP} = .1$)	1 1 1	3 1 1	4 1 1	4 1 1	4 1 1

A similar conclusion holds with respect to the increase of the per period patent rate. Some results of the simulations for the previous case are presented in Table 12.3.

Table 12.3

Discount rate ($R = 5$)	$\alpha = .30$	$\alpha = .50$	$\alpha = .70$	$\alpha = .90$
Risk-neutral manager	1 1 1	2 1 1	3 1 1	4 1 1
Risk-averse manager ($r_{AP} = .01$)	0	2 1 1	3 1 1	4 1 1
Risk-averse manager ($r_{AP} = .1$)	0	0	3 1 1	3 1 1

Tables 12.2 and 12.3 show also that the above results are independent of the

manager's behaviour towards risk. However, the less risk-averse is the manager the more he reacts to a change in the values of the parameters. On the other hand these findings seem consistent with the intuition about the expected behaviour of a risk-averse manager. Finally, from Tables 12.2 and 12.3 it can be noticed also that the change in the values of the parameters affects the amount of expenditure in the earlier stage of the research.

In the next section we consider if the present results still hold in the sequential case.

R & D EXPENDITURE ALLOCATION IN A SEQUENTIAL APPROACH

In the sequential case the manager adapts his decisions to the experiments' results. So according to the number of elements discovered in the previous stages he makes the optimal decision with respect to the number of experiments to be performed in that stage. The Table 12.4 can help to make clearer the nature of the manager decision in the sequential case here evaluated.

Table 12.4

Per period patent rate 1.00		Discount rate 0.90
Optimal number of experiments		
n/m	1	2
1	0	0
2	1	0
3	1	1
4	2	2
5	2	2
6	2	3
7	2	3

If we start with initial conditions of $n_1 = 2$, $m_1 = 7$, $R = 1$ and $\alpha = .90$ from the first period experiments' results the values of the parameters become $n_2 = 2$ and $m_2 = 4$; consequently the optimal number of experiments to be performed in the second period is two, etc. In this case the optimal behaviour consists in determining the optimal number of experiments in the next period, given the previous period's results. It may be useful to consider in more detail this latter aspect. In the predetermined approach the experiments' results affect the manager's decisions *ex ante*; that is, he takes account only of the possible results of the experiments. Since the latter do not change through time, the manager does not change his optimal allocation determined at the beginning of the research.

In the sequential approach the results of the experiments affect the manager's decisions either *ex ante* or *ex post*. It follows that the experiments' results may lead to a revision in each period of the optimal amount and allocation of experiments through time. So in the latter case the results of the experiments are effective in determining only the next period's optimal decisions.[8]

In Fig. 12.3 we present the results of the simulations for the sequential case. We can see that the qualitative results achieved in the previous paragraph with respect to the attitude to risk still hold.

The optimal number of experiments is inversely related to the manager's

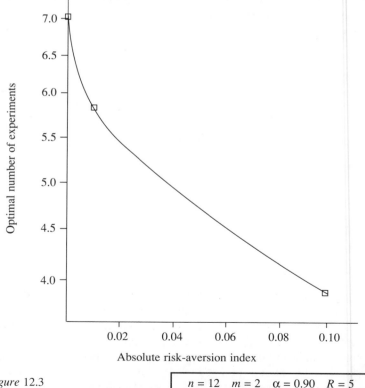

Figure 12.3

$$n = 12 \quad m = 2 \quad \alpha = 0.90 \quad R = 5$$

degree of risk aversion. Also, the conclusions of the previous paragraph concerning a different degree of reaction of a risk-averse and a risk-neutral manager with respect to a change in the values of the parameters are valid. So the nature of the project does not affect qualitatively the manager's behaviour with respect to the rate and allocation of R & D expenditure through time.

Finally we evaluated the effects of the nature of the project on the firm's expected profits. To this purpose we run the simulations for the same initial conditions in the sequential and the predetermined case. The optimal allocation of experiments through time and the correspondent expected profits are shown in Table 12.5 for both the risk-neutral and the risk-averse manager:

Table 12.5

| | Risk-neutral | | Risk-averse ($r_{AP} = .1$) | |
	Predetermined case	Sequential case	Predetermined case	Sequential case
Optimal number of experiments ($m_t = 7, n_t = 2$)	4 1 1	4	3 1 1	3
Expected utility of profits ($m_t = 7, n_t = 2$)	39.04	40.27	2914.80	3005.11
Optimal number of experiments ($m_t = 12, n_t = 2$)	6 2 1	6	4 2 1	4
Expected utility of profits ($m_t = 12, n_t = 2$)	34.89	35.72	2406.18	2453.33

The results of Table 12.5 are given for a value of the discount rate $\alpha = .90$ and the per period patent rate $R = 5$. As could be predicted, we can see that, independently of the degree of risk aversion, the expected profit for the sequential case is higher than the predetermined case. So there is an advantage when it is possible to perform the experiments sequentially, and then learn from the effective results, over the predetermined case. This latter result suggests some bias towards undertaking projects characterized by non-contractual costs. However, the analysis of the direction of the inventive activity is beyond the scope of the present work.

From Table 12.5 it can be noticed also that the expected utility of profits is higher for a risk-averse than a risk-neutral manager, whatever the nature of the project. This result suggests that risk-averse behaviour can prevail in expected utility of profit-maximizing managers.

Finally, comparing the expected utility of profits in the two initial conditions considered, we can see that this latter variable is inversely related to the values of n_t and m_t, leading to the conclusions that *ceteris paribus* there is a bias towards undertaking projects where there is an higher amount of initial knowledge available, irrespective of the degree of risk aversion. However this conclusion may be no longer valid when the projects differ with respect to the per period patent profit rate. So an extention of the present work could involve the analysis of the effects of the manager's attitude towards risk on undertaking projects characterized by the same expected revenue but with different per period patent profit rate.

CONCLUSION

In the present chapter we modelled R & D activity in terms of the search over a set of combinations. The discovery consists of performing the combination which contains the right elements. Within this framework we considered the rate and allocation of R & D expenditure through time. By simulation techniques, we addressed the question of the effects of the manager's attitude to risk on R & D activity. The general result is that the attitude towards the risk effects the rate and allocation of R & D expenditure in a crucial way. We found that more risk-averse managers spend less on R & D projects and relatively less in the earlier stages of the research. We found that this result is independent of the nature of the project involved. In turn, an expected utility of profits maximizer adopts a risk-averse behaviour, independently of the nature of the project. However, we should point out that due to the simulations techniques adopted, the results are of uncertain generality. However, since the present model involves a small number of parameters and we performed a large number of simulations, we believe our conclusions are not affected by the analytical tools adopted.

The above analysis has been carried out in a decisional theoretical framework. So a natural extension of the present work could involve strategic interaction considerations in the intertemporal allocation of R & D expenditure.

Notes

1. I thank Professor John Hey for the helpful comments on a previous version of this paper.
2. This way of handling the R & D activity may be considered appropriate to analyse the inventive process in specific sectors (e.g. chemical industry, pharmaceutical industry, etc.). If the elements in the combinations are considered in a wider meaning we believe the model presented in this paper could be addressed to capture even organizational aspects of firms' innovations.
3. So if the firm undertakes lines of enquiry which do not contain the right combination, m_t and n_t never will be null, whatever will be the number of experiments performed within the set of combinations considered.
4. Further possibilities could be semi-probabilistic or stochastic information. In the former the researcher is able to recognize from the experiment if there are correct elements but not which are the correct elements; in the latter the researcher is endowed with a probability distribution on the possible combinations and from the experiments' results he can only infer the likelihood of the probability distribution the combination comes from.
5. The research into the optimal decision function (i.e. the decision function which allows the biggest step forward in the discovery process, given the available information) is a central aspect of the economics of research.
6. The programs for the simulations can be obtained from the author. I thank Professor John Hey for the help he gave to me in writing the programs for the simulations.
7. For mathematical reasons we assume that m_t and n_t are continuous variables. However, the results are not affected by this assumption.
8. The sequential case can be then considered properly dynamic. In the predetermined case the dynamic aspect consists only in the multi-periodal context of the decision-making process.

References

ALCHIAN, A.A. (1950) 'Uncertainty, Evolution, and Economic Theory', *Journal of Political Economy* 58, pp. 211–21.

ALDRICH, C. and MORTON, T.E. (1975) 'Optimal Funding Paths for a Class of Risky R & D Projects', *Management Science* 21, pp. 491–500.

ARROW, K. (1962) 'Economic Welfare and the Allocation of Resources for Invention', in R. Nelson (ed.) *The Rate and Direction of Inventive Activity*, Princeton: Princeton University Press.

ARROW, K. (1970) 'Classificatory Notes on the Production and Transmission of Technological Knowledge', in K.J. Arrow, *Essays in the Theory of Risk-Bearing*, Amsterdam: North Holland, chap. 7.

BELLMAN, R. (1957) *Dynamic Programming*, Princeton: University Press.

BHATTACHARYA, S. and MOOKHERJEE, D. (1986) 'Portfolio Choice in Research and Development', *Rand Journal of Economics* 17, pp. 594–605.

CYERT, R.M., DEGROOT, M.H. and HOLT, C.A. (1978) 'Sequential Investment Decisions with Bayesian Learning', *Management Science* 24, pp. 712–18.

DASGUPTA, P. and STIGLITZ, J. (1980) 'Uncertainty, Industrial Structure and the Speed of R & D', *Bell Journal of Economics* 11, pp. 1–28.

DEGROOT, M.H. (1970), *Optimal Statistical Decisions*, New York: John Wiley.

DESHMUKH, S.D. and CHIKTE, S.D. (1977) 'Dynamic Investment Strategies for a Risky R and D Project', *Journal of Applied Probability* 14, pp. 144–52.

DOSI, G. (1988) 'Sources, Procedures, and Microeconomic Effects of Innovation', *Journal of Economic Literature* 26, pp. 1120–71.

HEY, J.D. (1979) *Uncertainty in Microeconomics*, Oxford: Martin Robertson.

JEWKES, J., SAWERS, D. and STILLERMAN, R. (1969) *The Sources of Invention*, 2nd edn, New York: Norton.

NELSON, R.R. (1959), 'The Simple Economics of Basic Scientific Research', *Journal of Political Economy* 67, pp. 297–306.

NELSON, R.R. and WINTER, S.G. (1982) *An Evolutionary Theory of Economic Change*, Cambridge, Mass.: Harvard University Press.

KAMIEN, M.I. and SCHWARTZ, N.L. (1982) *Market Structure and Innovation*, Cambridge University Press.

PAVITT, K. (1979) 'Technical Innovation and Industrial Development: The New Causality', *Futures*, 11, (6), pp. 458–70.

RAIFFA, H. (1970) *Decision Analysis*, Reading, Pa: Addison-Wesley pp. 1–300.

ROSENBERG, N. (1976) *Perspectives on Technology*, Cambridge University Press.

13 Market Structure, Firm Size and Innovation in Italy: An Integrated Approach to Testing Schumpeter[1]

Niall O'Higgins and Patrizia Sbriglia

INTRODUCTION

In this chapter we examine the Schumpeterian hypothesis that concentrated markets act as a spur to industrial innovation, examining evidence for Italy over the period 1981–5. The central idea underlying our analysis is that the testing of the Schumpeterian hypothesis on market structure and innovation needs to be modified in order to take into account the possibility of different responses of small and large innovators to changes in market concentration, barriers to entry, technological opportunities and demand conditions. The existence of such differences would support the claim advanced by Acs and Audretsch (1988) that in asymmetric market structures small and large firms may respond to different technological and economic regimes, and more or less competition may have a different effect on their incentive to innovate.

Failure to take into account variations in the responses of firms of different sizes to market conditions may lead to a mis-specification of econometric models employed to test the links between market structure and industrial innovation. Indeed, the bulk of the empirical literature in this area has considered the relationships between innovation and firm size, on the one hand, and between innovation and market structure on the other, as two separate issues. Apart from the recent work by Acs and Audrestch on industrial innovation in the United States (1987; 1988), little attention has been paid to a further element of interest: that is, the relationship between industry structure and innovation in small and large firms operating in the same market. If concentration acts as a spur to innovative activity, as has been claimed, does it affect small and large innovators to the same extent?

The reasons why this question is important are twofold.

Firstly, there is an increasing interest in the innovative activity of small firms and in the conditions under which small innovators emerge and challenge the technological leadership of large firms.

Secondly, the relationship between competition and technological advance, although greatly debated, is still somewhat unclear. It is, for instance, generally recognized that the perfectly competitive industry, even if better for consumers in the short run, would not allow technical advance, but it is still a matter of discussion how much 'imperfection' should be considered as optimal (especially in industries where firms differ in terms of size, cost and demand conditions) and the dynamic links between concentration and innovation are still to be fully explored, both in theory and in empirical analyses of industrial technical change.

In our chapter the possibility of analysing the different roles of small and large innovators arises out of an improvement in the available data provided by the recent surveys on innovation diffusion in Italian industry carried out by (ISTAT–CNR (Istituto Centrale di Statistica – Consiglio Nazionale delle Ricerche).[2] In these surveys, the innovative activity of firms of different sizes is explored in detail, which allows us to test the existence of differences in the response of small and large innovators to market conditions.

Applying a grouped logit model to the Italian data on innovative activity, we examine the relationship between market structure and innovation, allowing for variations in the responses of firms of different sizes. Controlling for other factors suggested by theoretical considerations as likely to affect innovative activity (barriers to entry, demand conditions, technological opportunities and appropriability) we find that firm size significantly affects the response of enterprises to such stimuli. In particular, a greater incentive for small firms to undertake innovative activity is found in concentrated industries with high technological opportunities and high barriers to entry, whilst, by the same token, concentration has no significant impact on the innovativeness of large firms. Thus the evidence presented below strongly supports the proposition that large and small innovative firms operating in the same industry structure respond differently to market stimuli. Although less innovative than their large counterparts overall, small firms seem to fit better the predictions of the Schumpeterian theory of technical advance that identify in product market concentration, technological opportunities and appropriability the structural conditions that favour innovation.

The chapter is organized as follows. In Section 1, we survey some of the literature on firm size and technological advance. Section 2 provides a description of the data employed, whilst Section 3 outlines the empirical model and results. In the conclusion, we suggest some directions for further empirical work in this area in order to provide a more general interpretation of the links between firm size, market structure and technological advance.

1 LARGE AND SMALL INNOVATIVE FIRMS AND THE EXISTENCE OF ALTERNATIVE TECHNOLOGICAL REGIMES

Despite the existence of a large body of empirical and theoretical literature on market structure and innovation, there is still very little understanding of the determinants of innovative activity in small and medium-sized firms and of how these determinants differ from those underlying the innovative activity of large firms in the same industry. There is also little understanding of what sort of innovative activity is generally carried out in small and medium-sized units, and how the size structure of the industry may influence the rate of technical change through a different propensity to undertake risky projects.

Evidence of the role played by small and medium-sized firms in determining the pace of industrial technical change is inconclusive. As far as innovative inputs are concerned, the greater part of empirical work in this area suggests that, overall, small and medium-sized firms are less innovative than large ones, investing less in research and development, relative to their size, than their bigger counterparts. This result seems to apply to all industries and to validate Galbraith's claim that 'bigness and fewness' are the conditions that most favour technological advance. However, if we consider innovative output (as represented by, for example, the number of innovations patented or introduced), the results of empirical work are less clear-cut. Indeed, looking at the number of innovations introduced and/or patented, small and medium-sized firms have performed well and, in the case of some specific industries, better than their larger counterparts.[3] The success often achieved by small and medium-sized innovators indicates that innovative activity carried out in small units deserves more attention than it has thus far been given. The evidence accumulated on the innovative performance of small firms suggests, above all, two things. Firstly, as noted by Kay (1987), although in general big firms are more innovative than small ones, the existence of some successful small innovators partially rejects the Schumpeterian hypothesis on firm size and innovativeness.

Secondly, the successful innovative performance of small firms achieved in some industries and in some countries confirms the idea that, as far as R & D departments are concerned, 'largeness' is not always synonymous with efficiency, since the nature of the teamwork that is related to innovative activity sometimes militates in favour of small and medium-sized units.[4]

One further element of interest in the analysis of the innovative performance of small firms lies in the study of the characteristics of their innovative activity and of the strategies pursued by small and medium-sized innovators. Studies investigating innovative strategies have in fact shown (see, for example, Caves and Pugel, 1980; or Freeman, 1982) that in some industries new small or medium-sized innovators aim to challenge the market leadership of large firms through technological advance, supporting more aggressive strategies, (competing for instance on completely new products) which, if successful, allow them to grow and to increase their market power. For this reason, it is possible to observe that in some industries, small and medium-sized firms carry out the riskiest projects, while larger firms tend to specialize in development activity that, requiring a larger capital outlay, is less feasible for small units.

Mansfield (1981) found that, whilst big firms seem to carry out a disproportionately large share of basic research in most industries, there is no statistical support for the hypothesis that they carry out a similarly large share of the relatively risky R & D or of R & D aimed at entirely new products and processes.

Although the results of empirical work on firm size and innovation still present an unclear picture, often relying on specific case studies, some general insights may be drawn. Firstly, small and medium-sized firms have a lower level of research intensity than large ones, implying that they generally undertake less innovative activity. On the other hand, even recognizing a scale disadvantage, it has been shown that small and medium-sized innovators can and do emerge, and, in some cases, perform better than large innovating firms. When this occurs, technological success is one of the main causes of firms' growth. Furthermore, when technological competition does take place between different sized firms, it is the small and medium-sized enterprises that tend to adopt the more aggressive R & D strategies.

One major point of interest is to understand which market and technological conditions are likely to raise innovative activity amongst small and medium-sized firms. In particular, are market concentration and barriers to entry likely to act as spurs or as deterrents to the innovative activity of small firms? Do the conditions which stimulate innovative activity differ according to the size of the firm?

Two recent studies (Acs and Audretsch, 1987; 1988) have looked at these questions by estimating econometric models in which a measure of innovativeness was regressed on several market characteristics, such as concentration, unionization, advertising expenditure, and the capital–output ratio. In Acs and Audretsch (1987), the dependent variable employed was the difference between innovation rates for small and large firms.[5] In the subsequent paper (Acs and Audretsch, 1988) separate regressions were estimated for small and large firms, using as their dependent variable the natural logarithm of the number of innovations introduced.[6] They employ as explanatory variables indicators of barriers to entry (capital–output ratio, advertising expenditure), unionization, the proportion of skilled labour employed, and demand growth.

In the first paper, the authors conclude that small firms have a comparative advantage in situations in which market structure was closer to the competitive model, whilst large firms tend to be favoured in industries which are capital-intensive, advertising-intensive, and with a concentrated market. The second, on the other hand, suggests that industrial concentration is detrimental, in terms of its effect on innovative output, for both large and small firms. Once again, however, small firms are more discouraged than large ones in concentrated industries.

The work by Acs and Audretsch has the merit of raising the important question of how to study market structures, taking into account the efforts of firms of different size. So far the problem of the role of market conditions in encouraging (or discouraging) R & D activities in small and large firms has been overlooked, being confined to models which do not allow for different responses. The improvement of the available data and of the theoretical analysis on the asymmetry of incentives may give a better insight into this area.

2   THE INNOVATION DATA

The measure of innovative activity employed in this paper is given by those firms undertaking R & D activity in the period 1981–5. The variable is divided into two and three digit classifications and into five size classes comprising firms with: 20–49, 50–99, 100–199, 200–499, and more than 500 employees. Table 13.1 reports the proportion of firms undertaking R & D broken down by the Industrial Sectors and by the five size classes employed in the empirical model below. The measure is derived from the first survey on innovation diffusion in Italian manufacturing industry (1981–5) carried out by ISTAT-CNR (1987).

In the questionnaire, firms were asked a number of questions on their innovative activities: firstly, whether or not they had undertaken any innovative activity over the period; secondly, they were asked whether the final aim of any such activity regarded product, process or organizational innovation (or some combination of the three). They were also asked for the source of their innovative activity. That is, whether it was based on 'in-house' R & D, purchase of innovative equipment, purchase of external knowhow or patents, use of innovations previously patented by the firm itself, and so forth.[7]

Table 13.1   Number of firms undertaking R & D in each industrial sector and in each size class

SIC		(A) No. of firms undertaking R & D	(B) Total no. of firms	Proportion of firms undertaking R & D = A/B
14	Mineral oil refining	12	41	.293
22	Prod. & prelim. proc of metals	42	391	.107
24	Non-metallic mineral products	174	1871	.093
25	(excl. 257) chemicals	288	714	.403
257	Pharmaceuticals	155	219	.708
26	Man-made fibres	8	17	.471
31	Manufacture of metal articles	228	3171	.072
32	(excl. 323, 327, 328) Mechanical Engineering	415	2437	.170
323	Textile machinery	28	142	.197
327/328	Misc. machinery	42	307	.137
33	Office & data proc. machinery	7	21	.333
34	(excl. 344, 345, 346) Electrical engineering	172	914	.188
344	Measuring & recording equipment	54	156	.346
345	Radio & TV equipment	63	209	.301
346	Domestic appliances	30	159	.189
35	(excl. 351) Motor vehicle bodies & parts	49	389	.126
351	Motor vehicles	5	14	.357
36	Other transport	40	280	.143
37	(excl. 372, 373) Precision instruments	33	129	.256
372	Medical & surgical equipment	13	75	.173
373	Optical instruments	19	104	.183
41	Basic foods	109	1181	.092
42	Sugar, drinks, tobacco & misc. food	84	598	.140
43	Textiles	141	2334	.060
44	Leather	56	459	.122
45	Footwear & clothing	73	2834	.026
46	Timber & wooden furniture	96	1967	.049
47	Paper & paper products	76	1300	.058

48	Rubber & plastics	160	1195	.134
49	Jewellery & musical instruments	42	473	.089

Size class
(no. of workers)

20–49	1073	14885	.072
50–99	564	4673	.121
100–199	449	2553	.176
200–499	358	1298	.276
500 and over	270	695	.388
Total	2714	24104	.113

Source: ISTAT (1987)

The survey was sent out to 37,188 firms with at least 20 employees, of which 24,104 (65 per cent) firms responded. Of the firms taking part in the survey, 16,701 (69 per cent) said that they had undertaken some form of innovative activity over the period 1981–5. These innovative firms were used as the basis for a second follow-up survey which went into a great deal more detail as to the nature of the innovations, their cost and their source(s).

The results of the first survey allow us to gain a general insight into the pattern of innovation in Italy, as well as to obtain specific information on the composition of the innovative inputs and outputs, the sectoral and size distribution of innovative firms, governmental support and the constraints to innovative performance. By introducing specific questions on the nature of innovative inputs and outputs as well as by the extent of coverage, the survey provides the most complete data source as yet available on innovative activity in Europe.

Of particular relevance to this study, the survey gives rise to the possibility of analysing the innovative performance of firms of different sizes. In as much as aggregate indicators, such as industrial expenditure on R & D (collected by the Organization for Economic Co-operation and Development) tend to underestimate the innovative efforts of small and medium-sized firms which often carry out R & D outside a specific R & D department, the new Italian surveys address the problem of inputs to the innovative process in a more complete and accurate way.

It has in fact been shown by statistical surveys carried out in other European countries, (see, for example, Kleinknecht, 1987) that aggregate statistics on R & D, usually employed to test hypotheses concerned with firm size and innovation, tend to be biased against R & D activity in small firms.

In smaller enterprises, R & D may be carried out in a more informal context than in larger concerns and without necessarily having a specific R & D department. It is also sometimes the case that in small firms, managers and technicians directly contribute to improvements in processes or organization or to the introduction of new products without having formal investment strategies regarding R & D. In this respect, a direct survey on R & D activity carried out by firms of different sizes may provide a better indicator of, in particular, innovative activity by small firms than the aggregate statistics.

Being the first direct inquiry into innovative activity in Italy, the survey is, of course, not without shortcomings. Of particular concern to this study, the survey tends to underestimate the size of innovative firms, in as much as it ignores the existence of subsidiary enterprises. Each company is considered as an independent unit without taking into account the possibility of flows of information and/or resources between groups of companies. This problem, which is a feature of all industrial data collected by ISTAT, may have important effects in so far as large companies with many partially independent subsidiaries are likely to undertake joint research activity which the survey cannot capture.

As regards the other variables employed in the analysis, data on industrial sales, capital investment and market concentration were drawn from the annual censuses of business carried out by ISTAT (*Fatturato, prodotto lordo, investimenti delle imprese industriali, del commercio, dei trasporti e communicazioni e di alcuni tipi di servizi*). Data on basic research expenditure was drawn from the annual ISTAT report, '*Indagine statistica sulla ricerca scientifica*'. Finally, data on patents were obtained from Archibugi (1988) and refer to the number of patnets awarded to Italian firms in the United States over the period 1969–84.

3   EMPIRICAL MODEL

We estimate a model relating a measure of R & D intensity to market and technological conditions, allowing these conditions to have different effects according to the size of the firm. The measure of R & D intensity employed is the proportion of firms in a particular size class and industry undertaking R & D over the period 1981–5. We prefer this as an index of innovative activity to the alternative available from the data, namely the proportion of firms introducing innovations over the period, for reasons hinted at above. Specifically, it appears that a large part of what was understood to be innovation was in fact the introduction of new products or processes developed outside the firm,[8] we felt that the number of firms undertaking R & D was, in practice, a more reliable indicator of 'innovativeness'. The extremely high proportion of firms responding yes to the question, 'Did you introduce any innovations over the period 1981–1985?' begs the question as to which interpretation was given by firms to the term 'innovation'. The question, 'Did you undertake Research and Development?' would appear to be far more clear-out in its meaning.

One might also argue that a more appropriate measure of innovative input would be an index of R & D expenditure or, alternatively the number of innovations introduced might be employed as a measure of innovative output. Unfortunately, although both types of data are available from the second part of the ISTAT-CNR survey, they are not yet available disaggregated by firm size, and therefore not useful for our main purpose: that is, to look at the differences in the response of firms of different sizes to market conditions. In support of our choice of dependent variable, it may be noted that, at the industry level, the number of firms undertaking R & D is highly correlated with the number of innovations in the industry (0.83); also, the 'effective' dependent variable, i.e. $\log(p/1-p)$,[9] is strongly correlated with R & D expenditure across industries (0.66).

Given that the basis for the dependent variable, whether or not a particular firm undertook R & D, is binary, we estimate a grouped logit model.[10] Thus, we interpret the proportion of firms undertaking R & D in a particular industry and size-class as the probability that a firm in that group will have undertaken R & D.

Turning to the principal independent variable, evidence of the effect of market structure on research intensity is not unequivocal. However, as noted by Kamien and Schwartz (1982), the majority of studies considering the issue find the relationship between market concentration and both research efforts and innovative output to be positive and non-linear (in the sense that increases in concentration act as a stimulus to research efforts up to a certain threshold, after which increasing concentration becomes harmful).[11]

How the effect of concentration is likely to differ in its effects on small and large firms is less clear. To the extent that small firms in concentrated industries might gain from technological spillovers and/or may be forced into technological completion with large concerns in order to survive, the effect of concentration on research intensity in small enterprises may be positive and indeed stronger than for their larger counterparts. However, if concentration implies a high level of technological competition amongst big firms, the relationship between concentration and innovative activity in small firms may be negative. In this paper we use an adjusted Herfindahl index as a measure of concentration derived from ISTAT sales data.[12] We include both the index itself and its square as independent variables in order to allow for the possibility of non-linearity in the relationship.

Pavitt and Wald (1971) found that an innovative advantage existed for small firms in industries in the earliest stages of the product cycle. With increasing market demand, opportunities for small firms seem to be higher, and the probabilities of small units becoming innovative to increase. For this reason, we included in our model a variable representing demand growth, expressed as the average annual nominal growth in sales, 1978–81.

We include also the capital–output ratio (averaged over the period 1978–81) as a measure of barriers to entry. On the one hand one would expect that high entry barriers would have a negative impact on R & D intensity, particularly for small firms. On the other, however, it should be remembered that the capital–output ratio is but one type of entry barrier, another obvious one being R & D intensity itself. It is highly likely, therefore, that there will be a strong positive correlation between capital intensity and our measure of innovative activity.

Following Scherer (1987) we control for differences in technological opportunities by using dummies for six different basic technologies (chemicals, electrical, traditional, raw materials, scientific instruments and engineering), and by including an index of the 'closeness to science'[13] of the industry. The index is defined as the ratio of expenditure for basic or

Table 13.2   Means and standard deviations of variables included in the regressions.

	Mean	*Standard Deviation*
R & D intensity	.1126	.0984
Basic	.0065	.0181
Patents	.0266	.0461
Capital intensity	.0461	.0144
Demand growth	.1862	.0258
Herfindahl	.0040	.0141
Herfindahl squared	.0021	.0599

NB   The patent ratio is multiplied by 1,000,000,000 and the square of the Herfindahl index by 10. The observations are weighted by the size of the industrial sector.

pure research to total R & D expenditure for the industry. We expect the coefficients on the technological dummies to vary across firm size, being greater for large firms, since they are in general more innovative than small concerns. In the same way, one would expect traditional and raw material industries to be intrinsically less innovative than the others. The effect of the 'closeness to science' index is expected to be positive and stronger for small firms than for large.

For an indicator of technological appropriability, we must once again rely an indirect measure. The extent to which firms succeed in appropriating the returns to their innovative activity does not form part of the ISTAT-CNR enquiry. Thus, we employ the ratio of patents to industrial sales as a measure of the degree of appropriability. Even if not ideal, this should capture some of the dimensions of the appropriability conditions in the industry. We would expect this variable to have a positive effect on research intensity, particularly for small innovators. As an aid to the interpretation of the coefficients we include the mean and standard deviation of each of the variables employed in Table 13.2.

We estimate a model in which all coefficients are allowed to vary across firm size. Firms were divided into five size classes according to the number of employees (20–49, 50–99, 100–199, 200–499, 500+) and a fixed effects model was estimated. That is, separate coefficients were estimated for each size class, although within the same regression using dummy variables to split the sample. Specifically, the probability that a firm undertakes R & D is estimated as:

$$p(\text{R \& D} = 1) = \frac{\exp(X\beta)}{1 + \exp(X\beta)}$$

where $X\beta = \sum_{j}^{5} \sum_{l}^{6} \alpha_{jl}\, S_j T_l + \sum_{j}^{5} \beta_{1j} S_j\,(\text{BASIC}) + \sum_{j}^{5} \beta_{2j} S_j\,(\text{PATENTS})$

$$+ \sum_{j}^{5} \beta_{3j}\, S_j\,(\text{CAPITAL}) + \sum_{j}^{5} \beta_{4j} S_j\,(\text{DEMAND})$$

$$+ \sum_{j}^{5} \beta_{5j}\, S_j\,(\text{HERFINDAHL}) + \sum_{j}^{5} \beta_{6j} S_j\,(\text{HERFINDAHL})^2$$

(S_j = size dummy; T_l = technological group dummy)

The difference between this and estimating five separate regressions is that the error terms in the single equation model are all assumed to have the same distribution. Indeed, estimating five separate regressions produces almost identical results.[14] The advantage of proceeding in this manner is

Table 13.3   General logit model of R & D infensity allowing for all size effects (standard errors in parentheses)

| | Size class (no. of workers) | | | | |
	20–49	50–99	100–199	200–499	500+
Intercept					
Traditional	−2.4678	−2.0823	−1.7284	−1.1673	−0.5032
	(.3044)	(.4791)	(.6054)	(.6613)	(.7398)
Raw materials	−2.6308	−2.0706	−1.5610	−1.2941	−0.3188
	(.3552)	(.5366)	(.6813)	(.7800)	(.9054)
Chemical	−0.8073	−0.6024	−0.4955	0.5263	1.6870
	(.3918)	(.6361)	(.7987)	(.8529)	(.9597)
Engineering	−2.5318	−2.6706	−2.5123	−1.4383	−0.3363
	(.3711)	(.5749)	(.7107)	(.7674)	(.8786)
Electrical	−1.8258	−1.7433	−1.5687	−0.6855	−0.2881
	(.2958)	(.4767)	(.5970)	(.6287)	(.7092)
Scientific	−2.2367	−2.3923	−2.3166	−2.8909	−0.2355
	(.4825)	(.7561)	(.9526)	(1.059)	(1.111)
Slope					
Basic	8.5699	6.1181	6.2249	2.7670	3.5702
	(2.480)	(3.679)	(4.561)	(5.166)	(5.344)
Patents	9.9405	13.108	14.260	13.197	7.4044
	(1.698)	(2.417)	(2.763)	(2.894)	(3.215)
Capital intensity	10.013	7.7139	7.4769	11.888	−1.9203
	(3.926)	(5.517)	(6.615)	(7.746)	(9.534)
Demand growth	−4.3154	−3.3954	−3.8222	−4.2986	−1.9144
	(1.311)	(2.096)	(2.729)	(2.902)	(3.097)
Herfindahl	15.694	57.127	123.65	28.874	−1.7886
	(6.549)	(26.06)	(35.08)	(9.457)	(7.446)
Herfindahl squared	−3.7548	−138.89	−419.03	−5.4537	0.4350
	(3.120)	(93.75)	(139.7)	(2.001)	(1.524)

Log-likelihood   = −6812.1

Cragg–Uhler R^2 = .196

that it allows us to straightforwardly carry out nested hypothesis tests on the existence of different regimes. In particular, we are able to allow the data to determine what, in terms of the response to the relevant influences, constitutes a large or small firm. The results of this procedure are reproduced in Table 13.3.

Looking at the results from the general model, we can see, reflected in the intercept coefficients, the stylized fact that large firms are more innovative than small ones. Secondly, both for slope and intercept coefficients, there appear to be significant differences between the responses of firms of different sizes. Indeed, the Neyman–Pearson likelihood ratio test rejects at the 99.5 per cent significance level the hypothesis that all slope and intercept coefficients are equal.[15]

Thus, having accepted that at least some coefficients vary across size, it is also immediately apparent from a brief examination of Table 13.3 that many of the coefficients are not significantly different from one another. The second stage of the estimation is to gradually reduce the number of coefficients in the model, by unifying size classes. Using the likelihood ratio and *t*-tests as a guide, the model was gradually reduced until such a

Table 13.4   Reduced logit model of R & D intensity allowing for some size effects (standard errors in parentheses)

| | Size class (no. of workers) | | | | |
	20–49	50–99	100–199	200–499	500+
Intercept					
Traditional	−2.2881	−2.2881	−2.2881	−0.8978	−0.8978
	(.2106)	(.2106)	(.2106)	(.2224)	(.2224)
Raw Mats.	−2.3134	−2.3134	−2.3134	−1.0049	−1.0049
	(.2435)	(.2435)	(.2435)	(.2694)	(.2694)
Chemical	−0.7731	−0.7731	−0.7731	0.8883	0.8883
	(.2715)	(.2715)	(.2715)	(.3339)	(.3339)
Engineering	−2.6428	−2.6428	−2.6428	−1.0679	−1.0679
	(.2496)	(.2496)	(.2496)	(.2687)	(.2687)
Electrical	−1.8081	−1.8081	−1.8081	−0.6565	−0.6565
	(.2071)	(.2071)	(.2071)	(.2384)	(.2384)
Scientific	−2.4248	−2.4248	−2.4248	−2.4248	−1.0873
	(.3319)	(.3319)	(.3319)	(.3319)	(.6622)

| | Size class (no. of workers) | | | | |
	20–49	50–99	100–199	200–499	500+
Slope					
Basic	6.3860	6.3860	6.3860	6.3860	6.3860
	(1.665)	(1.665)	(1.665)	(1.665)	(1.665)
Patents	11.618	11.618	11.618	11.618	11.618
	(1.052)	(1.052)	(1.052)	(1.052)	(1.052)
Capital Intensity	8.6037	8.6037	8.6037	8.6037	8.6037
	(2.576)	(2.576)	(2.576)	(2.576)	(2.576)
Demand Growth	−4.8538	−2.2161	−2.2161	−4.8538	−2.2161
	(.9119)	(.9185)	(.9185)	(.9119)	(.9185)
Herfindahl	27.767	27.767	152.02	27.767	−2.1185
	(5.512)	(5.512)	(22.59)	(5.512)	(6.188)
Herfindahl Squared	−30.257	−30.257	−538.14	−5.2555	0.5544
	(11.90)	(11.90)	(101.7)	(1.261)	(1.285)

Log-likelihood   = −6829.0

Cragg–Uhler R^2 = .193

point was reached at which any further reduction was rejected by both of these tests.[16] The reduced model is reproduced in Table 13.4.

The procedure adopted allowed us to reduce a model with 60 coefficients to one with 24. The main points to note from the reduced model are, firstly, that there exist clear differences between small and large firms, particularly with regard to the effect of technological opportunities. Secondly, the point at which a firm becomes large, that is, at which its response to market conditions alters, seems to vary across industries. Whereas scientific instrument industries have their cut-off point at 500 workers, all the others have a division at 200. This finding supports our choice of procedure in allowing the data to determine this 'cut-off' point rather than imposing it *a priori*.

The results for the slope coefficients are less straightforward to interpret. Basic R & D expenditure, patents, and capital intensity all appear to have a positive effect which is constant across size classes. Demand growth is, surprisingly, negative in its effect on R & D intensity. This may suggest that firms in industries with strong demand growth feel less need to undertake R & D in order to maintain or strengthen their market position.

The Herfindahl index performs more or less as was expected. For firms with fewer than 500 workers the effect is positive but decreasing. That is, market concentration provides a positive stimulus to R & D intensity; however, as such concentration increases, R & D intensity increases at a slower rate. For larger firms, the point estimate of the coefficient is reversed, although neither the Herfindahl index nor its square have coefficients which are significantly different from zero.

Since, employing a logit model, the effect of an explanatory variable depends both on the particular coefficient attached to that variable and on the values of all the other variables in the equation,[17] in order to get a clearer impression of the effect of concentration on R & D intensity we reproduce

Table 13.5a   Average elasticities of the probability of undertaking R & D with respect to the Herfindahl index (calculated using the general model)

	20–49	50–99	100–199	200–499	500+
Traditional	.026	.089	.190	.046	−.003
Raw materials	.026	.095	.193	.087	−.014
Chemicals	.069	.204	.285	.055	−.006
Engineering	.076	.184	.547	.202	−.034
Electrical	.119	.414	.756	.133	−.014
Scientific	.355	1.029	2.283	.656	−.028
All industries	.043	.140	.332	.099	−.015

Table 13.5b   Average elasticities of the probability of undertaking R & D with respect to the Herfindahl index (calculated using the reduced model)

	20–49	50–99	100–199	200–499	500+
Traditional	.046	.044	.239	.045	−.004
Raw materials	.045	.048	.248	.084	−.019
Chemicals	.118	.118	.325	.053	−.008
Engineering	.125	.124	.616	.195	−.040
Electrical	.204	.211	.925	.143	−.014
Scientific	.604	.507	2.823	.635	−.033
All industries	.074	.075	1.07	.097	−.017

in Tables 13.5a and 13.5b the elasticity of R & D intensity with respect to the Herfindahl index.

Two obvious points to note are that, firstly, that the elasticity is positive for firms employing fewer than 500 workers, whilst being negative for those above that turning-point. Secondly, a slightly more subtle feature which may be observed is that the elasticity is roughly constant or increasing until the turning-point of 200 workers above this point, the elasticity appears to fall with firm size.

4   CONCLUSIONS

In common with other empirical research in this area, one should be careful not to attach too much weight to the precise point estimates produced by the empirical model, particularly in the light of the difficulties with the data; however, the model does, we feel, provide some interesting insights into the problem of market concentration, firm size and innovative efforts. First and foremost, the estimation provides strong empirical support for the idea that firms of different sizes respond differently to market stimuli and technological conditions. With regard to market concentration, this would appear to act as a positive stimulus to research efforts for all but the largest firms. This finding adds weight to the notion that it is a mistake to analyse, both at a theoretical and an empirical level, technological advance in a context in which firms are assumed to all be the same size or, to all respond in the same way to market stimuli. Further, the existence of different 'cut-off' points in different industries, noted above, suggests that the arbitrary imposition of a definition of large and small firms is not justified.

At a practical level, the existence of several (implicit) models relating technical change to industrial characteristics has important implications for innovation policy. If the R & D activity of small and large firms is affected in a different way by the market structure characteristics and the state of technology in the industry, innovation policy may have discriminatory effects, favouring one type of innovator over another. An important question has, therefore, to be addressed by the economics of technical advance: that is, how to design well-balanced sets of policy instruments to improve the rate of technical change, and how to evaluate the innovative performance of different types of innovators.

Much work remains to be done. The forthcoming publication of data from the second part of the ISTAT-CNR survey will allow a greater insight into the problem to be gained. More information on the nature of innovations produced and resources expended in R & D will allow a more precise picture to be gained of the situation.

A second area which might usefully be examined in future work is the question of feedback effects between the different factors involved. That is, it is very likely that R & D intensity has effects on the market conditions themselves, and, notably market concentration is almost certainly affected by the rate of technical advance, as too is capital intensity. In as much as, in the model considered above, the causative factors considered temporally precede R & D intensity, the problem of simultaneity, or at least of feedback between the variables considered, does not arise. However, in so far as such feedback effects do exist, the model considered here must be seen as a short-run analysis. One obvious line for further research then would be to incorporate feedback, or at least the possibility of feedback, between the variables.

Appendix

Technological groups:

	SIC
Raw materials	14, 22, 24
Chemical	25, 26
Engineering	31, 32, 33, 35, 36, 37
Electrical	34
Scientific	37
Traditional	4

Notes

1. We wish to thank Malcolm C. Sawyer for useful comments and discussion on previous drafts and Dr Aldo del Santo of ISTAT for his assistance with data collection. P. Sbriglia acknowledges financial support from the Fondazione Ivo Vanzi Napoli. Responsibility for the views expressed and any remaining errors is of course our own.
2. ISTAT has carried out two surveys on innovative activity in Italy, for the period 1981–5. In this paper we use data from the first, more general survey, which we describe in section 2, since data from the second, more detailed, survey is not yet available at a sufficiently disaggregated level. We use data from the second survey to calculate the simple correlations reported below.
3. In this regard, see for example, Freeman (1981), Rothwell and Zegveld (1982), Kaplinski (1983), Acs and Audretsch (1988).
4. This point has been noted by Rothwell and Zegveld (1982) and Kamien and Schwartz (1982).

5. 'The large firms innovation rate (LIE) is defined as the number of innovations made with firms with at least 500 employees, divided by the number of employees (thousands) in large firms' (Acs and Audretsch, 1987, p. 568). Conversely, the small firms innovation rate is the ratio between the number of innovations and number of employees in firms with fewer than 500 workers.

6. The database used by Acs and Audretsch in both of their papers is provided by the US Small Business Administration and regards the number of innovations introduced by business firms in 1982.

7. Note that, in the first survey, firms were not asked to report the amount of resources devoted to innovation. Rather, the questions required a yes/no answer. Indeed, it is for this reason that the sensible model to employ in these circumstances is a non-linear probability (i.e. logit or probit).

8. This was particularly true for small firms. In the second survey, firms were asked to state the percentage of resources devoted to different 'innovative' activities. Whilst firms of over 500 workers reported, on average, as using 21.4 per cent of innovative expenditure on R & D with 43.5 per cent spent on productive investment, the smallest firms (under 50 workers) spent only 7.4 per cent on R & D with 73.1 per cent spent on productive investment. This tends to support the view that a large proportion of 'innovative' activity, particularly for small firms, involved the implementation of innovations outside the firm.

9. The logit model implies the relationship (omitting individual subscripts):

$$P = \exp(Z)/(1 + \exp(Z)) \qquad \text{with } Z = \sum_k \beta_k X_k$$

    Rearranging, this may be expressed as:

$$\sum_k \beta_k X_k = \log (P/1{-}P).$$

    Where in our case P represents the proportion of firms undertaking R & D, or, alternatively and more in keeping with the spirit of the logit model, the probability that a firm undertook R & D.

10. We prefer the logit over the probit model, given that the two models produce very similar results, because of the simplicity of formulation of the logit. Problems with a linear regression in a situation in which the dependent variable is binary are well known (e.g. Maddala, 1983). Principal amongst these is the fact that $E(P|X)$ may lie outside the range $(0, 1)$.

11. We do not take account of feedback effects or simultaneity in the analysis here. Whilst it is extremely likely that market concentration, and indeed other explanatory variables, are in turn affected by the level of R & D intensity, in as much as the explanatory variables precede in time the measure of R & D intensity, the issue does not arise.

12. The adjustment consists in using deciles of firms rather than the individual firms themselves as the base for the index. The rationale behind this step is to control for what we feel to be somewhat arbitrary divisions between the industrial sectors in the ISTAT data which imply arbitrary differences in the

size of industrial sector. Thus, the measure employed is:

$$H = \sum_{i=1}^{10} M_i^2$$

where M refers to the market share of the ith decile of firms. For example, in an industrial sector containing 200 firms, M_{10} would represent the market share of the largest 20 firms.

13. The index employed here is similar to the one used by Levin and Reiss (1984). The technological dummies are defined in the appendix.

14. These results are available from the authors on request.

15. The relevant chi-squared statistic is 694.4 which, compared with the critical value 77.2 (at 99.5 per cent significance level with 48 degrees of freedom) clearly rejects the null hypothesis of no variation in coefficients across size.

16. Use of such a procedure employing repeated specification tests is still not entirely uncontroversial, in as much as it lays such an analysis open to the charge of data-mining. However, in response, and without entering into a discussion of the efficacy or not of the procedure, we would argue that we followed a systematic use of the relevant tests. We would also argue that this is by way of being an exploratory analysis in an area where the underlying theory does not provide unequivocal predictions. Furthermore, whilst one might quibble over the precise final specification of the model, we feel that the central point that the response of firms does differ with firm size is so clearly established as to withstand any such criticism. Finally, it will be noted that we report results for both the general and the reduced models.

17. In the logit, as in the probit, model the effect of changes in one of the independent variables on the dependent variable depends not only on the value of the relevant coefficient, but also on the value of all the other variables and their coefficients included in the model. For the logit model we have the following relationship between the explained and the explanatory variable:

$$P = \frac{\exp(Z)}{1 + \exp(Z)} \qquad \text{with } Z = \sum_{k} \beta_k X_k$$

which differentiating with respect to any X_k gives:

$$\frac{\delta P}{\delta X_k} = \beta_k \frac{\exp(Z)}{(1 + \exp(Z))^2} = \beta_k P(1 - P).$$

Thus, it will be readily seen that the formula used to calculate the elasticities in tables 5a and 5b is given by:

$$\frac{\delta P}{\delta H} = (\beta_h + 2\beta_{h^2} H) (1 - P)P.$$

where H represents the Herfindahl index and the h, h^2 subscripts relate to the coefficient on H and H^2 respectively.

References

ACS, Z.J. and AUDRETSCH, D.B. (1987) 'Innovation, Market Structure and Firm Size', *Review of Economics and Statistics* 69, pp. 567–690.

ACS, Z.J. and AUDRETSCH, D.B. (1988) 'Innovation in Small and Large Firms: An Empirical Analysis', *American Economic Review* 78, pp. 678–90.

ARCHIBUGI, D. (1988) 'Concentrazione Innovativa per Imprese e Specializzazione Tecnologica Internazionale: Il Caso Italiano', *Economia e Politica Industriale*, no. 60, pp. 35–54.

CAVES, R.E. and PUGEL, T.A. (1980) *Intra-Industry Differences in Conduct and Performance: Vital Strategies in US Manufacturing Industries*, New York University Press.

FREEMAN, C. (1982) *Economics of Industrial Innovation*, Basingtoke: MacMillan.

ISTAT-CNR (1985) *Indagine Preliminare Sulla Diffusione Dell'Innovazione Tecnologica*.

ISTAT-CNR (1986) *Indagine Sull'Innovazione Tecnologica*.

KAMIEN, M. and SCHWARTZ, N. (1982) *Market Structure and Innovation*, Cambridge University Press.

KAPLINSKI, R. (1983) 'Firm Size and Technical Change in a Dynamic Context', *Journal of Industrial Economics* 32, pp. 39–59.

KAY, N. (1987) 'Industrial Structure, Rivalry and Innovation: Theory and Evidence', in H. Ergas (ed.) *A European Future in High Technology* .

LEVIN, R. and REISS, P. (1984) 'Tests of a Schumpeterian Model of R & D and Market Structure', in Z. Griliches (ed.), *R & D, Patents and Productivity*, University of Chicago Press.

MADDALA, G.S. (1983) *Limited Dependent and Qualitative Variables in Econometrics*, Cambridge University Press.

MANSFIELD, E. (1981) 'Composition of R & D Expenditures: Relationship to Size of Firm, Concentration, and Innovative Output', *Review of Economics and Statistics* 63, pp. 610–15.

PAVITT, K. and WALD, S. (1971) *The Conditions for Success in Technological Innovation*, Paris: OECD.

ROTHWELL, R. and ZEGVELD, W. (1982) *Industrial Innovation and Public Policy*, London: Francis Pinter.

SCHERER, F.M. (1967) 'Market Structure and the Employment of Scientists and Engineers', *American Economic Review* 57, pp. 524–30.

Author Index

313

Subject Index